LOSING THE PLOT

LOSING THE PLOT

POLITICAL ISOLATION OF WEST BENGAL

SUGATO HAZRA

PAPER MISSILE

NIYOGI BOOKS

Published by
NIYOGI BOOKS
Block D, Building No. 77,
Okhla Industrial Area, Phase-I,
New Delhi-110 020, INDIA
Tel: 91-11-26816301, 26818960
Email: niyogibooks@gmail.com
Website: www.niyogibooksindia.com

Editor: Sucharita Ghosh
Design: Shashi Bhushan Prasad
Cover design: Pinaki De

ISBN: 978-93-91125-21-9
Publication: 2021

Printed at: Niyogi Offset Pvt. Ltd., New Delhi, India

CONTENTS

BIRTH OF NATIONALISM

Ananda Math had defined nationalism for Indians in its formative stages, said historian S. Irfan Habib.[1] Bankim Chandra Chattopadhyay published the novel in 1882, about 40 years after the political upheavals known as Spring of Nations that broke out across Europe. The movements seen in Europe in 1848 were aimed at removing monarchies and creating nation states. This flame of nationalism reached the shores of Bengal since it had the closest connection with western thoughts due to the presence of the British rulers.

Bankim Chandra was the first Indian graduate from the newly established Calcutta University, a product of the British effort to educate its Indian subjects. In fact, even before writing the novel *Ananda Math*, Bankim had composed 'Vande Mataram', the national song which became the rallying cry for the Indian freedom movement. Judged by the overwhelming popular acceptance it may be safely said that the relatively nascent concept of nationalism, in the Indian context, had its birth on the soils of Bengal.

Swami Vivekananda, wrote historian Ramesh Chandra Majumdar,[2] had told a group of young men at Dacca some time in 1901, 'Read Bankim Chandra and emulate his *deshbhakti* (patriotism) and *Sanatan Dharma* (principles of the heroic band of Sannyasins as depicted in the *Ananda Math*). Your duty should be service to motherland.'

The nascent sense of nationalism was not confined to Bengal. Rabindranath Tagore set the poem 'Vande Mataram' to music and sang it during the 1896 session of the Congress in Calcutta. It was sung in 1901 five years later at another session of the Congress in Calcutta. Poet Sarala Devi Chaudurani sang the song in the Benares Congress session in 1905.

R.C. Majumdar wrote,

> During the long and arduous struggle for freedom from 1905 to 1947 'Bande Mataram' was the rallying cry of the patriotic sons of India, and thousands of them succumbed to the lathi blow of the British police or mounted the scaffold with 'Bande Mataram' on their lips. The main theme of the novel inspired the Bengali youths to supreme self-sacrifice during the hectic days of the Swadeshi movement.[3]

Bengal was the first to witness the great transformation since British rule was established here first. Historian Sir Jadunath Sarkar noted,

> If Periclean Athens was the school of Hellas, the eye of Greece, mother of arts and eloquence that was Bengal to the rest of India under British rule, but with a borrowed light which it had made its own with marvellous cunning. In this new Bengal originated every good and great thing of the modern world that passed on to the other provinces of India ... New literary types, reform of the language, social reconstruction, political aspirations, religious movements and even changes in manners that originated in Bengal, passed like ripples from a central eddy, across provincial barriers, to the farthest corners of India.[4]

Bankim Chandra, whose 'Vande Mataram' became a battle mantra and *Ananda Math* the inspiration, was a product of a wave of changes that swept Bengal. It all started with the spread of western education pursued relentlessly by personalities like Raja Rammohun Roy, Dwarkanath Tagore and Ishwar Chandra Vidyasagar to name just a few. The Hindu College was established on 20 January 1817 with active support from Sir Hyde East, then chief justice of the Supreme Court of Calcutta. It was an initiative undertaken by prominent Bengali families who met at Sir Hyde's residence and contributed money to set up an institution where their children could receive liberal education like the Europeans. According to R.C. Majumdar it was one Baidyanath Mukherjee, a prominent resident of Calcutta at that time, who had been the main force behind pursuing Sir Hyde East.[5]

The setting up of the Hindu College gave wings to the desire of Bengal to receive the best liberal education that was available in Europe. The Bengali Hindus in Calcutta were eager to learn English primarily to facilitate their discussions with English merchants in order to carry out their trading activities smoothly. In the beginning Bengalis did not have much fascination for the Englishmen as can be seen from what Raja Rammohun Roy wrote. Finding the Europeans 'generally more intelligent, more steady and moderate in their conduct' he gave up his prejudice against them.[6] In fact Roy started learning English only after this realisation. Bengalis took the initiative to learn English, with the majority acquiring a working knowledge in order to earn a living. The likes of Dwarkanath Tagore, Prasanna Kumar Tagore and Nilmoni Datta earned huge wealth through their association with the British. Some were employed in British establishments, some opted for trade and commerce, while others built up a fortune in law. The establishment of the Supreme Court in Calcutta opened up a new career opportunity for Bengalis. The economic prospect enticed the new generation of Bengal to seek English education which made them approach Sir Hyde East. That in due course this exposure to European education attracted them to the European concept of nationalism was a natural transition.

There was an interesting change in the attitude of Hindus in Bengal towards British rule. According to R.C. Majumdar the British victory at Plassey was viewed as yet another change of guard by the Hindus accustomed as they were to frequent changes in the then capital Murshidabad. 'The people of Bengal … looked upon the accession of Mir Jafar as one usurper and traitor succeeding another and it was beyond their wildest dreams to see in this event the beginning of British rule in Bengal, far less in India,' wrote Majumdar.[7] Essentially to the Hindus, who were the majority in Bengal, British rule was yet another foreign rule replacing the earlier one. To them the nawabs of Murshidabad were aliens. When Robert Clive entered Murshidabad triumphantly with a few hundred Europeans and sepoys, the people who gathered to witness his entry amounted to thousands. According to Clive had they cared they could have beaten back the Europeans even with sticks and stones.

The point to note is that when the British rule started there was no sense of nation state among the Bengali Hindus. They observed the change of guard and discerned certain benefits as was noted by Raja Rammohun. Hindus and Muslims used to live in proximity with two different beliefs and cultures. The feeling of distinct identities was deep rooted despite the fact, as was mentioned by Raja Rammohun in his 'Appeal to the King in Council', that under the Muslim rule, 'the natives of this country enjoyed every political privilege in common with Musaalman.' However under the British rule, despite loss of political consequence, the natives 'were consoled by the more secure enjoyment of those civil and religious rights which had been so often violated by the rapacity and intolerance of the Mussulmans …'[8]

When Bengalis were exposed to the idea of nationalism that was sweeping through Europe the thought that was uppermost in their minds was the violation of civil and religious rights during the 700 years of Muslim rule. *Ananda Math*, the hugely popular novel by Bankim Chandra, that served as the trigger for the nascent sense of nationalism in Bengal, was based on a central theme that was anti-Muslim, according to A.G. Noorani.[9] In the last chapter, Noorani wrote, there is a supernatural figure persuading the leader of the sanyasis, Satyananda, to stop fighting, 'The Muslim power is destroyed, there is nothing else for you to do … Hindu dominion will not be established now … The English will rule.'[10] Bengali nationalism started out as an anti-Muslim sentiment.

There are good reasons for this. 'When the British rule was firmly established in Bengal, the anti-Muslim and pro-British sentiments of the Hindus went on increasing,' wrote Majumdar.[11] He cited the views of Rammohun Roy who was arguably the most liberal man of his times and had accepted the superiority of Muslims in many respects. Yet according to Roy the British rule in India was a benign act of Providence. He referred to the despotic power of the Mogul princes who ruled over India in his 'Appeal to the King in Council'. He also referred to the religious bigotry and proselytisation of the Muslims that Indians suffered for nine centuries. Majumdar concluded that, 'The view of Muslims as alien rulers persisted throughout the nineteenth century among the Hindus …'[12] This explains the popularity of *Ananda Math* and ready acceptance of 'Vande Mataram' as the battle cry.

Curiously despite nearly 700 years of living under the Muslim rulers Bengalis disliked their rulers to the extent that they readily accepted the rule by people alien to their culture who came from faraway lands with the intention of exploiting the resources of their native land. One reason could be that the Moguls established their hold over Bengal after much struggle, and to maintain their control always appointed representatives from within their family or members from Upper India as governors of the state and other high-ranking officials. All these appointees looked forward to the day of retiring back to their homes. Bengal was thus a much-neglected province. The frequent changes of rulers immediately before the East India Company defeated Nawab Siraj-ud-daula had also alienated high-ranked Hindus from the rulers. Thus none of them from Siraj-ud-daula to Mir Jafar or even Mir Qasim could ensure loyalty from the Bengali Hindus. Instead Bengali Hindus won wealth by siding with the British traders. When they and their offspring opted for European education they nursed a soft corner for British rule. Thus the supernatural figure in *Ananda Math* told Satyananda, 'Who is the foe? There are no foes now. The English are friends as well as rulers.' This was the dominant sentiment among the Bengalis then and was not fabricated by Bankim Chandra Chattopadhyay just to please his English employers.[13]

Bengal's honeymoon with the British was evident during the Sepoy Mutiny of 1857 which was later considered as the first struggle for freedom from the British. Interestingly it was the soldiers at Berhampore (Murshidabad) who refused to use the cartridges made using beef and pig tallow. This was followed by the sepoys at Barrackpore where a sepoy Mangal Pandey had attacked a British officer. This apart there had been instances of sepoys revolting at Chittagong, Dacca and Jalpaiguri. Yet the vocal Bengali newspapers of the day and commentators did not support the mutiny. A meeting was held in Calcutta attended by prominent personages like Raja Radhakanta Deb, Kaliprasanna Sinha and Harendra Ghose where a resolution was adopted condemning the sepoys. *Sambad Prabhakar* a prominent newspaper wrote in its editorial, 'Some bands of irreligious, indisciplined ungrateful reckless sepoys having risen in revolt against the Government, the peaceful people are praying to God for establishment of immediate peace in the country by getting rid of the danger posed by the Mutiny.'[14] As early as in the 1850s Bengal held a view different from the rest of India, the upper provinces in particular where the Sepoy Mutiny had taken a serious form.

English education started at the behest of natives looking for opportunities to earn their living but was not confined to this narrow objective. The establishment of the Hindu College and the influence of Henry Louis Vivian Derozio ensured that the liberal ideas of the west along with patriotism and nationalism took roots in Bengal. Derozio was instrumental in setting up the Academic Association at the Hindu College where students used to freely discuss state, society, religion, patriotism, politics, etc., based on common logic which often enough militated against the then prevailing rigid rituals. Orthodox Bengalis who were behind the setting up of the Hindu College were agitated and saw to the ouster of Derozio from the college. Interestingly Derozio considered himself an Indian and wrote poems in English on nationalism. This was 'the earliest instance of a lyrical expression of an emotion of patriotism towards India as the country of one's birth.'[15] Much before Bankim Chandra's sanskritised poem 'Vande Mataram' it was Derozio who had expressed his love for India as his motherland.

Derozio's students became rebels and indulged in drinking and consuming forbidden meat. Rajnarain Bose, father of Indian nationalism according to historian R.C. Majumdar, wrote in his autobiography how they used to assemble near College Square to eat and drink. Some like Madhusudan Dutta even converted to Christianity. But more importantly these elite students despite their rebellion against orthodoxy were instrumental in the development of Bengali literature and also a sense of nationalism. The students of the Hindu College had set up the 'Sarbatatva Dipika Sabha' for the cultivation of chaste Bengali. Debendranath Tagore was its secretary. Clearly it was Derozio's disciples who lit the lamp of renaissance in Bengal even before Macaulay wrote his treatise. Bengalis did not learn English to become clerks but in order to enrich themselves with modern knowledge which included developing Bengali language and literature as well.

Interestingly Hindu College did not produce students who indulged in blind imitation of the Europeans. In an article read out at the Hindu Literary Society the author commented sarcastically,

> The Europeans on coming to this country were so much pained at the misery of the people that they at once set about to remove the same. They imported various kinds of alcoholic drinks – Rum, Gin, Brandy – and other accessories of modern civilization and within a surprisingly short time, managed to civilize this barbarous nation.[16]

The students of the college did not hesitate to criticise the British rulers for their lapses. In February 1843, Majumdar noted in his two-volume *History of Modern Bengal*, Dakshinaranjan Mukherjee read out an article on the police administration and justice system under the British East India Company in the presence of the principal of the Hindu College D.L. Richardson.[17] The principal objected to the article and called it seditious but he was overruled by the chairman Tarachand Dutta, a student of the college. English education did not create mere pen-pushing clerks in Bengal but free thinkers who excelled both in the liberal arts of Europe and traditional knowledge of India. Clearly the rebels of the Hindu College, such as Madhusudan Dutta, Rajnarain Bose and their other classmates like Iswar Chandra Ghosal, Prasanna Kumar Sen had taken up drinking as a mark of civilisation. They had later become major exponents of

Indian culture. Madhusudan Dutta was the first to use Bengali as a medium for expressing literary flavour. His first drama *Sharmistha* was written in verse and was based on the story of Yayati from the *Mahabharata*. The rebel who even converted to Christianity excelled in writing in his mother tongue based on themes taken from India's glorious past. Bengal thus served as the link between India's past and the most modern European philosophy.

Not that the intelligentsia that emerged from this environment of modern thinking did not have conflicts. An interesting discord was over banning polygamy where Bankim Chandra opposed Ishwar Chandra Vidyasagar's effort to stop the heinous practice. In fact, even the government was reluctant to enact a law banning such practices fearing that this would impact its control over the natives. When Vidyasagar along with the Maharaja of Burdwan petitioned the government to enact a law banning polygamy, Raja Radhakanta Deb opposed the same. In 1866 when the Bengal government appointed a committee of Europeans and Bengalis to examine the ban on polygamy, all Bengali members barring Vidyasagar opposed it and the issue was buried.

The Sepoy Mutiny of 1857 was seen by Bengal, busy as it was then with matters pertaining to larger human civilisation, as a threat. Rajnarain Bose had sent his family to Calcutta for their safety. Many Bengali families used to keep boats and other means of transport ready to flee in case sepoys reached their area. For the enlightened in Bengal the mutiny was merely a rebellion of a few thousands of sepoys against the crores who viewed the British rule as beneficial.[18]

Sri Aurobindo in a speech delivered on 19 January 1907 at the Bombay National Union said,

> Bengal once was drunk with the wine of European civilization and with the purely intellectual teaching that it

> received from the West. It began to see all things, to judge all things through the imperfect instrumentality of the intellect. When it was so, Bengal became atheistic, it became a land of doubters and cynics.

Aurobindo was aware of the sentiment prevailing in the rest of the country: 'You all know what Bengal used to be; you all know that Bengali used to be a term of reproach among the nations; when people spoke of Bengal, with what feelings did they speak of it? Was it with feelings of admiration?'[19]

Evidently the rest of India did not take kindly to Bengal's obsession with European education. But this changed due to various factors. Foremost among these, according to Aurobindo, was the influence of Sri Ramakrishna. According to Aurobindo, Bengalis had the faculty of belief:

> Belief is not a merely intellectual process, belief is not a mere persuasion of the mind, belief is something that is in our heart, and what you believe, you must do, because belief is from God. It is to the heart that God speaks, it is in the heart that God resides. This saved the Bengali. Because of this capacity of belief, we were chosen as the people who were to save India.

How did this belief come to influence the Bengali? This, Aurobindo said, was due to the birth of several religious men – 'men whom the educated world would not have recognised'. Of them the one who had the greatest influence and did the most to regenerate Bengal 'could not read and write a single word'. Aurobindo said that God sent this ignorant man to Dakshineswar in Calcutta, 'and from North and South, and East and West, the educated men, men who were the pride of the university, who had studied all that Europe can teach, came to fall at the feet of this ascetic. The work of salvation, the work of raising India was begun.'[20] 'There is a creed in India today which calls itself Nationalism, a creed which has come to you from Bengal', was the opening statement of Sri Aurobindo's speech. Clearly in 1907 Bengal was claiming leadership over India in its quest for nationalism.

Aurobindo was asserting the supremacy of Bengal while apologising for the alienation of Bengali intellectuals from the rest of the country. However the facts do not corroborate his feelings. Surendranath Banerjee wielded tremendous influence across India. In fact after Surendranath toured India in 1877, Henry Cotton, a member of the Indian Civil Service, observed that it was inconceivable that a Bengali could have so much influence across the nation (in Punjab for instance), from Dacca to Multan, and that a Bengali could build public opinion from Peshawar to Chittagong.[21] What is more, Allan Octavian Hume, who worked relentlessly to set up the Indian National Congress (INC), sought and received support from Surendranath which in turn ensured the success of INC's second session in 1886, compared to the lukewarm first session in Bombay the year before.

According to R.C. Majumdar, 'The fact that the educated young Bengalees became more concerned with securing a voice in the country's government than with social and religious reforms was due to Surendranath's clarion call to them and the new ideal that his oratory deeply implanted in their mind.'[22] This was, said Majumdar, perhaps the single most important contribution of Surendranath in the reawakening of Bengal. Bipin Chandra Pal, another tall leader of that era, and a member of the Brahmo Samaj, wrote in his *Memories of my Life and Times* that it was due to the influence of Surendranath that Bengali youth quit the socio-religious movement spread by the Brahmo Samaj and joined the political movement. Therefore one can say that the politicisation of Bengali youth owes its origins to Surendranath whom Bengal refers to as 'Rashtraguru'. There is a very important road in Kolkata named after him which has witnessed many a political agitation over the decades.

In 1876 the Indian Association or Bharat Sabha was set up at a meeting held at Albert Hall, present Coffee House, opposite Presidency College (now University). Surendranath was the star orator at the meeting attended by more than 700 people. Shyamacharan Sarma, a law lecturer in Calcutta University, presided over the meeting. Surendranath, then 28 years old, was deeply moved by the freedom struggles in Europe and particularly impressed by Joseph Mazzini. He had joined the British Indian Civil Service in 1871 but was dismissed for some petty official irregularity three years later. His appeal against dismissal was not accepted and Surendranath took up a teaching job at Metropolitan Institution, which was set up by Ishwar Chandra Vidyasagar (later renamed Vidyasagar College). His oratory deeply influenced the youth of Bengal. Bipin Chandra Pal was a student at that time and he has referred to two lectures in particular by Surendranath. One was on the rise of the Sikhs and the other on how Joseph Mazzini created the Young Italy movement.

Surendranath brought in a pan-India approach in his lectures with the intention of uniting Indians of all religions, speaking different languages and living across the country under a common national cause. In fact, after the first meeting of the Indian Association, pan-Indian opinion building was one of his major objectives. Consequently, he had to build a bridge between all communities particularly between the Hindus and the Muslims. Clearly this was a deviation from the 'anti-Muslim ruler' kind of nationalism that had been the story of *Ananda Math*. Interestingly *Ananda Math* was written about ten years after the first meeting of the Indian Association. At its very origin then, the flow of nationalism had bifurcated into two streams

– one as Surendranath thought was relevant and the other as was rooted in *Ananda Math* with the rallying cry of 'Vande Mataram'. The second, we have seen, was viewed as anti-Muslim, a stand shared by even modern-day commentators like A.G. Noorani.[23]

Historian S. Irfan Habib has shed light on the two streams of nationalism taking shape in Bengal in the late 19th century. 'In Bankim's historical novels, which were imaginary extension of real histories, the subjection of India was pushed back to include the rule of the pre-modern Islamic empires. This was a re-interpretation of Islamic rule as foreign conquest, an anachronistic extension of modern imperialism backwards into the past.'[24] In contrast Habib notes the forceful voice of Surendranath whom he acknowledges as a proponent of early liberal nationalism.

> In one of his many speeches and writings he [Surendranath] denies that there is any antagonism whatsoever between the two great races who inhabit this vast continent and who together form the Indian nation. He goes back to history particularly the past eight hundred years, to establish through some interesting instances that we have a shared past of goodwill and amity

writes Habib.[25] Bengal, to be more precise, Calcutta, saw the birth of nationalism, the secular nationalism as well as what later turned out to be Hindu nationalism and that too around the same time.

In the first meeting of the Indian Association Surendranath, as mentioned in his autobiography, had four objectives:[26] to build up public opinion in the country, to unite the people of different parts of India on the basis of political aim and objectives, to extend friendship between Hindus and Muslims, and to ensure that even the illiterate among the public can participate in political agitation.

R.C. Majumdar drew attention particularly to the third objective, that of friendship between Hindus and Muslims. In the second annual meeting of the Indian Association Nawab Mir Mahammad Ali was unanimously elected as president. The second objective, that of uniting all Indians, was due to the influence of Mazzini in Bengal.

The Indian Association received a tremendous boost from a new rule of 1876 regarding the Indian Civil Service examination. The maximum age for entering the examination was reduced from 21 to 19. The reason was the apprehension that large numbers of Indian students were entering the service otherwise. By lowering the age limit it was thought that Indian students would find it difficult to come to England and prepare for the examination. This was an opportunity for the Indian Association to whip up public sentiment. The Indian Association quickly gave it an all-India character. In fact, Surendranath toured important centres like Lahore, Amritsar, Delhi, Bombay, Madras, Lucknow, Aligarh, etc. Syed Ahmed had presided over the meeting at Aligarh. Thus, Surendranath had laid the foundation of a national political party with a common programme. According to R.C. Majumdar, 'A firm foundation for united action in the political field of India that was thus built up is an unforgettable phenomenon in the history of India of the 19th century and may be considered to be the greatest contribution … of Surendranath to India's struggle for freedom.'[27]

Apart from the amended civil service rule there were two more opportunities which came before the Indian Association. Three acts came as opportunities – the Vernacular Press Act, the Arms Act, and the Licence Act. The first one was aimed at muzzling the vernacular press which was turning uncomfortably critical of the British rule. The Arms Act made keeping of arms without licence illegal, and the Licence Act required businessmen to take out licences on payment of a fee. Protests against the Vernacular Press Act received support from all across the country culminating in a meeting at the Town Hall in Calcutta. The resolution passed was sent to William Ewart Gladstone, former prime minister of England and then leader of the Opposition. Gladstone moved a resolution in the British parliament which was defeated but the Vernacular Press Act was amended to some extent. The other notable achievement of the Indian Association was related to the Indian Civil Service rules. The association had sent Barrister Lalmohan Ghosh to England with expenses sponsored by the Maharani of Kashimbazar. The eloquence of Ghosh saw a new set of Rules for a Statutory Civil Service placed before the British parliament. On his way back Ghosh was accorded a reception in Bombay where he said, 'Public opinion in India which is flowing in a feeble current today will, by our united efforts, burst forth into a mighty river of national consciousness.'[28] The role of the educated middle class from Bengal, duly supported by certain wealthy persons, in building the first national consensus and giving shape to a national representative forum is acknowledged by historians like Irfan Habib who wrote, 'Surendranath Banerjea was one of our earliest liberal nationalists'. In his address in Dacca Surendranath said,

> Hindus and Mohamedans! We are brothers; and as brothers sometimes quarrel, so too they always make up their quarrels in the presence of the larger interests of the family. I ask you, Hindus and Mohamedans to forget your jealousies and your petty differences in the name of your common country and for the promotion of her dearest interests.[29]

The Ilbert Bill of 1883 was another landmark in strengthening the sapling of political consciousness among Indians. This law was meant to be an amendment of the infamous act of 1849 which assured that only an English judge could try an Englishman in an Indian court.

When Sir C.P. Ilbert, a member of Viceroy Ripon's council, drafted a bill to amend the provision, Englishmen took strong objection, used vile language and behaved unbecomingly. They abused and insulted Governor General Lord Ripon with perhaps tacit support from the members of the civil service. Given so much pressure, Lord Ripon did not pass the bill. However, the outcome was a charged-up atmosphere conducive to the growth of national political aspiration.

Around the same time a British judge, John Freeman Norris, a leader who was part of the agitation against the Ilbert Bill, asked a Hindu to produce his tutelary deity, a Salagram Sila, in court. This was vehemently protested by Surendranath in his paper *The Bengalee*. He even called Judge Norris as unfit to hold the office of a judge which was ruled as contempt of court by the judge. The majority of English judges held Surendranath guilty and jailed him for two months for contempt of court. A huge crowd that had gathered broke windows of the courtroom. The police had to sneak Surendranath out through a backdoor. Huge meetings of protests were held. In one such meeting at Beadon Square, a record 20,000 people gathered, the largest such gathering during those days. Protests were held even outside Bengal – at Agra, Faizabad, Amritsar, Lahore, Poona and many other places. Students had joined the movement in large numbers. These agitations had revealed the wider national unity and was the first instance of mass protest before the Swadeshi movement that took place 20 years later.

Realising the potential of a national platform Surendranath and the others felt the need for creating a national body since the Indian Association was after all a body created in Bengal. The association attempted to establish its presence in other parts of India and set up branches and associates in North India, Bombay and Madras. Meanwhile in 1883 the government arranged an international exhibition in Calcutta where many reputed regional influencers participated. With their support it was decided to hold a National Conference in the last week of December 1883. The second National Conference was scheduled in December 1885. The first conference was held at the Albert Hall where the stunning oratory of Surendranath and Ananda Mohan Bose paved the way for continuation of the forum. In fact, the second conference, again held in Calcutta in 1885, saw the participation of the British Indian Association as well as the Central Muhammadan Association. It was attended by members of the aristocracy or their representatives which included the envoy of the Maharaja of Nepal, Maharaja of Darbhanga, and distinguished citizens like Mahendralal Sarkar, Sibnath Sastri, Amir Ali and Girish Chandra Ghosh. At the same time when the second National Conference was being held the Indian National Congress (INC) had its first lacklustre meeting in Bombay.

Certain curious omissions in the manner in which the Indian National Congress held its first meeting cannot be overlooked. First and foremost, the organisers of the Congress knew well that the second meeting of the National Conference would be held in December 1885, the dates being decided at its first session in 1883. Yet they chose to go ahead with a parallel political set-up at the same time. Prominent personalities from Bengal like Surendranath Banerjee and Ananda Mohan Bose did not attend the first meeting in Bombay due to the more successful and much larger National Conference in Calcutta. Surendranath wrote in his autobiography,

> While we were having our National Conference in Calcutta, the Indian National Congress conceived on the same lines and having the same programme was holding its first session in Bombay. The movements were simultaneous, the preliminary arrangements were made independently, neither party knowing what the other was doing until on the eve of

> the sittings of the Conference and the Congress. Mr. W.C. Bonnerji, who presided over the Bombay Congress invited me to attend it. I told him it was too late to suspend the Conference and that as I had a large share in its organisation, it would not be possible for me to leave Calcutta and attend the Bombay Congress.[30]

The first session of the Indian Congress was perceived as an insult directed at Bengal. Rabindranath Tagore who was impressed with the successful arrangements and the scale of participation in the second National Conference was pained. In a letter to Priyanath Sen, Rabindranath wrote, 'I feel there is a work left for me to do … I feel I will do something for Bengalis … I don't like to leave the world with an insult.'[31] At the time of the National Conference Rabindranath was at Badora near Bombay nursing his father Debendranath Tagore who had fallen sick there. The absence of any prominent Bengali other than W.C. Bonnerjee in the first Congress session, helmed by Gujaratis and Parsis, had deeply hurt Rabindranath. He wrote a poem titled *Awhangeet* (Song to join the call) in which he lamented 'Where are you Bengali?' (*Koi re Bangali Koi*). 'The world over the trumpet has been sounded, hearing it, so many have come with their flags, but where is the Bengali?' The poet was crestfallen but did not give up hope. 'Rise the poet of Bengal, give life afresh in the mother tongue, the people of the world will drink nectar in that language' (*Utha bangakabi, maer bhasay mumurshere dao praan, jagater lok sudhar ashay se bhasa koribe paan*).[32]

This glaring omission was soon rectified by David Hume. Bipin Chandra Pal wrote in his autobiography that when Hume came to Calcutta in connection with his effort to organise the second session of the Congress he realised that Surendranath could not be ignored if he wanted Bengal to participate. In the first meeting in Bombay there were just 72 delegates while the National Conference in Calcutta had more than 100 participants even in its first meeting of 1883. What is more, Surendranath himself was magnanimous. The National Conference in Calcutta had sent a telegram offering felicitation to the first session of the Indian National Congress. When Hume approached Surendranath for joining the second session he readily agreed and worked towards the success of its second session which was presided over by Dadabhai Naoroji. Clearly Surendranath realised that the fledgling spirit of nationalism needed national integration and support from all sections. According to R.C. Majumdar, perhaps Surendranath understood that the English rulers would have greater respect for the martial races of the North and Punjab, and felt it would create a strong forum for Indians to bank on. Even before the first session of the Congress Surendranath had written,

> The Central idea was the promotion of unification between the different Indian peoples and provinces and of a feeling of friendliness between the people of Bengal and the material races of the North. We counted for nothing in those days. It was constantly dinned into our ears that our political demands, whatever they were, came from the deltaic Ganges, who did not contribute a single soldiers to the army and who were separated from the sturdier races of the North by a wide gulf of isolation, if not alienation.[33]

It was Surendranath Banerjee's commitment to the national cause that ensured that the insignificant launch of the Congress in Bombay was forgotten with a robust success in its Calcutta session. However, even his contemporaries felt that this self-abnegation did not serve the political interest of Bengal and in point of fact blocked the prospect of Bengal. Bipin Chandra Pal too observed that Surendranath committed political hara-kiri by joining the Congress.[34]

Rabindranath Tagore was a special invitee at the second session of the Congress. He wrote and sang '*Amra milechhi aaj mayer dake*' (We have assembled here today in response to the call of the mother).[35] It was a well-organised affair with delegates receiving all resolutions well ahead of the session. Compared to 72 in the first session 434 delegates attended the second session in Calcutta. But the animosity towards Bengal was visible as well with many considering the Congress as an organisation of Bengalis. The demands of the Congress reflected the political demands of Bengal, the naysayers claimed. Historian R.C. Majumdar wrote, 'Reacting to such a comment, Malik Bhagwan Das, a delegate from Dera Ismail Khan, retorted, "Do I look like a Bengalee Babu? Every intelligent man would demand the administrative reforms that the Congress is demanding."'[36] This anti-Bengali sentiment was cleverly used by Syed Ahmad Khan of Aligarh. An avowed critic of the Congress, before the third session in Madras he said in a meeting, 'If you want the Bengalees to rule the country, if you want the oppressed masses in the country to lick the feet of the Bengalees, then by all means get a ticket for Madras and board the train with the name of Allah on your lips.' Even the governor general Lord Dufferin wrote to the secretary of state that one reason why Muslims did not attend the Calcutta Congress was their feeling that they would be worse off under a Bengali Constitution.[37] According to author G.B. Malleson, who wrote on the Sepoy Mutiny and was quoted by Majumdar, 'Skillful in hectoring, the Bengalees are the founders of the Congress but the type of representative institution that they demand is hated by the martial races of India – Sikhs, Rajputs, Rohillas, Jats and the frontier Pathans.'[38] Clearly the superior skills of the Bengalis in communication and organisation had many detractors who received tacit support from the English administration. The sacrifice of Surendranath in person and that of Bengalis as a collective force perhaps made the detractors feel small. They harboured deep resentment towards the dominant Bengali leadership.

Meanwhile the Bengal leadership with its advanced political consciousness found the Congress lacking as a satisfactory representative body. Leaders in Bengal felt the Congress represented the rich and affluent, and the middle class, with little concern for the masses. Journals like *Bharatbasi*, *Garib* and *Dainik* were critical of the Congress even when it held its successful second session in Calcutta. The argument was that people who do not have food in their stomach or cloth on their bodies could not be concerned with the political demands of the Congress. Congress's chosen method of sending petitions to the government was also criticised. Aswini Kumar Dutta, an outspoken leader from Barisal, even called the Congress 'three days of fun'. Rabindranath Tagore who sang 'Vande Mataram' in the 1896 session of the Congress in Calcutta faced his share of discomfort when he was invited to join a dinner party after the session and sing a song. The poet had shown his disenchantment with the Congress leaders following the strict Western dress code and behaviour during the dinner. He wrote and sang a song titled, 'Don't ask me to sing' which was a veiled but severe criticism of the delegates all attired in western clothes while Rabindranath and other members of his family – Abanindranath, Samarendranath and Gaganendranath Tagore – were all wearing Bengali-style 'dhuti-chadar'. Abanindranath reminisced that so annoyed were the others that they gave them the nickname 'National dress'.[39]

The political maturity of Bengal was reflected in its literature, drama and publications. Bengal was way ahead in developing a sense of nationalism in India, followed by Maharashtra. There were other provinces where too the sense of nationalism was taking root. The Arya Samaj of Swami Dayanand was a prominent example. The Brahmo

Samaj in Bengal tried to attract Swami Dayanand into its fold but the inherent differences between them came in the way. Veneration of cows by the Arya Samaj was a major point of discord.[40] The Brahmo Samaj was influenced by the rational and liberal movements of the West while Swami Dayanand was not conversant with the English language and he appealed to the masses. Even within the Congress veneration of cows was an issue. In 1893 Cow Protection Society (Gorakshani Sabha) was set up in Maharashtra. In the same year there had been riots over cow slaughter in several places in Bihar. The anti-kine-killing movement resulted in Hindus rescuing cows from Muslim butchers. Rabindranath realised how the English rulers wanted this chasm to widen. He expressed his views in 1893, in 'Fear of the Englishmen' (*Engrajer Atanka*)[41] where he was clear in his thought that the differences between Hindus and Muslims over cow protection found favour among various sections of the Englishmen in India. One reason for that could be the observation of the English rulers that Indians were slowly coming together under the banner of the Congress. If Muslims too joined the platform it would be difficult for the English to rule India. Rabindranath had understood that the Englishmen wanted the Muslims to stay away from a united political platform. In addition, Tagore observed that due to many differences among themselves even Hindus found it difficult to unitedly take up a cause. Cow protection was an issue that could unite Hindus of all hues. Cow Protection Society, therefore, was viewed as a threat by the rulers. At the same time, cow protection served the purpose of keeping Hindus and Muslims separate, lessening the fear that Englishmen felt due to the rise of nationalism in the country. In short even in 1893 Rabindranath saw through the game of divide and rule and how divisive could be the Hindu urge of protecting cows. The cow protection movement however did not find many takers in Bengal or South India.

The educated Muslims felt that by joining the Congress the community would be handicapped due to their lack of education. Effectively the community would remain subservient to the more advanced Hindus. This inherent antagonism received further fillip, apart from the cow protection movement, due to two developments, both in Maharashtra. Bal Gangadhar Tilak started the Shivaji festival and revived Ganapati puja as a national festival. Tilak was also blamed for the cow protection movement but there was no evidence to back the claim. Both Ganapati puja and Shivaji festival served as a red rag of sorts to the Muslims. Liberal Hindus and orthodox Congress members did not favour these steps since both hurt their intention of creating Hindu-Muslim unity. Even in Bengal there were differences among the early nationalists. Surendranath tried his utmost to assemble everyone under one banner of nationalism. But others like Bankim Chandra lamented the Bengali Hindu's loss of freedom marking the year AD 1203 as the loss of liberty when Nabadwip fell to Muslim invaders. Bankim Chandra wrote in *Kamalakanter Daptar*,

> I have a memory of happy Bengal but I find no signs of happiness now. I remember the happy days but where shall I turn to find them? Where is Gauda? It is in ruins as the result of Muslim violence. Then look at Navadvip the cremation ground of Bengal's independence, where 17 Muslims conquered Bengal. When I remember my motherland, Bengal, I look at that cremation ground.[42]

Bankim was not alone. Bengali literature then was full of references to Muslim aggression. Rangalal Bandyopadhyay wrote in the context of Rajputs fighting Muslim aggression, 'who wants to live after losing freedom – who will agree to lead the life of a slave' – the most repeated lines by a Bengali nationalist since then.[43] Hemchandra

Bandyopadhyay lamented the fall of the ancient Hindu kingdoms, so did Nabin Chandra Sen. The popular literature of Bengal had taken it for granted that India's plight started only with the Muslims taking over. No one took note of any of the Muslim rulers who also had proud traditions of holding the country together. Rabindranath wrote *Shivaji Utsav* in 1904. He lamented that Bengal did not notice the message delivered by the saffron flag of Shivaji; instead later when the scales of the trader turned into a sceptre of the ruler, Bengalis welcomed it with the holy water of the Ganga. He felt it was now time for Bengal to join in the praise of the holy name of Shivaji which unified India. Tagore painted Shivaji as a great visionary, whose dream was to bind together the people of India, to create a unified Indian nation. Little did Tagore, who understood the divide-and-rule policy of the English rulers in the context of cow protection, realise that for a Muslim it would be difficult to say 'Jayatu Shivaji' without feeling the pain he inflicted on the Mogul Empire. Clearly the nascent idea of nationalism born in Bengal which spread across the country had in it a divisive thorn polarising the Hindus and the Muslims. Not just Tilak or Swami Dayanand, the liberal thinkers from politically advanced Bengal also had to tread along this sensitive line all along. Again there were differences of views in Bengal. *The Englishman*, at that time the leading organ of public opinion, was staunchly against the Shivaji utsav. In fact, the paper painted Shivaji as someone who gained prominence through treachery and assassination. *The Englishman* had no dearth of followers. Many well-established Bengalis who were afraid of bureaucratic displeasure kept away from the Shivaji utsav. In 1901 when several eminent Bengalis refused to chair the festival it was a much-anguished Swami Vivekananda who had offered to preside over the festival despite his extremely poor health.[44]

The spread of religion-centric nationalism which had several proponents in Bengal as also elsewhere such as in Maharashtra and

North India received a tremendous boost with the arrival of Swami Vivekananda. Though Swami Vivekananda was not involved in politics (perhaps the reason why S. Irfan Habib in his book *Indian Nationalism: The Essential Writings* did not include his contribution), he provided the much-needed self-respect to the Hindus due to his oratory in the Chicago Parliament of Religions in 1893, held in connection with the celebration of the 400th anniversary of the discovery of America by Christopher Columbus. Swami Vivekananda, an unknown, unheard of young man in saffron was joined by two other Bengalis on the dais – Mazoomdar of the Brahmo Samaj and Chakravarti representing Theosophy. Swami Vivekananda noted that both spoke well – 'Mazoomdar made a nice speech, Chakravarti a nicer one, and they were much applauded. They were all prepared and came with ready-made speeches.' Vivekananda had never spoken in public before and he was not even prepared. 'I was a fool and had none,' he wrote.[45] When it was his turn to be introduced and make a short speech, truly following the saying '*Mukam karoti bachalam*' – who maketh the dumb a fluent speaker – he started with 'Sisters and Brothers of America', instead of the usual salutations and 'a deafening applause of two minutes followed'. What followed had set the tone for Hindutva-centric nationalism.

> I thank you in the name of the most ancient order of monks in the world; I thank you in the name of the mother of religions; and I thank you in the name of millions and millions of Hindu people of all classes and sects ... I am proud to belong to a religion which has taught the world both tolerance and universal acceptance. I am proud to belong to a nation which has sheltered the persecuted and the refugees of all religions and all nations of the earth ... I fervently hope that the bell that tolled this morning in honour of this convention may

> be the death-knell of all fanaticism, of all persecutions with the sword or with the pen, and of all uncharitable feelings between persons wending their way to the same goal.

The media was stunned and wrote, 'But eloquent as were many of the brief speeches, no one expressed as well the spirit of the Parliament (of religions) and its limitations as the Hindu monk.'[46]

It was Swami Vivekananda who positioned Hinduism as the ancient liberal religion and placed Indian nationalism on the high pedestal of ancient glory. The western view of Hinduism was a bundle of superstitions, full of immoral customs and managed by evil institutions. The Hindu intelligentsia were always very sensitive to the criticism of the West, particularly the Christian missionaries, regarding the many evils and the shortcomings of the Hindu society and religion; they were always defensive and apologetic. All of a sudden, the tables were turned by an unknown sanyasi and the 'West joined in a chorus of applause at the hidden virtues of Hinduism which were hitherto unsuspected either by friends or foes.'[47]

Swami Vivekananda was called the father of modern Indian nationalism:

> O India! With this mere echoing of others, with this base imitation of others, with this dependence on others this slavish weakness, this vile detestable cruelty – wouldst thou, with these provisions only, scale the highest pinnacle of civilisation and greatness? Wouldst thou attain, by means of thy disgraceful cowardice, that freedom deserved only by the brave and the heroic? O India! .... Forget not that the lower classes, the ignorant, the poor, the illiterate, the cobbler, the sweeper, are thy flesh and blood, thy brothers. Thou brave one, be bold, take courage, be proud that thou art an Indian,

> and proudly proclaim, 'I am an Indian, every Indian is my brother.' Say 'The ignorant Indian, the poor and destitute Indian, the Brahmin Indian, the Pariah Indian, is my brother' … 'India's society is the cradle of my infancy, the pleasure-garden of my youth, the sacred heaven, the Varanasi of my old age.' Say, brother, 'The soil of India is my highest heaven, the good of India is my good.'[48]

The intensely patriotic Swami lamented the fragmented nature of the Hindu race. He felt that the only reason why a nation of 40 million had been ruling over 300-million Indians was this division among the people in India: 'You three hundred million have a will each separate from the other ... to make a great future India, the whole secret lies in organisation, accumulation of power, co-ordination of wills.' The ideal of nationalism as preached by Swami Vivekananda was based on four solid rocks:[49] the awakening of the masses who form the basis of the nation, development of physical and moral strength, unity based on common spiritual idea, and consciousness of, and pride in, the ancient glory and greatness of India. In later years Mahatma Gandhi had used these principles with suitable modifications to suit his politics and successfully built the foundation of an independent nation.

Bipin Chandra Pal, a member of the Brahmo Samaj, who along with Tilak and Lala Lajpat Rai had ushered in a change in the approach of the Congress, had called Vivekananda's teachings as neo-Vedantism.

> Under the influence of this Neo-Vedantism, associated to a large extent with the name of the late Swami Vivekananda, there has been at work a slow and silent process of the liberalization of old social ideas … But this movement has not only developed a strong spiritual note … it has struck a

> strong note of reality in Indian politics also, which it never had before. It has subjected the British policy in India to a rigorous analysis and has thus revealed its true character with almost cruel candor. It has completely demolished the idea that England is, and always been, in India mainly for the good of the Indian.[50]

While Bengal was leading in ideology it was Bal Gangadhar Tilak who infused action into the theory of religion-centric nationalism. He brought to the fore the failure of the administration in managing the plague epidemic in Poona (now Pune). In fact, even Swami Vivekananda had engaged his newly founded order Ramakrishna Mission in serving the plague affected in Bengal. But his was a non-political philanthropic act while Tilak's was a direct intervention by a politician. Tilak led a movement where the provisions of the Government's Famine Relief Code were explained to people inciting them to demand their rights under the code. Tilak urged people to demand work from the collector instead of selling land and paying rent – 'no rent campaign' as the British bureaucracy called it. The atrocities committed by British soldiers in Poona while enforcing preventive measures against the plague epidemic saw the British collector of Poona and another officer shot dead for which Tilak was held accountable and sentenced. The incident exposed the differences of opinion among the then leaders including within the Congress. Gopal Krishna Gokhale had tendered a humble apology to the government for his comments against the violent acts of the soldiers during the plague epidemic while Tilak had dismissed such a suggestion. Within the Congress these differences came to the fore in 1897 during its Amravati session. A special resolution supporting Tilak was shelved due to the opposition of the moderate sections of the Congress. Eloquent tributes were nevertheless paid by the president Sankaran Nair and also by Surendranath Banerjee who raised the bar at the session with his rousing oratory. But oratory on its own could not heal the widening gulf between the nationalists, within the Congress or outside.

Sri Aurobindo was a staunch critic of the Congress noting that it had lost connect with the masses:

> Like a consumptive patient, Bengal is advancing day by day towards its doom. W.C. Bonnerji, Lalmohan Ghose and other Congress stalwarts who move about in the rarified atmosphere of the Legislative Council have no contact with the youth of the land but the ardour of patriotism is gradually on the increase.[51]

Historians like R.C. Majumdar opine that Aurobindo was the most typical example of the new type of nationalism. 'What is Nationalism? Nationalism is not a mere political programme. Nationalism is a religion that has come from God: Nationalism is a creed in which you shall have to live … You must remember that you are the instrument of God for the salvation of your own country.'[52]

Rabindranath was also critical of the westernised meetings resorted to by the Congress and its provincial councils. He wrote, 'Our country is in the villages … The Ultimate objective of Political movements is to bring about unity of the heart all over the country.'[53] Rabindranath felt that the westernised meetings, that too in English, a language not understood by the people, were not the right approach. The likes of Aurobindo, Rabindranath and Bipin Chandra had provided the intellectual foundation to leaders like Tilak who, it is said, contributed more by his life and actions. It is believed that articles penned by Bipin Chandra gave rise to the extremist section within the Congress.

Clearly Bengal was the nursery of political thoughts and the idea of nationalism evolved in due course. What initially started out as meetings gave way to protests and actions by the turn of the century.

Endnotes

1 S. Irfan Habib, ed., *Indian Nationalism: The Essential Writings* (Aleph Book Company, 2017), Kindle edition.

2 Swapan Dasgupta, *Awakening Bharat Mata: The Political Beliefs of the Indian Right* (Penguin Viking, 2019), pp 167-8.

3 R.C. Majumdar, ed., *British Paramountcy and Indian Renaissance* Part II, tenth volume of *The History and Culture of the Indian People* (Bhartiya Vidya Bhavan, 2017), p. 478.

4 Ibid., p. 1.

5 Ibid., p. 33.

6 Ibid., p. 6.

7 Ibid., p. 2.

8 Ibid., pp 11-2.

9 A.G. Noorani, "Vande Mataram, A Historical Lesson," *EPW,* June 9, 1973, https://www.epw.in/system/files/pdf/1973_8/23/vande_mataram_a_historical_lesson.pdf.

10 Ibid.

11 Majumdar, ed., *British Paramountcy,* Part II, p. 4.

12 Ibid.

13 Noorani, "Vande Mataram".

14 R.C. Majumdar, *History of Modern Bengal: Part - One* (Tulshi Prakashani, 1978), p. 48.

15 Ibid., p. 93.

16 Ibid., p. 95.

17 Ibid., p. 96.

18 Ibid., pp 46-7 – written by Kishori Chand Mitra in 1858.

19 Habib, ed., *Indian Nationalism* – Speech of Aurobindo at Bombay National Union.

20 Ibid.

21 Majumdar, *Modern Bengal,* p. 391.

22 Ibid., p. 390.

23 Noorani, "Vande Mataram".

24 Habib, ed., *Indian Nationalism.* E-book location 169.

25 Ibid. E-book location 305.

26 Majumdar, *Modern Bengal*, p. 388.
27 Ibid., p. 391.
28 Ibid., p. 393.
29 Habib, ed., *Indian Nationalism.*
30 Surendranath Banerjea, *A Nation in Making* (Oxford University Press, 1927) quoted by Majumdar, *Modern Bengal*, p. 398.
31 Letter to Priyanath Sen and quoted in *Rabindrajibani* by Prabhat Kumar Mukhopadhyay (Visva-Bharati, Baisakh 1424), pp 228-9.
32 *Awhangeet* in *Kori o Komal* by Rabindranath Tagore, *Rabindra Rachanabali,* vol. 1 (Government of West Bengal, 1980), p. 275.
33 Majumdar, *Modern Bengal*, p. 400.
34 Ibid.
35 Prabhat Kumar Mukhopadhyay, *Rabindrajibani*, p. 244.
36 Majumdar, *Modern Bengal*, p. 399.
37 Ibid., p. 400.
38 Ibid.
39 Ibid.
40 Majumdar, ed., *British Paramountcy*, p. 109.
41 Rabindranath Tagore, *Rabindra Rachanabali*, vol. 13 (West Bengal Government 1990), p. 292.
42 Bankim Chandra Chattopadhyay, *Bankim Rachanabali*, vol. 2 (Dey's Publishing, 2018), p. 168.
43 *Swadhinata,* a poem by Rangalal Bandyopadhyay.
44 Sankari Prasad Basu, *Swami Vivekananda in Contemporary Indian News*, vol. II (Ramakrishna Mission Institute of Culture, 2007), pp 302-3.
45 Swami Vivekananda, *Swami Vivekananda on Himself* (Advaita Ashrama, 2006), pp 126-31.
46 Ibid. Swami Vivekananda quoted from the report in the *New York Critique.*
47 Majumdar, ed., *British Paramountcy*, pp 488-90.
48 *The Complete Works of Swami Vivekananda*, volumes 1-9 <www.ramakrishnavivekannda.info> e-book location 27527 to 545.
49 R.C. Majumdar, *Swami Vivekananda: A Historical Review* (Advaita Ashrama, 2016) quoted in Swapan Dasgupta, *Awakening Bharat Mata*, pp 161-70.
50 Bipin Chandra Pal, 'Hinduism and Indian Nationalism' in *The Spirit of Indian Nationalism* (1910) and reproduced in Habib, *Indian Nationalism.*
51 Majumdar, *Modern Bengal,* pp 1-2.
52 Habib, *Indian Nationalism* – Speech of Aurobindo at Bombay National Union.
53 Majumdar, *Modern Bengal,* p. 3.

CHARTING A DIFFERENT COURSE

The disenchantment with the Congress started almost since its inception. This was articulated forcefully by Aurobindo Ghosh who said in no unequivocal terms that the aim of the Congress was mistaken, its spirit did not reflect sincerity, and the methods it adopted were not right. Referring to the pro-Congress views held by Phiroze Shah Mehta and Manmohan Ghosh, Aurobindo quoting Ghosh's statement ('the Congress represents the thinking portion of the Indian people, whose duty it is to guide the ignorant') said that, '… the National Congress may be as national as you please, but it is not a popular body and has not in any way attempted to become a popular body.'[1] In fact, since its inception the Congress had never taken note of what Allan Octavian Hume wrote in the famous manifesto issued two years before the party was formed where he had appealed to educated Indians to make 'a resolute struggle to secure freedom for yourselves and your country'. The neo-nationalists among whom Aurobindo emerged as the most important voice declared, 'It is not in human nature to rest eternally contented with a state of subordination or serfdom … Tyrants have tried but have they ever succeeded in repressing this natural love of freedom in man?' What Tilak had shown through his actions Aurobindo had articulated forcefully.

The other point to note is that the armed revolution had its roots, not in Bengal, but in Maharashtra where the Chapekar brothers, Damodar and Balkrishna, shot dead the Poona collector

Walter Charles Rand and another British officer. The two Dravid brothers who were rewarded for informing the administration on the Chapekar brothers were murdered by the third Chapekar brother, Vasudev, with a friend in February 1899. The three Chapekar brothers and their friend were all hanged by the British court – the first four martyrs in the cause of a revolutionary movement. Aurobindo in his autobiographical sketch had mentioned a secret society started in Western India before the end of the 19th century. Vasudev Balwant Phadke, an independence activist, had even attempted to raise an armed rebellion thereby managing to control Poona for a few days. He was eventually captured and deported to Aden in Yemen where he died in 1883. That was two years before the Congress had its first session in Bombay. The revolutionary secret society which started in Bengal was the result of increasing frustration among the neo-nationalists. Anusilan Samiti was set up at the beginning of the 20th century. Aurobindo had tasked Jatindranath Bandyopadhyay to set up a secret society which later merged with the Anusilan Samiti. Differences of opinion among the members of the secret societies was a major hindrance for the growth of these organisations. For instance, Jatindranath and Aurobindo's brother Barindra Ghosh fell out which eventually led to Jatindranath quitting an active role in secret societies in Bengal. In later life he turned into a sanyasi and was known as Niralamba Swami. Aurobindo had helped Anusilan Samiti financially apart from his intellectual contribution to the cause of a revolt against the English rule. Anusilan Samiti launched the newspaper *Jugantar* under the editorship of Bhupendranath Dutta, younger brother of Swami Vivekananda. Aurobindo was the principal force behind the revolutionary movement though he remained in the background. Even as a student in England Aurobindo had revolutionary proclivity and was a member of a revolutionary society known as the Lotus and Dagger.[2]

The arrival of Lord Curzon as the viceroy in January 1899 contributed in no small way in shaping the nascent revolutionary ideas in Bengal into a movement of consequence. To begin with, Curzon had made no secret of his feelings of racial superiority. It is said that when Surendranath went with a few other leaders of the Indian Association to felicitate the newly appointed governor general, two members were sent back by the governor's A.D.C. for wearing pump shoes. Reportedly Curzon wrote to the secretary of state for India that he intended to dig the grave of the Indian National Congress before his term ended. Curzon having assessed the role played by Bengalis within the Congress, wanted to create a rift between them and even bribed the nawab of Dacca with a large sum of soft loan to win him over in bifurcating Bengal. This also served his objective of creating a Muslim majority Assam and East Bengal. The educated Hindu Bengalis who were a thorn in the side of the British administration thus became a minority both in the Muslim-majority East and in the other part comprising West Bengal, Bihar and Odisha. Evidently Curzon had studied his policies carefully and wanted to weaken the rise of nationalism in Bengal.[3]

Interestingly the arrival of Lord Curzon and Sri Aurobindo helped in the rise of the Swadeshi movement in Bengal – the latter shifted his base to Calcutta in order to help the nascent neo-nationalist revolutionary set-up. The Anusilan Samiti in Dacca had grown faster than its Calcutta counterpart. Later in 1917 when the British government appointed Sidney Rowlatt, a judge, to investigate political terrorism in India, the report had acknowledged the progress of the Dacca Anusilan Samiti.

> The Dacca Anusilan Samiti has had a quick expansion; its effectiveness was unique and the great courage exhibited by it in the execution of its programme is notable. The reason

> probably is that the average boys of East Bengal are far in advance of their counterparts in West Bengal in boldness and physical powers.[4]

Anusilan Samiti came into being when many centres of physical exercise were being set up under the inspired speeches of Swami Vivekananda who advocated that in order to attain greatness the people of a nation must acquire strength and courage first. Rabindranath mentioned one such society which had Rajnarain Bose as its president: 'Meeting of that Society used to be held in a dilapidated house inside a lane, in a dark room with closed doors; the members were initiated with sacred texts from the Vedas.' Such societies were effectively childish pranks, Rabindranath writing that these meetings were a 'farce and a mimicry of a display of heroism. The force is ended and not a brick of the Fort William has been displayed.'[5] Anusilan Samiti came up as one such centre of physical exercise. Barrister Pramathanath Mitra accepted the responsibility of leading the Samiti. To him came the representative from Baroda, probably Jatindranath Bandyopadhyay sent by Aurobindo, and a larger *samiti* was formed with Sri Aurobindo and Chittaranjan Das as vice-presidents and Surendranath Tagore as treasurer. Later when Aurobindo got deeply involved perhaps he felt the need to create a more active underground revolutionary cell to disrupt the English administration. Aurobindo's focus lay in teaching bomb-making and use of fire arms. Perhaps the hesitation of Pramathanath Mitra in such a radical move led to the separation of Anusilan Samiti. The newspaper *Jugantar* which had avid followers turned into a party of its own.

How did the old guard respond to the neo-nationalists? One revolutionary, Abinas Chandra Bhattacharya, recalled in his memoir how Surendranath reacted when he had visited Surendranath with a pamphlet titled 'No Compromise'. Surendranath went through the pamphlet carefully and concluded that no Indian could be capable of writing such language. Abinas Chandra then spoke of Aurobindo who had drafted the pamphlet. Surendranath had offered to support them financially but expressed his inability to join the movement; he was too old for that he had said. Clearly Aurobindo's revolutionary ideas were ahead of its time and too radical for the older generation of politicians like Surendranath to embrace.

The politics of Bengal took a sharp divergence from the majority view as reflected by the opinions of the top leaders of the Congress at that time. There were neo-nationalists elsewhere also. Tilak and Lala Lajpat Rai were two frontline leaders in India who were active in the Congress like Aurobindo from Bengal. With Curzon landing in Calcutta with a determination to teach nationalist Bengalis a lesson, this sharp political division came to the fore. The proposal to divide Bengal in two parts, a pet project of Curzon, changed the course of politics in India in more ways than one. First, as we have noted, it led to a sharp division within the Congress leadership. Second, thanks to Curzon's machinations, the seeds of communalism had been sown in Bengal, hitherto confined to intellectual ideas, that caused bloody riots later. Third, and no less important, the partition of Bengal was the first significant step, though affecting Bengal mainly, that eventually led to a nationwide anti-British call for independent India. As far as politics in Bengal is concerned the Swadeshi movement had paved the path for the deep-rooted deviation of Bengali political views from mainstream national politics, a tilt that is present even today.

Not that the Congress was not aware of the devious plan of Curzon to bifurcate Bengal and it took due notice of this proposal. In both 1903 and 1904 the Congress adopted resolutions, the most visible action of the party in those days, and attempts were also made to approach the government to persuade it to change its view of the Bengal partition. When the Congress thought in early 1905 that it would call upon the viceroy to discuss the issue of Bengal's partition, Curzon refused to receive the delegation and referred to the activities of the Congress in contemptuous terms. The leaders of the Congress in those days had tremendous faith in the British sense of justice and in their own ability to appeal to such sense. Clearly the response meted out to the Indian delegation which went to greet Curzon on his arrival did not teach leaders like Surendranath, who was in that delegation, a lesson. Not just that, when Curzon snubbed the Congress delegation, its leaders thought it advisable to go to England with an appeal to desist from partitioning Bengal. The Congress chose as its emissaries Gopal Krishna Gokhale, a moderate leader, and Lala Lajpat Rai, a supporter of the neo-nationalists. As expected, they came back with nothing to show for, 'sadder but wiser'.[6] This was evident in the speeches of Gokhale who was presiding over the Congress session at Varanasi in 1905. By then Bengal had been partitioned.

Curzon feared that Bengal would lead the nation in its first mass movement against British rule. This led to his unwavering resolve to weaken Bengalis by dividing the state. Curzon wrote to the secretary of state when the latter was not comfortable with the decision to partition the province, 'The Bengalees consider themselves a separate nation and indulge in driving away the British and putting a Bengalee Babu in the Government house as Governor General. The partition of Bengal would undermine their sense of superiority and destroy their dream and that is why they are agitating against it.'[7] By carrying out what he thought was right Curzon shaped the future course of Indian politics. Even a moderate leader like Gokhale said in the Varanasi session of the Congress that Indians needed self-government within the empire. He praised in glowing terms the Swadeshi movement that had taken shape in Bengal and said,

> The devotion to Motherland, which is enshrined in the highest (in) Swadeshi, is an influence so profound and so passionate that it's very thought thrills and its actual touch lifts one out of oneself. India needs today above everything else that the gospel of this devotion should be preached to high and the low, to Prince and to peasant, in town and in hamlet, till the service of Motherland becomes with us an overmastering a passion as it is in Japan.[8]

The delegates, according to Annie Besant, spoke in one indignant voice after another and expressed the anger and determination seething within. 'Not often has the National Congress witnessed such a sense of excitement,' she said.[9]

But that was only about the Swadeshi movement which had broken out in Bengal without any involvement of the Indian National Congress. Clearly the Congress session in Varanasi merely gave a post facto lip service to the spontaneous movement Bengal had launched. The problem arose when the Congress was required to voice its support for the boycott campaign that too was an integral part of the Swadeshi movement.

The call for boycott was given in the newspaper *Sanjibani* by its editor Krishna Kumar Mitra on 13 July 1905, a few days after the final decision of partition was announced by the government. Mitra suggested boycott of British goods and of government employees. In a meeting held at Bagerhat in the district of Khulna two resolutions were passed, the first one being boycott of British goods and the second being abstainment from amusements and festivities. Bengalis had realised that since armed rebellion was not possible, they would have to resort to other measures to put pressure on the government. Boycott emerged as a critical tool in the spontaneous Swadeshi movement.[10] Meetings held in all corners of Bengal overwhelmingly endorsed the resolution to boycott British goods. It was felt that the commercial loss of their merchants and mills would exert pressure on the British administration to rescind the decision on the partition of Bengal. How far such a feeling was correct could be seen from the quantum of loss suffered by the traders of imported goods. In a telegram sent (1 September 1905) to the Manchester Chamber of Commerce by the Marwari Chamber of Commerce in Calcutta, the Manchester Chamber was requested to exert pressure on the secretary of state in England to scrap Bengal's partition. Clearly boycott was hurting where it was intended to. But for the Congress there was a problem – the first major point of discord between popular opinion in Bengal and representatives of the Indian National Congress. An important point to note is that the movement in Bengal was a spontaneous one, where common men, students, zamindars, a section of the Muslims (despite Curzon trying to bribe the nawab of Dacca), and poets and writers led by Rabindranath Tagore came together. The Congress hardly played a role in this spontaneous movement. What the Congress in Varanasi was expected to do was to endorse the movement. However it failed to do so because of its reservations about 'boycott' as a policy.

While the delegates from Bengal and those belonging to the extremist section of the Congress (neo-nationalists) wanted the Congress to endorse boycott, the moderates who were in control of the party were averse to it. Resolutions had to be put before the Subjects Committee where it was debated acrimoniously. The Congress leaders were keen to pass a resolution welcoming the forthcoming visit of the Prince and Princess of Wales to India. In fact Gokhale had promised Lord Minto that there would be no boycott of the royal visit while delegates from Bengal and neo-nationalists refused to endorse such a resolution. The moderates had the numbers to pass the welcome proposal by majority vote but this would have taken away the grace and charm of the message. Clearly despite welcoming the Swadeshi movement and saying that India needed self-government within the empire, the royalty representing the empire meant more to the moderate leaders led by the Congress President Gokhale. As a compromise the Congress drafted a convoluted verbose resolution in support of boycott,

> That the Congress records its earnest and emphatic protest against the repressive measures which have been adopted by the authorities in Bengal after the people there had been compelled to resort to the boycott of foreign goods as a last protest, and perhaps the only constitutional and effective means left to them of drawing the attention of the British public to the action of the Government of India in persisting in their determination to partition Bengal, in utter disregard of the universal prayers and protests of the people.[11]

Lala Lajpat Rai, the nationalist among the senior Congress leaders, seconded the proposal and congratulated 'Bengal on its splendid opportunity of heralding a new political era for the country ... If other Provinces followed the example of Bengal the day was not far distant when they would win.'[12] On their part delegates from Bengal walked out when the resolution to welcome the prince was put to vote so that it could be passed without opposition. The Congress in Varanasi was a divided house and had failed to wholeheartedly endorse the heartburn of Bengal. Clearly the leaders found it difficult to join the Bengal nationalists enamoured as they were still of the fairness of British rule. The very first spontaneous national movement eventually was successful even without the National Congress formally joining hands with it. The other point to note is that the top leaders of the Congress then included persons like Surendranath Banerjee,

Rashbehari Ghosh, Lalmohan Ghosh, et al. None of these prominent Bengali leaders seems to have sided with the neo-nationalists from their home state. Clearly Bengal was yearning for a new leader, perhaps acknowledging Surendranath's admission when he said that he was rather old to take up the issues raised in Aurobindo's pamphlet 'No Compromise' mentioned earlier. The Swadeshi movement in Bengal was truly led by the entire province with just a token presence of Surendranath and the others. The stirring literature of the times aroused the entire Bengali-speaking population against the British decision of partition, an effect perhaps Lord Curzon did not foresee. Instead of breaking the morale of Bengal Curzon managed to unify the people under a single resolve – that of forcing the government to rescind its own decision and unify Bengal again.

The Swadeshi movement was truly led by the people of Bengal without any leader as such. The two most important influencers who had shaped the movement were Aurobindo Ghosh and the poet Rabindranath Tagore. According to historian R.C. Majumdar, Aurobindo not only expounded the religious and philosophical basis of nationalism but also presented it as a sublime sentiment in human life. Aurobindo wrote,

> Love has a place in politics, but it is the love of one's country … The feeling of almost physical delight in the touch of the mother-soil … music, poetry, habits, dress, manners of our Indian life, - this is the physical root of that love. The pride in our past, the pain of our present, the passion for the future are its trunk and branches, self-sacrifice and self-forgetfulness, great service, high endurance for the country are its fruit. And the sap, which keeps it alive is the realization of the Motherhood of God in the country, the vision of the Mother, the perpetual contemplation, adoration and service of the Mother.[13]

If Aurobindo was the high priest of the Swadeshi movement, Rabindranath was the poet who ignited the spirit among the Bengalis. His poems and songs in words of inimitable beauty proved more attractive than rabble-rousing speeches of any political leader. The song *Banglar mati Banglar jal* by Tagore stirred Bengal on 16 October 1905 (30th Asvin 1312 Bangabda), the day partition came into effect. Tagore wrote,

> Bengal is going to be severed by law on 30th Asvin but God has not separated them; remembering this and for proclaiming this, we shall observe the day as a day of unity for Bengalees and as a token of that shall tie yellow threads (Rakhi) on the wrists of one another, saying brothers shall not separate.[14]

Rabindranath led a huge procession to the bank of the Ganga where they bathed and then tied *rakhi*s on one another's wrists. Tagore's song *Banglar mati Banglar jal* was on everyone's lips. At Parsibagan the foundation stone for a Banga Bhavan was laid. Surendranath presided over the meeting. Rabindranath read out the resolution in Bengali:

> Ignoring the unanimous opposition of the Bengalees the British Parliament has severed Bengal into two: as a protest against this action we take this oath and resolve that we shall take all possible steps to neutralize the evil effects of the partition and to preserve the unity of the Bengalees. May God be our guide.[15]

This was the time when Tagore wrote several songs – one of which, *Amar Sonar Bangla,* is now the national anthem of Bangladesh. Political leaders of Bengal, however, were anything but united at that point. We have seen how the established Bengali leaders in the Congress were hesitant in providing unconditional support to issues like boycott of British goods. The only thing that bound them were the songs which Tagore had composed. Bengal followed the bard's song, *Jadi tor dak shune keo na aashe tobe ekla chalo re* (If nobody comes at your call walk alone).[16]

The reaction of the British administration to the Swadeshi movement led to a counter reaction from the revolutionaries who had been quietly working at Anusilan Samiti and its various branches. Aurobindo knew well enough that a few stray cases of violence aimed at public servants would not change a government but 'when a movement reflects public feeling it should not be opposed.' Aurobindo wrote,

> The Swadeshi movement generated disquiet and fear in the governmental circle resulting in a policy of repression. When imposition of fine on school and college students, expulsion, imprisonment, punishment and public flogging and similar measures of oppression mounted, the revolutionaries started thinking of redress and the cult of revolution gradually turned into terrorism.[17]

Even Barindra Ghosh in his confessional statement had said, 'We never believed that freedom could be achieved through political murder. But we believed that such murders were in tune with public opinion.'[18] The revolutionaries had by then mastered the art of bomb making. A bomb was planted under the railway track when Lt Governor Andrew Fraser was travelling by train from Cuttack to Calcutta (5 December 1907). The train had passed over the tracks without incident and some coolies from the neighbouring village were arrested and jailed. Clearly the police then had no clue about what a section of the revolutionaries had been planning. It was a rude awakening for the administration five months later (on 30 April 1908) when a bomb was thrown at a carriage in Muzaffarpur, killing instead of the target Magistrate Kingsford, the wife and daughter of lawyer Prince Kennedy. While Kshudiram Bose was arrested, his accomplice Prafulla Chaki committed suicide. Prafulla Chaki and Kshudiram were the first martyrs from Bengal. They became role models of sorts for Bengal with many songs composed remembering their self-sacrifice. Historian R.C. Majumdar wrote, 'The bomb thrown by Prafulla and Kshudiram exploded in Muzaffarpur but the sound of its explosion reverberated not only throughout Bengal but all over India and roused the country from its morass of lethargy.'[19]

The Muzaffarpur bomb blast saw the police acting against the revolutionaries owing allegiance to Barindra Ghosh and Aurobindo Ghosh. They were all arrested and the first phase of the revolutionary dream ended. The Alipore Bomb Case and the famous court battle that followed remained one of the most historical court proceedings that saw the rise of Chittaranjan Das, the lawyer whose oratory and legal skills resulted in the release of Aurobindo Ghosh, the top leader of the case. The Alipore Bomb Case trial changed the course of politics in the country and planted the seed of separation of Bengal mainstream politics from the politics pursued by the Indian National Congress.

The trial was preceded by several dramatic developments. First was the confession of Barindra which was opposed by his elder brother Aurobindo. Barindra felt that a confession would publicise the activities and the ideals of the revolutionaries influencing many others to follow the path. He knew well enough that freedom would not be achieved by killing a few Englishmen but 'what we wanted was to rouse the country from the torpor it was in, with the sound of bombs'. This objective was more than achieved by the Alipore Bomb Case. The overwhelming sentiment in favour of Kshudiram was captured by the popular song *Ekbar bidai de ma ghure aasi* (Mother, bid me farewell once, I will be back soon. Whole of India will watch me while I wear the noose smiling).

When Barindra in his confessional statement did not mention Aurobindo the prosecution managed to persuade Narendranath Goswami to implicate Aurobindo as the leader. This led the revolutionaries to kill Narendranath. Satyendranath Bose and Kanailal Dutta murdered him at the jail hospital at Alipore. Both were hanged, Kanai on 10 November 1908 and Satyen on 21st of the same month. When Kanailal's body reached the Kalighat crematorium, a huge crowd gathered. The outpouring of grief scared the administration and Satyendranath's body was cremated in a corner inside the jail. The objective of arousing the people was more than achieved by the revolutionaries.

No less important was Aurobindo Ghosh's trial in the Calcutta High Court in 1908. The defence had to engage Chittaranjan Das in place of celebrated barrister Byomkesh Chakraborty whose fee was difficult for the revolutionaries to meet. Chittaranjan's address to the bench remains one of the finest examples of courtroom oratory. In defence of Aurobindo he said,

> The charge against me is that I have proclaimed the ideal of freedom in the country and I admit the charge. It was for this that I came to Calcutta; it is for this that I live and labour; this is my only thought while awake and this is what I dream about in my sleep.[20]

Chittaranjan's closing statement has gone down in the legal annals of history:

> I appeal to you, therefore, that a man like this stands not only before the bar in this Court, but stands before the bar of the High Court of History ... Long after this controversy is hushed in silence, long after this turmoil and this agitation cease, long after he is dead and gone, he will be looked upon as the poet of patriotism, as the prophet of nationalism and the lover of humanity. Long after he is dead and gone, his words will be echoed and re-echoed not only in India but across distant seas and lands.[21]

Aurobindo turned towards spiritualism when in jail. In a speech delivered at Uttarpara on 30 May 1909, after his release, Aurobindo said, 'This Hindu nation was born with the Sanatana Dharma, with it, it moves and with it, it grows. When the Sanatana Dharma declines, then the nation declines, and if the Sanatana Dharma were capable of perishing, with the Sanatana Dharma it would perish. The Sanatana Dharma, that is nationalism.' He was talking of politics but with religious fervor, a change that perhaps occurred during his incarceration. Aurobindo clearly was confused and looked for guidance from the Almighty. In his own words,

> The storm that swept over the country has scattered them far and wide. It is I this time who have spent one year in seclusion, and now that I come out I find all changed. One who always sat by my side and was associated in my work is a prisoner in Burma; another is in the north rotting in detention. I looked round when I came out, I looked round for those to whom I had been accustomed to look for counsel and inspiration. I did not find them. There was more than that. When I went to jail, the whole country was alive with the cry of Bande Mataram, alive with the hope of

> a nation, the hope of millions of men who had newly risen out of degradation. When I came out of jail I listened for that cry, but there was instead a silence. A hush had fallen on the country and men seemed bewildered; for instead of God's bright heaven full of the vision of the future that had been before us, there seemed to be overhead a leaden sky from which human thunders and lightnings rained. No man seemed to know which way to move, and from all sides came the question, 'What shall we do next? What is there that we can do?' I too did not know which way to move, I too did not know what was next to be done. But one thing I knew, that as it was the Almighty Power of God which had raised that cry, that hope, so it was the same power which had sent down that silence. He who was in the shouting and the movement was also in the pause and the hush. He has sent it upon us, so that the nation might draw back for a moment and look into itself and know His will. I have not been disheartened by that silence, because I had been made familiar with silence in my prison and because I knew it was in the pause and the hush that I had myself learned this lesson through the long year of my detention.[22]

Aurobindo was bitter, bitter at the moderate leaders like Gokhale and Surendranath and minced no words about them in his writings. He called Gokhale the Bibhishan of the *Ramayana*,

> Till now many of us regarded Mr. Gokhale as a brother with whom we had our own private differences, but he has himself by calling for the official sword to exterminate us removed that error. He publishes himself now as the righteous Bibhishan who, with the Sugrives, Angads and Hanumans of

> Madras and Allahabad, has gone to join the Avatar of Radical absolutism in the India Office, and ourselves as the Rakshasa to be destroyed by this new Holy Alliance.

Aurobindo was severely critical of Gokhale's speech delivered at Poona in 1909 in which he had apparently called the nationalists to move back

> ... to recede to the position occupied by us previous to 1905. It is a forcible justification of repression and a call to Government and people to crush the lovers and preachers of independence. The time at which it comes lends it incalculable significance. The Morleyan policy of crushing the new spirit and rallying the Moderates has now received publicly the imprimatur of the leading Moderate of western India and that which was suspected by some, prophesied by others at the time of the Surat Congress, the alliance of Bombay Moderatism with officialdom against the new Nationalism, an alliance prepared by the Surat sitting, cemented by subsequent events, confirmed by the Madras Convention, is now unmasked and publicly ratified.[23]

Aurobindo bitterly wrote in *Karmayogin* (July 17, 1909) that he felt in Gokhale's view

> ... the ideal of independence was the beginning of all evil. The ideal of independence is an insane ideal; the men who hold it even as an ultimate goal, Tilak, Chidambaram, Aswini Kumar, Manoranjan, Bipin Chandra, Aurobindo, are madmen outside the lunatic asylum. Not only is it an insane ideal, it is a criminal ideal.[24]

According to R.C. Majumdar when Aurobindo attended the provincial conference at Barisal in 1909 Surendranath had approached him to join the Congress. Aurobindo asked for changes in the constitution that was adopted in the Surat Congress of 1907. This was not possible for Surendranath, the leader of the moderates, to accept. Later in 1936 when Sri Aurobindo was asked to explain his role in the Surat Congress and to clarify various rumours, he said,

> Probably they know nothing about it, as these things happened behind the veil. History very seldom records the things that were decisive but took place behind the veil; it records the show in front of the curtain. Very few people know that it was I (without consulting Tilak) who gave the order that led to the breaking of the Congress and was responsible for the refusal to join the newfangled Moderate Convention which were the two decisive happenings at Surat. Even my action in giving the movement in Bengal its militant turn or founding the revolutionary movement is very little known.[25]

The split in the Surat Congress was engineered by the moderates from Bombay. They wanted to dilute the resolutions adopted in the Calcutta Congress in 1906, the one after the Varanasi meet mentioned earlier. The nationalists, though still a minority, succeeded under the leadership of Tilak in imposing part of their political agenda on the Congress. The Congress consisting of both moderates and nationalists unanimously resolved to have Swaraj or Self-government as its goal and focus on Swadeshi, Boycott and National Education as the effective means for realising the goal. The moderates at the time did not raise any dissenting voice sensing the overwhelming national sentiment arising out of the partition of Bengal. However they seem to have felt that their position was somewhat compromised by these resolutions; and they had since then, been looking forward to an opportunity when they might return to their old position regarding ideals and methods of political progress in India. So in 1907 they managed to shift the session away from Nagpur, where the nationalists had a large presence, to Surat, a stronghold of the moderates. In the delegates count moderates assembled 1300 while the nationalists were less in number at 1100. A scuffle broke out when the delegates from Gujarat attempted to break a chair over Tilak's head and the nationalists in turn threw a slipper at Rashbehari Ghose, the president of the session. The young Mahrattas charged up to the platform to protect Tilak. Meanwhile the moderate leaders fled and after a short fight on the platform involving chairs the session broke up not to be resumed. Aurobindo's unflattering comments on Gokhale may be read in this context.

Aurobindo's views on Surendranath were less critical. In fact he was somewhat appreciative of his speeches delivered in England and wrote,

> Nevertheless it must be accounted as righteousness to Srijut Surendranath that he enforced the Moderate Nationalist view of things, – a very different view from Mr. Gokhale's which is certainly not Nationalism and hardly even strong enough to be called Moderatism, – to its utmost limits and did not leave the English public under the vain delusion that some paltry tinkerings with the Legislative Councils would satisfy the aspirations of an awakened India.[26]

Aurobindo was a harsh critic of the reforms of 1909 and said,

> The danger is that the older Moderates, trained in a much less exacting system of political agitation, may attempt to

> enforce the demand for control only in speech while in action conceding co-operation without control and thus giving away for some fancied and worthless advantage the vital position of the new movement. The reforms give no control, therefore the reforms must be rejected. Co-operation is our only asset, the only thing we can offer in exchange for control, the only thing by withholding which we can by pressure bring about the cession of control. It would be the height of political folly to give away our only asset for nothing.[27]

For the moderates in the Congress, Aurobindo's departure from active politics to an ascetic's life in Pondicherry was a reprieve. The short period of Aurobindo's political life was characteristic of the subsequent development of politics in Bengal. For Bengal's nationalists the end was more important than the means unlike the subsequent culture that was part of the Congress under Mahatma Gandhi. This was highlighted starkly in the case of Gopinath Saha, the martyr who attempted to assassinate the notorious Calcutta police commissioner Charles Tegart and instead killed one Mr Day, an Englishman working in a merchant office. Saha was caught and quickly hanged on 1 March 1924. Bengal had always expressed sympathy with the extremists but perhaps, for the first time, officially, the Bengal Congress declared itself formally sympathetic to Saha. In its provincial conference held at Sirajganj, a resolution was adopted on 1 June 1924 which

> … as a matter of form dissociated the Congress from all violence and reasserted the principle of non-violence as enjoined by Mahatma Gandhi, but which also put on record that the Conference appreciates Gopinath Saha's ideal of self-sacrifice, misguided though it was in respect of the

> country's interests, and expresses its respect for his great self-sacrifice.[28]

This was moved by Chittaranjan Das.

But Gandhi was annoyed and, in an interview given at the Sabarmati Ashram, described the Sirajganj resolution as 'unfortunate' and 'inconsistent' with the Congress creed. He said in an interview to *The Times of India:*

> I find it difficult to understand its meaning, because if the action of Gopinath Saha was worthy of condemnation, as in my humble opinion it was, what was the patriotism apart from the action for which the homage was deserved? I cannot, therefore, conceive the possibility of any political party subscribing to the moral underlying the homage paid to Gopinath Saha.[29]

In the 12 June 1924 issue of *Young India* Gandhi criticised the Sirajganj resolution 'as a travesty of non-violence'. Referring to the words 'while adhering to the policy of non-violence' he said:

> It would have been less undignified if non-violence had not been dragged in at all. Then patriotism of Gopinath Saha could only consist in the murder and not in the capital punishment which was the consequence of the murder. He was not out to die, but to murder one who was odious to him. The knowledge that he ran the risk of being hanged made him brave, but not necessarily patriotic. For every murderer knows that he runs such risk and may, therefore, be called brave. The patriotism, if any, therefore, consisted in the act of murder. Now murder is inconsistent with non-

> violence even when regarded purely as a policy. Non-violent suffering in one's person and violent injury to another cannot both be patriotic at the same time. The patriotism of every lover of his country demands that, whilst the country pursues a policy of non-violence, he does not disturb it by committing murder ... so long as the Congress creed stands as it is, every Congressman to be true to his creed is pledged to oppose and condemn in thought, word and deed every act of political violence.

Clearly Gandhi took offence and intended to make the Bengal Congress fall back in line. Armed with Gandhi's 12th June article and four resolutions as well as his call to Bengal Congress to dissociate completely from the Sirajganj resolution, the Gandhi loyalists in the Bengal Congress moved a resolution in its meeting at the Albert Hall on 21st June blaming Provincial Congress President C.R. Das for the Sirajganj resolution which was wrongly worded. C.R. Das defended the resolution and only eight Gandhi loyalists voted against the resolution of Das. Evidently Gandhi loyalists wanted to rewrite the record but failed.

Das explained how the mistake had taken place and how the correct version was published later. The resolution condemning the Provincial Congress Committee record lost by an overwhelming margin with only eight votes in its favour. There was another resolution placed before the house by the supporters of Deshbandhu Chittaranjan Das which criticised the Gandhi loyalists for moving the resolution and was passed with huge majority. Undaunted, the Gandhi loyalists moved another resolution condemning the Sirajganj resolution on Gopinath Saha. Again the Gandhi loyalists claimed that the Sirajganj resolution on Gopinath Saha violated the Congress policy of non-violence and that it was likely to mislead sensitive and immature minds into the paths of violence. This too was defeated by the majority who reaffirmed the Sirajganj resolution. Thus the ball was set for another round of fight a few days later on 29th June when the All India Congress Committee (AICC) met in Ahmedabad. In a resolution the AICC regretted the death of Mr Day, offered condolences to his family and unequivocally condemned political murders. Chittaranjan Das moved an amendment incorporating the expression of sympathy that was part of the Sirajganj resolution. He said that if the Congress had any sympathy for Bengal's sentiments it would vote in favour of his amendment. He lost by eight votes. A veteran leader from Maharashtra, Dr Paranjyape said sarcastically that Mahatma Gandhi was indeed one of the many saints of India, but he was trying to ram his saintliness down the throats of his less saintly countrymen.[30] Gandhi was unhappy that the resolution mooted by Das was defeated by a mere eight votes and talked of leaving the Congress. According to Nirad C. Chaudhuri the alienation of Bengal from Gandhian nationalism started from this juncture. Apparently he felt that the anti-Bengali feeling of Gandhi increased over the years 'and made him indifferent even to the real injustice inflicted on Bengal from 1932 onwards'.[31]

Bengal's bitterness over Gandhi's opposition to the resolution on the sacrifice of Gopinath Saha continued. Six years later when Bhagat Singh was sentenced to death, the Congress passed a similar resolution in Gandhi's presence. In fact, Gandhi had even approached the governor general to commute the death sentence of Bhagat Singh.[32] The breach between Gandhi and Bengal's freedom fighters did not heal.

That from the very beginning Gandhi did not hold Bengal in high esteem could be seen in the reminiscences of Surendra Mohan Ghose in a Publications Division collection of reminiscences on the 50th anniversary of the Non-cooperation movement. In fact, Gandhi was not even aware who was the top leader from the state. After his release from imprisonment, Ghose and his other friends wanted to hold a special session of the Congress for the political prisoners still suffering in jails. In order to seek Gandhi's support he went to meet him after his release from jail in 1920. Gandhi refused to hold any such session for the release of prisoners at a time when he was planning a movement that would send people to prison. Gandhi had also wanted to know from Surendra Mohan who the leader of Bengal was at that point. Gandhi was surprised when Ghose mentioned it was Chittaranjan Das and not a certain A. Chaudhury, who was the chairman of the Reception Committee.[33] Not that Gandhi did not know Chittaranjan. He was a member along with Chittaranjan of the committee of Congress that reported on the Punjab disturbances including the Jallianwala Bagh massacre. In the 1919 session of the Congress there was a bitter division over a resolution on the Government of India Act 1919, known as Montagu-Chelmsford Reforms. Gandhi felt the reform should be welcomed while Chittaranjan Das supported by Tilak wanted to reject it as inadequate. Finally a compromise was reached and a resolution drafted by Tilak, a modified version of Chittaranjan's, was adopted. It accepted the Montagu reforms till absolute Home Rule was not adopted. If despite knowing Das and his standing Gandhi still asked Ghose the question it was perhaps the shrewd politician in him who wanted to gauge the hold of Chittaranjan over Bengal. Such small gestures reveal a lot.

Gandhi and Chittaranjan had joined the Congress around the same time. While Das was busy in his legal defence of Bengal revolutionaries Gandhi came back from South Africa in 1915 and toured the country to understand the people. He also led the Champaran Satyagraha against the exploitative indigo farmers in 1917 as well as a movement of peasants at Kheda in Gujarat seeking tax concessions in the wake of a famine. Both the movements were in support of exploited peasants in particular regions and did not have any national significance. Earlier Gandhi had toured the country in support of enrolling people to fight on behalf of the British in the First World War. Das and Gandhi were two leaders with completely different personalities. Both rejuvenated a Congress which was effectively an organ of the British administration after the split between the nationalists and the moderates. It was moderate leader Gokhale who realised the need for a leader to revive the moribund organisation and invited Gandhi. While Bengal and Gandhi's disenchantment was mutual based on strong views held by both sides, a point that cannot be ignored is that Gandhi's firm belief in laying down observance of certain ideals went against the very core of Bengal's liberal attitude. Rabindranath Tagore's biographer recounts an incident that sheds further light on this. When Gandhi visited Santiniketan in March 1920 he suggested that students and teachers should be self-reliant and perform all chores like cooking, cleaning and washing. He also criticised the fact that students and teachers in Santiniketan used to follow the practices of the Hindu caste system instead of eating together. Rabindranath felt that something that would not come naturally from within could not be imposed, hence he did not ask the ashram residents to follow this. Gandhi perhaps did not appreciate this statement by Tagore.[34] The differences between Gandhi and Bengal were not merely political but also philosophical. The innately liberal sense of a Bengali, inculcated by their prolonged exposure to western education and philosophy was not appreciated by Gandhi, who was at heart an orthodox person. With Gandhi taking control of the Congress the national struggle now took an organised course along a route that the leader felt justified and his supporters followed in his footsteps. Meanwhile Bengal kept moving along its mixed course of revolutionary ideals and Gandhian philosophy tailored to suit its feelings. The same conflict and reluctant acceptance could be seen in Chittaranjan Das.

After its split in 1907 the Congress did not have any noteworthy contribution to the cause of the national movement till 1919. In fact, the speech of Lord S.P. Sinha as president of the Congress in 1915 was an embarrassment even for the moderate Congressmen who missed no opportunity to proclaim their loyalty to the British rule. Sinha said that the three provinces of Bengal, Punjab and North West Frontier were competing with each other to support England's war effort. These three provinces in reality were full of terrorism and hatred for the British at that time. Clearly the Indian National Congress at this point was an extension of the British administration. After the horrors of Jallianwala Bagh the Congress started rejuvenating itself. At this juncture in 1919 Gandhi participated actively in the Congress proceedings where he and C.R. Das had a disagreement which was finally resolved with Pandit Madan Mohan Malaviya's intervention.[35]

After joining the Congress, the first task Gandhi undertook was to amend the constitution that Gokhale had framed and to make it orderly as to the number of delegates to be nominated by each province and to have a machinery to run the party affairs between sessions. Clearly the Congress could not remain an annual session arrangement. Gandhi headed the three-member committee to draft the constitution and asked Das and Tilak to nominate their representatives. Evidently both did not attach much significance to this task and nominated two of their candidates neither of whom had the ability to persuade Gandhi on any matter. The constitution was passed unanimously and the Congress was handed over to Gandhi by the political naivety of Chittaranjan Das in particular. Clearly Mahatma Gandhi understood politics while Chittaranjan was more of an emotional nationalist. As a result, Das could not hold on to his views in the Congress and finally succumbed to Gandhi.

Sri Aurobindo had summed up the differences between Gandhi and Das in response to a question (17 May 1935):

> Politics, war, revolution are things of stratagem and ambush one cannot expect the truth there. From what I have heard Gandhi himself has played tricks and dodges there. Das told me it was impossible to lead men in politics or get one's objects without telling falsehoods by the yard and he was often feeling utterly disgusted with himself and his work, but supposed he would have to go through with it to the end. There is no necessity to reveal one's plans and movements to those who have no business to know it, who are incapable of understanding or who would act as enemies or spoil all as a result of their knowledge. Secrecy is perfectly admissible and usual in spiritual matters except in special relations like that of the shishya to the guru ... Gandhi talked about secrecy being a sin but that is one of his many extravagances.[36]

Politics in Bengal was more emotional than practical, cerebral than rational and altruistic than opportunistic. Such politics could not have built a national movement in a diverse country like India. No wonder Gandhian politics came to lead India with Bengal taking a backseat gradually. But before coming to how politics in Bengal shaped up in the 1920s and thereafter, mention must be made of the success of the Swadeshi movement and the annulment of the partition of Bengal. The movement had lost its backbone with the arrest of the leaders and enactment of repressive legislations. To stop bomb making the Explosive Substances Act was promulgated in 1908 which ensured that collecting material for bomb making, aiding in manufacture of bombs or possession of bombs would result in up to 14 years in jail. The newspaper control or Press Act of 1910 prohibited publication of anything that would incite murder or violence and three newspapers, *Jugantar*, *Bande Mataram* and *Sandhya,* were closed down. The Indian penal code was amended denying the accused certain rights and allowing detention without trial. This saw the arrest of nine leaders from Bengal which included Aswani Kumar Dutta, Raja Subodh Chandra Mallick among others, and they were lodged in jails far away from Bengal including in Burma. To exercise greater control over newspapers and other modes of communication the government was empowered to intercept any material viewed as suspicious. There was a long list of prohibited matters allowing a big leash to the administration. What is interesting is that when this bill was placed before the legislative council which was formed under the Reforms Act 1909, Gokhale was among the Indian members who supported the measures and this gesture was appreciated by Governor General Lord Minto. What is important for Bengal is that the Reforms of 1909 provided separate electorates for the Muslims and sowed the seed of the future partition of India. Two Muslim majority states suffered later – these were Bengal and Punjab. More changes came in 1910 and thereafter when Montagu was replaced as the secretary of state for India by Lord Crew and Hardinge took over as the viceroy replacing Minto. Despite repression the terrorist movement was continuing in Bengal and the administration was not happy about it. Hardinge and Crew realised that the partition of Bengal was the reason behind this and decided to undo that. The decision was announced on 12 December 1911 at the close of the Delhi Durbar. King George V announced annulment of the royal order of partition of Bengal. He also announced the shifting of India's capital from Calcutta to Delhi. The Swadeshi movement of 1905 which had by then lost steam but was still carrying on despite losing its leaders finally succeeded. The revolutionary who managed to continue the activities started at Muraripukur was Jatindranath

Mukherjee or Bagha Jatin who was an associate of Barindra Ghosh but escaped getting caught in the Alipore Bomb Case. Bagha Jatin was instrumental in collaborating with the revolutionaries in Bengal and other provinces and even reached out to set up collaborators in Canada, USA and Europe. Jatindranath was aware of the impending war in Europe and was looking for an opportunity to create an armed struggle to oust the British. That he was no small threat could be assessed from Hardinge's various despatches. Jatindranath and 46 of his associates were framed under the 'Howrah Gang Case'. This was when Inspector Shamsul Alam was killed in January 1910. Alam was investigating the activities of the revolutionaries and was close to cracking the case when he was murdered. Though 47 persons were implicated, Hardinge felt that only one was the 'real criminal'. But Jatindranath escaped with just a one-year prison sentence.

There was no evidence to nab Bagha Jatin. Clearly Bengal was on fire even without any prominent leader at the forefront. Bagha Jatin had the foresight to unite the revolutionaries and set up an international link with support from persons like Shyamji Krishnaverma, Rashbehari Bose and M.N. Roy. He had realised that global turmoil could be used effectively for the Indian nationalist movement. This was taking place at the same time when Mahatma Gandhi was busy preaching before Indians in supporting the British war effort. The Congress as mentioned earlier was loyal and supported the war efforts of the British government against political reform. India used to provide 15,000 soldiers every year to the British Army before the war started. During the four years of war about 50 lakhs of combatants and non-combatants were recruited from India. According to Montagu, the secretary of state, 12,15,328 Indian soldiers fought in foreign theatres of war and 1,01,439 of them died.[37]

Moderate leaders like Surendranath Banerjee, Bhupendranath Bose and Ambica Charan Majumdar realised that they were now in the minority within the Congress. In 1916 a patch up with the nationalists took place and in 1917 Annie Besant was chosen as president under pressure from the nationalists. Meanwhile Montagu had announced in 1917 that there would henceforth be responsible government and Indians would be associated with it. This was welcomed in the Calcutta session in 1917. But when the report came out the nationalists rejected it while the moderates found it progressive and satisfactory. Realising the prevalent mood the moderate leaders dissociated themselves from the Bombay session of 1918. This had created a vacuum in the political leadership in the country. The nationalists of Bengal were too uncompromising while the moderates who were ever willing to oblige the government with their support had lost their influence. Gandhi emerged to fill in this gap while the Bengal leadership was unfit to play any such role. Clearly Gandhi had several qualities which the leaders from Bengal lacked – Gandhi knew the pulse of the country as a whole and knew how to build a consensus; he was pragmatic and, most important of all, he knew how to create an organisation to move ahead. Gandhi took over the rein of the national movement while Bengal, which taught India nationalism, failed in carrying the whole country along with its idealism sans reality.

Chittaranjan Das had entered the political arena as a sympathiser of the revolutionary politics which was led by Aurobindo.

> A poet by temperament, emotion was the outstanding feature of this personality destined to dominate Indian politics eventually ... His early political association made a deep impression on his mind which never could get accustomed to the anti-revolutionary essence of Gandhism. In the closing days of his life, he was associated with an entirely different group of politicians, and tried to appear himself as a practical politician. But emotionally he always remained a

> revolutionary, and the mark that he left on Indian political history is that of an impetuous personality,

wrote M.N. Roy of Chittaranjan Das.[38]

There had been many important occasions when Das changed his views inexplicably. Historian R.C. Majumdar has pointed out occasions when Das had changed his views – between Calcutta and Nagpur Congress, at Gaya and later at Faridpur Provincial Congress.[39] After 1919 the Congress met at a special session in Calcutta in 1920, a few weeks after Tilak's death. The main resolution in the session referred to the treatment meted out to Turkey by the Allied Forces after the War, with secondary mention of the atrocities in Punjab. The resolution called for support of the Non-cooperation movement started by Gandhi and the work for the establishment of Swaraj. An amendment was placed by Gandhi for the promotion of the spinning wheel and khadi. Despite reservations of leaders like Chittaranjan, Jinnah, Madan Mohan Malaviya and Bipin Pal, Gandhi's amendment along with the resolution of non-cooperation even in the to-be-elected councils were adopted. The resolution had to be approved in the annual session held in Nagpur by the end of the year where Chittaranjan joined with a strong delegation from Bengal. It was expected that he would object to Gandhi's resolution. Das and Gandhi met the night before the Congress session. Nobody knew what they discussed but Chittaranjan supported the resolution which he had strongly opposed in Calcutta. It is said that Gandhi had appealed to the emotional nature of Das to bring in support of the revolutionary youth of Bengal for the success of the movement.[40] Surendra Mohan Ghose had mentioned in his reminiscences on the 1921 movement that the clinching argument of Gandhi was that since the council election was over, it was pointless to stick to the issue and consequently Das dropped his objection.

The Non-cooperation movement was much less successful than the spontaneous Swadeshi movement initiated in Bengal. Boycott of courts received lukewarm support with many lawyers continuing their legal practices. Burning of foreign cloth, as insisted by Gandhi, was opposed, a prominent voice in opposition being Rabindranath Tagore. Riots broke out in Bombay between Congress supporters and the English and Parsi communities. In Bengal Chittaranjan Das launched a civil disobedience movement. Chittaranjan made an emotional appeal to students after Lala Lajpat Rai was arrested, 'Lajpat is in prison. I want an open attack. Oh, you young men of Bengal! Will you still stand still and watch the activities of the Congress stop? Will you not respond to the call of your motherland?'[41] Das and his associates such as Subhas Chandra Bose, Abul Kalam Azad and Birendra Sasmal were arrested. A few days later Madan Mohan Malaviya met Das with a request from the governor general to withdraw the call for *hartal* or strike on the occasion of the visit of the Prince of Wales and offered in return to release prisoners and to organise a round-table conference with all political parties. Das and Abul Kalam favoured the proposal and sent a telegram to Gandhi who however said that the movement would be suspended only after satisfactory result of the proposed round-table conference. Chittaranjan was crestfallen at the loss of an opportunity 'which seldom comes in a lifetime'.[42] In the annual Ahmedabad Congress where Chittaranjan was selected as president but could not attend as he was in jail, Gandhi decided that he would start a civil disobedience movement at Bardoli in Surat district. But in a village called Chowrichowra near Gorakhpur when police opened fire on a procession the crowd retaliated and in the ensuing trouble 22 policemen died. An upset Gandhi suspended the civil disobedience movement, thereby losing his popular appeal and pushing the country to depression and occasional riots. Chittaranjan was much disturbed and said that in such a big country, incidents like Chowrichowra 'are bound to happen; that is no reason why the movement should stop in all provinces'.[43] Das had also called Surendra Mohan and Jatindra Mohan Sengupta to meet him in jail and advised them to oppose the move of suspension of the movement strongly in the Delhi session. But Ghose recalled that Malaviya's support saw to it that the Bengal lobby got defeated.[44] These two decisions of Gandhi overruling the sane advice of other leaders made Chittaranjan firm in his resolve to enter the council and oppose the government from within. In the annual session of the Provincial Congress presided over by Basanti Devi, Chittaranjan Das's wife, a resolution supporting council entry was passed. In the Gaya session of the Congress Chittaranjan announced as president that he would proceed to enter the council and 'shall wreck it from within by obstructing all its proceedings'.[45] But the resolution could not be passed. This did not deter Das. He formed a new political party – Swarajya party – with support from Motilal Nehru and many leaders of other provinces. The Congress a few months later decided that it would not object to any candidate standing for election to the Legislative Council with the object enunciated by the Swarajya party. According to M.N. Roy, after the loss of momentum post Bardoli, the no-changers led by Gandhi had no option but to look for an alternative and the Swarajya party gave them a chance to move towards constitutionalism.

The sudden death of Chittaranjan Das brought in several new dimensions to the politics of the province.

Endnotes

1 Majumdar, ed., *British Paramountcy,* Part II, p. 573.

2 Majumdar, *Modern Bengal*, pp 10-1.

3 Ibid., pp 12-7.

4 Ibid., pp 80-1.

5 Rabindranath Tagore, *'Jibansmriti – Swadeshikata' Rabindra Rachanabali* vol. 11 (West Bengal Government, 1989), p. 49.

6 R.C. Majumdar, ed., *Struggle for Freedom*, 11th vol. of *The History and Culture of the Indian People* (Bhartiya Vidya Bhavan, 2007), pp 78-96.

7 Majumdar, *Modern Bengal* Part Two, p. 20.

8 Ibid., p. 79.

9 Ibid.

10 Majumdar, *Modern Bengal*, pp 20-1.

11 Majumdar, ed., *Struggle for Freedom*, p. 80.

12 Ibid., p. 80.

13 Ibid., p. 65.

14 Majumdar, *Modern Bengal*, pp 25-7.

15 Ibid.

16 Mukhopadhyay, *Rabindrajibani*, vol. 2, pp 164-7.

17 Majumdar, *Modern Bengal*, p. 84.

18 Ibid.

19 Ibid., p. 88.

20 Ibid., p. 96.

21 Ibid., pp 95-6.

22 http://www.collectedworksofsriaurobindo.com/index.php/readbook/03-Uttarpara-Speech-Vol-08-karmayogin (accessed May 6, 2020).

23 http://www.collectedworksofsriaurobindo.com/index.php/readbook/19-Exit-Bibhishan-Vol-08-karmayogin (accessed May 6, 2020).

24 Ibid.

25 https://www.motherandsriaurobindo.in/#_StaticContent/SriAurobindoAshram/-09%20E-Library/-01%20Works%20of%20Sri%20Aurobindo/-01%20English/-03_CWSA/-35_Letters%20On%20Himself%20And%20The%20Ashram/-05_Political%20Career,%201906%20%C2%AD%201910.htm (accessed May 6, 2020).

26 *Karmayogin,* August 21, 1909.

27 http://www.collectedworksofsriaurobindo.com/index.php/readbook/30-Facts-and-Opinions-9-Vol-08-karmayogin#Srijut_Surendranath_Banerjis_Return (accessed May 6, 2020).

28 Nirad C. Chaudhuri, *Autobiography of an Unknown Indian - Part II* (Jaico Publishing House, 2008) Kindle edition, e-book location 5248.

29 https://www.gandhiashramsevagram.org/gandhi-literature/mahatma-gandhi-collected-works-volume-28.pdf

30 Chaudhuri, *Unknown Indian*.

31 Ibid., e-book location 5267.

32 Majumdar, *Modern Bengal*, pp 188-9.

33 V.V. Giri, 'Foreword' in *1921 Movement: Reminiscences* (Publications Division, Ministry of Information & Broadcasting Govt of India, December 1971), Kindle edition.

34 Mukhopadhyay, *Rabindrajibani* vol. 2, p. 501.

35 M.K. Gandhi, *The Story of My Experiments with Truth* (Rupa, 2011), Kindle edition, pp 500-3.

36 https://www.motherandsriaurobindo.in/#_StaticContent/SriAurobindoAshram/-09%20E-Library/-01%20Works%20of%20Sri%20Aurobindo/-01%20English/-03_CWSA/-35_Letters%20On%20Himself%20And%20The%20Ashram/-05_Political%20Career,%201906%20%C2%AD%201910.htm

37 Majumdar, *Modern Bengal*, pp 112-4.

38 M.N. Roy, *Men I Met* (Ajanta Publications, 1981), pp 21-5.

39 Majumdar, *Modern Bengal*, p. 134.

40 Ibid., p. 132.

41 Ibid., p. 171.

42 Ibid., p. 171-2.

43 Ibid., p. 173.

44 Giri, *1921 Movement*.

45 Majumdar, *Modern Bengal*, p. 173.

RIFT WIDENS WITH THE MAINSTREAM

Chittaranjan Das was the last tall leader who could control the complex political sentiment of Bengal. As Surendra Mohan Ghose had told Mahatma Gandhi when he met him in 1920 that 'if C.R. Das is with you the whole Bengal will be with you'.[1] If one looks carefully at the leadership of Gandhi during this period it can be seen that he knew he had to bring in Das with him, at least outvote him if it came to that. With the death of Tilak, Das lost an ally. It was easy for Gandhi to win over necessary support as and when he needed it to contain Das and his emotional brand of politics. As Nirad C. Chaudhuri, an eyewitness to all these developments, had recorded in the context of the resolution on Gopinath Saha, Gandhi was dismayed and felt disenchanted with Bengal thereafter. Every conflict needs a trigger, and the hanging of Gopinath acted as one such incident in the conflict between the two great personalities of that time. Das and Gandhi came from two completely different schools of thought. When Gandhi first landed in Bombay in 1915, after helping His Majesty's Government in the war effort, he was requested through Gokhale to meet Lord Willingdon, the governor of Bombay. Gandhi met him who in turn had requested Mahatma Gandhi to meet the governor general whenever the latter had any issue with the government. To this Gandhi had assured the governor that so had been his principle in South Africa and the faith that His Majesty's Government would not wilfully do any wrong sustained him (Gandhi).[2] Clearly Gokhale understood that Gandhi would manage to inject fresh purpose into the Indian National Congress which had become irrelevant under the moderates, and at the same time would not increase animosity with the administration as did the nationalists. Whether Gandhi was disillusioned with the Bengal brand of politics due to revolutionaries like Saha, as Nirad C. Chaudhuri recorded, or whether he came with a preconceived notion of taming the highly tempestuous Bengali nationalists cannot be ascertained now, after all these decades. However, in order to build a national movement Gandhi needed Bengal on his side.

The sudden passing away of Deshbandhu Chittaranjan Das in Darjeeling brought the entire Bengal out in mourning. Mahatma Gandhi was in the funeral procession and recorded how Calcutta was 'swept away by a wave of emotion'. Gandhi was present at the *sradh* (funeral rites) 14 days later.[3] Das had revived Bengal's nationalism. He admitted in his presidential address in the Bengal Provincial Congress meeting on 1 April 1917 that 'Hitherto all our (political) attempts have ended in huge failure, we have been able to achieve nothing, accomplish nothing'[4] and went on building the movement from there. He was critical of Surendranath for his westernised politics and also of Rabindranath for his internationalism which Das felt was a mere passing European enthusiasm. Gandhi stayed on in Bengal in June and July, merging his own political philosophy with Chittaranjan's and never omitting to mention Basanti Devi, wife of Chittaranjan Das, as an 'ideal widow'. The politician in Gandhi had realised that with the death of Das the Bengali spirit of nationalism reignited by Deshbandhu had to be channelled into the Gandhian politics nationally. He was keenly aware that with the passing away of Das an opportunity had presented itself to find a leader from Bengal who would not be a rebel to the Gandhian national politics. Clearly Gandhi was looking for a leader from the Swarajya party which at that point in time was of greater relevance than the Indian National

Congress. Gandhi wrote in *Young India*, 'A giant among men has fallen. Bengal is like a widow today.' He repeated how Deshbandhu was irreplaceable and quoted Acharya Prafulla Chandra Ray who said, 'If I could tell who could take Rabindranath's place as a poet, I could tell you who can take Deshbandhu's as a leader. There is no man in Bengal anywhere near Deshbandhu.'[5] Subhas Chandra Bose, one of Das's two close associates, was then confined in Mandalay jail.

Before his sudden demise, Das had been slowly coming to an understanding of sorts with Gandhi. This saw Gandhi being criticised for selling the Congress to the Swarajists. On the other hand, in his presidential address before the Provincial Congress at Faridpur, Das settled for Dominion status, denounced revolutionary violence, supported Gandhian constructive programme and promised cooperation with the government on the basis of some considerations. It is said that at that time Gandhi was busy promoting khadi rather than be involved in politics. Meanwhile the Swarajya party was taking the lead. Chittaranjan sensed that the government would invite him for a discussion in London and perhaps to facilitate the move he offered his olive branch through the Faridpur address. It is believed that Das was responding to a speech by Birkenhead, the secretary of state for India. Birkenhead had said that 'freedom would not be reached by violence'. He wanted the Swarajists to shun revolutionary terrorism in favour of an agreement between the government and the Swarajists.[6] Even Gandhi came and met Das in Darjeeling where the latter had gone for recuperation. Sadly within six weeks after the address Das passed away and the possible political course changed once again. Gandhi used this moment of loss to build his own influence and also to hold on to Bengal for the future course of the national movement. 'Gandhi stayed in Bengal in June and July 1925, speaking extensively on carrying on Deshbandhu's work. As one reads through the more than the one hundred pages of the

Mahatma's prose from this period … it becomes evident that Gandhi was practicing what might be called mourning politics.'[7] Bengal's loss was gain for Gandhi led rest of India.

The Swarajists entered the council with a thumping election victory. In the Bengal council out of a total of 57 candidates 40 won the election. Dr Bidhan Chandra Roy defeated Surendranath Banerjee, one of the founding stalwarts of the Indian National Congress, by a huge margin. Surendranath quit politics after the defeat of the moderates in the election. The Swarajya party members managed to reduce the salary of the Bengal ministers to one rupee per annum by 63 against 62 votes in March 1924. Put to vote again the resolution was carried and the ministers resigned. Lytton, governor of Bengal, had to suspend the constitution.[8]

Das had a huge following among the workers and was successful in organising a strike by the jute workers at Chandpur even in the face of opposition from the Bengal Central Labour Federation (BCLF) which owed its allegiance to Gandhi. Das's call for Swaraj for 98 per cent of the population had enthused many including the likes of M.N. Roy who was in the Soviet Union then working to set up the Communist Party of India. Chittaranjan said in the Lahore conference of All India Trade Union Congress (AITUC; an organisation set up in 1920 which had failed to win Gandhi's support) that labour includes 98 per cent of the population of India when we include peasants also. M.N. Roy was excited. He wrote,

> I thought that there was a man who shared the view that I was trying to introduce in the political life in India. The masses having been driven to primitive forms of revolt, Indian politics had undergone a radical transformation. Everybody talked about the masses. Under the new leadership of the Messianic Mahatma, the Congress experimented with mass

> action. It played, very circumspectly, with the inflammable material, only to be afraid of its own courage. But the general idea was that a new weapon had become available for the politicians. The weapon was the masses who were to be moved cautiously with the purpose of bringing sufficient pressure on imperialism, so that it could make some concessions to the elite of the nation. The point of the propaganda I was carrying on in that situation was stated in the word of Plekhanov[9] 'Revolution for the masses, not the masses for the revolution.' C.R. Das's demand for Swaraj for the ninety-eight percent appeared to echo the spirit I was trying to instil in the Indian political movement.[10]

Founders of communism in India viewed Chittaranjan as a person who could organise a movement of the mass and for the mass.

The Swarajists in the Bengal Council had burst their balloon of hope. The Swarajists had five big leaders calling the shots in the council. They were Tulsi Goswami, Nirmal Chandra Chunder, Bidhan Chandra Roy, Nalini Ranjan Sarkar and Sarat Chandra Bose. As soon as Das died they all became followers of Gandhi. What is more they represented the Calcutta-centric landed aristocracy, affluent middle class and the business classes. In December 1925, after Das's demise, when the government introduced a Tenancy Act Amendment Bill to give tenancy rights to the korfa ryots, the Swarajists opposed it along with the pro-British landlords. On the issue of providing mass primary education to children, the Swarajists felt that the provision of newspaper education to peasants would lead to ruin.[11] With the sudden death of Chittaranjan several anomalies present within the Bengal Congress and the Swarajya party came to the fore. Important among those was the equation that Das could build between the Hindus and Muslims in Bengal, a success which even he could not replicate in the rest of India. The Left-oriented former revolutionaries like M.N. Roy and those who had been working with him were also disheartened and looked for other opportunities which included infiltrating into the Congress. And what is perhaps most important is that the tussle for leadership in Bengal took an ugly turn in due course which eventually left Bengal without any able leader to steward the state in times of its greatest crisis – at the time of partition.

Das had three young associates: Jatindra Mohan Sengupta of Chittagong, Birendranath Sasmal of Midnapore, and Subhas Chandra Bose. There was a contest of sorts among the three contenders for the post of the chief executive officer of the Calcutta Corporation when Das became the mayor under the local self-government rule piloted by Surendranath Banerjee as minister for local self-government in 1921. Among the three, Sasmal was the frontrunner while Sengupta had fallen back due to his practice at the Calcutta High Court during the Non-cooperation movement. Bose was the youngest of them, hence not so much in the reckoning. The post of chief executive of the corporation was important since the entire power was vested in the officer though he remained a non-voting member of all committees. In the race for the post Sasmal was leading but Das was under pressure from two quarters – the erstwhile revolutionaries who had joined the Swarajya party and the Calcutta-based leaders of the party. The government intelligence bureau was carefully monitoring the activities of the erstwhile members of the Jugantar party and therefore of the Swarajya party as well. Sasmal was from Midnapore and the Calcutta-based leaders put pressure on Das for recruiting someone from the city to the post of chief executive officer of the corporation. The revolutionaries did not fancy Sasmal because of his views on revolutionary terrorism. It is said that he had even put forward his objection to Das on the entry of the revolutionaries into the party at that time. The decision to appoint Bose in place of the leading contender Sasmal underlined the stronghold of the Calcutta lobby on the Provincial Congress as well as the Swarajya party which even an undisputed leader like Chittaranjan Das could not overrule. The revolutionaries wielded influence due to their strong position in several districts with many revolutionaries holding posts of district presidents of the Congress. Das used to depend on village-level leaders as well for which Sasmal had proved his mettle. Chittaranjan's search for leadership beyond the Calcutta-based westernised aristocratic Muslim leadership saw men like Abdulah Bagi of Dinajpur, Maniruzamman Islamabadi of Chittagong, Akram Khan of 24 Parganas, Shamsuddin Ahmed of Kusthia and Ashraffuddin Ahmed Chowdhury of Tippera emerge as members of the Bengal provincial leadership. So Chittaranjan Das gave the post of Provincial Congress Secretary to Birendranath Sasmal but later could not appoint him as the chief executive officer of Calcutta Corporation. The struggle between the Calcutta coterie of the Congress and the rest of Bengal was visible even when Chittaranjan Das was the unchallenged leader. Sasmal lost interest after being snubbed in his bid for the post in the Calcutta Corporation.[12] But he continued working for the Congress and left politics a few years later. The exit of leaders like Sasmal shows how deep rooted was the infighting in Bengal politics then.

It is generally believed that in his endeavour to rally the Mohammedan elected members to support the Swarajya party, Das had formulated the Bengal Pact. But the initial proposal for an understanding between the Muslims and the Hindus came from the Muslim leaders themselves. By December 1923, Das was successful in coming to an agreement with the nationalist-minded Muslims on the Bengal Pact. The Muslims were promised a majority share in the administration and in the government of Bengal, once Swaraj was attained. The banning of music close to mosques, the permission of unrestricted cow sacrifice during the festival of Id, and the assurance of greater opportunities in the Swarajist-controlled Calcutta Corporation drew the Khilafatists, who had so long opposed council entry, to support Das and join the electoral battle. It was, however, not merely electoral politics that prompted Das to agree to the proposal. Chittaranjan's ultimate aim was for a Swaraj secured through Hindu–Muslim cooperation, and to make sure that 'no misapprehension, no doubts may arise as to whether it is going to be a Hindu or a Mohammedan Raj'. Chittaranjan felt that eventually the whole country would accept the pact though he was circumspect of the upcountry Hindus from Burra Bazar in Calcutta. The pact had antagonised a large section of the Hindu middle class along with the upcountry Hindu elements who dominated the Burra Bazar Congress Committee. They had consequently struck up a rapprochement with the No-Changer group in Bengal. The pact, wrote Partha Chatterjee, had aimed at a 'strange marriage of a religious-communal consciousness with institutional forms of representative politics.'[13]

After the sudden passing away of Chittaranjan Das, Mahatma Gandhi spent time in Bengal which helped him to understand in detail the political landscape which was complex, full of differences among Swarajists, Gandhians, Muslims and revolutionaries who had all come together under Das. On 28 June 1925, a meeting of the Bengal Provincial Congress Committee (BPCC) was held at the house of Chittaranjan Das in order to elect the president of the Provincial Congress. The names of Jatindra Mohan Sengupta, Basanti Devi, Lalit Mohan Das, who was then the vice president, were proposed. Revolutionaries like Sris Chatterjee, Basanta Majumdar were against the election of Sengupta as the president. The other name that came up for consideration was that of Maulana Azad. But both Basanti Devi and Azad explained their unwillingness to accept the office of the president which left Sengupta as the only suitable candidate for the post of the president of the Bengal Congress Committee. Sengupta was unanimously elected president of the Bengal Congress. Subhas Bose was then jailed at Mandalay.[14] The conflict within Bengal which the tall personality of Chittaranjan could sweep under the carpet now started raising its head time and again.

Birendranath Sasmal was ignored for the post of chief executive of the Calcutta Corporation at the behest of the Calcutta lobby and the revolutionaries. In 1926 there was once again competition for control in the Provincial Congress Committee which resulted in the creation of two rival executive councils of the Congress committees in Bengal: one headed by Jitendralal Banerjee and Biren Sasmal and the other by Sengupta and his group. Finally, the situation was resolved with the intervention of the All India Congress Committee. Then again in November 1927, a new Congress committee was constituted when Subhas Chandra Bose was elected the president on his release from detention. Satyendra Chandra Mitra and Maulana Akram Khan became the vice presidents and Kiran Shankar Roy was elected the secretary. Dr Bidhan Chandra Roy was appointed the treasurer and Nalini Ranjan Sarkar was the auditor. The new executive council was composed mainly of members from the anti-Sasmal group. Sasmal, who was elected from Midnapore, was not even included in the executive council. Eventually Sasmal lost all interest in the Congress. The domination of the Congress by the Big Five and their leader Subhas Chandra Bose was complete.[15]

Apart from the infighting and political rivalry, Bengal was not intellectually aligned to the Gandhian policy of Non-cooperation movement. Ashutosh Mukherjee and Rabindranath Tagore both had issues with certain calls that Gandhi made periodically. For instance, both were against the call to students to quit educational institutions and they criticised the new-found romanticism of students (by spinning the wheel India would get independence in six months).

Ashutosh who was then the vice chancellor of Calcutta University urged students to ignore such calls and engage in studies. This made him unpopular with students. Tagore also had reservations about burning foreign clothes. Bengal had called for both these steps during the Swadeshi movement and Ashutosh and Tagore were well aware of the consequences. The students, however, fascinated by the romanticism of the movement ignored both of them. When Sir Ashutosh passed away, there was a condolence meeting arranged at Calcutta University in which Tagore presided (14 August 1924). A section of the students turned unruly and disgusted with their catcalls Tagore left the condolence meeting.[16] Bengali intellectuals were uncomfortable with certain rigid views of Gandhi such as the compulsion to flout a set of laws. As Ramananda Chatterjee wrote in *Prabashi*, 'We are not afraid and we want Satyagraha. But we want men who may decide with their own conscience and intelligence which of the laws should be disobeyed.'[17] In fact, in the Calcutta Congress C.R. Das and Bipin Pal had placed an amendment that each province would decide on their course in the Non-cooperation movement. They wanted to substitute boycott of school, college, courts, legislative council with total boycott of British capital and industry. They had the backing of the rising middle class in Bengal but this was defeated. Clearly there was a difference of opinion between Bengal and the rest of India in the Gandhi led Non-cooperation movement.[18]

There was infighting in the Bengal Provincial Congress even when Subhash Bose was away in jail. On his release in November 1927 Bose was elected as the BPCC president. That was when Birendranath Sasmal was excluded and he lost interest in Congress politics. Under Bose the entire BPCC was under the control of the Calcutta-based elites like Kiran Shankar Roy, Nalini Ranjan Sarkar, Bidhan Chandra Roy et al. The infighting within the Congress was equally intense in the districts over occupying official posts in the Congress and also over joining elected offices in local bodies. In many districts new organisations started coming up and, depending on which splinter group had influence, these took up activities to suit the group leader's political tilt. A new organisation called the Congress Karmi Sangha ultimately came to dominate the politics of the Congress in Bengal. Initially it was formed 'to reunite the Congress workers in a solid and disciplined group, to consolidate their energy and influence and to bring about a common understanding for a cooperation among them.'[19] Karmi Sangha intended to function as a socio-political organisation which aimed to improve the conditions in the villages, form labour unions and peasant unions, reconstruct the rural economy and build up cooperative credit societies. But in the course of time, the Karmi Sangha attained such importance that it began to exert its influence in the decision-making process of the Congress. The political prisoners who were released joined the Sangha. It was with the help of the Karmi Sangha that Subhas Bose became the president of the BPCC and at the same time managed to cut away Sengupta's political support in Bengal.

However, at the beginning, Jatindra Mohan and Subhas Chandra worked together. In 1928 when the election for Calcutta's mayor came up Subhas contested it with support from Jatindra Mohan. But he lost to a candidate (B.K. Basu) belonging to the moderate section of the Congress. This broke the peace between Subhas Chandra and Jatindra Mohan. In 1930 when there was a sharp difference between these two leaders over who would be in the Congress Working Committee, Gandhi chose Jatindra Mohan and rejected Subhas Chandra. Gandhi's dislike for the rabble-rouser Subhas Chandra was consistent. This divided the Bengal Congress into two camps. Jatindra Mohan was viewed as Gandhi's 'yes man' and was strongly disliked by an influential section in the state.

The conflict between Bose and Sengupta which was simmering under the surface came to the fore with Sengupta gaining support of the members of Anusilan Samiti. In 1928 after Bose was elected president of BPCC, he was seen moving close to the Jugantar group which had upset the rival Anusilan Samiti and consequently they sided with Jatindra Mohan Sengupta. With Sasmal safely out of the way it was a contest of supremacy between the two leading personalities in Bengal. Till the Anusilan Samiti members put their weight behind him, Sengupta was organisationally weaker than Bose who had won over the support of almost all the competing factions of the party in the province. The equation changed with the Anusilan Samiti turning hostile to Bose. Instances of both the factions engaging in brawls and fights were many. The intense rivalry of the two charismatic leaders ended Bengal's prominence in national politics though their rivalry did not last long. Sengupta died in 1932 and Bose left for Europe in 1933 for medical treatment. Leadership of the Congress in Bengal fell on Gandhian Dr Prafulla Chandra Ghosh and Suresh Banerjee. Both hailed from rural Bengal and neither had a strong grip over the state politics. The weakness of the leadership coupled with several splinter organisations working often at cross purposes and even against each other left Bengal politically weak within the Indian National Congress. In fact, barring Subhas Bose with his revolutionary brand of politics, no other leader from Bengal could ever rise up in the hierarchy of the Indian National Congress since the demise of Chittaranjan Das.

When Das said that he wanted Swaraj for 98 per cent of the people of the country, people like M.N. Roy who were looking to set up a communist party and movement in India were excited. In fact, M.N. Roy wrote how he got in touch with Chittaranjan suggesting what should be the way forward in the then forthcoming Gaya Congress. Roy suggested that Das would do well to press for council entry as also beyond which would mean freedom with dominion status. The letter got leaked in the English language press through Reuters who loudly claimed a link between the Bengal leader and the Russian Reds. Roy felt that just entering the council would not attract people unless the plan was backed up with actions beyond. But Das took the safer approach and stuck to council entry which led to the formation of the Swarajya party.

Communists abroad were working on setting up a communist party in India. With the romanticism associated with the Russian revolution the idea was acceptable to those in Bengal in particular. Roy's effort to set up a farmers' and workers' unit within the Congress did not succeed. But his follower Muzaffar Ahmad tried to popularise the idea of communism in Bengal. In this he had support from some prominent literary persons of that time. Kazi Nazrul Islam was perhaps the most prominent personality associated with the cause. They set up Bangla Krishak O Shramik Samity (1924-25) and its mouthpiece magazine *Langal*. Between 1935 and 1940 many future communists started their political life in the Congress. Apart from Muzaffar Ahmad some other leaders were Promode Dasgupta, Somnath Lahiri, Harekrishna Konar, Biswanath Mukherjee et al. Many of them were even elected to responsible posts in the district and Provincial Congress committees. But these communists were eventually expelled from the Congress Socialist Party.[20]

The communists could attract the revolutionary terrorists since they wanted complete freedom from the British rule overthrowing the government violently. Its draft political actions stated that the Indian National Congress was a reactionary organisation and an ally of the British. This was viewed as dangerous by the British government.[21] Bengal, forever romantic and always eager to embrace new ideas, saw many prominent writers come out in support of the Bolshevik revolution. Apart from Kazi Nazrul there were other prominent writers like Nripendra Krishna Chattopadhyay who translated Maxim Gorky's novel *Mother* in Bengali. Sudhindranath Dutta started the periodical *Parichay* (1931) which opened up a platform for the expression of progressive literary ideas. Sailajananda Mukhopadhyay was another prominent literary figure in whose novels working-class characters found prominent positions. Like during the phase of spreading nationalism in the late 19th century, in the early 20th century Bengali literature and intellectuals played an important role in spreading the idea of communism along with nationalism among the youth. This was completely different from what Gandhian politics was and Bengal's divergence with the Indian National Congress took another direction. M.N. Roy, the person who had worked for the spread of communism in India, had returned to India after being expelled from the Commintern in December 1929 and had even joined the Karachi Congress of 1931 but was arrested immediately thereafter. Roy found himself drawn more towards Jawaharlal Nehru and did not play any major role in Bengal politics.

Gandhi's flipflop over Purna Swaraj (complete freedom) had turned many younger leaders restless. When the Simon Commission was appointed in 1927 to review the Government of India Act of 1919 with no Indian being asked to be a member, the country unitedly protested and decided to boycott the commission. A committee under Motilal Nehru was formed with the intention of drawing up a constitution. The committee placed the demand for immediate transfer of responsible government to the Indians. This was placed before the annual session of the Congress in Calcutta in December 1928. Subhas Chandra and Jawaharlal Nehru put forward a demand for complete independence. Gandhi drafted a resolution that if the government failed to honour the recommendations on administrative reforms by the Motilal Nehru committee the Congress would start a movement of non-payment of tax and other non-violent non-cooperation movements. Gandhi said while moving the resolution that if the government did not accept the proposal within one year, he himself would join the movement for complete independence. A section led by Subhas Chandra placed an amendment to the resolution stating that nothing short of complete independence would satisfy the Congress. Gandhi was not happy and even threatened to resign from the Congress if his resolution without the amendment was not passed. The amendment submitted by Subhas Chandra received 973 votes against 1350 votes in favour of Gandhi's resolution. By attracting so many votes against a seasoned politician and an unchallenged leader like Gandhi, Subhas Chandra made his mark as someone who could take on Gandhi, the Congress supremo. Naturally when Gandhi was selecting the Congress Working Committee member from Bengal he opted for Jatindra Mohan and discarded Subhas Chandra.

Two interesting factors emerged from the entry of the Swarajya party in the legislative assembly and legislative council. Motilal Nehru led in the legislative assembly in Delhi while C.R. Das chose to remain in the provincial council. Das was the person who spearheaded the move to join councils and Motilal supported him. That's how the Swarajya party was created. But Das chose to remain in Bengal clearly giving more importance to regional politics than the national assembly. This is an interesting trait among the leaders from Bengal, something that can be seen even long after those days.

The second development was the rise of communalism in politics. This was more prominent in Bengal, a Muslim majority state. When a no-confidence by way of an adjournment motion on the ministers was brought by the Swarajya party members (20 February 1924), a procession of Muslim boys reached the Town Hall, venue of the council meeting, with placards warning the Muslim members not to fall in line with the Hindu resolution of bringing down a

Muslim ministry. During the entire proceedings similar leaflets were distributed among the Muslim members. There was another instance when Nawab Musharaff Husain moved a motion that in all government appointments 80 per cent should be reserved for the Muslims till the total Muslim officials in the categories specified in the motion touched 55 per cent. This was the state of Hindu–Muslim amity even when C.R. Das was at the helm.[22]

The 1928 Congress session was another occasion where the dominant Bengal opinion and that of Mahatma Gandhi clashed. Subhas Bose was the emerging voice of Bengal by now. At his instance a volunteer force was created which dressed in military uniform with Subhas Bose leading as General Officer Commanding (G.O.C.) during a parade. The Congress president received an exuberant welcome 'enough to rouse envy of Rajas and Maharajas' wrote Bose. But the major point of disappointment was the dilution of a resolution on complete independence adopted in the Madras session of the Congress in 1927. Subhas Bose wrote,

> The Calcutta Congress resulted in a situation quite opposite to what was achieved in the Madras Congress … A keen excitement was evident all over the country at the beginning and everybody hoped that the Congress would now act with courage but though the country was prepared the leaders were not. The misfortune of Mahatma's countrymen was that he could not see any light anywhere to guide him and it was for this reason that the Calcutta Congress only wasted valuable time over a colourless Resolution of no consequence. None but an insane or a fool could ever believe that the all-powerful British government would agree to Dominion Status for India without demur. While the Congress session was on, a procession of 10,000 workers came to the pandal to express

> their solidarity in the struggle for independence and also to make an appeal for a consideration of the problems facing the hungry workmen but these signs of national upheaval were lost on the leaders.

Strong words but these explain the differences between the dominant opinions of Bengal and the national Congress politics shaped by Mahatma Gandhi. Bengal's deviation from the national mainstream was evident even in the 1920s.[23]

How far removed Bengal's political sentiment was from that of Gandhi was seen in the Gopinath Saha case. This was again seen when Jatindra Nath Das, a revolutionary who was arrested under the supplementary Lahore Conspiracy case and kept in Lahore jail, died after a protest fast of 68 days. The incident was compared to the sacrifice of the Irish patriot Terence MacSwiney who died similarly during Ireland's struggle for freedom from the British. On learning about Jatindra Nath's death the members of the MacSwiney family had sent a telegram: 'The family of Terence MacSwiney feels grief and pride at the news of death of Jatin Das – freedom is bound to come.'[24] A sense of deep grief engulfed the whole nation. Large crowds assembled at every station on the way when Jatindra Nath's body was being brought to Calcutta by train. The only person who was unmoved was Mahatma Gandhi. Neither did he say anything in sympathy nor did he write any article in his *Young India* mentioning Jatin Das's sacrifice. Clearly Gandhi wanted Bengal to fall in line before him. Any other philosophy was unacceptable to him. This was when the Congress was in inaction mode burdened with the toothless resolutions adopted. Jatin Das's sacrifice provided fresh impetus to the revolutionary activities.

Bengal was the hotbed of revolutionary activity. Several attempts on the lives of British officers, even governors, had taken place. Some notable ones were the attempt on the life of Governor Jackson of Bengal in the Senate Hall during the Calcutta University convocation in 1932 by Bina Das, the attack on John Robinson by a group of revolutionaries among them being Ujjala Majumdar on 8 May 1934, the attack on the Writers' Building, and also the Chittagong armoury raid in 1930. This had unnerved the British administration. The 2,500 young men who had gathered under the Bengal Volunteer Corps of Subhas Bose were thoroughly disheartened with Gandhi's resolution in the Calcutta Congress. They dispersed to different parts of Bengal. Among them were Ananta Singh, Ganesh Ghosh and Lokenath Bal. They came in touch with Surya Sen, a unique personality, who was a school teacher and formed 'Indian Republican Army'. They felt that small-time stray revolutionary incidences did not have a big bang impact. Lokenath Bal wrote in his memoires that the revolutionaries were looking for a showcase event of capturing power from the British and decided to place an example before the country from Chittagong. Accordingly they captured Chittagong from the British, burnt the Union Jack and hoisted the national flag. The British administration was unnerved by the audacious attempt by a group of young men and women. No other revolutionary activity had shaken the British rule as did the revolutionaries of Chittagong who kept it liberated for three days.

There is another aspect of the Chittagong armoury case. The revolutionaries could not escape the subsequent British determination to capture them. The award announced for information leading to capture of the revolutionaries was incentive enough. In addition Muslims were eager to assist the British rulers. Evidently the Hindu–Muslim divide that kept on widening with the introduction of electoral politics encouraged ordinary Muslims to help the administration. The communal award of the Simon Commission had widened the gap further. The perpetrators of the Chittagong armoury raid were nabbed from their hideouts all over the province by the British police with assistance from the Muslims. In fact, a revolutionary like Anant Singh had walked into the political police headquarter in Calcutta and surrendered. Nirad C. Chaudhuri wrote that so shocked were the policemen that they met Anant Singh fully armed. The reason why the revolutionaries surrendered was that they had nowhere to hide with the Muslims keen to inform of their whereabouts to the police. Even some Hindus fell prey to the lure of money. Netraranjan Sen, a zamindar, became police informer by betraying Masterda Surya Sen's hideout to the police, leading to his arrest. The British administration was so perturbed by the Chittagong incident that the Calcutta police chief Charles Tegart had even crossed into the French territory of Chandernagor in order to arrest Lokenath Bal and his associates. While the Chittagong armoury raid shook the British it did not even move the pen of Mahatma Gandhi, a prolific writer.

It cannot be said that Gandhi did not keep himself informed about developments in Bengal. In a letter to Tagore on 21 January 1934 Gandhi expressed his concern over martial law in Midnapore. He wrote:

> The news about the Government measures in Midnapur has dazed me. They appear to me to be worse than the Martial Law measures of the Punjab in 1919. I get here only The Hindu. Are you doing anything? Is Bengal doing anything? Our cowardice chokes me. Or do I see cowardice where there is none? Can you give me any solace?[25]

Midnapore was a trouble spot for the administration. When the civil disobedience movement started two policemen used canes to beat the picketers who got agitated and the police-in-charge was beaten to death while his assistant was never seen after the crowd carried him away. Three district magistrates, Peddy, Douglas and then Burge, were killed. The third one B.E.G. Burge was assassinated on 2 September 1933 when he went to play football under heavy security. The British administration was harsh and ruthless with all kinds of strict laws enforced in Midnapore. Gandhi solicited support from Tagore who was not in politics. In another letter to Jawaharlal Nehru on the same day he repeated his concerns and mentioned that he had written to Dr Bidhan Chandra Roy and Rabindranath Tagore.[26] Gandhi used to trust Ghanshyamdas Birla (G.D. Birla) more than any Congress member from Bengal. On 12 February 1934 Gandhi wrote,

> Bhai Ghanshyamdas, I had a talk with Miss Lester about Midnapore and asked her to see the Governor. She wrote a letter to him to which he replied by wire. She is now going. You should read the letter I have given to her. I have asked her to see you and learn all the facts. Give her all the information. If it is necessary, arrange for her to meet Dr. Bidhan and Satisbabu. She will leave on Friday to be back here with me. She has been given some money for the expenses and her ticket has been paid for. Shall I charge it to you?[27]

And again on 19th February Gandhi wrote to G.D. Birla,

> I am considering whether I should write to the Governor or not. The [compulsory] saluting in Midnapore has been stopped but there has been no admission of the error. Miss Lester has now asked the Viceroy for an interview. But these things can bring about no result at the moment. Still, we do not want to miss any opportunity of compromise. Whatever

> the Congressmen may say Bidhan Roy should make full effort to seek an interview.[28]

The Bengal leaders whom Gandhi mentioned had been Dr Bidhan Roy and Satis Chandra Dasgupta who was known as the Gandhi of Bengal. The Bose brothers or Prafulla Chandra Ghosh did not find mention.

The Gandhian faction in the Bengal Provincial Congress was fragmented. When Gandhi came on the scene a certain section of bright young men joined him. Among them was Dr Prafulla Chandra Ghosh, who later became chief minister of West Bengal (twice for brief periods). Around the same time in the early twenties another group of supporters all hailing from around the river Hooghly joined Gandhi. Important among them were Prafulla Chandra Sen and Atulya Ghosh. While both were influenced by the Gandhian ideology they maintained their separate identities. One reason could be that the group led by Dr Prafulla Chandra Ghosh hailed from the eastern part of Bengal while the Prafulla Sen faction was from West Bengal – the typical *Ghati-Bangal* conflict. Interestingly, none of these groups could lead the Bengal Congress due to the strong influence of non-Gandhi factions led by Subhas Chandra Bose who had connections with the revolutionaries as well. But after the death of Jatindra Mohan and the departure of Subhas Chandra to Europe, the Bengal Congress leadership weakened very substantially. Prafulla Ghosh lacked the appeal to lead and effectively the big five of the Swarajya party led by Bidhan Chandra managed the Bengal Congress with blessings from the All India Congress Committee till Subhas Chandra returned and took charge in 1937. Gandhi used to write to Bidhan Chandra but from his correspondences it seems he reposed considerable faith in G.D. Birla, his financier, keeping Satis Dasgupta by his side to assist him at the spinning wheel.

One year after the disappointment of the Calcutta Congress, Gandhi along with Motilal Nehru met the viceroy. The one-year suspension of activity as resolved by Gandhi was coming to an end. But as expected the viceroy did not promise anything on dominion status or administrative reforms. He merely said that decisions on the Simon Commission recommendations would be reached only after an all-party meeting in London. Gandhi had remarked that his boat was burnt while in effect there was no boat which was merely an individual illusion. The Lahore Congress, according to historian R.C. Majumdar, was unique for re-energising the nation as well as creating various complex issues for Bengal politics thereafter.[29] The Congress Working Committee had in July 1928 rejected a proposal of non-cooperation movement and boycott of legislatures. Both Jatindra Mohan and Subhas Bose had opposed it. But in December Jatindra Mohan broke rank and supported the same resolution. While the movement was approved no decision was taken on what would be the nature and course of the movement. With reference to the communal question, Gandhi's resolution assured that, 'no suggestion for resolving communal differences would be acceptable unless the same had the approval of the minorities'.[30] The resolution left the bar open and led to the minorities increasing their demands that led eventually to the partition of the country. For Muslim majority Bengal this spelled disaster in the long run. In addition, in order to ensure his hold on the Congress, Gandhi dropped leaders like Subhas Bose from the working committee giving no choice to dissenters or leaving room for any counter suggestions. The year 1929 was arguably a severe blow to Bengal delivered by none other than Mahatma Gandhi himself.[31]

In 1937 Gandhi wrote to Sarat Bose that he would accept the hospitality of the Boses during the forthcoming meeting of the AICC and Congress Working Committee in Calcutta.

> Of course, God willing, I am coming to Calcutta. I am not yet fit for meetings or discussions. I have a limited amount of energy which I would love to use whilst there for the detenus' cause, as also for questions that may crop up at the Working Committee meetings. For myself, I shall gladly be under your roof and have you as my guard against too many visitors and unnecessary interviews. You will also please save me from public demonstrations and meetings.[32]

Gandhi wrote to Subhas Chandra as well, 'I am trying to keep myself fit for Calcutta. I am praying to God to keep me fit. After I am there, you will have to see that I have no appointments or visits save about the Andamans prisoners and the Working Committee business.'[33] This decision of Gandhi to stay with the Boses, wrote Nirad C. Chaudhuri, caused considerable heartburn in Calcutta. Dr Bidhan Roy tried to get Gandhi shifted from the residence of Sarat Chandra Bose as did the Birlas. The Birlas had Gandhi's son Devdas Gandhi on their payroll to influence his father. An interesting point to note is that along with Gandhi, Jawaharlal Nehru too stayed with the Boses. Nehru had more influence on the Mahatma than did his son Devdas. Evidently Nehru was not too keen on G.D. Birla. Thus Gandhi stayed with the Boses. The stay was longer than planned since immediately after the meeting Gandhi had a heart attack and had to stay back for a couple of more weeks under the doctor's advice.[34]

There was a reason for Mahatma Gandhi to come to Calcutta and show his neutrality to the non-Gandhian faction of the Congress. The prisoners detained at the Andaman Islands had been on hunger strike and in August the CWC passed a resolution in support of them. The resolution noted, 'Public opinion all over India is agitated and strongly in favour of the release of the political prisoners there as they have already undergone many years of imprisonment under conditions which are far worse than those prevailing in Indian prisons.'[35]

There was also the issue related to 'Vande Mataram'. The CWC had taken a resolution that before the Congress sessions only the first two stanzas of the song would be sung and the rest of the song could depend on the decisions of the local bodies. This was done to appease the sentiments of the Muslim members. However, this had made Bengal unhappy. Gandhi knew well enough that he needed the Bose brothers on his side at this point in time. Clearly his decision to stay with Sarat Bose was politically strategic.

In a letter to Nehru dated 18 November 1937 Mahatma Gandhi explained how he had approached both the issue of the Andamans detenus and singing of 'Vande Mataram'.

> This I write to report to you what I have done about the prisoners in Bengal, and to ascertain whether it meets with your approval. The negotiations have been a taxing affair. Before entering upon them I had consulted the two Brothers (Sarat and Subhas Bose) as to the desirability of securing relief through negotiations ... The Brothers were emphatically for negotiations, whilst public agitation continued ... The Ministers have agreed to release what they call 'village and home domiciled' detenus almost forthwith, and inside of four months to release those in the detenu camps whom they may consider to be safe. For the rest they will accept my recommendation, if they are not earlier released. *My recommendation will depend upon my ascertaining the present belief of the detenus. If I am able to say to the Government that they do not believe in methods of violence for the attainment of independence and that they will pursue such Congress activities as are approved*

> *of by the Congress from time to time, they will release them* [emphasis added].

And on 'Vande Mataram' Gandhi wrote, 'The "Bande Mataram" controversy has not yet died out. Many Bengalis are sore at heart over the W. C. decision. Subhas told me he was trying to calm the atmosphere.'

It is apparent that Mahatma Gandhi did not deviate from his views on violence and had linked the release of detenus with their subscribing to the Congress approved non-violent activities. Meanwhile Mahatma Gandhi decided that in the next Congress at Haripura Subhas Bose would take over from Nehru as president. He wrote to Vallabhbhai on 1 November 1937, 'I have observed that Subhas is not at all dependable. However, there is nobody but he who can be the President (at Haripura Congress).'[36] On 23 January 1938 Gandhi sent a telegram to Bose, 'WELCOME HOME. GOD GIVE YOU STRENGTH TO BEAR THE WEIGHT OF JAWAHARLAL'S MANTLE. LOVE.'[37]

Politics in Bengal was complex due to factionalism not only within the Congress but among the Muslims as well. The Muslim League did not have much influence in Bengal. Instead the Bengal Muslim Party was more powerful but the most powerful among the Muslims was the Krishak Praja party led by Fazlul Huq. Even communist leaders like Muzaffar Ahmad had managed to reach out to the Muslims. Thus when the Congress contested the elections in 1937 with the decision that the party would form governments in provinces where it commanded absolute majority, it failed to take note of the position of Bengal politics. The election result was a hung assembly with Congress winning 60 out of 250 seats. The break-up of seats in the assembly was as under:[38]

Congress	60
Independent Muslims	41
Muslim League	40
Krishak Praja Party	35
Europeans	25
Independent Scheduled Caste Hindus	23
Independent Caste Hindus	14
Other Independents	12

The obduracy of the All India Congress helped the Muslim League. When Sarat Bose could not persuade the Congress to join a coalition with Fazlul Huq, the Muslim League took the opportunity to join hands with Huq. This helped the Muslim League to expand its influence in the province that eventually saw it divided. In December 1938 in response to Subhas Bose, Gandhi wrote a strictly confidential letter which was dictated in the presence of Maulana Azad, Nalini Ranjan Sarkar (who was then finance minister in the Huq cabinet) and G.D. Birla, where he mentioned that he had had exhaustive discussions with all three. He further wrote,

> I am more than ever convinced that we should not aim at ousting the Ministry. We shall gain nothing by a reshuffle. And probably we shall lose much by including Congressmen in the Ministry. I feel, therefore, that the best way of securing comparative purity of administration and continuity of a settled programme and policy would be to aim at having all the reforms that we desire carried out by the present Ministry. Nalini Babu should come out, as he says he would, on a real issue being raised and the decision being taken by the Ministry against the interests of the country. His retirement from the Ministry would then be dignified and

> wholly justified. I understand that so far as the amendment of the municipal law is concerned, separate electorate for the scheduled class is given up. There is still insistence on separate electorate for Mussalmans. I do not know whether opposition should be taken to the breaking point. If the Mussalman opinion is solid in favour of separation, I think it would be wisdom to satisfy them. I would not like them to carry the point in the teeth of the Congress opposition. It would be then a point against the Congress.

Gandhi then shrewdly mentioned the release of prisoners, a sensitive topic for Bose, and wrote, 'If my opinion is acceptable to you, the release of the Prisoners becomes a much simpler matter than it is today.'[39]

Mahatma Gandhi's letter illustrates several points. First, it shows that he had no faith in the most popular leader from Bengal who was then president of the Indian National Congress. Second, he reposed faith in three persons none of whom had any people connect but were there by virtue of being close to Gandhi. Third, and no less important, was his readiness to accept the demand for a separate electorate for Muslims. This arrangement extended to the Calcutta Corporation as well. Gandhi's decision was political naivety allowing Muslims to consolidate and move ahead with partition plans for Bengal. Subhas Bose was crestfallen upon receiving Gandhi's letter. What hurt him most was his leader giving more credence to three persons who had no role in running the Congress in Bengal. Subhas had had discussions with Gandhi at Wardha where the latter had agreed to a coalition government with the Krishak Praja party but changed his view after discussing the matter with three virtual outsiders to Bengal politics. Subhas predicted that the move to allow the ministry to run would strengthen the Muslim League and weaken the Congress but Mahatma Gandhi would not budge.

The difference between Mahatma Gandhi and Bengal was deep, not merely political. Historian Ramchandra Guha wrote an interesting article in *The Telegraph* (January 7, 2017) based on a letter he came across while working in the archives of the Sabarmati Ashram in Ahmedabad. This was sent by eleven young women of Calcutta.

> The letter was undated, but it appeared to have been written in January 1939. It was addressed to 'Most revered Mahatmaji', and was signed individually by the eleven women, all Hindus by their names. The letter was written in protest against an essay written by Gandhiji for his journal *Harijan*. Gandhiji's article, said these women, was 'not very inspiring', since it seemed to 'put the whole slur upon the injured female who suffers most due to the malevolent social custom'.[40]

Guha, who worked laboriously on Gandhi and Nehru, located the original article of Gandhi that had so offended the young women of Bengal. It was entitled 'Students' Shame' and was published in the *Harijan*'s issue dated December 31, 1938. This was Gandhi's response to a letter written by a college girl in the Punjab, complaining about the teasing and harassment she and her companions experienced at the hands of prowling young men. She had asked how in the circumstances 'girls can apply the principle of ahimsa and save themselves'. In response, Gandhi wrote in the *Harijan* and admitted that such molestation by men was a 'growing evil' in India. He suggested that such people should be named and shamed and also asked well-behaved men to chastise the deviants among their own flock. Despite his devotion to non-violence, in this case Gandhi thought that young women should 'learn the art of ordinary self-defence and protect themselves from indecent behaviour of unchivalrous youth'.

But in between Gandhi exposed his orthodoxy and preached that the dress code of the modern woman was also to blame. Guha quoted that Gandhiji wrote,

> I have a fear that the modern girl loves to be Juliet to half a dozen Romeos. She loves adventure. My correspondent seems to represent the unusual type. The modern girl dresses not to protect herself from wind, rain and sun but to attract attention. She improves upon nature by painting herself and looking extraordinary. The non-violent way is not for such girls.

Bengal's eleven girls did not take this gratuitous advice of Mahatma Gandhi kindly. They responded.

> Some may find modern girls' dresses and deportments a bit different than they wish them to be but to brand them as exhibitionistic generally is a positive insult to her sex as a whole. Strength of character and chaste behaviour are necessary not only for modern girls but for men as well. There may be a few girls playing Juliets to a dozen Romeos. But such cases presuppose the existence of half a dozen Romeos, moving around the streets in quest of a Juliet, thereby pointing out where the proper correction lies.

They informed Gandhi that his own unfortunate remarks

> … once again holds brief for that worn-out and un-becoming saying—'woman is the gate of Hell'. And naturally clouds of doubt gather over the much-vaunted progress that man has made since the birth of that saying. A Gokhale, a Tilak, a

> Deshbandhu would have surely hesitated to come out with such an ungenerous statement as you have done. Woman has been called a boa-constrictor, but that is in a different land and by a different man. What befits a Bernard Shaw with his hands touching the ground and legs kicking the air does not befit a Mahatma.

The young women added that they respected Gandhi as much as the others do but they resented 'To be hated or pitied' and added that they were

> ... ready to amend their ways if they are really guilty. Their guilt, if any, must be conclusively proved before they are anathematized. In this respect they would neither desire to take shelter under the covering of 'ladies, please' nor would they silently stand and allow the judge to condemn them in his own way. Truth must be faced, the modern girl of Juliet as you have called her, has courage enough to face it.

Guha located Gandhi's response which included printing parts of the letter leaving out the parts which had praised leaders like Tilak, Das and Gokhale and his tone, Guha noted, was defensive. He did not forget to highlight how he 'began service of India's women in South Africa more than forty years ago when perhaps none of them (the eleven girls from Bengal) were born'. But the response shows that Gandhi believed he could never have been wrong and repeated his assertion on the role women's dressing had: 'But in giving the diagnosis of the disease, I was bound, if I was to prescribe the right remedy, to mention all the factors which induced the disease'. This correspondence shows that Bengal was far too argumentative and modern for Gandhi. Bengal would not blindly accept his preachings which were gospel for his followers elsewhere. Gandhi's dislike for Bengal was more fundamental than a mere rift with certain personalities like Das or Bose.

When Gandhi was staving off criticism of the eleven young women from Bengal, he was fighting another battle with Subhas Bose, the final one that ended the role of a Bengali politician in the politics of the Indian National Congress. It started with the choice of Congress president for 1939 after the expiry of the one-year tenure of Subhas Chandra Bose. On 24 November 1938 Gandhi wrote to Nehru:

> Here is a letter delivered through messenger from Gurudev. I have replied saying my personal opinion was that he needed to be free from the Presidential work, if he was to rid Bengal of corruption. I have no doubt Gurudev will write to you directly or talk to you. You will give your own opinion.[41]

It seems that Tagore had asked for Subhas Chandra Bose's continuance as Congress president while Gandhi had brought in an excuse of corruption in Bengal to decline the request. Earlier in a letter (28 October 1938) to Maniben Patel, daughter of Vallabhbhai, Gandhi had written,

> What is happening regarding Subhas Babu is not out of my mind. That is why I discussed it in the Working Committee. But Father (that is Vallabhbhai) was of the view that we should wait till Jawaharlal's arrival, so I kept silent. There is bound to be some difficulty this time in electing the President.[42]

Mahatma Gandhi had been persuading Maulana Azad to take over from Subhas but he declined. Gandhi wrote to Nehru on 21 December

1938, 'Maulana Saheb does not want the crown of thorns. If you want to try again please do. If you won't or he won't listen, Pattabhi seems to be the only choice.'

The battle lines were being drawn, only in this instance the winner turned out to be the ultimate loser.

What Gandhi did not like was the way his resolution was handled by Congress President Subhas Bose on 23 September 1938. The resolution was against violence in political action and a clause restricting extent of civil liberties. It read:

> Inasmuch as people including a few Congressmen have been found in the name of civil liberty to advocate murder, arson, looting, and class war by violent means, and several newspapers are carrying on a campaign of falsehood and violence calculated to incite the readers to violence and to lead to communal conflicts, the Congress warns the public that civil liberty does not cover acts of or incitement to violence or promulgation of palpable falsehoods. In spite, therefore, of the Congress policy on civil liberty remaining unchanged the Congress will, consistently with its tradition, support measures that may be undertaken by the Congress Governments for the defence of life and property.[43]

The resolution was passed by the CWC in its session between 23rd and 25th September and was placed before AICC on the 26th, at which point a section walked out. Gandhi was not happy with the way the dissidents were allowed to speak out and wrote in the *Harijan*, (October 15, 1938)

> I understand the President went out of his way to let them make as many and as long speeches as they liked. Therefore the

> protest was against the majority refusing to accept amendments which cut at the root of the resolution which was regarded as vital to the existence of the Congress in its present form.[44]

Gandhi asked the opponents to stop their protest after the majority passed the resolutions and he insisted that the dissidents follow a certain discipline or they were free to go on their own.

It is pertinent to note that Gandhi claimed at that time that he was not in the Congress, one of the various on and off times for the Mahatma. Gandhi wrote in the *Harijan* on 23 January 1939: 'Though I am not in the Congress, I have not ceased to be of it. Congressmen still expect me to give the call when in my opinion the time for action has come.'[45] In a statement to the press on 31 January 1939 Gandhi said,

> Shri Subhas Bose has achieved a decisive victory over his opponent, Dr. Pattabhi Sitaramayya. I must confess that from the very beginning I was decidedly against his re-election for reasons into which I need not go. I do not subscribe to his facts or the arguments in his manifestos. I think that his references to his colleagues were unjustified and unworthy. Nevertheless, I am glad of his victory. And since I was instrumental in inducing Dr. Pattabhi not to withdraw his name as a candidate when Maulana Saheb withdrew, the defeat is more mine than his.[46]

This decisive victory by Subhas Chandra Bose was the last victory of any Bengali politician on the national stage and in any national political organisation (broken perhaps when Pranab Mukherjee was elected the President of India in 2012).

Endnotes

1 Giri, *1921 Movement.*

2 Gandhi, *Experiments with Truth,* p. 385.

3 Paul Greenough, "The Death of an Uncrowned King - C. R. Das and Political Crisis in Twentieth-Century Bengal" in *Comparative Studies in Society and History* 28, no. 3 (1986), pp 414–41, www.jstor.org/stable/178858 (accessed May 10, 2020).

4 Ibid.

5 Ibid.

6 Srabani Rai Chaudhuri, "The Swarajist Interlude in Bengal: Paradox of a Strange amalgam" in *The Indian Journal of Political Science* 51, no. 2 (1990), pp 242–59, www.jstor.org/stable/41855489 (accessed May 10, 2020).

7 Greenough, "C. R. Das and Political Crisis in Twentieth-Century Bengal", pp 414-41.

8 Ibid.

9 Georgi Plekhanov was a Russian revolutionary, philosopher and a Marxist theoretician. He was a founder of the social-democratic movement in Russia and was one of the first Russians to identify himself as a 'Marxist'.

10 Roy, *Men I Met,* pp 22-3.

11 Gautam Chattopadhyay, "The Real Face of 'Left' Nationalists of Bengal (1922-1929)" in *Proceedings of the Indian History Congress* 39 (1978), pp 733–9, www.jstor.org/stable/44139418 (accessed May 10, 2020).

12 https://shodhganga.inflibnet.ac.in/bitstream/10603/164577/8/08_chapter%205.pdf.

13 Ibid.

14 Ibid.

15 Ibid.

16 Tathagata Ray, *The Life and Times of Syamaprasad Mookerjee* (Ocean Books Pvt Ltd, 2008), Kindle edition.

17 Mario Prayer, "The 'Gandhians' of Bengal: Nationalism, Social Reconstruction and Cultural Orientations 1920-1942" in *Rivista Degli Studi Orientali* 74 (2001), pp 1–363, www.jstor.org/stable/41913060 (accessed May 12, 2020).

18 Ibid.

19 https://shodhganga.inflibnet.ac.in/bitstream/10603/155061/8/08_chapter%205.pdf.

20 Majumdar, *Modern Bengal,* p. 248.

21 Susnata Das, "The Empire Against Communism: Colonial Repression on the Marxist Revolutionaries in Bengal (1930-36)" in *Proceedings of the Indian History Congress* 72 (2011), pp 714–27, www.jstor.org/stable/44146764, (accessed May 14, 2020).

22 Majumdar, ed., *Struggle for Freedom*, pp 392-410.

23 Majumdar, *Modern Bengal*, pp 231-2.

24 Ibid., p. 233.

25 http://www.gandhiashramsevagram.org/gandhi-literature/mahatma-gandhi-collected-works-volume-63.pdf.

26 Ibid.

27 Ibid.

28 Ibid.

29 Majumdar, *Modern Bengal*, pp 234-5.

30 Ibid., p. 235.

31 Ibid.

32 https://www.gandhiashramsevagram.org/gandhi-literature/mahatma-gandhi-collected-works-volume-72.pdf.

33 Ibid.

34 Chaudhuri, *Unknown Indian* Part II.

35 http://www.gandhiashramsevagram.org/gandhi-literature/mahatma-gandhi-collected-works-volume-72.pdf. Congress Bulletin, No. 6, September 1937. File No. 4/15/37, Home, Political. Courtesy: National Archives of India.

36 Ibid.

37 http://www.gandhiashramsevagram.org/gandhi-literature/collected-works-of-mahatma-gandhi-volume-1-to-98.php.

38 Majumdar, *Modern Bengal*, pp 252-3.

39 Ibid.

40 http://ramachandraguha.in/archives/when-eleven-women-of-bengal-took-on-gandhi-the-telegraph.html.

41 http://www.gandhiashramsevagram.org/gandhi-literature/collected-works-of-mahatma-gandhi-volume-1-to-98.php.

42 Ibid.

43 http://www.gandhiashramsevagram.org/gandhi-literature/mahatma-gandhi-collected-works-volume-74.pdf.

44 Ibid.

45 Ibid.

46 https://www.gandhiashramsevagram.org/gandhi-literature/mahatma-gandhi-collected-works-volume-75.pdf.

BENGAL FLOATS ON ITS OWN

After the arrival of Mahatma Gandhi in the Indian political scene the collective decision-making process depended on the nod from the leader supreme, a tradition adopted as a part of the existence of the Indian National Congress thereafter. The victory of Subhas Chandra Bose over the candidate propped up by Gandhi in the election for the post of Congress president in 1939 should be seen in this context. Mahatma Gandhi, like many losers past, present and future, blamed the list of electorates as a reason for his loss. He put it subtly,

> There is one thing common between majority and minority, viz., insistence on internal purity of the Congress organization. My writings in the *Harijan* have shown that the Congress is fast becoming a corrupt organization in the sense that its registers contain a very large number of bogus members. I have been suggesting for the past many months the overhauling of these registers. I have no doubt that many of the delegates who have been elected on the strength of these bogus voters would be unseated on scrutiny. But I suggest no such drastic step. It will be enough if the registers are purged of all bogus voters and are made fool-proof for the future.[1]

In a letter to Subhas Chandra on 5 February 1939 Mahatma Gandhi effectively informed Bose that those whom he considered rightists, like Rajendra Prasad, Maulana Azad and others, would submit resignations from the CWC to let the newly re-elected president form his own committee. The tussle between Gandhi and Bose was viewed by many as ungracious in its approach to Bengal. Tagore wrote to Gandhi (29 March 1939), 'At the last Congress session some rude hands have deeply hurt Bengal with ungracious persistence. Please apply without delay balm to the wound with your own kind hands and prevent it from festering.'[2] But the Mahatma declined to assist Subhas without him accepting Gandhi's suggestions first. The deadlock in the Congress continued and in a letter on 14th May Gandhi informed Bose, 'The gulf is too wide, suspicions too deep. I see no way of closing the ranks. The only way seems to me to recognize the differences and let each group work in its own manner.'[3] He added that these views were his own and not influenced by any confidant of the Mahatma, 'You are wrong if you think that you have a single personal enemy among the Old Guard.' Perhaps the reference was to Sardar Patel with whom Subhas had a legal battle over the will of Sardar's elder brother Vithalbhai. When Vithalbhai was sick in Europe in 1933 Subhas had nursed him. In his will Vithalbhai had left three-fourth of his estate to Bose to be spent on publicity for India's cause in other countries. This led to cases which finally went in favour of Sardar and the estate went on to the legal heirs of Vithalbhai. This enmity perhaps carried on and Sardar was against Subhas being elected Congress president even in 1938.[4] As a result, Gandhi loyalists led by Sardar Vallabhbhai Patel ensured that Subhas got eased out as Congress president in 1939 despite his electoral victory. The Bengal leader lost to the two national leaders from Gujarat. The east and west of India could not work together.

The final breach between Subhas Chandra and the Congress came in August 1939 when a statement of Bose (this was after he was eased out as president) on prohibition, a pet theme of the Congress, was considered objectionable and as an act of indiscipline. Bose differed with two decisions of the Bombay government run by the Congress. One was prohibition which he felt would encourage illicit distillation and impose a restriction on the minority Parsis. The other was a stiff ten per cent property tax which Bose felt would adversely affect the Muslims. The opposition to decisions endorsed by the Congress, that too for the sake of the minorities mentioned by Bose, infuriated the Mahatma who in a statement to the press on 13th July criticised Bose for embarrassing the Congress ministers and said, 'Subhas Babu has played a most dangerous game by mixing up the communal question with such a purely moral reform as prohibition.'[5] The Congress president expressed his anguish, called for an explanation from Bose, and then on 11th August the working committee suspended Bose for three years: 'The Working Committee therefore resolves that for his grave act of indiscipline Shri Subhas Babu is declared disqualified as President of the Bengal Provincial Congress Committee for three years as from August 1939.'[6]

Politics in Bengal at the time was in a complex stage. With the departure of Bose, the Congress became significantly weak in the state. Even the official Congress organ 'Forward' accepted that the popular opinion was in favour of Subhas Bose and 'hence against the Indian National Congress'. The Calcutta Corporation election in 1940 had exposed this weakness beyond any doubt. Realising its weakness the Congress stayed away from the election. Bose and Syama Prasad Mukherjee-led Hindu Mahasabha initially tried to form an alliance of the Hindus but they failed. The Bose group won 21 out of 43 seats contested, and the Hindu Mahasabha 16 out of 33. Out of the 51,000 Hindu votes Bose and the Hindu Mahasabha won 41,000 votes. But the resulting acrimony between Bose and the Hindu Mahasabha, and the loss of the Congress made Subhas rethink and in a dramatic development he joined hands with the Muslim League to contest the various posts of the corporation. Three posts of alderman went to Bose, two to the Muslim League and the mayor's post went to a Muslim League MLA Abdur Rahman Siddiqui. Curiously Bose opted to be an alderman. He claimed that the tie up with the Muslim League was like the pact of C.R. Das and it was a continuation of the same noble policy.[7] This phase was marked by bitter exchanges between the Hindu Mahasabha and the Bose faction, resulting even in hooliganism in meetings. Syama Prasad was even injured in one such meeting. There was also an attack on a public meeting held at the Town Hall which was presided over by Ramananda Chatterjee, editor of *Prabasi*.[8] Political violence in Bengal was seen earlier too when there was a factional fight between Jatindra Mohan Sengupta and Subhas Chandra in the BPCC in 1930.

These incidents illustrate how politics in Bengal revolved around positions in Calcutta. Otherwise how can one explain Subhas Bose's decision to opt for the mere post of Alderman in the Calcutta Corporation! This also demeans considerably the political astuteness of Bose in sensing the dark clouds of Muslim politics eventually hurting the minority rights of Hindu Bengalis. Had Bose not left for Germany with a bigger mission for the cause of national freedom he would have remained consigned as a marginal leader of a faction in the national politics, judged by his role in Bengal immediately after being expelled from the Congress.

When Syama Prasad Mukherjee quit the post of vice chancellor of Calcutta University to take up the cause of Hindus in Bengal he had made efforts to build an agreement with the Boses. However at that time Subhas was the Congress president and had no interest in joining hands against the Muslims in Bengal. Both the Boses were not comfortable in being seen as mere Hindu leaders thereby giving up their secular position. Meanwhile Mukherjee along with prominent Bengalis like N.C. Chatterjee (father of politician Somnath Chatterjee) fought for the betterment of the Bengali Hindus.

Even the Muslim politicians were divided but taking advantage of this division the Muslim League managed to extend its influence and eventually divide Bengal. The seed of the problem was sown by the short-sighted Congress resolution in 1937 that the Congress would form governments only in those provinces where it would command absolute majority. Thus the Congress denied Bengalis the opportunity to form a Hindu majority government. Fazlul Huq, the leader of the Krishak Praja party, was keen on such a coalition. The Congress's refusal forced him to join hands with the Muslim League and dark clouds started hovering over the political fate of Hindu Bengalis. The plight of Bengal is an example of how the obduracy of a single powerful national leader could ruin the future of an entire state that in the past had introduced the concept of nationalism to India.

The politics of Bengal is a story of factionalism both among the Hindus and the Muslims, in the Congress and in the Muslim League. Even after refusing in 1937, the Congress could have joined a coalition with Fazlul Huq in 1938 as was suggested by Subhas Chandra Bose. However, Gandhi objected under the advice of G.D. Birla, Maulana Azad and Nalini Ranjan Sarkar, none of whom had any popular position in Bengal politics. According to Nirad C. Chaudhuri, who was then private secretary to Sarat Bose and was privy to inside views of the Bose brothers, G.D. Birla feared that a Hindu–Muslim government with support from the Boses would harm the business interests of the Marwaris. Unfortunately, Mahatma Gandhi opted to side with his financier ignoring the political advice of the most popular leader of Bengal.

If one probes deeply into the reaction or the lack of it of Mahatma Gandhi over the Bengal famine during 1942-44, the famines in Bengal (and Odisha) cropped up a few times but there was no effort to protest against the mishandling of the situation by the British administration or the Bengal government headed by Nazimuddin.

In December 1943 Gandhi had discussed with Devdas Gandhi, his son and an employee of G.D. Birla, the issue of distributing relief to the famine-affected areas. 'Some talk took place about the Bengal famine, and Mr. Devdas said that latterly some good arrangements were being made and the funds raised were used through public hands and not through Government.'[9] In March 1944 in a long letter to Viceroy Lord Wavell, Gandhi wrote, 'You are flying all over India. You have not hesitated to go among the skeletons of Bengal.'[10] In his speech to the Congressmen in Poona in June 1944 Gandhi mentioned the famine-related deaths in Bengal but said that though shocking it was negligible compared to the havoc the government had wreaked over the centuries. He admitted that many Congressmen had been pleading with him to do something,

> I have been receiving most depressing letters and also stimulating ones. Many Congressmen write to me saying that we must do something. Should we co-operate with the Government in the famine-relief work? The present deadlock, they say, must somehow be ended. Imitating the language of the Government, I would say, where is the deadlock? If the Government does not seek our co-operation, let it be so.[11]

In an interview to the press Mahatma Gandhi said that he had no doubt that the famine in Bengal was manmade. Curiously Gandhi never wrote or spoke explicitly against the section which was held guilty by the public and even by his confidant and friend Jawaharlal Nehru. Nehru wrote referring to the famine and cloth crisis in Bengal, 'According to the report of the Woodhead Commission, the black marketers made a profit of Rs 1000 per head out of the fifteen lakh starvation deaths in Bengal (a total of 15 crores of rupees).'[12] The Bengal famine has been reduced to a side note in the history of

India without delving into the uncomfortable details of the role of different personalities of that time. Janam Mukherjee wrote in his book *Hungry Bengal*, '... the effects that famine had on the politics and society of Bengal, and its deep entanglements in the broader history of India have been largely ignored.'[13] For an ordinary Bengali the loudest noise was the silence of Mahatma Gandhi on an issue that had rocked the then Bengal legislative assembly and had drawn the attention of the international media that too amidst the World War. In a letter to Gandhi (2 December 1943), the English industrial welfare reformer Agatha Harrison (who was close to Gandhi) wrote:

> As I write this letter, I have on my desk a cartoon by Low that appeared the other day in the Evening Standard. The caption reads 'Between the unhelpful and the helpless'. It depicts an Indian street: the pavements on each side are crowded with dead and starving men, women and children. In the middle of the road is a huge broken-down motor lorry labelled 'India-Food Distribution'. Two ropes are attached to the front of the lorry, one tightly bound to the straining figure of Lord Wavell. The other rope he is holding out with a beckoning hand to a seated Indian figure in front of him, who is reading a paper entitled 'Political Platitudes'.

Harrison reminded Gandhi of the help the Congress extended during the Bihar relief work in 1934 under Gandhi's leadership and implored him to cut the circle – that is the government-Gandhi deadlock – and join the relief work. That Gandhi did not find merit in the argument of Harrison could be seen in Gandhi's Poona address some six months later mentioned above.

The then Bengal governor Richard Cassey wrote on his experiences in Bengal at that time. He referred to the Marwari textile dealers who with an eye towards profit created artificial scarcity and then increased prices and bribed members of the legislative assembly, 'It is matter of great regret that a certain proportion of Muslim and scheduled caste politicians are seduced to defect from their party and do not hesitate to join another.'[14] Bengal's back was broken by a combination of factors: the failure of the Congress to stop the rise of Muslim politics and the taking over of the Muslim majority province by the Muslim League which initially did not have much influence there; infighting among the Congress leaders; lack of political sense among the Gandhians whose incompetence saw the party failing to contest even the politically important Calcutta Corporation election in 1940; the apathy of the Indian National Congress leadership led by Mahatma Gandhi himself; and the terrible famine in the province that had attracted international attention but could not move a leader in west India. The fate of Bengal as an influencer in national politics was sealed by the 1940s. The subsequent course of politics in the state, the division of Bengal, untold miseries faced by the Bengali Hindus, and the present political scene in the state nearly eighty years later can be examined in the context of this backdrop. The flicker of prominence that came Bengal's way due to Netaji Subhas Bose leading the Indian National Army (INA) and hoisting the national flag on Indian soil was effectively buried in the official record of the freedom struggle as just that – a flicker.

The politics in Bengal in the 1940s took two different courses. On one hand was the legislative politics in Calcutta which was full of infighting, corruption, personal political ambitions, and sectarian politics, while on the other hand was the freedom movement which saw selfless sacrifices of ordinary men and women. The Quit India movement announced on 8 August 1942 was a movement which was anything but non-violent and took place with no concrete action plan announced by the Congress or its supreme leader Mahatma Gandhi.

In Bengal the situation kept getting worse until people decided to take the law in their own hands. This deteriorating situation was aggravated by the food crisis late 1942 onwards. Even the tribals joined the uprising essentially out of food shortage. Industrial workers, municipal employees and port workers all struck work periodically, hard-pressed as they were by the war time inflation and price rise due to hoarding and black marketing. Suranjan Das mentioned that in Bengal where the Quit India movement had 'one of its best fruition did encompass a broad spectrum of social protest … Such popular outbursts mostly occurred independently of the Congress organisation. But they gained sustenance from the force of nationalism.'[15] Das pointed out how the restiveness in the rural sector saw spontaneous protests against the British administration. These protests saw the membership of the Marxists-led Bengal Provincial Kishan Sabha soar. The labour unrest had unnerved the administration. A joint secretary of the Indian Federation of Labour, a body sponsored by the Bengal government, wrote that Bengal was the most threatened province of the country. Though the communists had supported the British war efforts (once their patron nation the Soviet Union was attacked by Germany), E.M.S. Namboodiripad wrote how the communists were organising people against the suppression of the British rulers. There were instances where the members of the communist party and students joined hands in creating movements among the grassroots in different districts of Bengal – Birbhum, Pabna, Jalpaiguri, Nadia, etc.[16] This grassroot activism of the communists stood them in good stead later in the politics of divided Bengal which had borne the major brunt of the Partition.

Politics in Bengal in the 1940s therefore was a sorry tale of factionalism arising out of the self-interest of political leaders. The Bengal Cabinet crisis in 1945 which saw a fresh election and later

Suhrawardy assuming charge and presiding over the partition of the province is one such example. Fazlul Huq, a popular political figure at that time, chose his coalition partners based on his own personal ambitions on many occasions. Historian R.C. Majumdar opined that Huq was a vacillating character. He had seen through the politics of both the Congress and the Muslim League, both of whom were interested in the national scene even if the same went against Bengal's interest. Huq, writes Majumdar, 'was quite alive to the interest of Bengal ... and his view was that so far as the problems of a particular province are concerned, the central leadership should shape its policy in consultation with the local leaders of the party in the province.'[17] Clearly this did not suit the national leaders of either the Congress or the Muslim League. The continued interference in Bengal's politics by both Mahatma Gandhi and Jinnah had adversely affected the prospect of Bengalis. This was reflected when famine-affected Bengal was left to fend for itself in the absence of strong intervention by either of the central political parties.

In the provincial election of 1937 Huq's Krishak Praja party held the key to ministry formation. Despite the willingness of the Provincial Congress to join hands with Huq the central leadership refused to help Huq and paved the way for the Muslim League's penetration in the province. Huq had contested on regional issues unlike the Muslim League and the Congress. A major promise was abolition of the Permanent Settlement.[18] But due to the coalition with the Muslim League and Independent Caste Hindus, which included big zamindars, Huq had to dilute his promise. The hope of the people that the repressive laws would be diluted or scrapped, too, did not materialise. But more than 2,000 prisoners were released, many of whom were languishing in jail without trial. Among the prisoners who were behind bars for terrorist activities, 12 were released unconditionally, 41 with conditions, 7 had their sentences reduced, and 41 were not given any benefits. The terrorists were subsequently seen sympathising with the doctrine of communism and went on to stand by the peasants against the zamindars. In 1938 there was an attempt to form a coalition government between Huq and the Congress but Gandhi was not willing. When the Second World War broke out Huq had joined the Viceroy's National Defence Council. Jinnah was upset since Huq had not taken permission for the same. Huq's government fell in December 1941.

After Subhas Bose was expelled from the Congress he launched a movement for the removal of the Holwell Monument in Calcutta. He said that it was a symbol of national subjection and a mark of false accusation against Nawab Siraj-ud-daula. The movement was joined by both Hindus and Muslims. Subhas was arrested before the march to remove the monument could start. Despite his arrest the movement went on with students of the Islamia College playing a prominent role. Huq relented and assured that the monument would be removed. Prisoners were released except Subhas Bose. This was Subhas Bose's last movement on Indian soil.

Within a couple of weeks of resigning, Fazlul Huq formed his second ministry leaving the Muslim League out, with the support from members of the Subhas Bose faction of the Congress, now Forward Bloc, and the Hindu Mahasabha leader Syama Prasad. The second Huq ministry was hailed by many as a representative government which got rid of the communal caucus. Unfortunately the combined opposition of the British administration led by the then governor of Bengal Sir Herbert, the Muslim League, the Europeans, as well as the half-hearted attitude of the Congress led by Kiran Shankar Roy ensured that the government could survive only 16 months.[19] Problems started once the British administration discovered that belying their expectation that Syama Prasad was a pro-British man, he was seen acting against the Defence of India rules that Herbert wanted to impose. The response of Syama Prasad and his colleagues in the cabinet in organising a mass campaign against the invasion of Japan infuriated Governor Herbert. In addition, the Muslim League smear campaign that Huq was a hostage of the Hindu ministers ensured his loss of popularity in a communally charged atmosphere. Politically Huq was finding himself losing ground and for his survival wanted to move over to Delhi, even join the Viceroy's Council. Herbert, too, wanted Huq out. Huq was desperate and had even approached Jinnah to join as the head of the Muslim League in Bengal. The problem was exacerbated with the Quit India call by the Congress. When the food crisis took a severe turn the Muslim League introduced a censure motion against Huq in the assembly. To win over support Huq declared that the Government of India would ensure sufficient food supply to Bengal and would not export rice from the province. He also announced that he would set up an advisory committee under N.R. Sarkar, the then member food in the Viceroy's Executive Council. Post this, though Huq survived the censure motion, an infuriated Governor Herbert ensured that Huq resigned.[20]

Syama Prasad Mukherjee was an astute observer of political developments. Though not in politics he had observed the growing legislative measures against the Hindus in particular. Mention may be made of the change in recruitment rules. In 1938 the police recruitment rules were changed instructing the superintendent of police to ensure that while recruiting constables not less than 50 per cent were Muslims. A legislation stipulated that 60 per cent of all government appointments would be reserved for the Muslims against which the Maharaja of Burdwan led a delegation, in which Syama Prasad was a member, to meet the then acting governor of Bengal Sir John Reid. Their petition went to the viceroy and to the secretary of state but no protection to Hindus was offered. Then the government decided that the basic percentage of reservation for Muslims in all cases of direct recruitment would be 50 per cent, and in 1940 a special officer, called Communal Ratio Officer, was appointed to implement this decision.[21] This was when Subhas Bose was fighting for his political survival and was entering into a pact with the Muslim League in order to wrest control of the Calcutta Corporation. Clearly short-term personal political interests slowly acted against the interest of the Hindus at large in Bengal, a Muslim majority province.

Syama Prasad was not in politics when the Gandhi–Bose rift took place in the Congress. Upset over Gandhi's statement on Subhas's re-election, Syama Prasad wrote in his diary (2 February 1939),

> Read Gandhi's statement on Subhas Bose's election carefully. I cannot conceal my disappointment at its tone and content. Why should he be so upset at Subhas's victory? … Further he complains, Subhas's manifesto against the 'seven pillars of wisdom' was unjustifiable and unworthy. But what about the manifesto of these honourable gentlemen themselves; and what right had they to state that behind Subhas's back they (including Gandhi) had decided that it was unnecessary to re-elect him, and what is more, that Subhas's election would be harmful to the interest of India?[22]

History suggests that barring the leaders whose survival depended on blessings from Gandhi or his close associates, Gandhi's attitude towards Subhas Bose did not find much favour in Bengal. However this attitude of the Bengalis led the Congress national leadership to neglect the cause of Bengal, a fact that has not been clearly analysed by subsequent researchers. Any Bengali leader who made it on his own steam and not by virtue of loyalty to a leader, Gandhi in this case, did not find much virtue in the treatment of Bengalis by the Congress leaders including that of Mahatma Gandhi.

Syama Prasad Mukherjee, an educationist, joined politics when the Huq government brought in the Secondary Education Bill. The bill was meant to take away the control of secondary education from the Calcutta University and entrust the same to a Secondary Education Board. Given the Huq government's decisions to introduce quota in jobs for Muslims which even had a clause that for the vacancies meant for Muslims, candidates could be brought in from outside the province and even from outside the country, Syama Prasad lobbied actively to stall the Secondary Education Bill. His efforts eventually won over support of the majority of the Congressmen including that of Sarat Bose. For one long year, between August 1940 and September 1941, the assembly debated the bill but finally failed to get it passed.[23]

Another politically influential person in Bengal at that time was Jogendranath Mandal. Mandal was a scheduled caste leader who was with the Congress when Subhas Bose was in power but later in 1943 he joined the All India Scheduled Caste Federation of B.R. Ambedkar. Mandal sought reservations for the scheduled castes and was suspicious of the Congress led mostly by caste Hindus. He had even raised this question when he met Gandhi at Sarat Bose's residence in 1937. Mandal had developed a working rapport with the Boses and even accompanied Subhas to Barisal, his home district, when Subhas was expelled from the Congress and was working on his Forward Bloc. Later when the Huq ministry was eased out and Khawja Nazimuddin was invited to form a ministry, Tulsi Goswami and Barada Pyne joined the ministry ignoring the Congress directive. That politics in Bengal had several well-known wheeler dealers who could jump the ship at the slightest enticement was noticed even in undivided Bengal. Mandal who was expecting to be accommodated as a minister in the second Huq cabinet but failed to realise his hope, received a berth in the Nazimuddin cabinet. Mandal was pushed to this camp largely due to the failure of the caste Hindus, the Congress and the Hindu Mahasabha to recognise the needs of the scheduled caste population.

The formation of the Azad Hind Fauz by Subhas Chandra Bose and the march of the INA with the Japanese forces had alarmed the administration as also the ministers. Both the British administration and the Indian politicians had misgivings about the approaching Japanese forces. Nehru had said that if the Japanese came, he would go out to fight them with sword in hand. Syama Prasad wanted to raise a guerrilla force to fight the invaders. He even wrote to the governor Sir John Herbert (7 March 1942), 'Give us the right to have a Home Army for the protection of Bengal.'[24] Clearly none of the so-called national leaders had any idea of the possible role of Netaji's INA in the fast-moving political scene post the Second World War. When the trial of INA officers started in Delhi the sacrifice and gallantry of the Indian soldiers came to light. This generated huge public support and sympathy. In Calcutta trams, buses and police vehicles were destroyed and 40 persons were killed as a result of police firing. Not just the government but also the Congress which had supported prosecution of the INA officers initially were disturbed. The Congress changed its stance and even Nehru, who never practised in court, put on the robe and joined Tejbahadur Sapru and Bhulabhai Desai to defend the officers in the military tribunal. With Subhas safely out of the way, Nehru could change his position comfortably. Subhas Chandra Bose became a national hero in India's freedom struggle history. But the popular sentiment of the day did not much influence the official history written thereafter.

The second ministry of Fazlul Huq was running Bengal at arguably one of the most critical times of the Indian freedom movement. Britain was resorting to 'glorious retreat' in the face of aggressive Japanese troops supported by the INA. Singapore fell to Japan. Winston Churchill desperately needed US president Roosevelt's support. But after assessing the ground realities the Foreign Relations Committee of the US senate felt that a safe way to involve India, with its huge manpower, in the war was to declare it a full member of the United Nations. For Churchill this was one of the bitterest possible medicines. Helpless, he sent Sir Stafford Cripps to negotiate a settlement with Indian political leaders. This negotiation was destined to fail since the top two leaders – Mahatma Gandhi and Jinnah – were suspicious of each other's views. Further pressure from Roosevelt did not help since by then Cripps had left India.[25] This was when Gandhi gave the Quit India call, a movement which was not led by any member of the Congress since all of them were behind bars. Free from the guidelines of the Congress leaders the movement took its own course creating havoc for the British administration in the process. For the British government the most disastrous outcome lay in the Midnapore district of Bengal, where the district was virtually independent with its own government and administration. The last two jolts to the British rule in India came from Bengal – one on Bengal's soil in Midnapore while the other being the Bose-led INA progressing towards Indian soil.

In Midnapore it was a general uprising of all classes of people thereby crippling the British administration for nearly one and half years. The comprehensive administration that the revolutionaries established in Tamluk lasted from 17 December 1942 – that is, much after the failure of the Quit India movement – to 8 August 1944.[26] The British government's official report admitted the well-planned execution of the movement and described how the revolutionaries created Bidyut Bahini and Bhagini Sena Sibir (Band of Female Fighters) including their back-up support of informers, doctors and nurses. The recorded history of successful non-violent movement did not capture such movements in detail. History only mentions in passing how a 70-year-old Matangini Hazra courted death but did not let go of the Indian flag while facing police bullets.

Syama Prasad protested against the inhuman torture and reign of terror unleashed by the British administration which he had to observe helplessly as a minister of the Huq government. A cyclonic storm had ravaged the district but the British administration did not offer any relief to the people of the district as punishment for rebellion. Syama Prasad resigned as a mark of protest but his resignation letter was kept confidential.[27] Huq was forced to resign in March 1943 and a few days later on 4th April Khawja Nazimuddin was made the chief minister of Bengal. Sahid Suhrawardy was the minister of supplies under whose watch Bengal suffered the famine that saw millions of poor people dying of hunger. It was alleged that Marwari businessmen had bribed the supplies minister and staff to facilitate their black marketing. Even on the floor of the assembly Nalinakshya Sanyal made allegations against Suhrawardy which turned into a mutual name-calling exercise.[28]

The cabinet of Nazimuddin was a patch-up arrangement hoisted by the Bengal governor in order to oust the second Huq government. There were inner contradictions which were gleefully exploited by the hoarders and black marketeers. Even the then governor Cassey had observed how mysteriously essential commodities used to vanish from the shelves but magically reappeared immediately after the ministry raised prices due to shortages. When there was a motion against the Nizamuddin government in the assembly Suhrawardy claimed that since he had acted against the hoarders they were sponsoring the opponents to vote against the government. Actually the reason why the Nizamuddin government was voted out was the defection of Nawab Habibulla of Dacca who had been eyeing the post of the supplies ministry. This incident illustrates that corruption and money-making was the main pastime of the ministers and their supporting officials in Bengal. The ordinary people of Bengal were left to fend for themselves in one of the most unfortunate situations possible in a system where the elected representatives in concert with an administration whose members were merely counting their days exploited the people with no recourse in sight. This was the time when the Congress national leaders were in talks with the Muslim League national leaders on the post-British India situation.

In January 1944 came a new concept, that of a sovereign Bengal, from Sarat Bose, elder brother of Netaji Subhas Chandra Bose. It was actually a rehashed proposal that originally came from the communists who, influenced by the Soviet Union, opined that India was a big family of several nations. They proposed that each nation had a right of self-determination and advocated an all-India national assembly with no more authority than plenipotentiaries. Sarat Bose felt that by dividing the nation, the cohesive linguistic provinces would weaken and become happy hunting grounds of imperialists, communalists and reactionaries. The right prescription would be to have socialist republics on linguistic basis and then establish a Central Union of Socialist Republics. Evidently Sarat Bose was influenced by the communists and in 1945 had even praised Mao Tse-tung while criticising Chiang Kai Shek. Bose found support in Suhrawardy and Abul Hashim, secretary of the Bengal Muslim League, and even met Mahatma Gandhi to impress upon him their idea of a 'sovereign Bengal'. Suhrawardy visualised an independent, sovereign and undivided Bengal which would not remain a part of any Union of India. Abul Hashim felt that a divided Bengal would possibly be treated as a far-flung province, perhaps a colony, by an alien Indian imperialist government. Hashim had even predicted that the Hindus in Bengal would be reduced to daily wage earners. Sarat Bose drew up a six-point plan which included setting up a committee to frame the constitution of Bengal, establishment of an interim cabinet, and election of government through universal adult franchise. Bengal, Sarat Bose proposed, would be a socialist republic and the newly elected assembly would decide what would be Bengal's relationship with the rest of India. Sarat Bose formed the All Bengal Anti Pakistan and Anti-Partition Committee.

Jinnah was staunchly against any such proposal and wanted Bengal and Punjab as part of Pakistan. Akram Khan, a founding member of the Muslim League and a member of its Central Working Committee, dismissed Suhrawardy's sovereign Bengal dream. The working committee of the Provincial Muslim League dissociated itself from the sovereign Bengal proposal of Bose and reiterated its support for Pakistan and the leadership of Jinnah. The Sarat–Suhrawardy unity plan had created a sensation. Jawaharlal Nehru and Sardar Patel were dead against an independent Bengal. So were the businessmen backers of the Congress like G.D. Birla, Bir Badridas Goenka, B.L. Jalan, N.R. Sarkar, B.M. Birla and other industrialists. They considered the Indian Union as an economic unit and divided Bengal would be part of it. These businessmen were based in Calcutta with little economic interest in East Bengal. However they had units spread across the rest of India. So the concept of a sovereign Bengal threatened their business interests. In any case this was an idea which only had a few backers while its opposition was formidable – Jinnah, Nehru and Patel to name a few. In addition, both the Bengal Provincial Congress and the Hindu Mahasabha adopted the resolution of a divided Bengal for the Hindus as part of a divided India. Not that Sarat Bose was not aware of the Congress decision to accept partition. He made a press statement on the Congress decision (15 March 1947): 'I confess that the resolution has surprised me not a little. By accepting religion as the sole basis of the distribution of provinces, the Congress has cut itself from the moorings and has almost undone the work it has been doing for the last sixty years.'[29]

Both Nehru and Patel were unhappy with the Sarat–Suhrawardy plan. Patel wrote to Kiran Shankar Roy, 'It is incumbent on all Congressmen to set aside personal predilections and to stand united on the official policy of the Congress. Individual expression of views must fit into that policy, and there should not be any discordant note.'[30] While Kiran Shankar fell in line, Sarat Bose remained adamant. He told Patel that the Hindus of East Bengal were opposed to partition and reminded him that future generations would condemn 'us for conceding division of India'. Bose was right on both the points but the reality was not what he wanted to believe. What Sarat Bose refused to consider were the increasing instances of Hindu–Muslim riots in Bengal. Concerned with the emotional integration of two Bengals, even a few hours before his death (20 February 1950), Sarat Bose appealed to all Bengalis in the name of Bengal's past not to look at Delhi or Karachi but to look at their inner light and appealed to East Bengal to join the Indian union as a separate state.[31]

Bose was emotionally attached to a United Bengal but was not mature enough to appreciate the increasing divergence between the two communities especially since the 1920s. Even when he was campaigning in favour of a sovereign Bengal there had been severe riots going on in Noakhali where Gandhi had been touring to bring in peace. Even before that, in fact, one year before the British handed over power to the natives, Calcutta had witnessed one of the bloodiest riots in the history of India. If Bose was naive enough to believe that such bloody conflicts between the two communities can heal with the mere mention of historical and cultural bonds, he certainly matched Mahatma Gandhi who had offered simple and impractical solutions to riots in Calcutta or Noakhali. Despite the repeated instances of failures such emotions have not died in West Bengal politics even now.

In March 1946 election to the legislative assemblies in all provinces took place. The Muslim League won 115 seats out of 250 while the Congress bagged 84.[32] Congress President Maulana Azad was aggrieved at the poor performance of the Congress and repeatedly asserted that the elections were rigged. Fazlul Huq too joined Azad in alleging rigging, bribery and favouritism by the administration. Of course, Suhrawardy dismissed all such allegations pointing out narrow margins of victory of the Muslim League candidates in many constituencies. Suhrawardy refused Nazimuddin, the former chief minister, a ticket to contest the elections thereby making sure that Suhrawardy emerged as the leader of the Muslim League in the assembly. Suhrawardy offered the Congress a proposal for a coalition government which Congress President Maulana Azad accepted with conditions. It was suggested that consent of both communities would be taken on communal matters and it would require two-third majority to get passed by the assembly. The communist party had three members in the assembly. Jyoti Basu in a press release had welcomed the proposal of the coalition government between the Congress and the Muslim League.[33] However the coalition proposal was abandoned due to serious differences between the Congress and the League on the future administration of India. By the end of April 1946 Suhrawardy took over as the last chief minister of undivided Bengal.

In the 1946 elections both the Hindus and the Muslims had reposed their faiths in the two national parties. The support for the Congress in Bengal was so strong that even Syama Prasad Mukherjee lost the election from a Calcutta suburbs constituency by a massive difference. Mukherjee, the most popular leader of the Hindu Mahasabha, could receive a mere 346 votes against 10,216 votes polled by the victorious Congress candidate. Not only the electorates even leaders of the Hindu Mahasabha changed sides and won either on Congress tickets or supported the Congress after the election. In Bengal Sarat Bose reportedly took it upon himself the responsibility of ensuring Syama Prasad's defeat. The Bengali media, particularly the Ananda Bazar group with its Bengali and English newspapers, supported the Congress aggressively. Syama Prasad ended up as a lonely voice who came back strongly to contest the suicidal mission of sovereign Bengal launched by Suhrawardy and Sarat Bose.

The sharp differences over the Cabinet Mission proposals on transfer of power was the major political issue in the country at that point. The Muslim League reacted sharply stating that the Muslims of India would not be content with anything less than the immediate establishment of an independent and full sovereign state of Pakistan and announced that the Muslims would resort to Direct Action to achieve Pakistan. 16 August 1946 was marked as Direct Action Day, when Muslims throughout the country were to observe a *hartal* (strike). Even before the Muslim League National Council could work out the details of the day, the ministry in Bengal declared 16 August a public holiday. The Direct Action Day in Calcutta had been in preparation stage for some time. There had been speeches, statements by Muslim League leaders and circulation of inflammatory pamphlets by the lakhs. One such pamphlet in Urdu published under the signature of Muhamad Osman, then mayor of Calcutta and the district president of the Muslim League, stated:

> It was in this month of Ramzan that we were victorious in Mecca and exterminated the idolaters. It was in this month that Islam's foundation was laid. It is by the will of Allah that the All India Muslim League has decided to start Jehad for attainment of Pakistan in this month of Ramzan.[34]

When 16th August was declared a holiday, many were suspicious. Even the British members of the assembly had asked for withdrawal of the holiday. The newly appointed governor of Bengal had failed to see through the reason for declaring a holiday and let the holiday stand. On that day, a mass rally was planned at the foot of the Octerlony Monument near Dalhousie Square in Calcutta, where Suhrawardy, Khwaja Nazimuddin and other League leaders were to speak.

On 16th August, just about 50 days after the government took over, the Calcutta riots broke out. Historian R.C. Majumdar when assigned the task of writing the history of the freedom struggle in 1953, saw one document of the central intelligence officers on the Calcutta riots. This had clearly mentioned that Chief Minister Suhrawardy had planned and made arrangements for the riots. 'The reports mentioned the name of a goonda who directed the riots; he was arrested by the police; the report stated that the Chief Minister personally went and had him released.'[35] The document was classified and Majumdar was not allowed a copy by Prime Minister Nehru. On 15th August itself Muslims were seen shouting slogans such as '*Ladke Lenge Pakistan*' in Muslim majority areas. Arson, looting and killing started from the morning of 16th itself. Scared Hindus attempted to seek protection from the police but there was no response. According to Prakash Swarup Mathur, director of publicity of Bengal, in response to distress calls from some influential Hindus the then police commissioner Hardwick had said that when both the Hindus and the Muslims had been asking the British to leave the country he couldn't do anything. He derisively suggested that one could ask the Congress for help.[36] That was when Nehru was busy forming his cabinet in Delhi and could neither pay attention nor visit Calcutta afterwards. When carnage and riot in the capital city of Bengal, which was then the largest city in the country, failed to perturb Nehru, prime minister of undivided India, it is natural that in due course politics in the divided part of Bengal would eventually get alienated from the national politics.

A military report on the Calcutta riots despatched about a week later (24th August) stated:

> There is hardly a person in Calcutta who has a good word for Suhrawardy, respectable Muslims included. For years he has been known as 'The king of the goondas' and my own private opinion is that he fully anticipated what was going to happen, and allowed it to work itself up, and probably organised the disturbance with his goonda gangs as this type of individual has to receive compensation every now and again. It is difficult to estimate the number of casualties but I should say it is somewhere in the region of 2 to 3 thousand at least. There were corpses all over North Calcutta, they were in the river, canals, side lanes, in fact, everywhere. The number of shops looted and burnt must be somewhere in the region of 2 to 3 thousand. I personally think that the killings of both sides were fifty, fifty, or if anything, more Muslims than Hindus, but damage financially has been much greater to the Hindus than to the Muslims.[37]

Governor General Wavell who visited Calcutta a week after the riots had mentioned that there were 4,400 deaths, injuries to 16,000 and one lakh people were rendered homeless. Burrows, the governor of Bengal, had told Wavell that Suhrawardy was a cad and untrustworthy. Frederick Wavell had written of Suhrawardy, 'I have always had the impression that Suhrawardy was one of the most inefficient, conceited and crooked politicians in India.'[38]

After the riots the Congress brought in a no-confidence motion against the Suhrawardy government. The three communist members in a statement said they would not support the no-confidence motion but reiterated the need for the Congress–League united ministry for governing the province at a difficult time. While speaking on the motion in the house Jyoti Basu blamed British imperialism for deliberately creating the communal divide as also Suhrawardy for his failure to perform his responsibility of containing the riots sincerely. In fact, Basu felt that some Muslims had taken the call for direct action by their leaders quite seriously and had consequently taken necessary preparation to that effect. In other words, Basu blamed the one-party rule of the Muslim League for failing to control the riots. Clearly the communist party blamed the Muslim League for the 1946 communal riots in Calcutta.[39]

What is curious is that the same Suhrawardy in April 1947, less than one year later, was busy announcing a plan for creating an undivided sovereign Bengal jointly with Sarat Bose. The Sarat Bose–Suhrawardy plan illustrates how leaders like Sarat Bose were completely disconnected from reality and could easily be manoeuvred by cunning politicians like Suhrawardy. When Sarat Bose was busy formulating an undivided Bengal, Calcutta witnessed the Direct Action Day and Noakhali experienced untold atrocities two months later. The attack on the Hindus started on the day of Lakshmi Puja on 10 October 1946 under the leadership of a former local Muslim MLA Abdus (Golam) Sarwar. There was an arrest warrant issued against him and others who participated in the carnage but this was not executed. Initially the news of the massacre could be censored but the same later found its way into the media. This compelled Suhrawardy to make an aerial tour of the carnage-hit areas. Under pressure, the government had sent two independent officers for investigation. A report by Judge Edward Skinner Simpson was critical of the Muslim League and the government. The League government attempted to suppress it but a summary found its way into *The Statesman*, perhaps leaked by Mathur. The reports of atrocities on Hindus saw several leaders visiting Noakhali. Among them were J.B. Kripalani, who was then Congress president, his wife Sucheta Kripalani, Syama Prasad Mukherjee, Prafulla Chandra Ghosh and Sarat Bose who later joined hands with Suhrawardy for a sovereign Bengal. Mahatma Gandhi, too, reached Noakhali, a well-known historical event, which had no result.

On 7 November 1946 the Mahatma told the relief workers at Chandpur that what plagued the Hindus was cowardice and no police force or army could help cowards. It was not numerical inferiority that affected their cause said Gandhi,

> But even a few individuals are enough to terrorize the whole mass, if the latter feel helpless. Your trouble is not numerical inferiority but the feeling of helplessness that has seized you and the habit of depending on others. The remedy lies with you. That is why I am opposed to the idea of your evacuating East Bengal en masse. It is no cure for impotence or helplessness.[40]

Gandhi was unhappy with the retaliation by the Biharis against the Noakhali carnage, an incident that halted the atrocities in Noakhali. According to Gandhi, 'If the Biharis wanted to retaliate, they could have gone to Noakhali and died to a man. But for a thousand Hindus to fall upon a handful of Mussalmans—men, women and children—living in their midst is no retaliation but just brutality.'[41] Nehru, too, was in Bihar and so were other leaders like Kripalani, Rajendra Prasad and Jayaprakash Narayan. Though the Congress led by the Mahatma himself was upset with Bihar for avenging Noakhali, an act that probably forced the masterminds of Noakhali to rethink, the fact remains that Gandhi's presence there, despite good publicity, had little or no effect on the marauding Muslims. The Muslims were fed up with Gandhi. They started putting obstacles in Gandhi's course as he travelled from one village to another as recorded by Nirmal Kumar Bose who was with Mahatma Gandhi during these months: 'In the meantime (February 1947) Muslim protest against Gandhiji's stay in Noakhali gradually became stronger … Towards the end of February it turned vulgar. The path Gandhi would tread used to be deliberately dirtied every day and the number of Muslims attending his meetings decreased day by day.' He further mentioned, 'Gandhiji advised the Hindus to follow non-violence and not to hurt the assailant when attacked … Whatever effect his exhortations might have had on the Hindus, his appeal to the common Muslims seemed to bear even less fruit.'[42]

The commissioner of the Chittagong division in a confidential report on 13 May 1947, that is, a few months after Gandhi's departure from Noakhali said,

> Though outwardly Noakhali is quiet, the Hindus there are still panicky; the reason for the panic is the petty oppression of the Hindus by the Muslims in the countryside away from the towns and the abuses they are subjected to … The Gandhi Camps and other volunteers did not succeed in affording much relief to the distressed people.[43]

When Mahatma Gandhi was in Noakhali engrossed in weaving a fantasy of Hindu–Muslim unity, Syama Prasad along with the Ramakrishna Mission were engaged in a realistic endeavour. The Ramakrishna Mission published a booklet, signed by the general secretary of the Mission, Swami Madhavananda, on reconversion of Hindus, a home *wapasi*. This had the endorsements of leading Hindu religious schools, religious leaders and even a judge of the Calcutta

High Court.[44] For the first time perhaps the Brahminical society took back the Hindus who were forcible converted, a small step initially that expanded in later years.

The Noakhali riot was engineered by hard-core elements in the Muslim League led by former MLA Golam Sarwar. Noakhali, wrote Amalesh Tripathy, had several seminary-educated Muslim persons who had studied at Deoband and Azamgarh. They were a strong supporter of the Khilafat movement and were a backbone of sorts in the movement then. However once the movement was suspended they fell out with the Congress.[45] With just about 20 per cent Hindus and due to the sensitive nature of communal feelings, as was seen in the Calcutta riots just a couple of months ago, the Muslims thought it incumbent on them to force the Hindus to either convert or leave or die. Since they had a supportive administration they had no qualms in doing what they felt was right. When Noakhali happened, about a month earlier on 2nd September, a new government took oath under Nehru in Delhi. Sarat Bose was a member in that cabinet. On 19th October after the news about Noakhali broke, Sarat Bose made an aerial visit to Noakhali. Bose was fully aware of the communal designs of the party Suhrawardy represented. Despite that he fell into Suhrawardy's trap and voiced the demand for a sovereign Bengal. The riots in 1946, both in Calcutta and in Noakhali as also in Bihar, had shown how the two dominant political parties, the Muslim League and the Indian National Congress, had failed to protect the minorities in their respective strongholds. Perhaps the carnages alarmed the central Congress leadership and Patel in particular took a hard stance in favour of a divided Bengal for the persecuted Hindus. Patel had also requested the viceroy to dismiss the Bengal government for its failure to maintain law and order in the state. In fact Viceroy Wavell had toured Noakhali on 1st November but he refused to take over the administration of Bengal from the Muslim League government.[46]

When the Muslim League government led by Suhrawardy was busy unleashing communal violence after the call of 'Direct Action' by his party why did he join Sarat Bose and place a demand for a United Bengal? The Calcutta riots had clearly indicated the numerical superiority of the Hindus. Even after meticulous planning and clever support of Chief Minister Suhrawardy the Calcutta riots had turned against the Muslims from the second day onwards. Suhrawardy realised it would be difficult for the Muslim League to take control of Calcutta as a part of divided India. But Jinnah was keen to have Calcutta in Pakistan and told Mountbatten, 'What is the use of Bengal without Calcutta? They had much better remain united and independent; I am sure they would be on friendly terms with us.'[47] This was when Suhrawardy met Mountbatten on 26 April 1947, demanding a United Bengal. Apparently his idea of a United Bengal would be within the Commonwealth and serve as a base for British capitalism. When Suhrawardy was asked in a press conference in Delhi on 27th April if the United Bengal would join Pakistan, he had evaded the question. Evidently the issue of United Bengal was raised in order to separate Calcutta, the largest city in the subcontinent, the largest port as well as the largest industrial and business centre, from India and eventually conjoin with Pakistan. It was not very difficult to see through the larger plan. It is strange that Sarat Bose, overwhelmed by pure emotion, did not think through these developments and played into the hands of a wily politician.

However, the political situation was more complex than envisaged by Suhrawardy. Akram Khan was a strong opponent. He had pointed out how a United Bengal would snowball into demand for many other separate independent provinces, like the North West Frontier Province. Jinnah tried to explain that undivided Bengal and Punjab would remain within Pakistan. Jogendranath Mandal, who had joined the central cabinet as a nominee of the Muslim League, too objected on the ground that in undivided Bengal the scheduled caste population would remain subservient to the caste Hindus as before. Meanwhile Jinnah clarified that he did not approve of the move by Suhrawardy to opt for an independent Bengal.

On 26th April when Suhrawardy was meeting Mountbatten, Syama Prasad was in Delhi in a meeting with Bidhan Chandra Roy and Kiran Shankar Roy of the Congress. It was agreed that the Bengal Provincial Congress would join the Hindu Mahasabha in their demand for the division of Bengal. The Hindu Mahasabha launched a strong movement in favour of a truncated Bengal as a part of independent India. Prominent intellectuals of Bengal, the likes of Suniti Chattopadhyay, Jadunath Sarkar, Ramesh Majumdar, Meghnad Saha and others, sent a cable to Mountbatten expressing no-confidence in the Suhrawardy government and urgently demanding the partition of Bengal.[48]

Earlier, on 23rd April, the widely read English newspaper of Calcutta the *Amrita Bazar Patrika* published the result of a poll conducted on the question: 'Do you want a separate Homeland for Bengali Hindus?' An overwhelming 98.3 per cent voted in favour and a mere 0.6 per cent against. The newspaper reported that 99.6 per cent Hindus and 0.4 per cent Muslims supported a separate Homeland for Hindu Bengalis.[49]

When the AICC accepted the proposal of the Cabinet Mission on 6 January 1947, it had expressed concern over difficulties that the proposal entailed with regard to Assam, the North West Frontier Province, as well as to the Sikhs. But nobody bothered to think of the Hindus of Bengal and the difficulties they had to face, before, after and long after partition of the province. Clearly this was a glaring instance that 'Bengal wielded no influence in the political field of India at the time'.[50]

Jinnah had suggested that there should be an exchange of population after the partition and the Hindus and the Muslims would move to the respective areas where they were a majority. Gandhi opposed it. This was effected in Punjab, of course, through a pool of blood. It also was effected in Bengal, but mostly in one direction with Hindus leaving their homes and rushing for refuge in West Bengal. When Hindus were being driven out of East Pakistan after the Partition, there was a movement in West Bengal which demanded rehabilitation of the refugees by sending equal number of Muslims from West Bengal to Pakistan. This had infuriated Nehru. He felt that in secular India this would be an unthinkable demand. He asked the West Bengal chief minister Dr Bidhan Chandra Roy to stop entry of East Pakistan refugees into West Bengal. 'The two letters which made the above suggestion will be treated for all times to come as an example of extreme cruelty and callousness on the part of Jawaharlal Nehru,' wrote Majumdar.[51]

Concerning the demand for undivided Bengal the then director of publicity P.S. Mathur had an interesting anecdote, based on the conversation he had with Altaf Hussain who was the editor of the *Dawn* in Karachi. Hussain told Mathur that the Muslim League would never accept the Suhrawardy plan of independent undivided Bengal since it was against the two-nation theory. Also, the Muslim League leader Liaquat Ali Khan was opposed to it. The principal authors of the proposal were Suhrawardy, who had no past, and Sarat Bose, who had no future. There was another proposal on the issue of division of Bengal. Governor Burrows recommended that Calcutta would be made a free city and port, an industrial and commercial enclave, under a governor deputed by the British government. This was a desperate attempt to save British investment in the subcontinent but it failed to generate any enthusiasm. There was no voice in favour of such a proposal and it was dismissed by Mountbatten.

The debate surrounding independent sovereign Bengal was put to rest when both the Congress and the Muslim League accepted the Mountbatten plan of 3rd June that was clearly based on the partition of India. In the Bengal legislative assembly the results were interesting. In the joint session the majority supported undivided Bengal. But in separate sessions the representatives from the Muslim majority constituencies voted in favour of undivided Bengal with 106 voting against partition and just 35 in favour. The representatives of the Hindu majority constituencies voted in favour of partition by a majority of 58 to 21. The voting based on territorial representation, not exactly divided between Hindu and Muslim areas, clearly shows that undivided Bengal was the dream of those from the Muslim majority areas while those from the Hindu majority areas were scared of Muslim domination and the resultant ignominy that they had to suffer during the Muslim rule 1937 onwards. What hurt them most perhaps was the biased administration of justice and management of law and order when communal disturbances broke out. It was decided that when voting separately even if one house voted in favour of partition it would be accepted. Some historians have blamed the caste Hindus for diverting the movement from nationalism to communalism since the 1930s which eventually saw the province partitioned. What such historians ignore is the rise of political Muslims and how their politics was moulded by the sectarian incentives of the British. It was an easy option for them to seek votes on communal lines. One important factor that had made the Muslims in favour of undivided Bengal as part of Pakistan was clearly the position of Calcutta which was certain to go to India. Communalism in politics is the product of people tending to cast votes as a community. The representative politics since 1937, therefore, started in the Muslim majority Bengal along communal lines. In the process the Hindus suffered, both the upper castes and the lower castes. Leaders representing the lower castes such as Jogendranath Mandal sided with the Muslim leadership believing that would benefit their community. However, they were eventually disappointed. Jogendranath's return to India from Pakistan explains that the political choice of the Muslims was to remain close to their own community. The course of politics in divided Bengal was founded on the interplay of such secular-communal divide.

Endnotes

1 Statement to Press, January 31, 1939, https://www.gandhiashramsevagram.org/gandhi-literature/mahatma-gandhi-collected-works-volume-75.pdf.

2 https://www.gandhiashramsevagram.org/gandhi-literature/mahatma-gandhi-collected-works-volume-75.pdf.

3 Ibid.

4 https://www.hindustantimes.com/columns/the-forgotten-rivalry-between-patel-and-bose/story-qctC1zkNRCNc6eF024x4EO.html.

5 Statement to Press, July 13, 1939, https://www.gandhiashramsevagram.org/gandhi-literature/mahatma-gandhi-collected-works-volume-76.pdf.

6 https://www.gandhiashramsevagram.org/gandhi-literature/mahatma-gandhi-collected-works-volume-76.pdf.

7 Pranab Kumar Chatterjee, "Bose-League Pact in the Calcutta Corporation in 1940" in *Proceedings of the Indian History Congress* 41 (1980), pp 547–53, www.jstor.org/stable/44141879 (accessed May 21, 2020).

8 Ray, *Dr Syamaprasad Mookerjee*, Kindle edition, e-book location 1744.

9 https://www.gandhiashramsevagram.org/gandhi-literature/mahatma-gandhi-collected-works-volume-83.pdf.

10 Letter to Lord Wavell, March 9, 1944, https://www.gandhiashramsevagram.org/gandhi-literature/mahatma-gandhi-collected-works-volume-84.pdf.

11 https://www.gandhiashramsevagram.org/gandhi-literature/mahatma-gandhi-collected-works-volume-84.pdf.

12 Majumdar, *Modern Bengal*, p. 288.

13 Janam Mukherjee, *Hungry Bengal: War, Famine, Riots and the End of Empire* (Harper India, 2015), pp 2-3.

14 Majumdar, *Modern Bengal*, p. 288.

15 Suranjan Das, "Nationalism and Popular Consciousness: Bengal 1942" in *Social Scientist* 23, no. 4/6 (1995), pp 58–68, www.jstor.org/stable/3520215 (accessed May 22, 2020).

16 Ibid.

17 Majumdar, *Modern Bengal*, p. 258.

18 M.K.U. Molla, "The Bengal Cabinet Crisis of 1945" in *Journal of Asian History* 14 no. 2 (1980), pp 127–48, www.jstor.org/stable/41930376 (accessed May 23, 2020).

19 Manzur Ahsan, "The Fall of Fazlul Huq's Second Ministry" in *Proceedings of the Indian History Congress* 60 (1999), pp 811–27, www.jstor.org/stable/44144152 (accessed May 23, 2020).

20 Ibid.

21 Ray, *Dr Syamaprasad Mookerjee*, Kindle, e-book location 1474.

22 Ibid., e-book location 1772.

23 Ibid., e-book location 1801.

24 Ibid., p. 272.

25 Majumdar, ed., *The History & Culture of The Indian People*, vol. 11, *Struggle for Freedom*, pp 637-41.

26 Majumdar, *Modern Bengal*, p. 265.

27 Ibid., pp 273-5.

28 Ibid.

29 Amalendu De, "Sarat Chandra Bose on Indian National Question: A Plea for Sovereign Bengal" in *Proceedings of the Indian History Congress* 37 (1976), pp 389–95, www.jstor.org/stable/44138998 (accessed May 25, 2020).

30 Ibid.

31 Ibid.

32 The communists had three elected members in the assembly. They were Jyoti Basu, Ratanlal Brahma and Rupnarayan Ray (courtesy of *Nirbachita Rachanasangraha* by Jyoti Basu).

33 Jyoti Basu, *Jyoti Bosur Nirbachita Rachanasangraha* vol. 1 (National Book Agency, 2010), pp 16-7.

34 Majumdar, *Modern Bengal*, p. 299.

35 Ibid., pp 299-300.

36 Ibid.

37 https://www.nationalarchives.gov.uk/education/resources/the-road-to-partition/#introduction.

38 Majumdar, *Modern Bengal*, pp 300-3.

39 Basu, *Nirbachita Rachanasangraha* vol. 1, pp 36-40.

40 1946 Talk to Relief Workers, https://www.gandhiashramsevagram.org/gandhi-literature/mahatma-gandhi-collected-works-volume-93.pdf November 7.

41 Ibid.

42 Majumdar, *Modern Bengal*, pp 313-4.

43 Ibid., pp 315-6.

44 Ray, *Dr Syamaprasad Mookerjee*, Kindle, e-book location 3948-58.

45 Amalesh Tripathy, *Swadhinata Sangrame Bharater Jatiya Congress (1885-1947)* (Ananda Publishers, 2012), p. 449.

46 Ibid., p. 453.

47 Bidyut Chakrabarty, *The Partition of Bengal and Assam 1932-1947* (Routledge, 2004), p. 137.

48 Ibid., p. 458.

49 Haimanti Roy, "A Partition of Contingency? Public Discourse in Bengal, 1946-1947" in *Modern Asian Studies* 43, no. 6 (2009), pp 1355–84, www.jstor.org/stable/40285016 (accessed May 26, 2020).

50 Majumdar, *Modern Bengal*, p. 321.

51 Ibid., pp 322-3.

PARTITION AND BIRTH PANGS

When Subhas Bose was eased out of the Congress, the Working Committee got an opportunity to revamp the Bengal Congress according to their preference. In December 1939, the Working Committee dissolved the Provincial Congress Committee of Bengal, and constituted an ad hoc committee with eight members and Maulana Azad as its chairman. Of the three major factions – Gandhian, Hooghly group and Jugantar – the third was left out and the first was brought to the helm. But since Bose was the popular leader there was stiff opposition from several quarters and Azad failed to set up even an office of the ad hoc committee. He perhaps realised that without the assistance of the powerful groups, especially the Jugantar, it would be difficult for him to function. Azad was an outsider to Bengal politics. This helped the Surendra Mohan Ghosh-led Jugantar group to emerge as a strong faction of the Bengal Congress.

The Congress constitution had a fixed number of delegates based on the population in a district. This allowed 344 delegates from East Bengal and 200 from West Bengal. Even though there were more Congress members in East Bengal,[1] this number did not play any role till strong leaders like Chittaranjan or Subhas Bose were leading Bengal. When Bose was ousted the East Bengal Congress leaders had emerged more powerful and remained so even when Prafulla Ghosh, a staunch Gandhian, and a leader of the Gandhi faction, had voted against Bose in 1939 and had supported Pattabhi Sitharamaiya. When

Rajendra Prasad took over as Congress president after Bose resigned, Prafulla Ghosh was accommodated in the Congress Working Committee. Ghosh was also very close to Acharya Kripalani who was the Congress president in 1947. Thus when it was decided that there would be an interim chief minister and a shadow cabinet after the partition was finalised, both Surendra Mohan Ghosh and Prafulla Ghosh emerged as contenders. Kripalani negotiated with the Congress MLAs and Prafulla Ghosh was chosen as the leader. Surendra Mohan remained the Bengal Congress president and he refused to join the shadow cabinet. Reportedly Ghosh had also requested Dr Bidhan Roy and Syama Prasad Mukherjee to join his cabinet but both had excused themselves. Factionalism in the Provincial Congress raised its head even before the country was independent.

On 30th June Gandhi wrote to Prafulla Ghosh, 'Sardar has sent word that there should be a Marwari in your Cabinet, either Badridas Goenka or Khaitan. I think it will be proper to do so, improper not to.'[2] Ghosh was surprised since he had shown his choice of cabinet to an approving committee where Patel was a member. Gandhi's request shows the Marwari business community's influence on the Father of the Nation. The community used to generously fund Gandhi. Ghosh's refusal to honour Gandhi's request gave his opponents in Bengal opportunities to rally against him later. Ghosh took oath on 3rd July without any Marwari presence in the shadow cabinet.

Within three days of Independence Ghosh had his hands full with a curious problem. When the country was partitioned and attained independence a crucial decision was not made public. That was the boundary decision or the Radcliffe Award which was kept on hold by none other than Mountbatten.[3] The momentous decision was made public only on 17th August. Without a clear understanding of the territorial division there was utter confusion. On 14 August 1947, the Pakistani flag was hoisted in the district towns of Murshidabad and Malda. On 15 August 1947, the Indian flag was hoisted in Khulna. The report of the Boundary Commission of the two Bengals as well as the Radcliffe Award on 17th August had placed the entire Khulna district as part of East Pakistan, and some part of Murshidabad and Malda districts along with the main city of Malda and Murshidabad had become part of West Bengal. This created tension in the two Bengals. Under the circumstances, P.C. Ghosh along with Khwaza Nazimuddin, the Muslim League chief minister of East Bengal, made a joint statement. The essence of the joint statement was that if there was a necessity to change the Radcliffe Award, it must be done with the consultation of the governments of both Bengals and, until and unless it had not been done, the people of both sides had to respect the boundary line. Gandhi welcomed the joint statement as statesmanlike and sagacious. But Sardar Patel, the first home minister of India, did not like the joint statement. Later the Government of India formed a five-men committee in order to consider the demands of the people, but the result was meaningless and futile.

The Boundary Commission for both Bengal and Punjab had Sir Cyril Radcliffe as chairman. The reason for a common chairman was perhaps to compensate loss of one party in one province by gain in another, an idea of Mountbatten's.[4] Nehru recommended a quick decision by the commission so that any disagreements post the award could be settled through mutual discussion between the two governments. Nehru's recommendation that the Boundary Commission would be instructed to 'demarcate the boundaries of the two parts of Bengal on the basis of ascertaining contiguous majority areas of the Muslims and the non-Muslims … taking into account other factors' was accepted by Mountbatten.[5]

In Bengal the Muslim cause was represented by the Muslim League faction managed by the shadow chief minister Nazimuddin.

Two other possible groups, one headed by Suhrawardy and the other supporting the Congress, were left out. Suhrawardy was rejected because he had pleaded for sovereign independent Bengal, and the Congress-affiliated Muslims were also ignored since they were against partition as such. The Muslim League chose to simply go by contiguous areas so as to maximise its territorial gains and effectively recommended that only the districts of Midnapore, Burdwan, Bankura, Birbhum and parts of Hooghly – excluding the jute mills – should go to India. Clearly even at that stage the aim of the Muslim League was to include Calcutta in their part of Bengal.

But there was a problem in the Hindu group. The smaller parties like the Hindu Mahasabha with even smaller parties had ten members in the Central Coordination Committee to recommend the Hindu claim before the Boundary Commission while the Congress which had a much larger political stake had only two members. The smaller parties wanted as much territory as they could lay their claim on and even demanded a few Muslim-majority districts to be part of West Bengal. Their political motive was simple – to establish that for the Hindu cause they had managed to win the larger territory which by their claim worked out to four-fifth of undivided Bengal, perhaps more preposterous than the claim of the Muslim League. The Congress watered down the claim and reached out with two proposals. One was called the Congress Scheme which claimed 57 per cent of the territory for 46 per cent of the people. In this proposal the claim made to Muslim-majority districts of Malda, Jessore, Rajsahi were shortened to only Hindu-majority *thanas* (police stations). The other was called the Congress Plan which was created keeping contiguousness in mind. But conflict arose since the majority, consisting of smaller political voices like the Hindu Mahasabha, voted in favour of the scheme that advocated for 57 per cent of territory. Finally the shadow chief minister Ghosh had to intervene. Within the Congress a group emerged under the leadership of Atulya Ghosh among others that left out Muslim-majority districts and opted for only Khulna, Hooghly, Midnapore, Burdwan, Bankura and Birbhum.[6] Clearly this group was focused on their future political comfort and even left out the economically important North Bengal with its rich tea plantations and Murshidabad which was critical for regulating the flow of water to the river Hooghly, therefore affecting Calcutta. Joya Chatterjee has mentioned how keen was Bihar and Assam to have the North Bengal districts within their respective states while Atulya Ghosh and the others, representing the Hooghly group in the Congress, were looking only at their future electoral bases. The drawing of borders for the future West Bengal among the various political interest groups were in effect a precursor to how politics would evolve in West Bengal after Independence. The Partition had opened up several problem areas, such as the majority population of one community suddenly finding themselves part of a region where they were a minority, a problem which Ghosh and Nazimuddin attempted to assuage.

Mahatma Gandhi had seen the sorry state of affairs in the Bengal Congress during these days. He lamented that there was not a good man to be found among those who formed the Bengal Provincial Congress Committee. 'Apart from seeking personal interest and partisan interest, no other efforts may be said to have been visible in Bengal during the last 20 years,' Gandhi wrote in 1947 before his assassination, '... unless there is a radical change in its programme of work, there is no escape from a steady deterioration of its affairs in the next twenty years to come.'[7] How prophetic was Gandhi. Exactly twenty years later in 1967 the Congress lost the state of West Bengal to a coalition of opposition parties. It never came back to power alone barring a massively rigged election in 1972.

When Prafulla Ghosh took charge of the newly truncated province of West Bengal he had to face three kinds of problems –

internal politics of the Congress, inflow of displaced persons from East Pakistan, and frequent communal flare ups. Since Dr Ghosh did not belong to any lobby of Bengal and was an outsider it did not take long for his detractors to ease him out just in six months. As Gandhi said, personal and partisan interest triumphed and West Bengal ushered in a new chief minister before the end of January 1948.

Political infighting started almost within a week after the country became independent. When Ghosh went to Delhi to meet the Congress president on 23rd August, rumours surfaced in Calcutta that the chief minister intended to drop certain ministers and reconstitute his cabinet. His supplies minister Radhanath Das, a member of the Hooghly group, was facing charges of corruption and had to resign. This had upset the politically strong faction who were anyway opposed to accepting someone from East Bengal as their leader. In quick succession two more ministers owing allegiance to the Hooghly group resigned. One of them did so after the Midnapore District Congress Committee had urged its member who was minister of irrigation and waterways to resign. Congress President Kripalani intervened and the machinations to embarrass Ghosh stopped for some time. Ghosh was meanwhile elected to the assembly from the Seuri constituency in Birbhum by defeating his rival from the Hindu Mahasabha (November 1947). He had also handled the impeding food crisis successfully. But with generous support of his detractors from within the Congress problems kept on mounting. One was the demand for advance salary by the drivers of the food supplies department which was led by a Congress trade union leader Maitriyee Basu. When the same was denied on administrative grounds there was a strike by the drivers. Ghosh and his supplies minister managed to challenge the strike by taking help from private drivers. In addition to all this, there was the continued communal problem in Calcutta and elsewhere.

Just before Independence Gandhi reached Calcutta on his way to Noakhali where he wished to be on the day of Independence. But there was communal tension in Calcutta and at the request of Muslim leaders who were worried that Hindus would attack them in retaliation for Noakhali where Hindus were under constant threat, Gandhi had agreed to stay in Calcutta. Suhrawardy, who was in Karachi, on his return, requested Gandhi to stay back. Gandhi decided to stay at Beliaghata and had invited Suhrawardy to stay with him. When he reached 'Haidari Mansion' at Beliaghata his entry was blocked by young men who were waiting for him with black flags. When Suhrawardy came to join Gandhi they became even more agitated. They blamed Gandhi for not being in Calcutta in 1946 and for his failure to stop the attacks by the Muslims. Gandhi had to use all the persuasive skills at his disposal to diffuse the situation. But the truce was temporary.

On 1st September Gandhi wrote to Patel of his experience on the previous evening:

> Someone received knife wounds in Machhva Bazaar. No one knew who stabbed him. People brought him here for demonstration. Perhaps they wanted to attack Shaheed Suhrawardy, but they could not find him; so their anger was turned on me. ... I was in bed about to go to sleep. Our Muslim landlady came in to have a look as she was afraid I might come to harm. I sensed danger and got up. I broke my silence. My vow permits me to break it on such occasions. I went to face the crowd but the girls would not leave my side. Other people also surrounded me. Glass windows were being broken and they started smashing the doors also. There was an attempt to cut the wires of the electric ceiling fans but only a few were snapped. I started shouting at the crowd,

> asking them to be quiet. But who would listen? I could, moreover, speak only Hindustani and they were Bengalis … The Superintendent of Police came soon after and the youngsters dispersed after causing considerable damage to the house. Prafulla Babu and Annada arrived. Prafulla suggested the posting of more police guard but I objected. Everyone suspects the Hindu Mahasabha [was behind the attack]. I have asked them to see Syamaprasad and Chatterji (N C Chatterjee) before arresting the mischief-makers and not to do anything in a hurry.[8]

In the meanwhile, Punjab had been burning and there were requests made to Gandhi to be there. But he chose to remain in Calcutta and decided to use fasting as a weapon to bring back sanity. In a statement to the press, Gandhi said,

> But now that the Calcutta bubble seems to have burst, with what face can I go to the Punjab? The weapon which has hitherto proved infallible for me, is fasting. To put an appearance before a yelling crowd does not always work. It certainly did not last night. What my word in person cannot do my fast may. It may touch the hearts of all the warring elements even in the Punjab if it does in Calcutta. I therefore begin fasting from 8.15 p.m. to end only if and when sanity returns to Calcutta. I shall as usual permit myself to add salt and soda bicarb to the water I may wish to drink during the fast.[9]

Due to the continuing law and order problem, the West Bengal government decided to bring in the Security Bill in December. The communists started agitating against the bill. Ghosh's opponents in the state Congress assisted them. In a violent demonstration in front of the assembly the police had to resort to firing in which an employee of the Relief and Welfare Ambulance Corp died. Gandhi was pained by these developments. In his speech at the prayer meeting on 12th December Gandhi said,

> According to newspaper reports there has been rowdyism in Calcutta. It seems that we have got used to thinking that we can take what we want by resorting to rowdyism … The Government in Bengal is our government. It is run by Congressmen. They should not have been subjected to such behaviour. Supposing they have made a mistake — I personally do not know where their mistake lay — rowdyism is not the way to point it out. Why should we indulge in barbaric behaviour? There were students among those who indulged in rowdyism. They are well-educated. It hardly behoves them to stop the members of the Assembly from entering the Assembly, to block all the entrances and, not stopping there, to get into the Assembly itself. But that is what they did. It seems to me that if we persist in this kind of thing the Government cannot be carried on for long. The demonstration was intended to make the Assembly desist from enacting the Bill that the demonstrators did not want. The Bill proposed by the Government is meant for preventing people from indulging in violent activities. Even if the demonstrators did not like this Bill, they should have expressed their opposition in a peaceful way. They should not have indulged in rowdyism. We did not do such things against the British, if any people did so I used to admonish them. We always behaved as gentlemen — I for one even used to undertake fasts.[10]

The incident was a trailer of sorts of the future political course in West Bengal.[11]

Jyoti Basu was the main voice of opposition to the Special Powers Bill, raised by Dr Ghosh on 27 November 1948. So keen was Basu that even before the proposal to table the bill was placed he rose and objected to it. The suggestion of the communist party was that the bill should go for a referendum for a decision. He had added that earlier in undivided Bengal Suhrawardy wanted to bring a similar bill but was vehemently opposed by the Congress then. On this particular bill Jyoti Basu spoke 60 times on different occasions and had placed 60 amendments. Finally, on 15th January, it was passed by 47 votes in favour and 12 against.[12] After Independence this bill was perhaps the first most bitterly contested one in the West Bengal assembly even attracting comments from Gandhi and necessitating a public meeting by Sardar Patel.

Apart from the factions in the Bengal Congress the business lobby led by G.D. Birla himself was acting against Dr Ghosh. In December Birla had met the chief minister at his official residence and had submitted a paper signed by the majority of the Congress MLAs seeking Dr Ghosh's resignation. That was when the chief minister was engaged in getting the security legislation passed. He had even invited Sardar Patel to speak before a huge crowd in Calcutta in support of the bill. In the meeting Patel had accepted that Ghosh did not have much administrative experience and mentioned that if there was opposition to Ghosh as chief minister the CWC could be approached but agitation on the road was not the process to go about it. The message to Ghosh was clear and after the security bill was passed he tendered his resignation to the governor. Within ten days Dr Bidhan Chandra Roy assumed charge of the state. He had invited Dr Ghosh to join his ministry but Ghosh refused since earlier Roy had refused to join Ghosh's ministry. Their acrimony continued with Ghosh losing no opportunity to criticise the Bidhan Roy government. But in the factional politics of West Bengal Ghosh had no base. Moreover the wily Hooghly group led by Atulya Ghosh knew well that the personal charisma of Dr Bidhan Roy would ensure his acceptance by the central leadership as also would play a decisive role in case of opponents seeking his ouster. There was such a move by the Jugantar group supported by the Gandhians. They objected to the presence of 'outsiders' like Nalini Ranjan Sarkar who was always in some group or other which helped him to hold some ministerial post. Out of 13 members of the Roy cabinet, 7 were from the Hooghly group, 3 from Jugantar, and 3 did not belong to any group. There was no representation of the Gandhian group nor anyone from the Calcutta Marwaris backed by G.D. Birla. But the Marwaris did not find any reason to object. Now the Gandhian group joined hands with the Jugantar group and requisitioned a meeting of the Congress Legislative Party. This was within three months of formation of the ministry. Out of 55 members 52 attended and 30 voted in favour of Dr Roy. The minority 22 who had supported the resolution of forming a new ministry under Surendra Mohan Ghosh withdrew the motion, in effect conceding defeat. In the faction-ridden Bengal Congress the Hooghly group emerged victorious, sidelining the Congressmen who had their origins in East Bengal.[13]

The Hooghly faction realised that in order to ensure their control over the power structure they had to restructure the Pradesh Congress Committee (PCC) in such a way that the numbers of the East Bengal lobby were reduced. Control over the PCC would ensure selection of ministers from the group as also selection of candidates during elections so as to ensure control over the legislative party. The Congress leaders were well aware of the tricks of the electoral political game. The restructuring of the West Bengal PCC was due since the province was reconstituted after the Partition. Accordingly in April

1948 the AICC decided to liquidate the Congress committees of East Bengal. The CWC directed that those members of the PCC who were elected from different constituencies belonging to the territory of West Bengal would sign and submit prescribed membership forms in order to be eligible for participating in the general meeting of the PCC. Those members who were returned from the constituencies belonging to East Bengal too would continue as members of the PCC provided that they had signed and submitted prescribed membership forms together with a declaration that they had made West Bengal their homes by 30 April 1948 and that they were not members of the legislature or the constituent assembly of Pakistan or of any political organisation in East Pakistan. This would have ensured that all 346 members from the East would continue to be in PCC and the Hooghly group would still remain numerically less in the 576-member PCC. The Hooghly group approached the Congress president and placed before him the statement that since the Hindu residents of the East were part of Pakistan, if the same number of representatives from the East controls the Congress in West Bengal there would be less representatives for the residents of West Bengal. The Congress president accepted their logic and felt that the CWC decision should be reviewed. In order to showcase their numerical strength, the Hooghly group organised a conference of West Bengal Provincial Congress Workers in Midnapore in which 151 out of a total 230 members of West Bengal PCC participated. The conference even expressed extreme views such as the East Bengal Congressmen should not even come to West Bengal. Clearly the target of the Hooghly group was to take over the reins of the PCC from the Jugantar group. Surendra Mohan Ghosh, the tall leader of the Jugantar group, was then the president of the state Congress.

As a compromise the CWC suggested that two categories of Congress members from East Bengal be included in the PCC.

The first category would be those who were residents of West Bengal but had been elected from East Bengal constituencies and had provided their West Bengal address. The second category were those who had migrated before 30th April and had already applied for membership. CWC appointed a Scrutiny Committee headed by Working Committee member Acharya Jugal Kishore and two Congressmen, one from West Bengal (Atulya Ghosh) and another from East Bengal (Amar Ghosh). In all 179 applications were received out of which 48 belonged to the first category. From the second category 35 applications were voluntarily withdrawn and 101 applications were accepted. After the exercise, the East Bengal Congressmen had 149 members in the PCC against 346 earlier.[14] The total number of members in the PCC came down to 312.

The groupism in West Bengal Congress did not end with the reconstitution of the PCC. In the presidential election the Hooghly group tied up with the Gandhians after the Gandhians and the Jugantar group fell out over the choice of the state Congress president. While the Jugantar group wanted Surendra Mohan to continue the Gandhians led by Dr Ghosh wanted one among their group as president. The Hooghly group used this opportunity and came to an understanding with the Gandhians. While Dr Suresh Banerjee of the Gandhian group was elected president, Atulya Ghosh took over as the secretary. He packed the executive committee with his group members – out of 91 more than 50 belonged to the Hooghly Group.[15] But again trouble started brewing when the Gandhians switched sides and joined the Jugantar group in the struggle for controlling the PCC. In May 1949 they gave a requisition for a fresh meeting of the PCC for revamping the organisation. Out of 312 members 107 had signed the requisition. Atulya Ghosh delayed calling the meeting since a bye-election was being held for the South Calcutta constituency where the sitting Congress member

Satis Chandra Bose had passed way. His brother Sarat Bose was contesting the seat but as a Socialist Republican Party candidate and he won the seat on sympathy vote mainly.

After the election Atulya Ghosh called the meeting. Out of a total 312-member PCC, 294 attended the meeting. Dr Prafulla Chandra Ghosh, the leader of the Gandhian group, moved the proposal that in the interest of 'better organization and service' the present executive committee of the PCC and its office bearers be removed. This was carried by 172 to 121 votes, one member remaining neutral. Next the Jugantar group moved the proposal that Surendra Mohan Ghosh be elected president of the PCC. Bijoy Singh Nahar on behalf of the Hooghly group proposed the name of Bepin Behari Ganguly. Surendra Mohan Ghosh received 172 against 121 and took over as PCC president. Charu Chandra Bhandari of the Gandhian group was elected as secretary replacing Atulya Ghosh. In the reconstituted executive committee of 91 members, only about 20 were from the Hooghly group. Now was the turn of the Hooghly group to criticise Surendra Mohan Ghosh for packing the executive committee with his own supporters. Atulya Ghosh issued a statement, 'It (the PCC executive) is a packed house consisting of a large number of the opted out members of East Bengal who have neither any constituency nor any stake in this province and his own partisans. We expected a bold lead from Sri Surendra Mohan Ghosh.' In response Amar Ghosh, a follower of the Jugantar group, remarked: 'I have always held that the differences which Sri Atulya Ghosh and his group and associates always seek to make between East Bengal and West Bengal delegates is mischievous and inimical to harmonious and united action by all Congress workers who are now citizens of West Bengal.'[16] Amar Ghosh felt that such differences would act as a serious disruptive force. Perhaps this rush to seize control of West Bengal politics right after Independence saw the dominant Hooghly group ignoring the cause of the Hindu Bengalis of East Pakistan and the rehabilitation of those who left their homeland in search of safety for West Bengal. This group rivalry could be one reason why the apparent stepmotherly approach of the Central government for the relief and rehabilitation of East Pakistan-displaced persons went uncontested in the initial days of Independent India, a factor which saw West Bengal politics moving away from the mainstream of the national political course.

Results of the South Calcutta bye-election which took place on 12th June, two days before the PCC reconstitution, went against the Congress. Dr Bidhan Roy passed on the blame to the PCC which he felt had 149 members from East Bengal who had no connect with the people of West Bengal. Thus the Congress party in West Bengal had been far removed from the people of West Bengal and the party candidate did not receive much support from the PCC president and other members of his group. The statement of Bidhan Roy exposes that he himself belonged to the West Bengal-based Hooghly group and encouraged factionalism. Also, he blamed Surendra Mohan as PCC president for the defeat while PCC was a coalition between the Hooghly and Gandhian groups till 12th June. Surendra Mohan, the PCC president, called the chief minister biased towards his own group (Hooghly group) and said that Roy's bias

> … had made him blind to his obligations as the chief minister and he has added some bitterness to the issue already bitter. A section of Congressmen have raised the question of East Bengal and West Bengal, just as the Muslim League raised the two nation theory; both have inspirations in hatred and jealousy.[17]

In the heat of their bitterness both the tall leaders of Bengal's freedom movement – Dr Roy and Surendra Mohan Ghosh – glossed over the fact that the South Calcutta constituency was held by Netaji's brother and won by none other than his 'mejda' Sarat Bose. More than party affiliation the Bose family name and influence was the reason for the Congress's defeat. Yet the two mighty leaders, holding the two key posts of chief minister and PCC president, kept exchanging bitterness in public. Clearly the Congress in West Bengal was born weak which served the cause of regional political sentiments and its eventual domination in the state.

What the Congress leadership had failed to address, busy as they were in factional feuds, was the interest of ordinary people. Jyoti Basu had in his opposition to the state's budget in the assembly on 20 February 1948 exposed these weaknesses clearly. He had blamed the government for pursuing the interests of the businessmen while ignoring those of the common people such as the workers and farmers. He raised the issue of unemployment and the problems plaguing the public distribution of food.[18] On 3 March 1948, Pandit Lakshmikanta Maitra, Congress member from Nabadwip, raised the issue of the plight of refugees coming from East Bengal in the parliament. Maitra mentioned that more than 20 lakh people had crossed the border and moved over to West Bengal. In Calcutta, he mentioned, there were 61 lakh ration cards against a population of 21 lakhs as per census of 1941. Clearly there were huge numbers of fake ration cards but due to the influx of so many people the then population of Calcutta would be around 50 lakhs. The city could offer hardly any facility to its residents. In the small town in Nadia district from where Maitra hailed, the usual population was 40,000. But due to the influx of at least 110,000 people from East Bengal, the town was inundated with people. When a Congress member was busy pointing out the plight of the people coming from across the border, the leadership of the West Bengal Congress including its chief minister Bidhan Chandra Roy was preoccupied with factional feuds.[19]

Sarat Bose's victory in the bye-election created ripples in the Central Congress too. It was reported in the media that Nehru in a speech expressed the view that the West Bengal ministry should resign.[20] The activities of the West Bengal Congress embroiled in groupism was not encouraging with new recruitment for party membership at a standstill indicating loss of popularity of the provincial cabinet of Dr Roy. While West Bengal was not politically as important as undivided Bengal it still was the premier province economically with Calcutta being the major port and business centre of the nation. Central Congress was naturally disturbed. In addition, riots inside jails by communist prisoners and processions in support of communists exposed the growing weakness of the Provincial Congress. The general secretary of the Congress stated that the condition of the state Congress warranted the intervention of the most powerful leader to set the house in order.[21]

Meanwhile B.C. Roy left for Switzerland on 23rd June and Nalini Ranjan Sarkar was holding the fort in place of Roy. Nehru came to West Bengal on 12th July. The opponents of Roy and the Hooghly group met Nehru and submitted a memorandum providing 17 instances of discredits faced by the Roy ministry. A few days later the CWC met in Delhi to deliberate on West Bengal. Nehru proposed that the West Bengal legislature and the PCC should be dissolved. CWC called the warring factions of West Bengal to come and place their respective views. As expected the Hooghly group led by the acting chief minister Nalini Ranjan Sarkar placed arguments against dissolution of the assembly and election at a time when the state had been undergoing several problems. The opponents, the Jugantar group and the Gandhians, supported the call for fresh election assuming with that there would be change in government.

The CWC adopted a resolution on 28 July 1949 which recommended inter alia interim election in West Bengal, a new government and reconstitution of the PCC. But it kept the final decision in abeyance till the return of Dr B.C. Roy from Switzerland. Roy returned on 2nd September and met Sardar Patel to assess the situation. Patel was then in complete charge of the Congress party. It should be remembered that it was Patel who had asked Prafulla Ghosh to induct a Marwari in the cabinet which Ghosh had declined and this refusal eventually saw the ouster of Ghosh. There are reasons to believe that Patel's tacit support was in favour of Dr Roy hence the CWC decision was kept in abeyance till his return. Roy called a meeting of the Congress Legislative Party (CLP) immediately on his return to Calcutta. In a resolution out of 50 members of the CLP, 34 expressed confidence in the leadership of Roy (with only 14 voting against) and requesting the CWC to reconsider its decision of installing an interim ministry. Armed with the support of the CLP Roy met the CWC members who agreed with Roy and asked for the continuation of his ministry as also maintenance of status quo of the PCC. However the CWC maintained its stand on an interim election in the state. It was not very difficult to postpone the decision of holding an interim election since by then the constituent assembly had nearly completed the task of drafting the Constitution and a national general election on the basis of universal adult franchise was expected to take place. In such a scenario to hold an election with restricted electoral rolls on the basis of the 1935 Act was uncalled for. In view of this and also keeping in consideration various administrative issues Nehru announced that holding an election in West Bengal when a national election would be conducted in the next few months was unwarranted. Clearly the personal equation of Bidhan Roy both with Nehru and Patel and his charisma helped the Hooghly group to weather the storm and continue its control over the Congress administration in West Bengal. It is evident from the developments that Roy had complete supremacy in administrative matters while

Atulya Ghosh was busy manipulating different political factions in order to keep the stronghold of the Hooghly group intact. Both Bidhan Roy and Atulya Ghosh needed each other for maintaining their supremacy in post-Partition Congress politics of West Bengal.[22] It is argued that Bidhan Roy took over as chief minister of West Bengal at the request of the Congress Legislative Party and stood above political factionalism in the state. But this argument does not hold much water if one takes into account his comments on the state Congress president after the loss of the Calcutta bye-election as also his role in influencing the CWC in cancelling its resolution on change of government in West Bengal. Clearly Dr Bidhan Roy knew how to handle state politics well enough without being seen as an active participant in the murky game. Atulya Ghosh provided able support to Dr Roy while Atulya Ghosh too benefitted from the influence and stature of Dr Bidhan Roy in order to meet the challenges posed by Gandhians like Dr Prafulla Ghosh or Jugantar group head Surendra Mohan Ghosh. Atulya Ghosh did not enjoy the confidence of the Congress high command like either of the Ghoshes.

That Bidhan Roy was a shrewd politician could be judged from his choice of Kiran Shankar Roy as his home minister one-and-half months after forming his cabinet. Perhaps he had a hidden agenda for that. Jyoti Basu's speeches in the West Bengal assembly were tarnishing the image of the government. His stinging attack on the first state budget in the assembly, calling it a friendly move for the business classes and industry, 'You cannot fool people not tomorrow, not even today. Soon enough people would ask you to give up your cushy posts and engage others to formulate a people centric budget,' had perhaps overwhelmed the state government. The communist party had its second congress in Calcutta between 21 and 26 February 1948 and within one month on 26th March CPI was banned in the state of West Bengal.[23] The charges against the party were that the party was resorting to violent activities and creating anarchy among the workers and farmers. Clearly Kiran Shankar would not have taken such a decision, especially knowing well Nehru's possible objection to such a move. In fact Nehru wrote to the state chief ministers in his fortnightly letter dated 1 April 1948 that the West Bengal government 'has banned the communist party without any reference to us (Union Cabinet) ... this procedure is undesirable because any such action leads to repercussions.'[24] Later, one day after the adoption of the Constitution in 1950, the Calcutta High Court dismissed this order of the West Bengal government.

A problem that leaders including Nehru wanted to sweep under the carpet was the constant flow of refugees from East Bengal. When Nehru wrote his first fortnightly letter to the state chief ministers on 15 October 1947, he recorded his satisfaction over resolving the problems faced by the divided province of Punjab, but there was no mention of the plights of the Hindus of East Bengal. Later when Pandit Lakshmikanta Maitra had highlighted the problems of the refugees and their resettlement, around that time Nehru was engaged with Dr Roy on the continued inflow of refugees from East Bengal. It seems that Nehru had full faith that the Hindu Bengalis of East Pakistan would opt to stay put there like a large section of Muslims in Bengal did. In a letter (16 August 1948) to Dr Roy, he even went on to say that every effort should be made to stop inflow of Hindu Bengalis into West Bengal.

> I think it was very wrong thing for some of the Hindu leaders of East Bengal to come to West Bengal. In spite of our efforts it is difficult to induce most provinces to absorb more refugees. We have been pressing them to do so for a long time. I think in spite of every difficulty in East Bengal it is far better for our people to face the situation there than to come away.[25]

In another letter to Roy, Nehru said that he was determined to stop migration even at the cost of war. Clearly Nehru had no solution for the possible Hindu Bengali migration from East Pakistan.[26] Either he was naive or he did not care for the Bengalis. This desperation to stop refugees from East Bengal, perhaps, led to Nehru signing an agreement with the Pakistan prime minister Liaquat Ali Khan, an issue which saw Syama Prasad Mukherjee the then industry minister quitting the cabinet.

While Nehru was firmly ensconced in his belief that migration of Hindus from East Pakistan was temporary in character and those who came would go back after some time he was rudely shaken out of his make-believe world when riots broke out in Dacca in February 1950. On 10th February after the Friday namaz, Muslim clerics called for a meeting. After the meeting a procession was taken out. It shouted anti-Hindu and anti-India slogans and looted shops belonging to Hindus. The violence spread in no time to other districts of Mymensingh, Comilla, Chittagong, Noakhali, Rajsahi, Khulna, Barisal and Sylhet. More than 10,000 were killed and there was an influx of an estimated 11,72,928 people into West Bengal.[27] For Nehru this was completely beyond his imagination. He dashed to Dacca and met the Pakistan prime minister Liaquat Ali Khan. An agreement was signed on 8 April 1950, the much-debated Nehru-Liaquat Pact. The pact stated:

> The Government of India and Pakistan solemnly agree that each shall ensure, to the minorities throughout its territory, complete equality of citizenship, irrespective of religion, a full sense of security in respect of life, culture, property and personal honour, freedom of movement within each country and freedom of occupation, speech and worship, subject to law and morality.[28]

The nicely drafted document failed miserably in execution of the intent. The change in the population ratio of the Nadia district is an example. Immediately after the Partition, Nadia was a Muslim majority district with 52.65 per cent of its total population of 9,01,272 being Muslim. By 1951 the population of Nadia increased to 11,44,924 and the share of the Hindu population stood at 77.03 per cent while those of Muslims declined to 22.36 per cent. Subhasri Ghosh in her presentation before the Indian History Congress has cited several instances where the letter and spirit of the pact were violated in Nadia district and Muslims were persecuted.[29] There is no reason to believe that such instances were isolated only in the border district of Nadia and also to think that persecutions of Hindus in East Pakistan went unavenged in West Bengal. But the fact remains that the nicely drafted and well-publicised pact was more effective in assuaging the sentiments of the political leaders rather than helping the minorities in either Pakistan or in India.

The Nehru-Liaquat Pact had an important political reaction in India. It came from Syama Prasad Mukherjee, the most important Bengali representative in the Nehru cabinet. Syama Prasad wrote to Nehru:

> The reason for my resignation, as I have communicated to you, arises out of the policy pursued regarding Indo-Pakistan relationship, especially relating to Bengal. The Agreement which, I suppose, will be finalised today does not touch the basic problem and is not likely to offer any solution. I can under no circumstances be a party to it. Apart from the fact that it will bring little solace to the sufferers, it has certain features which are bound to give rise to fresh communal and political problems in Bharat, the consequences of which we

> cannot foresee today. In my humble opinion, the policy you are following will fail. Time alone can prove this.[30]

Subhasri Ghosh's research cited above merely endorses what Syama Prasad Mukherjee had said.

Even Nehru did not have any misgiving that the pact would be warmly welcomed. Therefore there was a blitzkrieg of publicity launched by the government beginning with Nehru himself speaking to the nation through the All India Radio.[31] In his inimitable style, full more of sentiment than logic, the prime minister told the nation how he had discussed with his counterpart of Pakistan for a full week. He said, 'Hundreds of thousands of people have been uprooted from their homes in Bengal and suffered intolerable agony. Millions have lived under the dark shadow of fear and insecurity.' Clearly Nehru wanted to apply a balm on their sufferings – his first recorded effort to address the plight of Bengalis arising out of the Partition. Nehru had no doubt that the prime minister of Pakistan 'will exercise his great influence in the fullest degree to help in implementing this agreement and in producing those conditions of peace and security and good living for the minorities in Pakistan.' Evidently Jawaharlal Nehru had decided to wipe out the memory of the Noakhali riots of October 1946 when the country was not yet divided as well as the role of the Suhrawardy government in protecting the interests of the minority Hindus. Or perhaps he felt for some reason that there had been a miraculous change of heart since then. Nehru knew that the pact had weaknesses and also accepted that the success would depend on how the pact would be implemented by Pakistan, 'I do not expect some magical change suddenly because of this agreement. I do not expect the great exodus to stop …' He appealed to his critics, pointed out the welcome mats that came from abroad over the pact, and expected Bengal's youth to work for its success. The only critical point that the Indian prime minister left to fate was that the source of the problems were the fundamentalists across the border who could be handled only by a government there. No amount of speeches in India could have addressed the problem of millions of Bengalis displaced from East Bengal. On 21st April, Sardar Patel, the home minister, spoke in support of the pact. He dwelled on his ill health and how despite that he was in West Bengal to support the government and the people there, how he had tried to persuade the two Bengali ministers, Syama Prasad Mukherjee and K.C. Neogy, to remain in the cabinet and help the Bengali refugees. He reiterated that there was no way of going back on a pact that had been signed:

> Public opinion throughout India outside West Bengal and the State Governments have almost unanimously and wholeheartedly accepted the concluded arrangements, and are determined to work the Agreement to the best of their ability and competence. Would it then pay the people of West Bengal to have a different or contrary line even partially? Let not West Bengal isolate itself and alienate the rest of India.

It was a not-so-veiled threat to West Bengal from Sardar Patel.[32] In April itself there were 19 addresses through the All India Radio in support of the pact, in May another 20. The aim was to make West Bengal agree to the pact while on the other side of the border movement of persecuted Hindus went on unchecked. Clearly West Bengal was born isolated from the heart of India.

Not that there was no discussion in the Parliament on the plight of East Pakistan-displaced persons. Nehru had mentioned the unfortunate riots in various districts of East Pakistan as well as the retaliation carried out in West Bengal. On 27 February 1950 Nehru ruled out a proposal of exchange of population between the two

Bengals calling it vague and unrealistic. Nehru said in a statement, 'The proposal for an exchange of population was completely antagonistic to India's political, economic, social and spiritual principles. It was a question of breach of trust.' In response to this statement Syama Prasad Mukherjee said,

> When Pandit Nehru himself had arranged the exchange of population in Punjab, he had kept this question of breach of trust in cold storage. At the present moment it would be proper for him to keep the question of breach of trust in cold storage again and face the reality like an experienced politician.[33]

Clearly Nehru had two separate yardsticks for the plight of refugees due to the Partition of India, and West Bengal suffered the most as a result. In the constituent assembly, Renuka Ray had spiritedly taken up the question of central grant for the refugees from East Pakistan. When discussing grants with the relief and rehabilitation ministry Renuka Ray had strongly objected to the interventions of Sucheta Kripalani who perhaps wanted to fix responsibility on the state.[34] Not just Nehru, the plight of Bengal did not find much merit among the other leading politicians of the day. Sucheta Kripalani's indifference was particularly shocking because she had travelled to Noakhali in 1948 with Acharya J.B. Kripalani, the then Congress president, and had witnessed first-hand the plight of the Hindus in East Bengal.

The resignation letter of Jogendranath Mandal, the leader of the scheduled caste Namasudras, a large community in East Bengal, and a minister in Pakistan, submitted on 8th October, six months after the Nehru-Liaquat Pact, exposed the futility of the agreement in redressing the problems of Hindus who stayed back in East Pakistan. Mandal had cited instances which made it clear why the East Pakistan government and the Muslim League had hardly any inclination to honour the pact. The Nurul Amin government in East Pakistan was weak and had appointed Dr N. Barari as minister in charge to oversee the implementation of the agreement. Dr N. Barari was known for his divisive, communally charged views. Mandal knew that the fate of the Nehru-Liaquat agreement was sealed. Mandal pointed out how East Pakistan was replicating the success of West Pakistan in eliminating Hindus from their country. He wrote,

> Apprehension of launching of a movement for re-union of East and West Bengal by both Hindu and Muslim leaders made the East Bengal Ministry and the Muslim League nervous. They wanted to prevent such a move. They thought that any large-scale communal riot in East Bengal was sure to produce reactions in West Bengal where Muslims might be killed. The result of such riots in both East and West Bengal, it was believed, would prevent any movement for re-union of Bengals.[35]

According to Mandal, the Nehru-Liaquat agreement had made it clear to the Hindus seeking refuge in India that they had no future in terms of relief or rehabilitation in West Bengal or for that matter in the rest of India. In desperation some came back to East Pakistan but this did not in any way prove that they felt safe or hopeful after the agreement. Mandal had cited several instances where Hindu professionals like doctors, lawyers, educationists, and merchants were being harassed and made to feel subservient to the Muslims. Even Mrs Nellie Sengupta, wife of late Jatindra Mohan Sengupta, who stayed back in Pakistan, had mentioned such instances. Clearly the faith reposed in the Pakistan administration by Nehru did not reflect any understanding of the ground reality of Bengalis in Pakistan nor did he take note of how Pakistan had been internationalising the Kashmir issue at that time.[36] The Nehru-Liaquat agreement was a sop handed over to West Bengal by the first national Indian government on as Patel said 'take it or else' basis. That politics in West Bengal would not move in sync with the rest of India, particularly that in the Hindi heartland, was reflected in the treatment meted out to the state immediately after India won its hard-earned Independence.

This differential treatment was pointed out by K.C. Neogy also. In a statement from Kalimpong he said that from his personal experience he had seen how even small issues raised by the refugees from West Pakistan kept the rehabilitation minister and the prime minister busy in resolving. These refugees of West Punjab were in Delhi and the surrounding areas. Naturally the central government was busy redressing their problems and had little or no time for the refugees from far away Bengal.[37] Syama Prasad Mukherjee in a public meeting in Calcutta (4 September 1950) said that Pakistan had been using a strategic tool of warfare by forcing out Hindus from East Pakistan into West Bengal. In Kashmir Pakistan used arms and in West Bengal a clever policy of hidden warfare. Prime Minister Nehru, according to Syama Prasad Mukherjee, should have adopted a similar diplomatic stand against these two different means of aggression used by Pakistan.[38] Unfortunately there was no political compulsion for Nehru to pay attention to such sermons.

The stepmotherly treatment of Bengal could also be gauged from the regular flow of complaints against Dr Syama Prasad Mukherjee stating he was partial to the cause of Bengal officers. In an undisclosed letter (1 December 1948) Prime Minister Nehru wrote to Mukherjee that there was considerable talk in the constituent assembly and among the general public that Syama Prasad was converting his ministry into a miniature Bengal. Nehru had enclosed a letter from a member of the constituent assembly whose complaint was that Mukherjee was running the ministry with help from Bengali officers. In response Mukherjee provided a list of the officers. The three senior-most officers – the secretary and two joint secretaries – were from South India. He went on to enumerate the names of senior officers and the method of appointment – either with cabinet approval, or through recommendations of the Federal Public Service Commission (FPSC was the predecessor of UPSC), or by departmental promotion and strictly as per seniority. Syama Prasad also pointed out that in temporary posts filled on ad hoc basis refugees from West Pakistan were favoured with hardly a few posts going to those from East Pakistan. He requested the prime minister to draw on the surplus officers that West Bengal had. Syama Prasad also suggested to the prime minister to immediately call for a statement 'showing complete list of appointments to all higher posts made in all ministries since August 15, 1947, detailing the procedure adopted in each case and also the percentage of persons belonging to various provinces.' The calumny did not stop there though. In another letter dated 13 February 1950, Nehru sent a list of gazetted appointments made in the industry and supply ministry between 15 August and 22 December 1949 which indicated that the number of recruitments from Bengal was rather high. Syama Prasad responded by providing a detailed outline of the procedure of recruitment which was by a duly constituted departmental selection committee which had a member from the FPSC. He emphasised that the minister had merely accepted the recommendations of the selection committee. He also highlighted that out of 605 gazetted appointments 188 were from Bengal, 115 were from Madras, and the rest were from other provinces. He again requested the prime minister to stop such a campaign of calumny and to ask for a list of all appointments by all ministries since Independence and the provincial distribution of the same.[39] There is no record of Prime Minister Nehru making any effort to seek such information from all the ministries. The bias against Bengal was evident from the very first ministry formed in Independent India. K.C. Neogy, who too was a minister in the same cabinet and had resigned along with Syama Prasad in protest against the Nehru-Liaquat agreement, had mentioned how the problems of refugees from West Pakistan received priority in Delhi while Bengal was neglected.

The unfair treatment of Bengal had several manifestations. When the issue of central grant to West Bengal for the relief and rehabilitation of the refugees came up, Chief Minister Bidhan Roy was always at the receiving end of red tape. Frustrated with the unequal treatment of West Bengal compared to those where refugees from West Punjab settled, Bidhan Roy wrote to Nehru on 1 December 1949,

> You are under the impression that your government gave us a large grant for the purpose of relief and rehabilitation. Do you realise that the total grant received for this purpose from your government in the two years 1948-49 and 1949-50 was a little over 3 crores, the rest about 5 crores was given in the form of loan? Do you realize that this sum is insignificant compared to what has been spent for refugees from West Pakistan?

In the same letter, accusing Nehru of a stepmotherly attitude, Roy was emotional about 'the exodus of 1.5 millions of people who belong to upper and middle class Hindu families, who came here hungry and starved, having lost all including their hope of finding subsistence in the new place.' He added,

> For months, the Government of India would not recognize the existence of refugee problems from East Pakistan, and

> therefore, would not accept the liabilities on their account. The provincial Government had to carry on as best as they could. And for these refugees, a magnificent sum of Rs.20/- per capita has been granted by the Centre in two years.[40]

Meanwhile in the 1950 election for the post of Congress presidentship Kripalani, supported by Nehru, contested against Purushottam Das Tandon, a candidate of Sardar Patel. Kripalani's loss reflected Patel's sway over the Congress party. A disheartened Kripalani quit the Congress and formed the Krishak Mazdur Praja party. His friend Dr Prafulla Chandra Ghosh left the Congress with him. Ghosh's departure removed one of the warring groups in West Bengal and weakened the Jugantar group considerably. In September 1950 when the election for PCC was due, the Jugantar group too did not put up a fight. Atulya Ghosh was elected as state Congress president unopposed. Finally the Hooghly group had won complete control over the Congress in West Bengal. Marcus F. Franda in a brief sketch on Atulya Ghosh wrote that the political organisation that he created in West Bengal was

> ... held together and motivated by desire for personal gain based more on personal gain rather than by political principle or ideology. It is dependent upon patronage, precinct workers and ward heelers, honest graft, ignorant and pliable voters, cohesion within the boss's faction, and all of the other phenomenon generally associated with machine politics.[41]

This tradition could be seen in non-Congress ruling parties later.

In the first three years after Independence it was clear that West Bengal kept on losing its importance in national politics. The small state of West Bengal did not match the huge influence that the undivided Bengal had over the national political scenario. Once electoral politics took root even before Independence, the strengthening of the Muslim vote bank and as a result consolidation of the Muslim League political power in Bengal resulted in the Indian National Congress losing its foothold in the state. What is more, with the arrival of Gandhi the Bengal leadership, beginning with Chittaranjan, had some issue of discord or the other with the national Congress ruled by Gandhi and his followers. The other reason for Bengal to lose its political weight was intense factional rivalry which was seen even before modern politics took root in India. The politics of Subhas Chandra Bose was more emotional than logical or strategic. Meanwhile even Chittaranjan Das on some occasions reconsidered his stand and reframed his steps. Subhas Chandra on occasions moved precariously breaching political discipline. His aggressive stance in 1939 not only harmed his own position in the national Congress but also ended any prominence Bengal had in the freedom movement despite it leading from the front even in the unregulated Quit India movement, the last flicker of freedom struggle that the Congress had led. Syama Prasad Mukherjee was not a freedom fighter nor was he from the Congress. His personality was more suited to parliamentary discourse than grassroot political movements. This was seen in the result of the 1946 elections when the Hindu Mahasabha fared miserably. Sarat Bose, another mighty personality, got lost in various political crosscurrents. Gandhians like Dr Prafulla Chandra Ghosh or Jugantar group leader Surendra Mohan could not form a greater coalition even within the province of Bengal. In politics it is the number that counts. Dr Bidhan Roy, too, was not exactly a *street* politician but rather a person with the ability to handle complex issues, best suited for parliamentary democracy. Thus when Bengal was looking for charismatic leaders to create a resistance of sorts to oppose the rising power of the

Muslim League, sadly there was nobody who could stand out. In addition, Gandhi's myopia and his dependence on his coterie of well-wishers such as G.D. Birla or Nalini Ranjan Sarkar, an eternal position seeker, did not allow Bengal to develop a robust coalition politics for the Hindu-dominated Congress. Bengal being a Muslim majority province, only a coalition could have helped the Congress to rule the state and perhaps counter the rising communal politics of the Muslim League. That Bengal was friendless could be seen during the famine in 1942-43 as also during the various communal riots which had been a regular occurrence in different parts of the province. For the Indian National Congress leaders the politics of the Hindi heartland was more important than faction-ridden Bengal. Thus when the most critical time in the life of Bengali Hindus came there was no tall leader to back them up in the arena of national politics. On the other hand, the leaders who emerged, Atulya Ghosh for instance, were busy scheming for the hegemony of their own group. In the process West Bengal suffered from its very birth.

Endnotes

1 Babulal Bala, "Congress in the Politics of West Bengal from Dominance to Marginality 1947-1977" (PhD., North Bengal University, 2017), https://shodhganga.inflibnet.ac.in/bitstream/10603/256841/11/11_chapter%202.pdf, http://hdl.handle.net/10603/256841.

2 https://www.gandhiashramsevagram.org/gandhi-literature/mahatma-gandhi-collected-works-volume-95.pdf.

3 Joya Chatterji, "The Fashioning of a Frontier: The Radcliffe Line and Bengal's Border Landscape, 1947-52" in *Modern Asian Studies* 33, no. 1 (1999), pp 185–242, www.jstor.org/stable/313155 (accessed May 27, 2020).

4 Ibid.

5 Ibid.

6 Ibid.

7 Majumdar, *Modern Bengal*, p. 340.

8 https://www.gandhiashramsevagram.org/gandhi-literature/mahatma-gandhi-collected-works-volume-96.pdf.

9 Ibid.

10 https://www.gandhiashramsevagram.org/gandhi-literature/mahatma-gandhi-collected-works-volume-98.pdf.

11 Ibid.

12 Basu, *Nirbachita Rachanasangraha* vol. 1, pp 62-4.

13 Prasanta Kumar Sen Gupta, *The Congress Party in West Bengal: A study in Factionalism 1947 to 67* (Calcutta University, 1982), http://hdl.handle.net/10603/165137.

14 Ibid.

15 Ibid.

16 Ibid. Sen Gupta has given details of the infighting in his above referred study.

17 Ibid.

18 Basu, *Nirbachita Rachanasangraha* vol. 1, pp 66-75.

19 Arpita Basu, *Udbastu Andolan o Punarbasati Samasamayik Patra Patrikaye* (Gangchil, 2013) – quoted from *Ananda Bazar Patrika*, March 6, 1948.

20 Bala, "Dominance to Marginality 1947-1977".

21 Richard L. Park, "Congress Defeat in West Bengal" in *Far Eastern Survey* 18, no. 15 (1949), pp 178–9, www.jstor.org/stable/3024356 (accessed June 3, 2020).

22 Ibid., and also see Sen Gupta, *The Congress Party in West Bengal.*

23 Basu, *Nirbachita Rachanasangraha*.

24 Madhav Khosla, ed., *Letters for a Nation: From Jawaharlal Nehru to his Chief Ministers 1947-1963* (Penguin Kindle edition, 2015); letter dated April 1, 1948.

25 Ibid.

26 For details check Joya Chatterji, "'Dispersal' and the Failure of Rehabilitation: Refugee Camp-Dwellers and Squatters in West Bengal" in *Modern Asian Studies* 41, no. 5 (2007), pp 995–1032, www.jstor.org/stable/4499809 (accessed January 28, 2021).

27 Subhasri Ghosh, "The Working of the Nehru Liaquat Pact: A Case Study of Nadia District, 1950" in *Proceedings of the Indian History Congress* 68 (2007), pp 853–62, www.jstor.org/stable/44147893 (accessed May 31, 2020).

28 https://mea.gov.in/Portal/LegalTreatiesDoc/PA50B1228.pdf.

29 Ghosh, "The Working of the Nehru Liaquat Pact".

30 https://nationalistspeeches.wordpress.com/2019/06/07/resignation-letter-of-syama-prasad-mookerjee/.

31 http://pibarchive.nic.in/archive/ArchiveSecondPhase/BROADCAST%20 TALKS/1950-JAN-DECBRODACAST-TALKS/PDF/BRO-1950-04-10_012.pdf.

32 http://pibarchive.nic.in/archive/ArchiveSecondPhase/BROADCAST%20 TALKS/1950-JAN-DECBRODACAST-TALKS/PDF/BRO-1950-04-21_017.pdf.

33 Debate in Lok Sabha on 27 February 1950 and quoted in Bala, "Dominance to Marginality 1947-1977".

34 Basu, *Udbastu Andolan* – quoted from *Ananda Bazar Patrika*, September 7, 1950.

35 https://www.spmrf.org/wp-content/uploads/2020/01/J-N-Mandal-Resignation-Letter.pdf.

36 https://wikilivres.org/wiki/Resignation_letter_of_Jogendra_Nath_Mandal.

37 Basu, *Udbastu Andolan* – quoted from *Ananda Bazar Patrika*, March 24, 1950.

38 Basu, *Udbastu Andolan* – quoted from *Ananda Bazar Patrika*, September 4, 1950.

39 Ray, *Dr Syama Prasad Mookerjee*, Kindle edition.

40 https://shodhganga.inflibnet.ac.in/bitstream/10603/256841/12/12_chapter%203.pdf.

41 Marcus F. Franda, "The Political Idioms of Atulya Ghosh" in *Asian Survey* 6, no. 8 (1966), pp 420–33, www.jstor.org/stable/2642469 (accessed June 1, 2020).

THE EARLY DAYS AND GROWTH OF THE OPPOSITION

Jyoti Basu was a major opposition leader in the West Bengal assembly despite there being just two members in the communist party and Basu being the only one who was articulate. After the ban imposed on the party was revoked Basu again became active in the assembly proceedings. His staunch criticism of the Bidhan Roy government on two bills – one on the Calcutta Corporation and the other on the Calcutta Tramways Company – were scathing. When the nation had decided on election on the basis of universal adult franchise, Roy opted for election for the Calcutta Corporation on the basis of restricted voter list. Strangely the election to the corporation took place in March 1952, that is, after the national election held on the basis of universal adult franchise. Looking at the parliamentary election results the worry of the West Bengal Congress over its support base in Calcutta seemed justified. Out of the four Lok Sabha constituencies Congress could bag only one – the Calcutta South West seat while the other three went to opposition Bharatiya Jana Sangh, CPI and RSP. However in the assembly election the Congress had managed to win majority of the Calcutta seats. The single most important factor in the first national election in West Bengal was the success of the communist party. Even after its ban and the arrest of its leaders including Jyoti Basu, a moderate and parliamentary communist, CPI could win 28 seats in the 238-member assembly. Certain big names in politics had to bite the dust. Important among them were Prafulla Chandra Sen from Arambagh constituency which elected two members and saw both INC nominees losing to an independent and a CPI candidate, and the other was former chief minister and KMPP leader Dr Prafulla Ghosh from Tollygunge North assembly constituency. Jyoti Basu won the Baranagar seat by a margin of nearly 22 per cent of valid votes cast, while the winning margin of Bidhan Roy from Bowbazar constituency was less, 17 per cent of total valid votes. Many thought that Bowbazar would prove to be tough for Bidhan Roy. In fact, he did not spend time campaigning in his constituency, busy as he was elsewhere. But in the last two days of the campaign he arranged a *padayatra* and managed to tilt the scale in favour of the Congress. Atulya Ghosh and Surendra Mohan Ghosh were elected to the Lok Sabha, as were Syama Prasad Mukherjee, N.C. Chatterjee, Tridib Chaudhury and Hiren Mukherjee. In West Bengal the two Hindutva parties Jan Sangh and Hindu Mahasabha won just 3 seats, while the Left parties CPI and RSP won 7 seats, and the remaining 21 seats went to the Congress. In the assembly election the Congress captured 150 seats out of 238, but its two ministers Prafulla Chandra Sen and Kalipada Mukherjee lost in the election. The success of the CPI was a setback for the Congress. The ban on the party was lifted only after the order of the Calcutta High Court that too just about a year before the election. Also many of its leaders were still behind bars, some even contested when on parole. Nevertheless, the CPI captured the second highest number of seats.

The election had seen formation of groups by the opposition in order to challenge the overpowering presence of the Congress. In West Bengal there were four major opposition groups: the Communist Party of India, the Jan Sangh led by Syama Prasad Mukherjee, United Socialist Block including KMPP, RCPI, Forward Bloc (Marxist) and the Bolshevik Party, and the fourth was the Socialist Party led by Jayaprakash Narayan and their allies like Forward Bloc and RCPI (Saumyendranath Tagore group). But they were united only in anti-Congressism and did not project either a common programme or a common campaign divided as they were by ideological and personal differences. Problems arose when Roy was forming his cabinet. The view of the Congress high command was that no defeated candidate should find place in the cabinet and Roy was adamant in accommodating at least two of them – Prafulla Sen and Kalipada Mukherjee. He got both elected through the Upper House, the council, and formed his ministry two months later despite opposition from Nehru. He also inducted Renuka Ray, who was also defeated in the Lok Sabha election, as refugee relief and rehabilitation minister. Jyoti Basu had been scathing in his criticism of the induction of defeated candidates in the cabinet through the backdoor of the Upper House.[1]

While Bidhan Roy had the charisma and control over the Congress party and had used the same effectively in managing the affairs of West Bengal, Jyoti Basu had developed into an effective parliamentarian creating difficulties for the ruling party in the state. The very fact that the West Bengal government had resorted to banning the communist party in the state, despite Nehru's reservations, illustrates how Bidhan Roy had viewed the CPI as an opposition. When the CPI emerged as the largest opposition party with the requisite number of seats to be recognised as the official opposition with Basu as the leader of opposition, the assembly speaker ruled that since the CPI did not have the number to form a government even in case the state government lost its majority, hence the party would not be recognised as official opposition party but suggested that the CPI could be accepted as the principal opposition party only.[2] Clearly democracy in West Bengal was what its top leader Chief Minister Bidhan Roy wanted. The Congress in the state had no qualms in suppressing any opposition inside or outside the assembly by reinterpreting rules and often enough, as was seen in the ban imposed on the CPI, violating the same. Dr Roy was a law unto himself and used to run the government as per his wishes. Jyoti Basu wrote bitterly about how the legislative session used to depend on the schedule of Dr Roy – got delayed or postponed based on his availability. There were hardly any rights of the opposition to raise questions, even if raised there was no guarantee that answers would be provided. On every Friday individual members could introduce private member's bills but the permission for the same depended on the whims of the speaker. Also there were no privileges of the members, no estimate committee where budgetary issues could be discussed and what was most glaring, according to Basu, was that Bidhan Roy used to speak on behalf of any minister even if the minister was present in the house. In short, Basu recounted how Dr Bidhan Roy used to trample over the well-laid-down parliamentary processes and ran the government completely based on his wishes.[3]

The stamp of Dr Roy's domination or maybe the complete nonchalance of Prime Minister Nehru was evident in the formation of the Central ministry. West Bengal's representative was Charu Chandra Biswas, minister of law and minority affairs, who was made a member of the Upper House, the Rajya Sabha though two senior leaders like Surendra Mohan Ghosh and Atulya Ghosh were elected to the Lok Sabha. Clearly a non-political person was eminently suitable both for the West Bengal chief minister and the prime minister. The same process was adopted even while forming the cabinet after the 1957 election. Perhaps due to the influence of Bidhan Roy the newly elected Lok Sabha member Asok Sen was appointed minister of state for law.

It was clear that in the first election post-Independence, the CPI emerged as the most successful opposition both in West Bengal and in the Lok Sabha. After the 356 seats won by the Congress, the CPI was the second political party with 16 seats – independents had won a total of 36 seats. Jyoti Basu had picked up the legislative process fast enough to emerge as an almost one-man army against the formidable chief minister of West Bengal. Basu knew well enough how to use the power of crowds mixed with his legislative intervention and put pressure on the government. Thus despite the wide gap between the Congress and the CPI in number, in the assembly Jyoti Basu emerged as a force to be reckoned with.

After the first national election Basu made an effort to bring the opposition together under a common programme. He had excluded Jan Sangh and Hindu Mahasabha and called upon all the rest of the political parties to join hands against the Congress government. Some of the common agenda included withdrawal of the draconian Peoples' Safety Act which helped the administration to arrest political opponents even without legal process, to put an end to the food crisis in the state, rehabilitation of the refugees and giving all refugees the right to citizenship, appointment of the governor through election, curbing the power of the government to issue ordinances when the assembly was not in session, etc. Clearly the CPI under the able leadership of Jyoti Basu in the legislature and Promode Dasgupta in organisation was looking for a long-term position in the politics of West Bengal. That the communists were a rising force was seen again in the municipal election held in Howrah and Calcutta immediately after the national polls. The Congress managed to win both – in Howrah the Congress got back the municipality from the United Progressive Bloc of the Left but in the Calcutta Corporation the margin of victory for the Congress shrunk to just 4 from 28 earlier. *The Economic Weekly* (predecessor of *Economic and Political Weekly* or *EPW*) in a weekly comment wrote that these 'two elections make it abundantly evident that the citizens of Calcutta dislike the Congress and the Congress administration'.[4]

The CPI came up with a smart move – during the period 1951-53 the CPI organised movements in favour of a consistent peace policy. Thus in early 1951 the party organised mass movements demanding withdrawal of foreign troops from Korea, withdrawal of all American troops from Taiwan, and recognition of the People's Republic of China as member of the United Nations. CPI even observed 24 August 1952 as 'sympathy day' for the struggling people of Malay. CPI leaders in numerous public meetings criticised Nehru's foreign policy. Then again 27 February 1953 was observed in West Bengal as 'halt Eisenhower day' and a procession of 5,000 people demonstrated against the arrival of four American warships which were returning from the Korean War in Calcutta and they burnt the effigy of Eisenhower. The CPI protested against the visit of US Secretary of State Dulles and supported 'Vietnam's Liberation struggle'. Whether such protests made any bit of difference globally or could make Prime Minister Nehru shift from his diplomatic stance were immaterial since such moves had tremendous appeal to Bengal's intellectuals and made them embrace the party warmly. The Congress was at a disadvantage since as the ruling party in the state and at the Centre it could not have used the romanticism of Bengal in adopting the causes of people of distant lands. The provincial committee of the CPI, on the other hand, took these peace movements seriously. It created one broad front 'Shanti Samsad' with representatives from all political parties, mass organisations and eminent citizens, and directed all party members within the peace movement to treat 'Shanti Samsad' as a mass front. The peace movement saw the CPI managing to bring together eminent scientists, doctors, teachers, poets and actors. As a result, the movement became very powerful in West Bengal and this in turn helped the CPI to increase its popularity among students, intellectuals and middle-class people in general.[5]

West Bengal politics was especially sensitive to the nature of relationship between India and East Pakistan. The Jan Sangh and Hindu Mahasabha concerned with the fate of the Hindus in East Pakistan were in favour of a stringent stance against Pakistan. In fact, some leftist parties, Forward Bloc, Revolutionary Socialist Party, Praja Socialist Party, were also in favour of an economic boycott of Pakistan. Curiously, the provincial committee of the CPI laid emphasis on normalisation of relations between India and Pakistan. In numerous meetings and signature campaigns the party urged the immediate withdrawal of the passport system between the two states. Perhaps the party sensed the sentimental attraction for a United Bengal and the belief among many that sooner than later the two Bengals would unite. This stance, though against the then prevailing political tide, had takers particularly among the middle class and Bengal's intellectuals. The peace committees for peace in distant lands that a Bengali could never visit and see only on maps, and the barrier-free border with East Pakistan were two important tools that helped the CPI to create a strong political foundation in the state.

Post-election, the CPI collaborating with other opposition parties organised movements on the crying issues of the day. Important among them were the food movement, struggle against enhanced tram fare and also the movement for increased pay by the school teachers. The food movement in 1952 was marred by the division of the movement into two blocs – one was CPI-led Khadya Avhijan Committee and the other led jointly by the Forward Bloc, RSP and KMPP called Sanjukta Durviksha Pratirodh Committee (SDPC). In a public meeting organised by SDPC on 7 June 1952, the CPI was invited to join but was not given the opportunity to speak. The opposition to the West Bengal Securities (Extension) Act was led by Jyoti Basu. The government claimed that the act was necessary to stop the CPI from collecting arms and engaging in violent movements. However the most noticeable movement was over the hike in tram fares in Calcutta. Calcutta Tramways Company was a British company which was granted a 20-year extension by the Bidhan Roy government in 1951. Jyoti Basu led a spirited debate against the benefits given to the British company and sought instead nationalisation of the asset. His objection was based on the fact that the agreement between the state government and the tram company was brought to the assembly for endorsement and that too with an understanding that there would be no changes made in the agreement reached. Basu read into this the British company's desire for a safeguard of sorts, calling the agreement not with the government but with the concurrence of the elected representatives as well.

In 1953 the tram company increased the second class tram fare by just one paisa – from three paise to four paise – or by 33 per cent. The opposition formed an anti-fare increase committee to lead the protest. For nearly a month Calcutta was in turmoil. The acting chief minister Prafulla Chandra Sen was so disturbed that he contacted Bidhan Roy who was then in Vienna for his eye operation. At one point it seemed that Roy would postpone his eye surgery and come back to Calcutta. On 1st July the increased fare was scheduled to be charged. People started picketing at the tram terminuses and they were also refusing to pay the increased fare. On the third day the situation escalated further. On 4th July a strike was called and the leaders of the movement – Jyoti Basu, Subodh Bandyopadhyay, Ganesh Ghosh et al. – were arrested. The tram company sought help from the police to stop the movement and this resulted in direct conflict between the people and the police. Some interesting aspects of the tram strike were the violence, the widespread participation of the young people from the refugee communities, and later a sort of competitive participation of the rowdies from the north and south of Calcutta. The movement had gone out of control even for the anti-fare movement committee which had to issue a statement against the violence. The tram company staff also joined the movement and stopped working. The tram fare movement brought back memories of revolutionary politics in Bengal during the freedom struggle. The only difference was that here the students and participants of the movement were fighting against their own elected government and police of Independent India. Both sides were hurling ammunitions against each other – the police were attacked with bricks, acid bulbs and bombs who in turn retaliated with liberal use of sticks and even firing at mobs. The movement had eased a bit towards the end of July but finally stopped when Bidhan Roy came back to Calcutta and met the leaders on 30th July. The proposed fare hike was stopped and finally trams started moving after the end of July. Tram fares were increased two years later.[6]

The movement, nicknamed movement of burning trams and buses, took a permanent shape in any peoples' movement in Calcutta since then. For six months after the tram-burning movement there was relative peace barring protests against shortages of food. But these paled in significance when the teachers hit the streets demanding a raise in their salaries. At that time a primary school teacher used to be paid Rs 37 per month in rural areas and Rs 43 in urban centres. The secondary school teachers used to receive Rs 60 out of which Rs 10 was as dearness allowance (DA). Though primary school teachers were worse off the movement of teachers started for rise in salary of secondary teachers under ABTA (All Bengal Teachers' Association). Teachers demanded a salary as per the recommendation of the Secondary Education Board and DA of Rs 35. On 10 February 1954, the teachers started an indefinite strike and from the next day onwards they started squatting on the eastern side of the Governor's House. It was declared that on 15th February they would move towards the Assembly House.

On that day the governor, Harendra Kumar Mukhopadhyay, was scheduled to address the assembly. The intention of the striking teachers was to hand over their memorandum to the governor. On 15th February the assembly of teachers increased manifold with many other teachers joining the strikers. Students, workers from the industrial sector and even ordinary citizens too joined the teachers in support. Jyoti Basu requested the governor to accept the memorandum from the teachers who were squatting on the street for five days at a stretch but the governor refused. Basu and other opposition leaders walked out of the governor's address and went to address the striking teachers. The movement took a dramatic turn with ordinary people expressing solidarity with the striking teachers. Food, fruits and other provisions were sent for the teachers, and even decorators came and erected tents for the teachers. It was transforming into a peoples' movement. On 16th February the teachers walked towards the Assembly House, where they were stopped by the police and suddenly the movement took a violent turn. When the movement was spiralling out of control, in the assembly the government announced a hike in salary of teachers which was accepted even by the opposition members. But by then the movement had turned violent. As was the trend then, street fight between police and the protesters stopped life in Calcutta, the police resorted to lathi charge and firing in response to the rowdies using bricks and bombs. Many teachers including the leaders of the movement were arrested. Finally on 21st February the movement was called off. Not that the teachers were happy at the rowdyism during the movement but by then the participation of the huge number of young unsettled refugees (at least five lakh of them were living in various refugee camps), had made Calcutta sit on a powder keg waiting to be detonated.[7] This became the nature of subsequent political movements in West Bengal.

The CPI used the traditional cultural heritage of Bengal effectively to build a strong foundation of the party. Given the plight of the people, since the famine in 1943, then the Partition and the resultant uprooted people, the plot was strong enough to arouse the sensitive souls of artists, writers, poets, dramatists, actors and all kinds of creative persons residing in West Bengal. The CPI channelised these sentiments effectively in creating an ideological movement to help its political expansion. Coupled with its peace initiative the party emerged as the choice of the Bengali intellectual like nationalism was at the dawn of political movement in India. When the ban on the party was revoked by an order of the Calcutta High Court, the CPI had to rebuild itself. Here the cultural wings like the Indian Peoples' Theatre Association (IPTA) and Progressive Writers' Association (PWA) played a critical role. By the end of 1951 a provincial preparatory committee of IPTA was formed in West Bengal. In 1953 (31s August and 1st September) a provincial conference was held at Naihati which adopted a resolution that called on writers and artists in West Bengal to join IPTA in creating a national culture and in combating illiteracy, superstition, communalism and provincialism. It was not confined to narrow provincialism but had the attractive spice of international causes like calling the creative persons to dedicate themselves to the causes of Asian and world peace and a culture based on the struggle of people for a better life. IPTA also resolved to work against the government crackdown on protesters in order to encourage them to join the movements which were in full flow then in West Bengal.

The West Bengal government was naturally concerned and imposed restrictions on the growing cultural activities of the IPTA using the British administration's Dramatic Performance Act of 1876. The police commissioner of Calcutta served a notice to the secretary of IPTA asking for printed manuscripts of 54 dramas staged by them. In the list were well-known writers and their equally famous stories – for instance *Mahesh* by Sarat Chandra Chattopadhyay, *Gora* and *Bisarjan* by Rabindranath Tagore, and *Nil Darpan* by Dinabandhu Mitra. Chief Minister Bidhan Roy in the assembly said that altogether details of 59 dramas were asked for in order to ascertain the character of the dramas and motivations of the CPI. He added that IPTA was governed by the CPI.[8] From the nature of the administrative steps it seems that the Congress government merely took over from the British administration without much change in the character of governance. Its inability to meet the aspirations of the people, particularly those of the refugees fleeing from East Pakistan and, what is more, its failure to form a considerate and sympathetic administration for the people to back it strongly turned into an adversarial relation with the intellectuals, at least a large section of them. It was a glaring political failure of the Congress as a political party in West Bengal particularly at a time when the chief minister was at the forefront of several developmental projects in the state. The Congress party under the leadership of Atulya Ghosh as Marcus F. Franda wrote was a party held together for personal gains not by ideology. The organisation that Ghosh oversaw depended 'on the ability to satisfy (and reconcile) private desires and interests of influential citizens throughout the state and does not hesitate to "starve" or "deprive" those politicians who refuse to cooperate with the wishes of the "boss" or the "ring".'[9]

The counter steps taken by the state administration merely helped the cause of the CPI and IPTA. In response the IPTA along with 50 theatre associations formed a broad committee called the 'United Drama Movement Committee' and organised seminars, meetings, and signature campaigns for the withdrawal of Dramatic Performance Act of 1876, sought exemption from amusement tax and pre-censorship, and demanded building of a national stage open to all without any bias regarding their ideology.

The CPI and its mass fronts and eminent personalities of West Bengal strongly criticised the police offensive of the government against cultural activists. Being agitated over the government's policy the IPTA in order to plant its roots in the very depths of the hearts of the people of West Bengal came out with innumerable cultural programmes directed against the establishment. Thus at the time of tram fare resistance movement the IPTA marched with the people with a poster drama on the current movement and performed every evening before the teachers squatting in Calcutta at the time of the teachers' movement. In order to foster the trend of radicalisation of the masses against the Congress Government in West Bengal, the IPTA came out with a number of programmes like Bhadu gan, Kabi gan, Ghetu gan, dance, Ballets like Ahalya - a story about the pregnant peasant woman who was killed by the police in the background of peasant movement in 1949, number of revolutionary songs, movies like Ritwik Ghatak's Dalil - a drama about a refugee family from East Pakistan and his struggle for existence, dramas like Bhuter Bhet of Purnendu Pal - an agitational sketch exposing the 'hypocrisy' of the Congress rule, Natak Nay - problems of the middle class society of the city, Annya and Akal - agitational sketches exposing the Government's policy during the food movement and struggle for existence against the backdrop of a famine, Haripada Master - depicting the aspiration and struggle of a school teacher and with a number of poster plays. These programmes of the IPTA helped the CPI and its mass fronts to penetrate among the masses.[10]

The violence in agitations had been a result of the frustration of the people who had failed to receive assistance from the state that they had hoped for. There were several instances of negligence and apathy particularly on the part of the central government. When during the winter session of 1952, Renu Chakravarty, CPI Lok Sabha member from Basirhat, raised the issue of notice to vacate served on refugees living at Bandhavnagar Colony at Dum Dum, the rehabilitation minister A.P. Jain called it an attempt to seek publicity by the member. Syama Prasad Mukherjee strongly condemned the effort of the central minister to trivialise the plight of the refugees struggling to 'rerail' their lives. Even the deputy speaker who was presiding at that time took umbrage at the frivolous remark made by the minister. Clearly the rehabilitation of Bengal's refugees was not priority for the Union ministry and even voices of elected representatives – cutting across party lines – were muzzled.[11] Syama Prasad presided over a conference of All India Displaced Persons held in December 1952 and mentioned the plight of an estimated 45 lakh persons evicted from East Bengal. Not only had the government failed to rehabilitate the refugees, there were many instances of eviction of hawkers from the streets and subjecting them to penalties and even jail terms as per the amended provision of Bengal Highways Act of 1925. These short-sighted policies acted as the precursors of the last rites of the Congress party in the state.[12]

The influx of refugees into an already densely populated West Bengal created the twin problems of rehabilitation of the huge number of displaced persons and creating suitable employment opportunities for the people. The state government had bitter exchanges with the Centre. Nevertheless the support from the central government fell short of the requirements. A comparison of the Centre's rehabilitation record for the refugees from West Punjab created additional heartburn in West Bengal. The province which had a tendency to tread along its own course even during the freedom struggle and had drifted apart from the mainstream Congress leadership had good reasons to move further away from the mainstream national politics. The failure of the newly created Bharatiya Jana Sangh (BJS) by Syama Prasad, a champion of East Bengal Hindus, to create a firm base in West Bengal needs some introspection. In 1952 out of the three seats the party could win, two were from West Bengal. But this was more due to Syama Prasad's presence than any faith the Bengalis had in BJS. In any case BJS was a new experiment to create a political alternative to the Congress that would uphold the cause of the Hindus. RSS chief Guru Golwalkar and Mukherjee sorted out various issues and the party was created. One must acknowledge Syama Prasad did not join politics through any political movement, rather his was a lateral entry into politics. He was an effective parliamentarian but for creating a national political party Syama Prasad lacked the necessary skill in Hindi. In any case his unfortunate and suspicious death in J&K ended a promising opposition in India's parliament. He was the last Bengali who stood tall in the parliamentary politics of the nation. Also West Bengal was too preoccupied with its survival because of the complicated socio-economic problems posed by the Partition and therefore politicians who came to prominence during those days used to focus on West Bengal only. For the opposition, particularly the rising CPI, it was quite logical since their influence was confined to certain pockets of the country. Also they neither had the resources nor the ability to match the tall politicians in other states, particularly to dent in any manner the image of Jawaharlal Nehru. In West Bengal they had another charismatic personality to contend with but Bidhan Roy was more into administration and managing the assembly than grassroot politics which was assigned to Atulya Ghosh. Therefore the communists had an opportunity here to strengthen their political base further.

The State Reorganisation Commission appointed in 1953 submitted its report on 30 September 1955. Earlier Bidhan Roy had argued that a part of Bihar – districts of Purnea, Singbhum, Manbhum and Santhal Paragana – and Assam – Goalpara district – should be made part of West Bengal so as to help the state administration and also partly solve the state's problem of population pressure worsened by influx of refugees. While discussions were on to sort out disputes over the allocation of parts of Bihar districts to West Bengal, the chief minister of Bihar (Srikrishna Sinha) and that of West Bengal agreed to merge the two states and call it Purva Pradesh. Even Prime Minister Nehru and the CWC welcomed the foresight of the two leaders. A movement against this merger started in West Bengal. West Bengal called for a bandh on 24th February while the Bihar assembly approved the proposal the very next day by an overwhelming majority. Meanwhile two bye-elections to the Lok Sabha from West Bengal had been scheduled – one was Midnapore and the other Calcutta North. Asok Sen, a lawyer close to Bidhan Roy, was the Congress candidate in Calcutta. Mohit Moitra, the secretary of the anti-merger committee, contested the seat with support from the opposition including the CPI. Bidhan Roy had turned the election into a referendum of sorts for the merger. Asok Sen lost the seat by a huge margin and Roy promptly suspended the merger proposal. Based on the recommendation of the Reorganisation Commission, the Purulia subdivision of Manbhum and parts of the Kishengunj subdivision of Purnia were handed over to West Bengal.

Anti-Congress sentiments shrouded the outcome of the second national election in 1957. The most striking feature of the election was how the chief minister of West Bengal Dr Bidhan Chandra Roy just managed to scrape through from his home constituency of Bowbazar. Many old Left leaders who were part of the student wing of the undivided communist party then had claimed that it was an orchestrated rigging by the Congress helped by Gopal Mukherjee, a known businessman of the Bowbazar area (dealing in goat meat and also known for creating the Hindu resistance force during the 1946 great Calcutta riot), that finally tilted the scale in favour of Roy. The opposition candidate was Md. Ismail of the CPI who polled 15,010 votes against 15,550 of Dr Roy. Postal votes tilted the scale for Bidhan Roy. There may be some truth in the role of Gopal Mukherjee since he had taken an active part in the campaign with the chief minister. Due to his presence the Muslims stayed away from casting votes for the Congress. The atmosphere in the constituency was tense – rumours floated that if Md. Ismail won he would be the chief minister and West Bengal would merge with Pakistan. All these baseless rumours helped Bidhan Roy to somehow retain his seat.[13] The other interesting outcome was the electoral loss of the Congress in Calcutta. The party could win just 8 seats while CPI bagged 12, PSP won 4, independents 3 and Forward Bloc (M) 1. In 1957 the CPI bagged 46 seats with the Congress taking 152 out of the total 252 seat assembly.[14] The combined strength of the opposition was 100 and Basu became the leader of the opposition, a position denied to him in 1952. In the Lok Sabha, the Congress could bag only 1 seat from Calcutta out of 4, 2 went to the CPI, and 1 to an independent candidate who defeated the Congress candidate from Calcutta South West constituency. Out of 36 seats in West Bengal, the Congress won 23 and the CPI 6 in the second Lok Sabha.[15] The election result revealed how the Congress had lost its appeal in Calcutta and surrounding areas while it retained its appeal in the districts. In the central cabinet Asok Sen joined as minister of state for law. There was no minister of cabinet rank from West Bengal. The CPI had bagged 26 Lok Sabha seats but its maximum number (9) came from Kerala. In fact, in Kerala the Left had formed the first non-Congress government after the second national election. Politically West Bengal's influence remained on the fringes.

One reason for the success of the Congress in rural areas could be agricultural reforms undertaken by the state government. In 1953

Zamindari Acquisition Act and in 1955 Land Reforms Act were passed. Provisions were made to protect the share croppers. Peasants in West Bengal were satisfied with abolition of the Permanent Settlement and this was reflected in the Congress success in the districts during the 1957 polls.

The Nehru government's decision to transfer a part of Jalpaiguri district – a four square km land – Berubari – to Pakistan was another instance of rift between West Bengal and the national government. Prime Minister Nehru arrived at an agreement with the Pakistan Prime Minister Feroze Khan Noon in 1958 which provided among other things for 'Exchange of enclaves on the basis of enclaves for enclaves without any consideration of territorial loss or gain' (9th Amendment of Constitution act, 1960, Article I and Part I of First Schedule). As a result of this agreement Dahagram and Angorpota came to Indian territory and resulted in transfer of 11.29 sq. kms of southern half of Berubari to Pakistan. There was vehement opposition in West Bengal. Nehru had justified his decision on the basis of 'recommendation of revenue officers of West Bengal'. But this was not true. Bidhan Roy had to issue a clarification in the West Bengal assembly that revenue officers had no role in giving such recommendations nor were they empowered to do so. A unanimous resolution of the West Bengal assembly was sent to Prime Minister Nehru against the handing over of the state territory to Pakistan. When the two houses of the Lok Sabha and the Rajya Sabha passed the amendment bill all elected members of the Congress including Asok Sen, the law minister, stayed away. In any case international treaties, according to the Constitution, rest with the central government with states having no authority. Thus despite its opposition West Bengal could not influence the two agreements signed by Nehru – one with Liaquat Ali Khan in 1950 and the other (though of not similar significance) with Feroze Khan Noon in 1958. This difference between the Centre and the state raised its head in subsequent years also – river-water sharing for example.

Food crisis was a nagging problem in West Bengal since the 1940s. Even after Independence the scarcity of food refused to die down. In fact, food shortage was looming large in many parts of India as well. Bidhan Chandra had earlier managed the crisis by rationing food grains, a move that was removed in 1955. In 1958 the food crisis started worsening and the opposition formed a Price Rise and Famine Prevention Committee. A political embarrassment for Dr Roy was the sudden resignation of Judicial Minister Siddhartha Shankar Ray who strongly criticised the management of the food crisis and attributed the reason for the base and inefficient nature of administration to the base and inefficient nature of the leadership. He resigned from his Bhowanipore assembly seat and contested it supported by the opposition. He won the seat with increased margin. Taking advantage of the resignation of the minister the opposition brought in a no-confidence motion. Jyoti Basu in his speeches had attacked the food minister Prafulla Sen. Even Siddhartha Shankar Ray in his resignation had criticised Sen. The no-confidence motion was defeated by voice vote due to the huge majority of the government. But the motion and the charges by the opposition tainted the state government. The food crisis worsened due to lack of rainfall across the country. The government attempted to impose levy and bought rice from farmers and resorted to mass distribution of food. But the price fixed on levy rice was lower than the ruling market and farmers and rice mill owners started hoarding rice. This led to a sharp rise in food price as well as an increase of scarcity. The government even attempted to remove levy and restrictions on the food market but already the price had sky-rocketed. People started migrating to cities from villages in search of food. Due to the famine-like situation the food minister Prafulla Sen started being called the Famine Minister. The entire opposition joined hands in the movement for food.

On 31st August the opposition called for a rally which was attended mostly by people coming from the villages. After the rally a procession moved towards the Writers' Building, the administrative headquarter of the government. Top leaders were either arrested or went underground to avoid getting arrested. Like the earlier movements – anti-tram fare increase and salary increase for teachers – this too turned violent with matching police brutality. The food movement played a significant role in shaping up the politics of West Bengal. The administration was much more harsh on the protesters than the earlier two occasions. The most interesting overview of the food movement was provided in the *Economic Weekly* issue dated September 12, 1959.

> When the Price Increase and Famine Resistance Committee, an uneasy combination of parties and individuals in the Opposition in the West Bengal Legislative Assembly, first thought of launching, or reviving, a campaign against the Government, the price of rice was in fact rising. By the time the movement got moving, in which there was delay ... prices were in fact falling. As the 'Statesman' wrote, there was by then no famine to resist.[16]

Even Jyoti Basu in his reminiscences had accepted that when the movement was launched the situation was improving and the administration had initiated release of prisoners. The movement was primarily political and had served, at least the politicians felt, interests of all political elements. For the opposition was divided – they were on different sides of the fence in Kerala where the coalition government led by the CPI was dismissed by the Centre. But not the entire opposition group in West Bengal was part of the dismissed CPI-led coalition. Evidently for the CPI it was politically imperative to show that Kerala was not the only issue they were up against – the food movement therefore came as an opportunity. For the other opposition parties the food movement was a plank they had refused to hand over to the CPI, as has been mentioned earlier when in the Calcutta rally over food scarcity the CPI representative did not receive an opportunity to make an address.

The movement was characterised by lack of organisation as well as any plan of action on the part of the opposition leadership. Most of the leaders were either in hiding or behind bars while people enticed by their shrill oratory ended up as victims of brutal lathi charge by the police. Many villagers who came to join the rally had to bear the brunt while the ruffians managed to hurl brickbats, soda bottles and bombs at the police who retaliated with lathi, tear gas and firing at mobs. Setting fire to trams, buses and ambulances was a patented activity of any movement in Calcutta by then. 'Citizens of Calcutta have learnt to take such things in their stride and give them no more than a passing thought. Such things have happened before and will happen again,' opined the *Economic Weekly*. Even the prime minister called Calcutta the nightmare city, perhaps with sufficient justification. The situation was explained succinctly by the *Economic Weekly*.

> The Opposition's demand is moderate; it only wants a separation between Prafulla Sen and the portfolio of food. The Government is weak because not only have all its policies failed but its Ministers also are unrespected. It had better be known that non-Bengalis think more of Dr B C Roy than Bengalis, who know him better. As for P C Sen, he is not thought of - except as someone to be got rid of. The Congress

> Party? It recently reminded the people of its continued existence by issuing a pamphlet on the misdeeds of the Communist Party of India, some of them going back to what now seems pre-history. The Congress Party's deeds have been so conspicuous by their absence (or invisibility) that Atulya Ghosh really had to fall back upon this trick. It didn't work, as indeed Atulya Ghosh would have known if he were not so singularly ignorant of what Bengalis think today. Let me sum it up in one short sentence: There is not a single institution or individual in Bengal today that the Bengali instinctively loves or respects.[17]

The *Calcutta Diary* summed up the condition of West Bengal –

> The Government, the Corporation, the University — these are the dominant institutions in the bourgeois world of Calcutta, and they are all rotten. Dr Roy has the largest Ministry of all State Governments in India, and the record of the Government is impressive only in the matter of multiplying the State's problems … There are few creative channels in which the energy of the Bengali (which is greater mentally than physically) can find opportunities of flowing … The Bengali has no sense of participation in what Nehru calls the mighty adventure of building the new India. He Is 'The Outsider' in Indian life today. And In only recites Yeats's terrible line: 'Things fall apart; the centre cannot hold.'[18]

This was written in September 1959. Since then more than 60 years have elapsed.

The resignation of Siddhartha Shankar Ray as judicial minister in the West Bengal cabinet opened up another round of factional fight within the state Congress. A group of Congressmen contended that the Hooghly group which was managing the party uninterruptedly since Independence had kept its eyes shut in matters of corruption and also that the party had failed to win popular support. The group came to be known as the Ginger group which wanted to 'revitalise' the Congress by reducing the dominance of the Hooghly group within the PCC. Evidently the members of the Ginger group had realised that complete dominance of the Hooghly group would hamper their prospect within the party. Among the Ginger group members were Pratap Chandra Chunder, Jehangir Kabir, Jagannath Kolay, Kanailal Goswami and others, composed of Congressmen from different parts and it was not a very cohesive faction. Unlike the other previous factions like the Gandhians or the Jugantar group these members were not together just because of their loyalty to a single leader but because they wanted to curb the domination of the Hooghly group for their political future. The Ginger group approached the Congress central leadership with their grievances. But this did not help them much since the Hooghly group had the blessings of the charismatic Dr Roy, the chief minister, and was managed by the wily Atulya Ghosh as the state PCC president. Around that time the election for state Congress was due by the end of 1958. When Nehru's attention was drawn to the fact that Atulya Ghosh and Bijoy Singh Nahar had been PCC president and state PCC secretary respectively for nearly 10 years, he accepted that rotation of leadership was good in principle though he was satisfied with the good work of the PCC president. The CWC advised all members of parliament who were office bearers of PCCs to vacate one post following which Atulya Ghosh resigned and with him another 18 PCC executive committee members also submitted their resignations.

The Ginger group was not a cohesive group and lacked widespread support. It was easy for the Hooghly group to manipulate the outcome of the new PCC executive committee election. The choice of the Hooghly Group was Bijoy Singh Nahar as president but the Ginger group wanted a neutral leader. Both the groups met Dr Roy and agreed to elect Jadavendranath Panja, a veteran Congressman from Burdwan, as the president. Though Panja was not associated with any group he knew who called the shots and chose his team accordingly. Atulya Ghosh became a vice president, Nahar the treasurer. The Ginger group failed in its objective of loosening the stranglehold of the Hooghly group in the PCC.

The allegations against the state government was summed up by Jyoti Basu during his speech on no-confidence motion in 1958. He had explained how electoral malpractices helped the ruling party leaders to win their seats. An example was how election dates were fixed. The Congress, Basu alleged, had clear ideas on which seats they might lose. Accordingly with support from the electoral officer the election dates were fixed. Basu alleged that the date of election for Calcutta was placed at the end and its results also were last to be announced. The reason could be that the Congress knew the opposition would win many seats in Calcutta metropolitan areas. 'Had the results come earlier and we would have gone to the rural West Bengal with those success reports, Congress would have been sitting in the opposition today,' said Basu.[19] Basu also pointed out how funds got sanctioned for the benefit of select constituencies from where senior leaders of the Congress contested. Prafulla Sen was singled out by Basu. In 1956-57 when there was an estimated shortage of three lakh tonnes of food grains the food minister had earmarked a sum of six and a half crore rupees. But after the elections were over, for 1958-59 the allocation was just above Rs 14 lakh for meeting a shortfall of seven lakh tonnes of food grains. From this Basu alleged that the excess amount allotted for less procurement was to incentivise the election-funding machinery of the ruling party. There was more. A sum of Rs 2 lakhs was sanctioned for spending in the Hooghly district – out of this Rs 1.90 lakh was spent in Khanakul constituency where Prafulla Sen was the candidate. In addition the food minister sanctioned installation of 296 tube wells out of which 226 went to Khanakul. Basu had also cited instances of nepotism when work was allotted to people known to the chief minister even flouting norms surrounding tenders. In short, by the time of the second national election in West Bengal, the opposition had cited several instances of misuse of government money to facilitate victory of the ruling party candidates.[20]

The third general election in 1962 too was a smooth sailing for the Congress. But this time the charismatic chief minister Dr Bidhan Chandra Roy did not take any chances and contested from two constituencies – Saltora in Bankura district and Chowringhee in Calcutta. He had switched over from his Bowbazar constituency which he had barely retained in 1957. Bijoy Singh Nahar was nominated from Bowbazar which he won without much ado. Bidhan Roy won both the seats, the media called it 'scoring a double'. The Congress maintained its record, in fact it won 157 seats in a 252-member assembly, 5 better than in 1957. What is more, the 28 constituencies in Calcutta tracked here above in 1957 returned more Congress candidates in 1962. Against 8 in 1957, the Congress won 15 seats. The CPI won 9, 3 less than in 1957. The CPI had improved its position but marginally – it won 50 seats. Before the election the CPI had formed the United Left Front in electoral alliance with Forward Bloc, RSP, RCPI and Bolshevik Party. They bagged 72 seats. But in 1962 the Congress continued to maintain its electoral supremacy in the state. It also bagged 22 out of 36 seats in the Lok Sabha from West Bengal. The year 1962 saw the passing away of Dr Bidhan Chandra Roy in July and Prafulla Chandra Sen, the much-vilified food (famine) minister, taking over the mantle of the state. Since Sen was the number two in the Roy cabinet there was no problem with the transition. Dr Bidhan Chandra Roy had steered the political fortunes of the Congress effectively during some of the most troublesome years of the newly partitioned state.

This was when the communist party was having internal differences over what should be its political approach in India. Amidst the differences in views the election result was not satisfactory with the party winning just 29 seats, two more than what it did in 1957. The electoral outcome was not very encouraging in West Bengal also. The loss of seats which the CPI had bagged in 1957 to the Congress in Calcutta and other urban and industrial locations was disheartening. But the fact that the CPI could penetrate in rural areas where it failed in 1957 was encouraging. The leftist parties were in the majority in the districts of Burdwan, Birbhum and Cooch Behar. This was due to the party acting on its slogan of 'turn your faces to the villages' and sending 'students-squad to the villages'. While the CPI in West Bengal had managed somewhat to overcome its urban bias and also to penetrate the villages, the party realised its organisational weaknesses in urban centres of Calcutta, Howrah and 24 Parganas. The ideological differences that were seen in party congresses could be a reason. In the West Bengal provincial council Promode Dasgupta placed a 'Draft Report on Party organisation in West Bengal' in which 40 members joined the deliberations. It was mentioned in the draft that there were some differences of opinion on some vital issues within the party, and also how revisionist bourgeois outlook had infiltrated the party. The document gave a call of relentless ideological struggle in all mass-fronts against the danger of revisionism. The document urged to build up the party organisation and cadres in a conscious way and to change the class composition of the party by recruiting more and more members from the working class and poor peasants. It claimed that building up of the peasant movement and peasant organisation was the main task of the party. Clearly it was a move to change its focus from urban and industrial bases to farmers and rural areas – a decision that helped the communists in no small way. At the same time, the West Bengal unit decided to strengthen its trade unions and circulated a draft document on the trade union activities.[21] Meanwhile the border clashes with China rattled the communists. The CPI executive committee of West Bengal asked its members to remain vigilant over price rise and black marketing taking advantage of the war. But the National Council of the CPI had differences over what should be the party's stance on the Indo-China border clashes. While the CPI National Council adopted a resolution calling all to 'unite to defend our motherland against China's open aggression', a section within the party wanted a peaceful settlement of the dispute and to stop anti-China hysteria. There were differences of views on the issue of importing arms from abroad – while the resolution supported it, the opponents felt that this move would make India dependent on imperialist powers. Jyoti Basu called for minimisation of discord. The West Bengal CPI was not exactly in agreement with the party's National Council resolution and opted to pursue an independent course. Promode Dasgupta adopted a tactical line which included participation in mass committees for the defence of the nation and pressing for release of communists booked under the preventive detention act. It was felt that this would give the party an opportunity to tell people what their view was on the border issue.

But the West Bengal chief minister Prafulla Sen was not humoured by this gesture. He made it amply clear that no CPI representatives would be part of the 'Deshraksha Committee' and increased police raids on and arrests of CPI leaders and activists. During the course of November 1962 almost all of the members of the state secretariat and two-thirds of the state council were arrested under the Defence of India Rules. The Congress, PSP and other anti-communist forces launched an anti-communist campaign and in numerous places CPI offices were ransacked. The communists in West Bengal faced a new problem to contend with. Simple anti-Congressism would not be sufficient for the communists to contest the supremacy of the party in the polls. The other interesting point to note is that even in the communist party, where discipline receives more attention than other political parties including in the Congress, Promode Dasgupta, a brilliant political strategist, opted to deviate from the central guideline and create his own standard operating process. That West Bengal did not share similar political thoughts as the rest of the country was clear to Dasgupta.

> The West Bengal Council thought that anti-Chinese hysteria would accelerate the crisis and the Western military aid even on commercial terms would make India dependent on the imperialist powers. The West Bengal unit, therefore, emphasized the urgent need of peaceful settlement of the disputes through discussions and negotiations. The National Council thought that the West Bengal Council in the name of 'peaceful discussion' was defying the all-India Resolution. The West Bengal Council thought that by extending uncritical and unqualified support to the Nehru Government on the border war the national leadership was following a new tactical line, repudiating its earlier adopted line, of general united front with the Congress. In other words, there was a 'general inclination in the provincial party organisation in West Bengal towards a stand in opposition to the one advocated by the all-India Party'.[22]

Even within the Congress similar tendencies were seen when West Bengal protested against handing over of Berubari or when the CWC had failed to impose its decisions on many occasions to change the leadership of the state government. In matters of dissension AICC had always remained loyal to the ruling coteries of the PCC. The failure of right-wing national parties like the Hindu Mahasabha and the Jan Sangh or even socialist ones like the PSP to create a strong base in West Bengal was for want of a charismatic face in their parties or the refusal to take up Bengal-specific issues to attract mass support. Politics in West Bengal was dominated by local issues primarily even in the early years of its independence.

The West Bengal State Council of the CPI felt that the party's central council was tilting towards the viewpoints of the Soviet communist party. It is not that there was unanimity in the West Bengal CPI. There were leaders like Bhawani Sen, Somnath Lahiri, Renu Chakraborty, Biswanath Mukherjee, Geeta Mukherjee, Indrajit Gupta, etc., who favoured political cooperation with the progressive section of the Congressmen. For them Nehru was a progressive leader and needed support. They supported the government's stand on Indo–China armed clash in 1962. They were viewed as the 'Right faction' of the West Bengal CPI. The other and dominant set of opinions were led by Promode Dasgupta, Harekrishna Konar, Muzaffar Ahmed, Niren Ghosh, Benoy Choudhury, Charu Majumdar, Ratanlal Brahaman et al. who belonged to the 'Left faction' of the CPI. They were against any cooperation with the bourgeoisie and the Congress, and favoured the stand of the Chinese Communist Party on certain issues. In the state the 'Left faction' was stronger than the 'Right'. The restive nature of Bengal's political culture and ready acceptance of agitational activities made it easy for the Left of the CPI to build up a strong base in the state. But between these two positions there was a third section which was called 'vacillating' by the Leftists. Prominent among them was Jyoti Basu. These leaders were against any cooperation with the Congress but found merit in both the

'Rightist' and the 'Leftist' viewpoints. It was easy for the Leftists to win over the vacillating group led by Jyoti Basu since many of the leaders belonging to the Left group were arrested under the Defence of India rule. Also, Chief Minister Prafulla Sen did not let the CPI join the 'Deshraksha Committee'. The strong adversarial personal relation between Sen and Basu, as was seen on many occasions in the debates in the West Bengal assembly, too, perhaps made Basu shun the 'Rightists'. The most prominent opposition leader of West Bengal's move towards the Leftists had strengthened the party and they could issue a formidable challenge to the Rightists within the CPI. But the central leaders of the CPI did not accept the indiscipline of the West Bengal 'Left' group. The elected provincial secretariat and the state council were dissolved, and a new 7-member secretariat and Provincial Organising Committee (POC) was formed with the 'Right faction' under the patronage of the central leaders.

While the Left faction was working from inside and outside the jails, it blamed the newly appointed POC for working as per the wishes of the West Bengal government. Their mutual distrust escalated and the CPI was almost on the verge of a split. The question was how would this affect the two factions politically. But that was a distant issue at that point in time caught as the party was in stringent anti-communist campaign in the background of the Sino–India war. Chief Minister Sen along with PSP, a major opposition party then in the state, lost no opportunity to harm the political prospect of the communist party. Sen had a score to settle also and did not let go of the opportunity.

The 10-year period of legislative politics of West Bengal had clearly established that the CPI succeeded in channelising the grievances of the people to its advantage. The party had skilfully used the economic issues faced by a group of people for creating broad-based political agitation both inside and outside the assembly. The CPI had used well-known persons of the day who were not party members to head many committees created to lead peoples' movements. Thus eminent persons like Dr Meghnad Saha, Hemanta Kr Bose, Amar Bose and Mohit Maitra who were not associated with the CPI at that time were made presidents or secretaries of movement committees. The party had used a bottom-up approach in raising issues – generating public opinion through its local leadership and local organisations and bringing the same to the capital city of Calcutta and the assembly floor. Their policy received a boost due to the short-sighted policies of the ruling Congress. The administration treated all issues as simple law-and-order problems and used police force which helped the hooligans to join the street fight. The pent-up frustration among the people who had to leave their homes in East Pakistan and who were still living in abject conditions found expression in violence against the administration. It was seen on certain occasions that when Chief Minister Dr Roy had shown a reconciliatory approach the agitation could be tackled easily. But similar leadership was lacking among the other leaders of the Congress which had helped the politically savvy Left leaders to capture the political initiative. The CPI was also keen on forming a broad-based opposition alliance against the Congress. Immediately after the first general election Jyoti Basu had made this intention clear through a media statement. Even during the first national election when the CPI had just regrouped after a near 2-year ban it attempted to form an electoral alliance against the Congress.

The CPI-led electoral alliance, namely, United Socialist Organisation of India comprising FB, SRP, BPI, was the largest opposition group in the assembly and had secured 42 seats in total, out of which the CPI bagged 28 seats. The alliance received 27.5 per cent of valid votes out of which the CPI's share was 10.76 per cent. The alliance formed at the time of the first general elections was also carried forward in the election of autonomous bodies and mass movements were organised. But two Left parties namely RSP and PSP were outside the alliance and they joined the CPI-led electoral alliance only in the second general elections.

The United Left Election Committee had RSP, FB, FB(M), SRP, BPI and PSP and emerged as the only political platform of all opposition parties against the Congress in West Bengal. As a result of the inclusion of RSP and PSP in this front, the support base of the electoral alliance improved and the alliance secured 75 seats out of which 46 seats went in favour of the CPl. The Front got 36.8 per cent of the total valid votes, out of which the share of the CPI was 17.8 per cent. The third general elections of 1962 were held at a time when on the question of border dispute between China and India, the relation of the CPI with other Left political parties was getting tense and difference of opinion on various issues harmed the alliance formation. The United Left Front led by the CPI was formed with RSP, FB, FB(M), RCPI and Bolshevik Party but PSP did not join it. The alliance secured 63 seats with the CPI winning 50 of them. The United Left Front won 36.1 per cent of the total valid votes, marginally less than in 1957, but the CPI improved its share to 25.2 per cent. Clearly when Dr Roy passed away, the CPI had emerged as the major political rival for the Congress. With the split in the CPI the balance was expected to move back in favour of the Congress but there were other political developments in the offing.

Endnotes

1 Basu, *Nirbachita Rachanasangraha* vol 1, p. 98.

2 Ibid.

3 Ibid.

4 https://www.epw.in/system/files/pdf/1957_9/14/calcutta__verdict.pdf.

5 Susanta Bhattacharyya, 'The CPI and Radicalisation of Politics in West Bengal 1950_1962', http://hdl.handle.net/10603/65827 https://shodhganga.inflibnet.ac.in/bitstream/10603/65827/8/08_chapter%203.pdf.

6 Sandip Bandyopadhyay, *Bikhhuvdha Bangla – Paschimbanger Birodhi Rajniti (1947-2007)* (Radical Impression, 2014), pp 30-7.

7 Ibid.

8 Bhattacharyya, 'The CPI and Radicalisation of Politics in West Bengal'.

9 Marcus F. Franda, "The Political Idioms of Atulya Ghosh" in *Asian Survey* 6, no. 8 (1966), pp 420–33, www.jstor.org/stable/2642469 (accessed June 6, 2020).

10 Bhattacharyya, 'The CPI and Radicalisation of Politics in West Bengal'.

11 Basu, *Udbastu Andolan* – quoted from *Ananda Bazar Patrika*, December 7, 1952.

12 Basu, *Udbastu Andolan* – quoted from *Dainik Basumati*, November 11, 1953.

13 Bandyopadhyay, *Bikhhuvdha Bangla*, p. 54.

14 Election Commission Statistical Report on General Elections 1957.

15 Ibid.

16 https://www.epw.in/system/files/pdf/1959_11/37/things_fall_apart_the_centre.pdf7.

17 Ibid.

18 Ibid.

19 Jyoti Basu's speech in the assembly on 27 March 1958 reprinted in Basu, *Nirbachita Rachanasangraha*, vol 1, pp 146-73.

20 Ibid.

21 http://shodhganga.inflibnet.ac.in:8080/jspui/handle/10603/65827.

22 Bhattacharyya, 'The CPI and Radicalisation of Politics in West Bengal'.

DISCONTENT SPREADS ACROSS THE STATE

The split in the CPI went through an acrimonious process to finally materialise in 1964. In a last-ditch effort the two factions met at the residence of Bhupesh Gupta in Delhi. The anti-establishment group was represented by E.M.S. Namboodiripad, who was then party general secretary, Promode Dasgupta, Jyoti Basu and Harkishan Singh Surjeet. But the Shripad Amrit Dange-led establishment was adamant and demanded that first the dissenters would have to accept their conditions before initiating any negotiation. Anil Biswas wrote that after this the two factions moved along their own designated courses.[1] Thirty-two members of the CPI National Council left the meeting and called for establishing the 'true' communist party of India. In July 1964 the splinter group met at Tenali in Andhra Pradesh and decided to hold their 7th party congress sometime in October 1964 in Calcutta. The congress held between 31st October and 7th November decided to form the 'true' communist party, and thus ending 10-year-long ideological differences (1954-64), the Communist Party of India (Marxist) known as the CPI(M) was formed. In 1963-64 when the party was going through the split, its candidate Binoy Chaudhury won the Burdwan assembly seat in a bye-election. Binoy Chaudhury was part of the group that split and called itself the CPI(M).

One issue that had escalated the rift with the CPI was the letters written by S.A. Dange to the viceroy – these were published in the magazine *Current* (March 7, 1964). The party alleged that these letters were fake while three members led by Jyoti Basu inspected the documents. The letters written in 1924 by Dange requested the viceroy to transfer him from the jail in the United Province to Bombay. There were three more letters in which Dange assured that he would not get involved in any anti-government activity if he were released from jail. After inspecting the documents, the three members which included Jyoti Basu, Saroj Mukhopadhyay (then editor of *Ganashakti*) and Niranjan Sengupta (MLA, West Bengal) issued a statement on 12th April that they felt the letters were genuine. Jyoti Basu had also alleged that Dange had acquired *benami* shares worth Rs 30,000 of the publishing company of *The Patriot* which also published the magazine *The Link*. It had been decided a few years back in the party that no party member would keep any contact with the magazine *The Link*. The supporters of Dange claimed that the letters were forged and released to the media by the disgruntled group. In response on 13th April Basu told the National Council of the CPI to file a defamation case against the magazine *Current*. They had earlier asked for an investigation which was ignored. Basu felt that the alacrity with which the Dange group was rushing to the media to deny the veracity of the letter instead of adopting the correct and legal steps was suspect.[2] There were four letters written by Dange in 1924 from Kanpur jail – two to the district magistrate, one to the governor general and the fourth one to the inspector general of prisons – requesting consideration of his letter written to the governor general.[3]

Character assassination had been an oft-used tool in politics. So had been the use of the media. In 1962 the Bengal media led by the Ananda Bazar Group was critical of the dissenting group of the CPI. The magazine *Desh* had even questioned the silence of film director Satyajit Ray on the border war with China, 'Why are you silent, Satyajit Ray?' Criticising the popular play *Angar* on the life of coal mine workers, then being staged at the Minerva theatre, *Ananda Bazar Patrika* derisively referred to it as coming from the leftist brand. Later in 1965 there was an effort to stop staging of *Kallol*. *Desh* had even started a column on 'Freedom of an Artist' (*Shilpir Swadhinata*) to provoke those who kept quiet on the question of nationalism.[4] In the West Bengal assembly a resolution was raised by Congress member Dr Pratap Chandra Chunder on 16 November 1962. The resolution inter alia mentioned,

> The House requests the Government of India and the Government of West Bengal to take serious notice of those persons in this country, who abuse the freedom granted by our Constitution and who, in their extra territorial allegiance and loyalty, help the enemy, directly or indirectly, by their speech and action, discourage defence efforts and endanger the freedom of our country, and also cautions the people of this State regarding the activities of such anti-national persons.[5]

The entire house was against the members of the CPI who went against the party line. Within a week after the assembly resolution all leaders of the group were arrested under the Defence of India Act. Basu was released one year later in December 1963.[6] The ideological difference within the CPI blew up into a war between nationalists and communists who deviated from the central party line of the CPI. Interestingly post the split the new faction emerged stronger as was seen in the bye-election result. The *Economic Weekly* wrote on 4 January 1964,

> What the people are considering increasingly necessary is that the ruling party should be reminded every now and again that the people do not wholly accept the Congress

> version of the country's progress and that, Chinese aggression or no, the Communist Party of India, though divided, has a useful role to play.[7]

The question that remained to be answered was post division which group would emerge stronger than the other. The election result of the Kerala assembly in 1965 had the answer – the CPI could win only 3 seats against 40 by the CPI (Marxists) (CPI(M) for our reference henceforth) which had emerged as the largest single party in the assembly.

After Nehru's demise Gulzarilal Nanda took over as the home minister in the Lal Bahadur Shastri cabinet. On New Year's Day in 1965 Nanda addressed the nation over the All India Radio in which he attacked the Basu faction of the communist party. Nanda accused the faction as working, at the behest of China, for peoples' democracy which he said was antagonistic to parliamentary democracy. The allegations of Nanda were based on the theme that the faction was looking forward to organising an armed revolution like the Telangana uprising seen earlier taking advantage of the border clashes with China. Basu in a statement to the Calcutta media on 12th January rubbished the statement of the home minister calling it superficial and full of lies.

The newly separated CPI(M) had the entire machinery of creating agitation as well as a competent leader like Jyoti Basu to lead them in the assembly. The allegations against the CPI(M) leaders that they were anti-national did not influence the voters of Kerala or even West Bengal during the bye-election at Burdwan. What is more, this was when the nagging food crisis hit the state again. The food movement of 1965-66 was characteristically different from the one witnessed in 1959. This time the movement was not confined to Calcutta and its neighbourhood but had spread to rural areas too. By now the incompetence of the chief minister was thoroughly exposed since there was no buffer like Bidhan Roy any more. In his inimitable way Chief Minister Sen committed several crucial mistakes. His first and major false step was the suggestion that Bengalis change their food habits, recommending wheat instead of rice – a suicidal recommendation of sorts. Secondly, he added spice to his first mistake by suggesting that green banana could become a dietary supplement since it contained more protein. Immediately the former famine minister Sen was given a new nickname – 'kanchakala' (green banana) minister. Taking advantage of the war with Pakistan the state government had put several CPI(M) leaders behind the bars. But the party had the organisational base of creating movements on economic issues. An example was the movement against the tram fare increase in July 1965. Even a one-day bandh was organised in Calcutta on 31st July. Due to the war with Pakistan the government could suppress the movements though this respite did not last long.

In early 1966 the food crisis gave rise to a fierce food movement in the state. There was short supply of kerosene and coal also – both were important sources of energy then. Long queues and black marketing of such essential items made people angry which the administration attempted to subdue by using force – a repeated failure of the Congress-led state government. Unlike earlier movements it did not play out on the streets of Calcutta but spread across the districts and was more spontaneous than the food movement of 1959. The fire was ignited on 16 February 1966 when police fired on the agitators at Swarupnagar and killed a 15-year-old schoolboy, Nurul Islam, during a demonstration against the scarcity of kerosene and the steep prices of essential commodities. The movement spread like wildfire across the state touching Bashirhat, Habra, Krishnanagar, Ranaghat, Chakdah, Hindmotor, Uttarpara, Asansol, Plassey, Beldanga, and

Berhampur. West Bengal witnessed spontaneous and incessant processions, demonstrations, blockades of roads and railways, destruction of state properties, closure of schools resulting in clashes between the agitators and the police. The crisis and its abject mishandling by the government acted as a strong enough stimulant for the newly created CPI(M) erasing all criticisms directed against its leaders for being anti-nationals.

Trouble does not come alone as could be seen in the West Bengal Congress. A senior Congressman and minister in the Sen cabinet Ajoy Mukherjee revolted against the state leadership at this juncture. This was the first dissension after the failure of the Ginger group towards the end of the 1950s. Unlike the earlier dissent this was stronger since Mukherjee had several followers in the state Congress. Ajoy Mukherjee knocked at the door of the central leadership but no one paid attention to him given the influence of Atulya Ghosh in the Congress Working Committee. The total breakdown of the rationing system angered the people who joined in peaceful mass processions even without any party or leader in the lead. The students bared open their shirts before the lifted rifles of the police, asked them to shoot as many times as they like and face the power behind them. Effectively the state was taken over by lawlessness. The morgue of the Krishnanagar hospital was broken into and the dead body killed in police firing was taken out by force by the mob who organised a funeral procession. Buildings of Congressmen including the house of a minister were ransacked. In other districts, too, violence and attacks against Congressmen and the police disrupted the administration. For five or six days, the whole state was in a state of automatic bandh converging in the historic march of the people in Calcutta on 10th March. The important leaders and ministers of the Congress had to take shelter in a posh Calcutta hotel to save their skin. The situation on the streets was reflected in the assembly budget session when

30 members were arrested and 16 MLAs were ousted forcefully for disregarding the order of the house.[8]

Between 1964-66 food grain production in the country had actually decreased due primarily to drought conditions. In addition, there was inflationary pressure built up in the economy. The retail price index of rice in Calcutta rose sharply to 186 in 1966 from 138 in 1961. The West Bengal government planned for extensive procurement through state cooperatives and the government agencies. After procuring as much food grain as it could from the stocks of the central government the state government aimed at maintaining a rationing system. But the Congress government's procurement policy was destined to fail under an inept and corrupt administrative system. Besides there was resistance to the scheme from the support base of the ruling party – the big landlords and the rice mill owners. Thus their stiff resistance, the inefficiency of the administrative system, and the rampant corruption ensured that the government initiative failed miserably.

That the Congress was failing to win the support of the people was sensed by senior politicians like Ajoy Mukherjee. He even went to Delhi to meet the Congress national leaders to apprise them of the ground reality. His efforts were construed as another attempt to revolt against the dominant Hooghly lobby led by Atulya Ghosh. Control of Ghosh in the central Congress was significant and he ensured that nobody among the Congress senior leadership give any audience to Ajoy Mukherjee. The hero of the Tamralipta Jatiya Sarkar during the movement against the British rule, Ajoy Mukherjee was a minister in the Bidhan Roy cabinet but was shunted out as a part of the Kamraj plan in 1963. This was when Prafulla Sen was the chief minister and it gives the impression that Ajoy Mukherjee was a misfit in the schemes of Atulya Ghosh to exercise complete hegemony over the West Bengal Congress and the government. Naturally

Mukherjee's effort to reach out to the central Congress leadership was futile. There are some who change the fate of events while there are others who play a significant role as a pawn during the course of change. Ajoy Mukherjee fell in the second category. His conflict with the West Bengal Congress leadership arose when the state had been passing through severe food crisis and facing sporadic movements across West Bengal. What is more, the large peasants who were the traditional support base of the Congress, had revolted against the imposition of steep levy by the Sen government. Mukherjee emerged as a leader of this traditional support base of the Congress.[9] Once separated from the Congress mainstream Mukherjee had to float with the tide and ended up playing contradictory roles during the 5-year period between 1966 and 1971. In three consecutive elections between 1967 and 1971 Mukherjee was the chief ministerial choice before he faded from the scene.

The general election of 1967 was a game changer – nationally as well as in West Bengal. Nationally it sounded an alarm bell for the Congress though the party maintained its parliamentary majority. But in West Bengal it was more than an alarm – the Congress failed to win a majority in the state assembly. The political background was loaded against the Congress government – the food movement and unrest spreading across the state, and the separation of Ajoy Mukherjee, a well-respected Gandhian, from the party were two major issues the Congress had to contend with. But on the positive side for the party was utter political disagreement in the opposition camp. The state Congress leadership of Sen-Ghosh was hopeful of electoral success once again. But the fact that they were nervous could be seen in an early release of its list of candidates. And also in the fact that Atulya Ghosh, the strong man of not only West Bengal but nationally in the party organisation, switched his constituency from Asansol to Bankura.

If the scene was uncertain for the Congress it was no more certain for the opposition. Negotiation for an opposition unity was protracted and yielded only confusion. Though negotiation for seat adjustments started early in June 1966 no workable formula could be arrived at. Finally, there emerged two opposition fronts: the United Left Front consisting of CPI(M), SSP, RSP, SUC, RCPI, Workers' Party and Forward Bloc (Marxist); and the Peoples' United Left Front with Bangla Congress, CPI, Forward Bloc, Bolshevik Party, Gorkha League and Lok Sevak Sangha. The *Economic and Political Weekly* wrote on the political uncertainty prevailing in West Bengal. It predicted that the rural votes would be the deciding factor and wondered which combination could emerge strong enough to win away the traditional Congress hold over the rural votes. This feeling perhaps led the politically shrewd Atulya Ghosh to switch to the Bankura Lok Sabha seat, an overwhelmingly rural constituency. The only unpredictable element in the election was how the new entity Bangla Congress would influence the rural votes. The magazine observed that Bangla Congress was, '... a body of dissident Congressmen who have been visibly gaining in strength. The defeat of the Congress, however, would not necessarily mean a left government. There is the question of achieving a workable left coalition, for the alternative of President's rule is always there.'[10] There were several reasons for doubting the success of a non-Congress coalition since Ajoy Mukherjee was known as an ardent anti-communist in the same mould as that of Prafulla Sen and there was grave doubt how long the coalition between the Left and Bangla Congress would last. And Mukherjee was not the only one who could have created trouble later on. The *Economic and Political Weekly* wrote: 'Jatin Chakraborty has never been known to be an easy person to accommodate in any alliance; the same could be said of Hemanta Basu, Forward Block Marxist, whatever that means.'[11] Unlike any other state, West Bengal's political parties and the leadership did not enjoy unrestrained support across the state so as to claim to be a unifying force for opposition unity. Even within the Congress with the passing away of Dr Bidhan Roy there was no leading personality who could have commanded respect across constituencies. The election of 1967 was clearly tough for the ruling Congress while experts had doubts over a viable non-Congress government coming to power. The election result was as predicted. Congress won 127 seats in a 280-member assembly falling short of the halfway mark to form a government. CPI(M) emerged as stronger than CPI – winning 43 seats – the second highest after the Congress, and the CPI could bag 16 only, less than the third placed Bangla Congress which bagged 34 seats. The most important result was at Arambagh where the sitting member, Chief Minister Prafulla Sen, lost to challenger Ajoy Mukherjee by a margin of 881 votes. This win made Ajoy Mukherjee the opposition's choice to lead the coalition government. Atulya Ghosh lost the Bankura Lok Sabha seat by nearly 30,000 votes. The Congress could win 14 Lok Sabha seats out of 40 while the CPI, CPI(M) and Bangla Congress won 5 each. The electoral outcome of 1967 was marked by the Congress defeat – the dominant Hooghly group which could not be ousted by several rebel groups in the past was finally tamed by the people of West Bengal.

The period after the fourth general election was marked by behind-the-scenes political maneuvering by the Congress party, like they did successfully in Kerala in 1957. But in West Bengal this strategy did not succeed. Instead a precedence was set where the governor was shown by the legislature who was supreme in formation of a government. The significant change that had swept the nation in 1967 was that half of the electorate had been below 35 years of age.[12] In West Bengal the new voters were children of post-Independent India, many were from the families which had to flee from East Pakistan. The loyalty of young Bengali voters towards the Congress was less robust than the elderly ones. For them the daily struggle for jobs and livelihood mattered more than any historical loyalty. In any case Bengal's loyalty for the Gandhian Congress was never particularly strong. The communists with their agitational politics attracted the economically unsettled population easily while the Congress with its political mismanagement and use of police in tackling all popular movements did a great disservice to its political future. Eric Da Costa, director of the Indian Institute of Public Opinion, wrote in *The Economic Times* on 30 January 1967,

> The Indian electorate, believed inert and incapable of dramatic choice, is showing signs of a revolutionary change. The young, the less educated, and particularly the illiterates, the minorities, and most unpredictable of all, the lowest income groups are all rewriting their basic loyalties. To the candidates this is, perhaps, a struggle for power. To a political scientist … the beginning of a break with the past.[13]

The election result of 1967 was inconclusive and the government put together did not last. However this was the beginning of the end of rule by any national party in West Bengal leaving aside the 5-year period of Siddhartha Shankar Ray as chief minister which was another aberration of sorts.

Jyoti Basu joined the Ajoy Mukherjee government as the deputy chief minister with charge of finance and transport. The sensitive food portfolio was given to Prafulla Chandra Ghosh, who was the first chief minister of the state. Food continued to be the problem area for the administration since West Bengal was a deficit state and had to depend on the Centre. There was allegation that the Centre was discriminating against West Bengal, a complaint that was muted when Dr Bidhan Roy had taken up the issue of rehabilitation of refugees with Nehru and Patel, but with an opposition coming to power this allegation came to the fore once again. Since then on many occasions West Bengal has complained against the Centre citing its stepmotherly treatment and it has become a patented slogan of sorts in the state politics. In its report before the 11th meeting of the CPI(M) state council there was mention of mistreatment by the Centre – Rs 10 crores due to the state was not paid by the Centre. New Delhi reduced the supply of food grains to West Bengal from an average 130,000 tonnes to just around 60,000 tonnes. Only after pressure was created by the opposition the food supply was increased marginally to 100,000 tonnes.[14] Clearly the aim of the Centre was to create problems for the opposition-led government and then get it removed.

One important decision of the first United Front (UF) government was nationalisation of the Calcutta Tramways Company. This was an issue which Jyoti Basu had raised in the assembly when in 1951 the Bidhan Roy government brought up an agreement entered into with the British company that the terms of its continuation would be extended by 20 years. Basu had argued in favour of state ownership which was supported by the tram workers. Thereafter the increase in tram fare had remained a contentious issue between the people (led by the Left) and the government. On 14 July 1967 Jyoti Basu as transport minister of the United Front government placed before the assembly a bill on taking over of management of the tram company. The refusal of the company to pay salary to employees, not even to accept state government guaranteed bank overdraft till fare was hiked led to the bill of management takeover that had support of all members of the assembly. The British government through its deputy high commissioner had put pressure on the United Front government. In reply Basu responded that Her Majesty's Government should ask the tram company to work in the interest of the people. Prime Minister Indira Gandhi did not intervene in the tram company acquisition by the West Bengal government.

The year 1967 is politically significant for West Bengal for several reasons. First, it exposed the internal contradictions of a coalition assembled only to oppose the Congress. Second, the year saw further split among the communists – CPI(M) had a disgruntled section and the Naxalbari movement took root. The movement had brought in several elements in West Bengal politics even after the movement turned into a chapter in the political history of the state. Third, and no less important, had been the message that was delivered on limitation of the jurisdiction of the central government exercised through the governor by the then speaker of the West Bengal assembly Bijoy Banerjee – the views expressed later were formalised by the Supreme Court in its famous S.R. Bommai judgement delivered on 11 March 1994.

'At first sight organizational politics in West Bengal seems a hopeless maze of confusion,' wrote Marcus F. Franda.[15]

> Of the more than fifty political parties that have contested elections to the State Legislative Assembly since 1947, many represent mere factions that have broken with the older parties, many are splinter groups from the various factions, and some of the splinter groups have in turn split two or three times themselves.

This was repeated during the United Front rule when some members broke away from the newly split CPI(M).

The much-expected internal contradictions in a coalition, full of persons with conflicting ideologies and in some cases bitter differences where ideologies were not violently different like between the CPI and the CPI(M) did not take long to surface. The election of 1967 was characterised more by the effort of securing the position of the leading opposition party tag by the two communist parties. The non-Congress government was thrust more by the voters who wanted to see the back of the 20-year-long Congress rule than any design by those who received the mandate eventually.

> History has seldom seen such a reluctant march to authority. The dominant section in the leadership of the CPI (Marxist), the largest party in the coalition, had at an early stage of the pre-election palavers explicitly stated it did not envisage an alternative government in the State; its unconcealed strategic objects were consolidation of its own position as the principal opposition party in the State legislature (and, thereby, outside the legislature too) and inflicting maximum damage possible to the Right CPI in the process. The Right CPI and its closest ally, the Bangla Congress, both representing break-away sections of their parent organizations in the State, were too concerned with their survival to consider anything so grandiose as an alternative government seriously,

wrote the *Economic and Political Weekly* (*EPW*).[16]

It was a triangular contest among the two coalitions formed by the CPI(M) and CPI and the ruling Congress. The prestige fights were mostly between the two communist parties. Analysts estimated that the two fronts sacrificed as many as 39 assembly and 6 Lok Sabha seats by splitting each other's votes. Despite that Congress managed to win 127 seats which electoral analysis suggests was due to infighting among the opposition. But for the Congress, government formation was not difficult given the internal conflicts among so many opposition parties and the unsteady alliances they formed. What went against the party perhaps was the state-wide jubilation at the electoral loss of the two top leaders – Prafulla Sen and Atulya Ghosh. Most places in West Bengal saw delirious processions hailing their defeats with green bananas (*kanchakala* – nickname given to Sen) and brinjals (*kana begun* – insect-eaten brinjal – nickname given to Atulya Ghosh) – a shocking enough message for the Congress not to stake claim and an encouraging one for the rag-tag coalition partners to join in an effort to form the government. The election outcome had clearly shown that in the battle between the two communist parties the CPI(M) was the peoples' choice. CPI had managed 16 assembly seats largely due to its alliance with Bangla Congress that helped it to win 8 seats from Midnapore, the stronghold of the Bangla Congress. In the Lok Sabha, however, CPI proved to be the giant killer since its candidate unseated the Congress strong man Atulya Ghosh who had shifted to this seat (Bankura) expecting it to be an easy win for him.

The internal contradictions of the United Front government were easy to manipulate. There were several loose ends, the chief minister Mukherjee himself being one. He was uncomfortable with the agenda of the CPI(M) since it militated against his principal support group, the landholders. Mukherjee was also embarrassed by the representatives of the CPI(M) in the Front's coordination council, who were aggressive in handling the food situation and harsh towards the food minister Ghosh.

> Seeing that Ajoy babu was becoming increasingly frustrated by the internal discord and dissatisfaction, some Congressmen started wooing him back into the party. The idea was that if the 34 MLAs of the Bangla Congress joined hands with the 127 Congress MLAs, the group would form a majority in the assembly,

wrote Pranab Mukherjee.[17]

It was decided that Mukherjee would resign on 2 October 1967, the Congress would withdraw its expulsion order on Mukherjee and his fellow members of Bangla Congress and a Congress government under him would be formed. But the information was leaked to Barun Sengupta of the *Ananda Bazar Patrika* and a meeting of the UF partners was held where the CPI(M) assured that the party would not embarrass the chief minister in future.

While Mukherjee was thus placated, the weakest point, the food minister Prafulla Chandra Ghosh, a staunch Gandhian with no love lost for the communists, was not satisfied. He left the Front with 17 supporters. CPI(M) wanted the government to take over wholesale trade of rice but leave the retail trade untouched, called for stringent action on hoarders and large farmers, as also put intense pressure on the Centre to restore supply of food grains to the earlier level. P.C. Ghosh was not keen to act against the large farmers and wholesale traders.[18] The government lasted for 8 months and faced a crisis when Ghosh resigned as minister.

While dissention was a problem arising out of the coalition, the CPI(M) itself faced a problem of dissent when its peasant leaders in North Bengal led by Charu Majumdar went in for armed struggle by peasants to forcefully acquire lands and take the rice cultivated there. Harekrishna Konar, minister in the United Front cabinet, came forward for reconciliation so that the coalition government was not embarrassed but by then the party in the region had gone out of the control of the state leaders.[19] Even the political and organisational report in the 11th state assembly had recorded the sudden and foolhardy decision of the peasant leaders and how the same created problems for the party. Naxalism played an important part in shaping the politics of the state since then.

The resignation of P.C. Ghosh on 4th November was preceded by drama in the Bangla Congress where the legislators were uncertain of which course to take – left, right or centre. The Congress too was divided since there was a section which was loyal to Atulya Ghosh who did not want formation of a government by the party since that would help his opponents to thrive. But events moved faster than what various contenders planned. 'It was undoubtedly ordained by deeper social forces,' wrote *EPW* (December 2, 1967).

> It is significant that P C Ghosh's resignation, accompanied by the defection of 16 other MLAs, most of whom belong to the landed gentry synchronised with the finalisation of the UF cabinet's policy of foodgrain levy. Equally notable are the facts that both the ministers who were sworn in along with Ghosh (Ghosh was sworn in as chief minister on 21st November by the state Governor Dharamvira after dismissing the Ajoy Mukherjee government) are scions of jotedar families and the first policy indications given by the new ministers related to the abolition of levy and re-introduction of free-trade in foodgrains. One of the first acts of the new Government, alongside the arrest of more than three thousand UF supporters was the release of a big food grain trader who had been imprisoned by the previous regime for manipulation of the market.[20]

Confusion ruled the dismissal of the UF government and swearing in of Ghosh as the chief minister. It saw Atulya Ghosh joining in the issue and assuring the support of all the Congress MLAs to the newly sworn-in chief minister though an important member of the Congress opposed the 'operation topple'.

The installation of the P.C. Ghosh government led to a unique tussle between the governor and the state assembly speaker. When the governor called the assembly session on 29th November after dismissing the Mukherjee government and installing P.C. Ghosh, the speaker of the state assembly called the action of dismissing the earlier government and also calling the assembly session at the advice of an illegally installed government unconstitutional. Speaker Bijoy Banerjee adjourned the house sine die. The house was prorogued by the governor and summoned again on 14th February. The speaker Banerjee again adjourned it repeating his earlier ruling. Curiously the governor did not move the court as done in a similar incidence in the Punjab assembly in 1968. The governor Dharamvira knew that he was on an uncharted territory on the issue. According to India's former attorney general M.C. Setalvad, the governor had the power to dismiss the ministry 'if he is satisfied that the Ministry was in a minority and it was not prepared to hold an Assembly session within a reasonable time'.[21] That was the reason why three hours before the Mukherjee government was dismissed the governor through the chief secretary had asked the chief minister to call for an assembly session which was earlier called on 18th December but within three hours of seeking preponing of the session, the government was dismissed. Two questions came up. 'Did the Governor have a right to dismiss the ministry without an adverse vote in the Assembly?' The question forgotten was: 'Was the Governor right in dismissing the UF ministry on his mainly personal guess that it had lost its majority?' Apparently the Congress at the Centre knew they were standing on a very thin line as far as Constitutional propriety was concerned. Therefore after the house was adjourned sine die for the second time in February, West Bengal was placed under the President's rule. Apart from the desperate move of the Congress to topple the first UF government the incidents of 1967-68 had shown clearly that the reason for ousting the government was to assist the hoarders and large farmers, and that big money would go to any extent to subvert the wish of the people. The massive protest against the move did also have few precedence. Clearly the move to dismiss the first UF government without a floor test was a mistake for which the Congress had to pay dearly in West Bengal. The stage that was set for a mid-term poll in

West Bengal could not have helped the return of the Congress. In any case the Congress was a divided house – the scheme of toppling the UF government apparently was hatched by Gulzarilal Nanda, and Atulya Ghosh was kept out of it. There were also differences between former chief minister Prafulla Sen and Atulya Ghosh and none of the groups had control over the people. Therefore the Congress aimed at buying time before calling for a mid-term poll in West Bengal.

Finally the day of reckoning had to be fixed. Election to the West Bengal legislative assembly was scheduled after festivals such as Durga Puja were over, harvesting was completed and there were no other distractions to the shrill election campaign. Compared to two years earlier the Congress was in a better shape – it was no longer a divided house and could win back part of its rich rural support base due to fragmentation of the Bangla Congress in some 6 parts or so. Moreover both Prime Minister Indira Gandhi and Home Minister Y.V. Chavan spent time in campaigning for the Congress, hopefully rejuvenated. For the Left there was one major gain – they had managed to put together a united front thus ruling out the chances of splitting votes which saw them losing some 30 seats in 1962. The people of West Bengal had seen the result of a fragmented mandate and the utter chaos that affected them. They had also been told by a certain group called the 'Naxalites' to boycott the polls since it yielded no benefit which an armed struggle would. The stage was set for a critical mid-term election in West Bengal which redefined the state's political landscape.[22]

The people of West Bengal delivered their verdict in no uncertain terms. The Congress was routed, losing the position of the largest political party in West Bengal to the just about 5-year-old outfit CPI(M). The boycott campaign of the Naxalites helped to increase the polling percentage from 63 to 68 per cent. It had its effect in the North Bengal areas, where Naxalites were active, which did not return a single CPI(M) candidate. Prafulla Sen could win back his Arambagh seat by defeating Ajoy Mukherjee by a substantial margin of more than 15,000 votes. But all defectors including Prafulla Ghosh and his ministers were shown the door. In the end the United Front tally reached 218 and that of the Congress a miserable 55, clear enough signal to the national party of what West Bengal thought of the party ruling the nation. The election result of 1969 had demonstrated West Bengal's breach with the politics of the Hindi heartland. What is more, politically sensitive Calcutta and its neighbourhood gave a clear thumbs down to the Congress. The Congress tally in Calcutta was 5 out of 23, it was 4 out of 50 in 24 Parganas, 1 out of 16 in Howrah, and 2 out of 18 in Hooghly. In the other well-developed district of Burdwan, it got only 2 out of 25. In Midnapore, the second most populous district of the state, the Congress won 6 out of 35 seats. In the two western-most districts of Birbhum and Bankura, it got no seats at all. In about 40 constituencies from the Asansol-Raniganj-Durgapur area and in the sprawling industrial belts on both banks of the Ganga where industrial workers constituted a majority, the Congress won just 1 seat, the railway township of Kharagpur.[23] In terms of votes polled however Congress did marginally better than in 1967, winning 41.32 per cent of votes polled against 41.13 per cent in 1967. While the CPI(M), the largest party, improved its poll percentage by less than two per cent – of course it contested just 97 seats in 1969 against 135 in 1967.[24] Clearly CPI(M) gained both by coalition formation which did not split its votes and also from increased popular support. Despite the sweeping election victory, the 1969 poll was still in a work-in-progress stage for West Bengal's isolation from the national mainstream politics that one witnessed later. One reason was the elements within the United Front – like the Bangla Congress – which were ideologically more aligned with the Congress than with communism. The poll saw complete wiping out of right-wing elements like Bharatiya Jana Sangh or communal political parties like Hindu Mahasabha; even the Progressive Muslim League could not make much headway since people voted more on political ideological line than along communal lines.

The very fact that the coalition partners of the first UF government stuck together in 1969 illustrated, according to Marcus F. Franda, '... the culmination of attempts at unity on the part of the non-Congress parties of West Bengal.'[25] The difference in poll percentage between the Congress and the United Front was about 9 per cent (49.7 per cent for the UF against 41.32 per cent of the Congress). Political polarisation between the Congress and the communist-led front was evident in the loss by any other alternative that attempted to contest against these two. There were 5 parties which attempted to do that hoping to benefit in case of yet another hung assembly. 'The extent to which these parties were rejected by the electorate can be seen from the fact that, out of 372 candidates contesting for these five parties, only four were ultimately victorious ... more than 90 per cent of them forfeited their deposits ...' The number of independents contesting in 1969 was only 90 (compared to 602 in 1952, 346 in 1957, 324 in 1962, 327 in 1967) and only 10 per cent had cast votes for independents or candidates from the 5 parties who were outside the Congress or the communist-led front. Thus what started in 1967 post-election due to voters opting for non-Congress alternative, took a firm political root in 1969. Only there were some more glitches since even the United Front was not formed on the basis of political ideology but compulsion to oppose the Congress – a compulsion that hoisted a Gandhian and anti-communist Ajoy Mukherjee as the chief minister again.

This period had seen three important developments which had shaped the politics of West Bengal – increase in lawlessness in West Bengal, split in the Congress at the national level, and freedom of

Bangladesh. For the growth in lawlessness the rise and eventual demise of the Naxal movement had contributed in no small measure. The eternal romanticism of Bengal of waging war that was seen at the dawn of nationalism received new impetus from the success of the Chinese communist party. By then the Soviet Union had lost its shining edge to arouse even an ever-willing Bengali youth to take up arms or pens in fighting the state. The debate within the undivided communist party over the Soviet ideology or the Chinese one – both completely couched in jargons and lucid enough only for a gullible to digest – created a third group of converts who wanted to opt for violent overthrow of the state. Some of them chose farmers of villages like Naksalbari, Kharibari and Fansideoa to join in armed struggle against the landowners, to take over their land forcefully and cultivate there. Chief Minister Ajoy Mukherjee had expressed concern over such lawlessness before the media on 17 May 1967. Meanwhile on 24th May trouble started under the police station of Naksalbari when a group of armed farmers went to occupy and cultivate land of a large farmer. To diffuse the situation when the police reached the area, they were attacked and an inspector Sonam Wangdi was fatally injured by arrows thrown on the force. The next day when a meeting was being held by the farmer protesters near Naksalbari market Assam Rifles which was patrolling the area fired on the crowd and 11 persons mostly women and some children were killed as a result. This was the beginning of the Naxal movement.[26] Earlier in 1965 there were issues between a group of students and the authorities of Presidency College over demonstration organised in front of the USIS office in Calcutta apparently against a certain comment by a US councillor in a conference. The dispute escalated and a few student leaders were expelled from the college. Later after the United Front government came to power their expulsion was revoked. These students were not comfortable with the CPI(M) and later when CPI(ML) was formed in

1969 they joined it. A section of these students had shifted to villages in Midnapore – Debra and Gopiballabhpur – and created Naksalbari type movements. Kanu Sanyal along with some other colleagues had even visited China via Nepal to seek Chinese endorsement. 'Spring thunder over India', an article in *People's Daily*, China (July 5, 1967) hailed the groups creating a Red area in Naksalbari. The Chinese communist party welcomed these movements while the then United Front government failed to initiate strong administrative measures to quell the resultant lawlessness. The police, too, was hesitant since their political masters were divided and confused. West Bengal was caught between the devil of romanticism of communism and the deep sea of lawlessness.

The curtain raiser of the administration's weakness was seen when a group of policemen raided the state assembly with the body of a colleague who was killed by 'anti-social' elements in the district of 24 Paraganas. Some in uniform broke furniture, tore papers, raised slogans, chased the speaker and even beat up some members. When a police contingent from the headquarters arrived they left. Jyoti Basu who was the home minister and deputy chief minister blamed certain Congress members for instigating the police personnel to create problems for the newly formed UF government.[27] This perhaps was one of the first signs of politicisation of the law enforcing agency in West Bengal, a tradition that continues even now. Factionalism has been an in-built characteristic in any organisation in Bengal – political parties too could never escape the trap. When the Naxals in the garb of struggling for the poor invaded the villages they were greeted as 'Zulum' party by many villagers. In fact, with the active support of village resistance groups many of them were nabbed by the police.

> Even the most sympathetic assessment of the movement could not help but agree to the fact that activities of the

> Naxalites in the furthest villages could continue for some times only because the UF Ministry allowed it to. The Police was ordered either to stay away from the disturbed zones or avoid confrontation. This attitude was prevalent even during the peak period of Naxalite activities in Birbhum, Gopiballavpur and Debra.[28]

One characteristic of militancy in West Bengal witnessed during the period was that militancy thrived only when it was backed by the administration. This was best seen when in later years the CPI(M) government was removed and a Congress government under Siddhartha Shankar Ray ruled the state. The legacy of the UF government in West Bengal was a weak law administration authority, marred by political favouritism and armed inter and intra party rivalry. The deep-rooted ailment was nurtured and carefully nursed by the political parties since this proved to be the key to political authority. West Bengal's factional politics and failure to integrate with the national mainstream, therefore missing out on opportunities for development, created an intractable isolation of the state in the Indian Union.

The year 1969 saw a major split in the Indian National Congress which had its effect on the politics of West Bengal as well. Prime Minister Indira Gandhi was uncomfortable with the 'syndicate' of senior party men eager to control her. She had the opportunity to strike at them when incumbent President Zakir Hussein passed away and a new president had to be elected. The Congress nominated its veteran member N. Sanjiva Reddy as its candidate. While Indira Gandhi had signed his nomination paper she asked her party men to vote according to their conscience. The then vice president V.V. Giri resigned and filed his nomination also. A third candidate C.D. Deshmukh too came up in the arena. Before the election on 20th July

Indira Gandhi had nationalised 14 major commercial banks. With her support V.V. Giri was elected the president.

> The overwhelming majority of the Congress Parliamentary Party and its Legislature parties have turned against the old, discredited dados sitting in cabalistic control of the Parliamentary Board and Working Committee. The Congress President, who was to have wielded the whip against the 'rebels' is reduced to a pathetic, garrulous figure who does not know his own fate. The revolution we have witnessed over the past few weeks has placed the reins of power firmly in the hands of Indira Gandhi,

wrote Romesh Thapar in the *EPW*.

There was one worry however. Whether Prime Minister Indira Gandhi would be a hostage of the Left like West Bengal Chief Minister Ajoy Mukherjee was then. '... the rather patent attempt by a lot of opportunist leftist parties to make an Ajoy Mukherjee out of Indira Gandhi is being taken note of in quarters which are knowledgeable.'[29]

In West Bengal it took less time than expected for the political contradictions to surface. 'The simulated honeymoon is over. The stark reality of intense social tensions and collisions is surfacing,' wrote the magazine *EPW* in July 1969.[30] The incidences of clashes over the recovery of vested lands began during the first UF government and escalated during the second term of the UF government. Such clashes, wrote *EPW*,

> ... have been revived on a bigger scale and have spread quickly, particularly in the districts of 24 Parganas, Burdwan and Midnapore. There have been quite a number of incidents in the countryside involving physical clashes. Sometimes

> jotedars and their associates have met the advancing kisan jathas with firearms and even inflicted death. On other occasions the jotedars have been overwhelmed by superior force and have paid the supreme price for resistance. There have been cases of individual murders in the dark too.

Politics in West Bengal since then has been engulfed in violence with the scales of democracy held by those having enough muscle power. The trouble in rural West Bengal had its roots in the past.

> Bengal was the earliest and a classic case of permanent settlement. As early as in 1883, the British Lieutenant-Governor of the province observed that 'almost every vestige of constitutional claims of the peasantry [if ever such existed beyond a small privileged class] was lost in the usurpations and encroachments of the landlords.' It is also known and recorded in official reports and reviews that the Congress brand of agrarian reforms stopped far short of a proper redressal of the historical inequities that have been the lot of the majority in the countryside.[31]

When in 1955 the Bidhan Roy government introduced abolition of zamindari many large farmers managed to transfer their landholding to other family members and made innovative arrangements of evading the law. The West Bengal media cited the case of a former Congress minister who managed to transfer his huge landholding to family members and their henchmen and even after that he converted the excess land he had into fisheries on paper thus evading the act. 'They received about Rupees seven lakhs as compensation, while retaining within the family's possession whatever land they owned originally.' (*The Statesman*, Calcutta, April 5, 1968.) According to a survey conducted by the University of Calcutta, the total area involved in mala fide transfers in the state of West Bengal excluding the districts of Purulia and Darjeeling on the eve of the enforcement of the act exceeded 1,00,000 acres.[32]

The inefficiency and corruption of the bureaucratic system helped the rural rich to have the cake and eat it too. This was the reason why the farmers' wing of the communists was agitated and some broke away from the CPI(M) and took law and order into their hands. The Naksalbari movement was a result of this desperation of the landless peasants. Under political pressure of the *kishan* wing who had no link with the rural rich, CPI(M) joined the move to forcibly occupy such *benami* land. Not that there is evidence of much land getting recovered and redistributed but the demonstration effect of such movements was immense. The rural peace was shattered and with the police being restrained due to political interference West Bengal turned into an island of chaos. Two adversarial political interest groups emerged – the radicals led by the CPI(M) and the conservatives backed by the Congress which was keen to protect its political turf after a sound electoral defeat. Caught in between were parties like the Bangla Congress, and Ajoy Mukherjee in particular who had been watching helplessly the unrest across the state with little political strength to call the shots. It was clear that eventually the second UF government was destined to go and this was a matter of time. Two factors, in addition to the daily collisions in West Bengal, hastened the fall of the second Mukherjee government. One was the newly rejuvenated Congress led by Prime Minister Indira Gandhi and the second were the incidents taking place across the border in Pakistan. The survival of the Congress government at the Centre depended on the communist party's support, since the Indira faction did not command majority. However this was not a strong enough rope for the CPI(M) to entangle the Congress in West

Bengal. Politics in the state moved along its own course irrespective of the compulsions of the central government.

The year 1969 had seen a different political culture that had swept across the 'Gandhian' Congress. Atulya Ghosh, the strong man, who had been at a waning stage since 1967, was finally out along with his conservative friends in the Congress syndicate. Even before that he was not seen calling the shots in the 1969 mid-term election in West Bengal. Ghosh had lost relevance since his idea of 'orderly development of society by non-violent means' had yielded place to 'mobocracy'.[33] The orderly development that Ghosh advocated was an orderly way of protecting the henchmen and maintaining the political hegemony while people at the grassroots were restless. Ghosh's theory that communists would appeal to the local people in terms of personal gains and not due to any higher principles proved right – poor peasants joined the movement of forcible occupation of land for redressal of their abject economic state and not because they had been moved by certain documents penned in Moscow, Beijing or by any of their ardent admirers in India. Similarly the Congress had built a coalition with rich farmers, landowners and businessmen for its political interest. The violence that erupted across West Bengal after the UF government came was the desperate move of the conservatives who were the traditional support base of the Congress to protect their turf. While Atulya Ghosh had predicted the outcome correctly he had failed completely to strategise any defence to save the Congress from the avoidable decimation. The mid-term election and the split in the Congress thus ushered in a new era of social conflict and political structure in West Bengal.

That the CPI(M) was concerned about the future of the United Front government could be sensed from the political and organisational report placed before the party's state-level plenum held between 9 and 15 February 1970. The UF government was receiving critical attention in the national media for various violent incidents in the state. This was adversely affecting the party's image. The party was also concerned over certain elements in the UF who, the party report felt, were keen on returning to the Congress led by Indira Gandhi now that the syndicate had separated from the grand old party. The CPI(M) blamed both the CPI and Bangla Congress for their support of the Indira Congress. The party was bitter about Mukherjee calling the CPI(M) a party of uncivilised barbarians.[34] Clearly the party was aware that despite the huge majority of the UF, the government's days were numbered. However it was looking for the continuance of the government so as to prepare for eventually staking its claim to form the government as the largest party in the assembly. Promode Dasgupta in his response alerted his party of the events in East Pakistan in particular, as well as cautioned the members not to underestimate the political acumen of Indira Gandhi. Clearly Dasgupta was aware of the possible problems that would plague the party once the UF government collapsed.

The most significant event in the subcontinent during the period was what Dasgupta had mentioned, the movement that had started in East Pakistan. Under public pressure Pakistan President Ayub Khan had released Sheikh Mujibur Rahman arrested under Agartala conspiracy case in 1968 and called for a round table conference on 10 March 1969. The conference did not resolve the issue of mass agitation in East Pakistan. Ayub Khan handed over the reins to General Yahya Khan but failing to stop political volatility he declared a national election to be held on 7 December 1970. In New Delhi Indian Prime Minister Indira Gandhi was observing the developments closely. She knew well enough the importance of West Bengal in case India was drawn into the internal problems of Pakistan. In case of an all-out freedom movement in East Pakistan India could not have remained a mute spectator. At the same time, a volatile West Bengal would not have been conducive for the Indian forces. Politically Mrs Gandhi knew she had to act and was getting ready to strike at an appropriate time. The rift within the United Front government was an opportunity which a sharp politician like her was not expected to miss. The fall of the UF government was summed up in the *EPW*:

> The United Front in West Bengal had given up the struggle for life long ago; the proclamation of President's rule, following formal resignation by the Chief Minister, only buried the decomposed corpse. The surprising tenacity with which the contending factions of the Front clung so long to the lifeless body was due to the obvious impossibility of any minifront - with or against CPI (M) - to fill the vacuum created by the disintegration of the 14-party coalition.[35]

The fall came as a surprise to the Front partners barring the two major adversaries – the CPI(M) and the Bangla Congress. These parties attempted to resurrect the Front once more since that was the only way to avoid election and cling to power. But they failed to read the political positions of the three major parties – CPI(M), Bangla Congress and the Indira Congress. Since a mini-front was not feasible in West Bengal, the best option for the Congress was the central rule in the volatile province during a possible volatile development across the border. An early mid-term election looked attractive for the CPI(M) since certain steps the UF government had taken had helped it to consolidate its vote bank. Even the CPI acknowledged the political advantages that came from the good work done due to the 32-point agenda that was adopted by the UF government, and criticised the Bangla Congress for failing to appreciate the same in its official paper *Kalantar*. Politically not only the CPI(M), which had taken credit for the success of populist measures, but also other partners would have gained from the work done by the UF government. It was clear that in case of election these parties would gain by sticking to the CPI(M). For the Bangla Congress there was hardly any future but to stick to the Indira Congress. For the Centre the immediate need was to set up an effective administrative machinery under the governor – a necessity both to address the developments across the border and to impose rule of law in the state of West Bengal which was plagued by political violence as well as Naxalism. The violence brought everything to a standstill despite imposition of a modified Public Detention Act – the West Bengal (Prevention of Violent Activities) Act, 1970. The streets of the state, Calcutta in particular, witnessed murders at regular intervals. People were disgusted and 'the demand was rising for the use of preventive detention powers - to break the back of those who were violent and the disorderly. Those who had earlier opposed the granting of such wide powers to the executive authority were no longer vocal in their opposition.'[36] According to government statistics, 178 people had died since April 1970 as a result of political conflicts. The violence was so rampant that many of the acts of violence were taking place in broad daylight and even in the presence of large numbers of witnesses. These were brutal to say the least. For instance, an off-duty policeman travelling with his wife in a rickshaw was dragged out and stabbed to death in a crowded street, in front of his wife and scores of people. People were so scared that nobody came forward either to protect the victim during the attack or to identify the assassins afterwards. There were many such cases unfolding nearly every day in Calcutta and elsewhere in West Bengal. The Naxalite violence was directed towards members of the CPI(M) – the party had claimed that between 18th March and November they had lost 170 members of the party either at the hands of the Naxalites or in police firing. The party however was guilty of committing a 'showcase' violent act on 17 March 1970, the day CPI(M) had called for a Bangla Bandh in protest against the resignation of Chief Minister Ajoy Mukherjee the day before. A procession of the party while passing through a middle-class locality at Burdwan killed two brothers and their friend in the presence of the family members. However, as long as the Naxalite violence was directed against the cadres of the CPI(M) it served the interests of the other political parties who could argue against holding a mid-term poll citing the violence. West Bengal had the unworthy distinction of hogging the headline news in the rest of the country for all the wrong reasons. Political violence since then remained a well-accepted fact in the political life of a Bengali.

Endnotes

1 Anil Biswas, ed., *Banglar Communist Andolan Dalil o Prasangik Tathya*, vol. 4 (National Book Agency, August 2005) pp 336-9.

2 Basu, *Nirbachita Rachanasangraha* vol. 1, pp 251-4.

3 Biswas, ed., *Banglar Communist Andolan*, pp 287-94.

4 Ibid., p. 13.

5 Basu, *Nirbachita Rachanasangraha* vol 1, pp 216-7.

6 Ibid.

7 'Democracy, their Democracy,' *EPW*, January 4, 1964, https://www.epw.in/system/files/pdf/1964_16/1/democracy_their_democracy.pdf.

8 Sajal Kumar Basu, 'Politics of Violence Studies with reference to West Bengal', http://shodhganga.inflibnet.ac.in:8080/jspui/bitstream/10603/162993.

9 https://www.epw.in/system/files/pdf/1986_21/22/obituary_ajoy_mukherji.pdf.

10 https://www.epw.in/system/files/pdf/1966_1/10/electoral_prospects.pdf.

11 https://www.epw.in/system/files/pdf/1966_1/X/a_calcutta_diary_white_caps_in_the_ring.pdf.

12 Norman D. Palmer. "India's Fourth General Election," in *Asian Survey* 7, no. 5 (1967), pp 275–91, www.jstor.org/stable/2642657 (accessed June 11, 2020).

13 Ibid.

14 Biswas, ed., *Banglar Communist Andolan*, pp 524-5.

15 Marcus F. Franda, "Electoral Politics in West Bengal: The Growth of the United Front," in *Pacific Affairs* 42, no. 3 (1969), pp 279–93, www.jstor.org/stable/2753899 (accessed June 12, 2020).

16 'The Reluctant Rulers', https://www.epw.in/system/files/pdf/1967_2/10/the_reluctant_rulers.pdf.

17 Pranab Mukherjee, *The Dramatic Decade: The Indira Gandhi Years* (Rupa Publications, 2015).

18 Biswas, ed., *Banglar Communist Andolan,* report placed in the 11th state council meeting of CPI(M), pp 520-7.

19 Amar Bhattacharya, *Lal Tamsuk* (Gangchil, second print June 2014), pp 63-4.

20 'The Jotedars' Coup,' https://www.epw.in/system/files/pdf/1967_2/47/from_our_correspondents_west_bengal_the_jotedars_coup.pdf.

21 S. Mohan Kumaramangalam, 'Governor's Power to Dismiss a Ministry,' https://www.epw.in/system/files/pdf/1968_3/1-2/capital_view_governors_power_to_dismiss_a_ministry.pdf.

22 'Bangla in Disarray,' https://www.epw.in/system/files/pdf/1969_4/5/west_bengal_bangla_in_disarray.pdf.

23 'Beyond the Triumph,' https://www.epw.in/system/files/pdf/1969_4/8/west_bengal_beyond_the_triumph.pdf.

24 Election Commission data base.

25 Franda, "Electoral Politics in West Bengal."

26 Bhattacharya, *Lal Tamsuk*, pp 57-9.

27 Speech of Basu on 1st August in the assembly, reprinted in Basu, *Nirbachita Rachanasangraha*, vol. 2, pp 24-30.

28 Basu, 'Politics of Violence Studies.'

29 Romesh Thapar, 'The Ferment of Today,' *EPW*, August 30, 1969, https://www.epw.in/system/files/pdf/1969_4/35/capital_view_the_ferment_of_today.pdf.

30 'Into the Open,' *EPW,* July 1969, https://www.epw.in/system/files/pdf/1969_4/28-29-30/west_bengal_into_the_open.pdf.

31 Ibid.

32 Ibid.

33 Marcus F. Franda, "The Political Idioms of Atulya Ghosh," in *Asian Survey* 6, no. 8 (1966), pp 420–33, www.jstor.org/stable/2642469 (accessed June 14, 2020).

34 Biswas, ed., *Banglar Communist Andolan*, pp 627-31.

35 'The Squeezed Middle,' *EPW*, March 28, 1970, https://www.epw.in/system/files/pdf/1970_5/13/the_squeezed_middle.pdf.

36 Romesh Thapar, 'The Shadow of Calcutta,' *EPW*, December 5, 1970, https://www.epw.in/system/files/pdf/1970_5/49/capital_view_the_shadow_of_calcutta.pdf.

POLITICS IN WEST BENGAL TAKES ITS SEPARATE COURSE

The people of the state who had dreamt of freeing the nation from British rule through some localised revolution by killing government servants here and there were now ready to worship democracy through inter-party violence – a unique position adopted in West Bengal politics since then. When Prime Minister Indira Gandhi went for an early national election in 1971, the much-awaited mid-term poll of the West Bengal assembly too was scheduled along with that. The election outcome of 1971 had put on record the divergence of West Bengal politics from the national mainstream. The inter-party violence, which was vitiating the political atmosphere of West Bengal for more than 18 months, received a further impetus and took 'a big leap forward, both quantitatively and qualitatively.'[1] On one single day, on 17th January, West Bengal recorded 14 deaths in political skirmishes. Due to widespread violence it was getting increasingly difficult for the Election Commission to enrol election staff – according to media reports just 4,000 persons had volunteered against the total requirements of 1,75,000. In West Bengal since then politics became a continuation of war by other means, with due apology to Carl von Clausewitz, the Prussian general. Politics is a struggle for power between several opposing forces. It is said that political events and outcomes are rarely, if ever, the product of any single actor's conscious intentions. But intelligent politicians can shrewdly manipulate the scenario and set the background carefully for a favourable outcome, like Indira Gandhi did in 1971.

But politics is also complex particularly in a country like India with diverse cultures of different regions. West Bengal in 1971 is a case in point. While the Indira wave swept the nation returning her with a majority that even Jawaharlal Nehru could not achieve, West Bengal remained confined to its chaotic politics involving competing political parties busy in saving the ground they had occupied and expanding the same during the hustlings. Naturally the intense emotion for survival ended up in violence like never seen before. The *EPW* wrote,

> The aggravated violence is only the surface reflection of the intensified deadlock underneath. The various political parties, and the social forces they represent, have been caught in the net of their distorted politics and the more they struggle to escape from the snare, the further they get entangled in their twisted politics.[2]

There were efforts by the CPI(M) in particular to present the party as innocent victims of violence. The killing of three young men who were at the most small-time, local-level supporters of the Congress at Burdwan had hurt the party's image badly. Even now whenever the issues of political murder in West Bengal come up for discussion the Sain Bari case comes up as a reference. The embarrassment of the CPI(M) could be read in the footnote added in the letter written by Jyoti Basu on 4 May 1970 to the governor S.S. Dhawan protesting against the police action on party members suspected to be involved in the Sain Bari case. The footnote mentions that there was a bomb attack on a procession of the CPI(M) organised in protest against the resignation of Ajoy Mukherjee as chief minister of the second UF government. This had resulted in a scuffle when the 'people' attempted to defend themselves and as a result some people died. In order to defame the CPI(M) the incident was distorted.[3] How deep rooted was the embarrassment could be seen in this falsehood propagated even after so many years of the murders. An immediate event at Patna railway station on 31st March, two weeks after the Sain Bari incident, was, many believed, stage managed to influence people away from the case – CPI(M) claimed that there was an attempt made on the life of Jyoti Basu when he got down from a train at Patna railway station to address a rally there. A party member Ali Imam who was standing nearby died in the firing. CPI(M) had organised a rally on the very next day, on 1st April, protesting against the attack on its leader. The Patna railway attack on Basu was more prominent in CPI(M) publications than in contemporary literature.

Political violence in West Bengal was widespread and so intense that even Hemanta Kumar Basu, a well-respected senior leader and former freedom fighter, was killed. The CPI(M) said that this was done to malign the image of the party and pass on the blame to it. The party had been bitterly complaining against the police actions, especially the use of the Central Reserve Police Force (CRPF), to stop political violence. Caught amidst such a violent political struggle, on one side from the extremist elements like the Naxals who intensified their campaign against the election, and its electoral oppositions who the CPI(M) alleged were also taking not exactly the roles of spectators in the political theatre of violence, the party found that election was thrust on them since Mrs Gandhi used a political tactic never used before. Political opponents as well as the analysts were flummoxed by her decision to prepone the Lok Sabha election which effectively untangled the Lok Sabha poll from the elections to the state assemblies. The electoral success of the ruling Congress depended entirely on how Mrs Gandhi would steer the campaign. The entire opposition lacking in any magic mantra for a successful campaign got busy in a contest that they never anticipated. But in West Bengal the picture was different since the principal political actor, the CPI(M), cornered though it was due to violence and multiple opposition from ultra-left to ultra-right, had deep connections with the peasants, factory workers and urban employees. To transform this readiness into another electoral battle was not difficult.

The election result of 1971 had shown how politics took shape in West Bengal by then and how different it was from what was practised in the rest of the country. In the Lok Sabha out of 520 seats which went to poll, the Congress led by Mrs Gandhi captured a record 352 seats; enough seats to allow it even to amend the Constitution. For amending the Constitution it required two-third majority support which the Congress had in the fifth Lok Sabha. CPI(M) emerged as the second largest party with 25 seats, two more than its rival the CPI. Out of these 25 seats as many as 20 came from West Bengal. Despite its huge electoral success nationally the Congress could win just 13 out of the 40 seats in West Bengal.[4] Clearly the state had less concern with a strong national government that was necessary to meet the impending challenges coming from the struggle in East Pakistan. It had no impact on the voters choosing the state assembly as well. In the West Bengal assembly the CPI(M) emerged as the largest party with 113 seats while the Congress bagged 105. Calcutta voted against the CPI(M), electing 16 members from the Congress, 1 from the CPI and just 5 from CPI(M), the CPI(M) paying the cost of violence. Perhaps due to widespread violence there was not a single woman candidate put up in the assembly. The United Left Front under CPI(M) had 123 members. A government was formed led by Ajoy Mukherjee whose party the Bangla Congress had just 5 members with Bijoy Singh Nahar of Congress as deputy chief minister. It survived just 3 months facing the assembly only once for 10 days.[5]

The Congress realised that continuation of a weak government under Ajoy Mukherjee would harm the national interest especially in view of the freedom movement for Bangladesh across the border.

Also the Centre needed to have a strong administration since continued political violence especially Naxalism would have harmed the national interest once the war with Pakistan broke out. Moreover the government led by Prime Minister Indira Gandhi was strong, in fact strongest since Independence judged by its majority in the Lok Sabha and therefore could take a strong decision. West Bengal thus came under the central rule for the fourth time in four years. Siddhartha Shankar Ray was appointed Union minister in charge of West Bengal – a clear enough message that the central government meant business. For the first time in the history of the state a strong action was initiated by New Delhi. Ray had called for all-party meetings to decide on the future course of action on the raging violence in the state. The modus operandi of the administration was seen in the mass killings of 12th and 13th August in the Cossipore and Baranagar areas of Calcutta. 'There is no parallel to these killings in even Calcutta's recent violence-ridden history; for an appropriate parallel one has to hark back to the great Calcutta killings of 1946.'[6] Reportedly the killings continued for 17 long hours from the evening of the 12th, and the police both local and central were not deployed. In a public statement on the murder of officially admitted 27 young persons, Ray had said that the killings reflected mass anger and people in the area had expressed satisfaction at the clearing out of Naxalites and anti-social elements. Curiously not a single political party which had joined the all-party meetings convened by Ray said anything in protest. The era of strong-arm politics in West Bengal with the police as bystander could not have a more auspicious beginning than just two days before the 24th Independence day of India.

The strong-arm tactics of the Congress went on unchecked. In fact, in due course, it increased manifold so much so that even leaders of the Congress ally the CPI were heckled for voicing disapproval of the violence against the opposition. It was cold blooded and calculated annihilation of the opposition by the Congress when even undertrial prisoners and detenus lodged in jails could not escape brutal attacks. The Congress ally CPI adopted a resolution condemning the violence. It blamed new recruits in the Congress who were anti socials or came from the Naxalites fold for various criminal acts. The CPI was also disappointed that the *jotedars* in rural areas were harvesting crops depriving the share croppers under police protection. The state-backed attack on the Left was so widespread that Left parties like the RSP and Forward Bloc joined hands with CPI(M) in local elections.[7] Post 1969 the Congress was rejuvenated and had taken position to win the next assembly election at any cost. The mid-term poll in 1972 that saw the Congress return to power for the last time was the harbinger of use of violence in rigging elections in the state. The widespread use of violence in the poll in West Bengal was a one-off tactic used by the rejuvenated Congress emboldened by a massive national electoral success in 1971, just a year before, and also by the swift victory over Pakistan during the Bangladesh freedom struggle. West Bengal was in rejoice mode and a huge crowd had gathered when Prime Minister Gandhi did a joint rally with the prime minister of Bangladesh Sheikh Mujibur Rahman to pay respect to the two heroes who created history. West Bengal had three reasons to tolerate the Congress bullying in the election to the state assembly. Firstly, the people were fed up with an annual ritual called election and were looking for a stable government. Secondly, they were also keen to have a strong government that would stop the continued blood bath on the streets. The Congress led by Mrs Gandhi was an obvious choice. Thirdly, and no less important, the people of West Bengal wanted to gift their votes to the party led by the leader who got them a free land for Bengalis, even though that land was not part of India. What is more, during the 20-odd election meetings in West Bengal Prime Minister Gandhi had assured more funds for the projects in the state, such as the Haldia port, the Second Hooghly Bridge, and a metro rail project, as well as the Centre's help in reviving the state's industries. The media in West Bengal had accepted this as a cue to encourage Bengal to opt for the Congress.[8]

But one cannot ignore the fact that the main rival the CPI(M), though subdued due to certain external factors, had its support base not much impaired. Out of a total of 13.35 million valid votes (59.84 per cent of the electorate), CPI(M) collected 3.65 million or 27.45 per cent as against 6.34 million or 47.52 per cent collected by the Congress (R).[9] CPI(M)'s share in the total had dropped by 5 percentage points from the peak reached in 1971. It received nearly 36 per cent of valid votes in the constituencies the party contested. Along with its coalition partners the CPI(M) had received one third of the valid votes polled, a significant share despite an election that was evidently not free or fair. In 1972 there was a Left coalition put together by the CPI(M) which had all the Left parties in West Bengal barring the CPI. The Left alliance won just 20 seats with the CPI(M) winning a mere 14 against 113 it did in 1971.

How true was the allegation of electoral malpractices that the CPI(M) had raised? Even before the election, on 31st January the parliamentarians hailing from the CPI(M) had handed over a list of 34 constituencies where the party was strong and where they alleged the police and para military forces were acting in a partisan manner. Jyoti Basu in a report on West Bengal election mentioned that Prime Minister Gandhi called the allegation false.[10] Basu cited several instances where prominent Left candidates were forced to stay outside their constituencies and how even complaining to the chief election commissioner did not help. In total he cited instances of massive rigging in 51 constituencies where the Left candidates were in a strong position. Apparently there was an Intelligence Bureau report which had indicated that the Congress was not exactly in the driver's seat in West Bengal; hence this was the poll tactic used by the Congress. The allegations both before and after the election were ignored. Jyoti Basu mentioned the various types of rigging that were resorted to. Before election the Left supporters were driven out of the constituency. Its election agents were threatened. Many polling booths did not have election agents from the Left which helped the Congress camp to cast false votes. During vote counting, with the help of counting officials, ballots in favour of the Left candidates were damaged so that these were rejected. The combined effect of such a well-planned election management was seen clearly in several constituencies where the Left had been traditionally strong. In Baranagar, Jyoti Basu lost by 38,987 votes, a margin of 39 per cent of votes polled. Basu received 30,158 votes which was less than 43,340 votes he had polled in 1971. The startling increase was in the number of votes polled by the opposition CPI candidate – he received 69,145 votes, more than double that of the opposition candidate polled in 1971. The polling percentage in the constituency was 87.4 per cent, more than 15 per cent higher than in 1971. If this looks normal one can cite the cases of Kalna, Nadanghat and Dum Dum. In Kalna, a CPI(M) stronghold, the party's candidate received 952 votes against 31,896 votes polled by the party one year ago. Similarly there was huge drop in votes polled by the party at Nadanghat (from 34,288 in 1971 to 2,621 in 1972) and Dum Dum (received 15,036 votes against 40,736 in 1971). There are many such examples. But what was curious, Jyoti Basu mentioned in his pamphlet, was that certain constituencies which were viewed as a strong bastion of the Congress, recorded increased polling for the CPI(M). That there was truth in what Basu claimed cannot be denied. It could be that taking a lesson from the 1972 election the Left too adopted the same system subsequently in the state which had helped its uninterrupted rule from 1977 till 2011.

The Congress election manipulation of 1972 was an innovation that stayed on in the state since then and used as and when this was necessary. Some Congress leaders however claim that this was not exactly an innovation but was used in limited extent by political parties, particularly the CPI(M) during elections.[11] Political violence in West Bengal since then became more organised and targeted towards electoral gain, a unique character that explains the isolation of West Bengal from the national political trend. The Congress model was adopted by the state's ruling party thereafter – the model of keeping the contenders away by hook or by crook.

The Congress administration between 1972 and 1977 was known for the party's internal problems. After decimating the rival Left the party cadres paid attention to each other intensifying the group rivalry which regularly ended in violence. There were several factions; the younger the leaders were the more intense were their brawls. Political murders were common, so was corruption. The wheat bran scandal had even hurt the image of the chief minister Siddhartha Shankar Ray since it had exposed involvement of his close relations along with Food Minister Kashi Kanta Maitra. It all started with the arrest of an official close to Maitra with a large amount of unaccounted money. The root cause of the scandal started with Maitra giving permits of wheat bran sale to his party cadres ignoring government procedures. To rope in cooperation of the youth Congress, he created a wheat-bran distribution committee in West Bengal in which he included people like Sudip Bandyopadhyay, the then Youth Congress president of West Bengal, Somen Mitra, Debaprosad Roy, etc. Price rate of wheat bran doubled from Rs 20-22 to Rs 40-44 per maund. In addition, wheat bran mixed with atta was passed off as food for human consumption. The black marketeers reaped huge profits with resultant gains for the politicians. Kashi Kanta Maitra had given the license for distribution of wheat bran to Jaydeep Mukhopadhyay, India's ace tennis player and nephew of Chief Minister Siddhartha Shankar Ray. But Ray did not hesitate to continue with the investigation which led to the arrest of Jaydeep's father Adhish Mukherjee. Maitra had to resign. Less than a year later, in June 1974 Sudip Bandyopadhyay, the Youth Congress chief, and Kumud Bhattacharya of the Chhatra Parishad (student wing of Congress) in a press conference brought in corruption charges against 5 ministers. Ray formed a one-man commission under the former chief justice of India K.N. Wanchoo to investigate. In January the report was submitted with two ministers resigning while complaints against three senior ministers were dismissed. The Pandora's Box of dissent in the state Congress was opened after this. Ray's close connection with Prime Minister Indira Gandhi ensured that he continued the full term in office. Factionalism in the Congress had plagued Bidhan Chandra Roy and he survived because of his own charisma and connect with the Centre; it was the same with Siddhartha Ray. In West Bengal, the Congress remained a circus of factional politics. After coming to power in 1972 through massive manipulation, the party remained thereafter consigned to the opposition benches. With the only national party being sidelined politics in West Bengal assumed its own course, in isolation from the national mainstream.

The Siddhartha Shankar Ray government had another unique distinction – that of running the state assembly without any opposition. The entire Left bloc – some 20 MLAs – had boycotted the assembly since this, they claimed, was created trampling over the democratic right of free election. It may be recalled that in 1977 the Congress had an alliance with the CPI in West Bengal and on paper it was the government of the Progressive Democratic Alliance (PDA). But the CPI was not always supportive; for example when there was an all India Railway strike called by the opposition parties in May 1974 the CPI joined in that strike. The CPI passed a resolution asking its MLAs to function as the opposition. The party blamed Chief Minister Ray for all the troubles. Ray was unhappy since he felt that certain central ministers wanted to embarrass him and were instigating the breakup of the PDA. The problem of the Congress government was both internal and external. The external one came from a movement against the Indira Gandhi government led by the veteran leader Jayaprakash Narayan. The internal one was intensified with Sanjay Gandhi taking an interest in politics. Sanjay had developed a strong antipathy towards Siddhartha Shankar and worked towards weakening his position with the prime minister. The disgruntled elements in the state Congress merrily joined hands with the anti-Ray campaign. Ray did not enjoy control over the state Congress structure. In addition, many who had benefitted from his support earlier now turned against him.

The genesis of factional fighting in the state Congress was in the way many senior Congressmen were denied tickets to contest elections and instead young leaders who came from the Yuva Congress and Chhatra Parishad were accommodated. In West Bengal the Congress led by Mrs Gandhi was popularly known as Naba (New) Congress. The leaders of the Chhatra Parishad and Yuva Congress had played a very crucial role in positioning Naba Congress in the state and had emerged as the driving force of the party. As many as 80 MLAs of the 216 Congress members in 1972 were at an average age group of not above 30. There were differences among these new leaders as well – an influential MLA from Calcutta Prafulla Kanti Ghosh (Sata Ghosh) fell out with Subrata Mukherjee. This led to two clear groups in the Chhatra Parishad – Mahajati Sadan and Siksha Banchao (Save Education). Their rivalry on many occasions resulted in bomb attacks on College Street, home of the Calcutta University, Presidency College, and Calcutta Medical College. The group rivalry could neither save *siksha* (education) nor the Congress in West Bengal. It is said that Sanjay Gandhi, in order to curb the influence of Ray, actively helped the disgruntled elements to approach the prime minister and complain against the chief minister. Pranab Mukherjee wrote that till 1975 Ray was a dominant figure. It was Ray who gave the idea of imposition of emergency to the prime minister. Mukherjee claimed that Mrs Gandhi had told him later that she had no idea of the possibility of declaring emergency on the grounds of internal disturbance.[12]

After the declaration of emergency from the second half of 1975, Sanjay Gandhi started getting actively involved in politics. The anti-Ray group in West Bengal used Sanjay's anti-Ray stance to create trouble for him. Those who were in the anti-Ray group included A.B.A. Ghani Khan Choudhury, Tarun Kanti Ghosh and Prafulla Kanti Ghosh, with support from the two central ministers D.P. Chattopadhyay and Pranab Mukherjee. Even T.N. Seshan, the then private secretary to the prime minister, had called up Ray to inform him about conspiracies being hatched behind his back. Ray was disgusted and wanted to resign but his supporters, the youth brigade, like P.R. Das Munshi, Subrata Mukherjee, Sougata Roy, Sudip Bandyopadhyay, Kumud Bhattacharya persuaded him to stay back. Thus while chief ministers like Nandini Satpathy and Hemabati Nandan Bahuguna were removed from Odisha and UP, Ray stayed put in West Bengal, but with reduced authority over the party. This was seen in the choice of candidates for the 1977 election.[13] The Congress was by then a family-run political party. Different factions were taking advantage of their proximity to certain members. This helped the rise of different leaders even in West Bengal. For their political gains the aspiring leaders of the Congress were more keen on maintaining their bases with the 'family' and its coterie instead of the people who were expected to vote for them. This ended the

Congress's prospects in the politically advanced and volatile state of West Bengal.

The Allahabad High Court judgment which unseated Prime Minister Gandhi for failing to follow electoral rules was the reason for the desperation of Mrs Gandhi. The judgment came on 12th June and on 25th, less than two weeks later, 'emergency' was declared. Much before the court judgment, the honeymoon of the people of India with Mrs Gandhi had been marred. Amidst growing discontent among the common people throughout the country due to gradual price rise of necessary commodities and rampant corruption, agitations started in each and every state of the country against the government as well as the Congress party. The mid-term poll results were grim for the Congress. Veteran leader Jayaprakash Narayan (popularly known as JP) was busy creating a movement against the government for addressing the woes faced by the people. The threat of 'total revolution' aroused political parties like CPI(M) to assemble under the umbrella offered by JP. Since early 1973, Basu was in touch with JP. JP came to Calcutta and had addressed a big rally in preparation for a movement in West Bengal. His presence unified the opposition – Jyoti Basu and Prafulla Sen both were on his side while different factions of the Congress also joined hands in demonstrating against the veteran national leader. When JP came to Calcutta on 2 April 1975 to address a convention of youths and students in the University Institute Hall, there was a violent demonstration in front of the proposed venue and JP was stopped from addressing the convention. JP received a taste of the violence unfolding in West Bengal. JP's car was gheraoed and certain Chhatra Parishad supporters practised their dancing skills on the bonnet of his car. It is insinuated that one such protester was Mamata Banerjee. The experience of Calcutta was quite a shock for JP. He later said in Bihar,

> What happened there, and of which I myself was a victim, was naked hooliganism and gangsterism in the presence of a West Bengal Minister, a West Bengal M.P. and posse of police officers and police force. West Bengal would be doomed unless the State is rid of Yuba Congress Chhatra Parishad gangsterism.[14]

Unknown to JP, by 1975 West Bengal had adopted its unique style of politics, not to be rid of the hooliganism, rather adopting it.

With the declaration of emergency there was no longer any need for counter demonstration against opposition leaders since all movements were now stopped. Emergency was the last nail in the Congress coffin in West Bengal. Though West Bengal did not experience atrocities like other parts of the country which became prominent in the opposition election campaign after emergency was lifted, the sentiment was overwhelmingly anti-Congress. When election was declared in 1977, the people of West Bengal were preparing to respond to the massive electoral rigging of 1972, Congress infighting, and violence seen in many parts of the state. The election results of 1977 were loud and clear.

When emergency was lifted and election was declared, West Bengal was unusually quiet despite some rallies by the United Opposition in Calcutta and some other centres. 'Absent today is the political passion that used to animate the people during the past three decades on the eve of the general elections and even critical by-elections,' wrote the magazine *EPW*.[15] Clearly the silence on the surface had a loud message underneath. The 5 long years of violence on the opposition had its toll. The period up to 1977 had witnessed several instances of liquidation of Naxalites as well as of supporters of the main opposition party, the CPI(M). Even after rigging the election of 1972, the CPI(M) was the target of systematic two-pronged attacks – one from the law-enforcing agencies and the other from the extra-legal gangs under the control of the government. Thus when election was declared CPI(M) was virtually confined to some offices only, with no signs of the party on the streets. Numerous local offices of the CPI(M) and trade unions, about 300 according to the party, were either physically occupied by Congress supporters or remained closed. About 1,000 of its cadres were killed, nearly 20,000 party members and activists were forced to flee their localities for fear of their lives. Only a fraction of them, not more than four to five thousand, could come back to their old bases for electioneering. They were under constant threat since they were sternly told to keep clear of politics. The terror unleashed since the 1972 election had unnerved a large part of the party's cadres. For them the 1977 Lok Sabha election was a curtain raiser of sorts – if an event could create history and unseat a Congress government in the country, they too had chances of returning home in West Bengal. There were enough reasons for the Left supporters to help the campaign in a muted way.

While the unthinkable happened nationally, in West Bengal the Congress ended up with just three seats – Darjeeling, Katwa and Barrackpore. The average polling in the state was just above 60 per cent while the polling percentage in Barrackpore, from where Saugata Ray, youth leader of Congress, won was more than 72 per cent. Saugata Ray seemed to be immensely popular in the constituency – he received 64.6 per cent of votes polled. The constituency stood out for huge polling and also defying the trends of all neighbouring constituencies where opposition candidates got elected defeating heavyweight candidates of the Congress and CPI. None of the Congress big names – Pranab Mukherjee, Maya Ray (wife of Siddhartha Ray), Priya Ranjan Dasmunshi, Sudip Bandyopadhyay – could win. Saugata Ray remained an exception, so was the huge polling in his constituency in his favour. The

CPI(M) won 17 Lok Sabha seats, its allies from the Left, Forward Bloc and RSP won 3 each, the Janata Party won 15, the Congress only 3. The CPI(M) received 26 per cent votes in the 20 seats it contested, the Congress 29 per cent in 34 seats. The Left parties received 34 per cent votes in the 26 seats they contested while the Congress with ally CPI won 36 per cent votes polled across the state. The Janata party which contested 15 seats, winning all, with support from the Left parties, received over 21 per cent votes polled. A mere look at the polling data shows that in 1977 clearly the Left parties had an edge over any other party in West Bengal.[16] The assembly election in 1977 was held under such circumstances.

What intrigues any analyst is whether there was no effort to indulge in malpractices during the 1977 Lok Sabha poll? After tasting success and with unchecked authority in the state it was reasonable to feel that the Congress would have liked to replicate its successful formula of 1972 again. It was reported that there were gaps in the draft electoral rolls almost everywhere in the state; perhaps there was a systematic attempt to drop a section of voters from the voters' list.[17] The draft roll for the Siliguri assembly constituency 'looks like' a 'study in chaos and confusion'.[18] The names of many people who had cast their votes in earlier elections and had been permanent residents of the town were missing. The election commission could not offer any plausible explanation. But the circumstances had changed in 1977. Due to misuse of the democratic process awareness of democratic values had ruled the Lok Sabha election especially in the media. Even officials were unwilling to blindly overlook electoral processes. The media's exposure of violence resorted to by the Congress-CPI alliance forced the Central Election Commission to order re-polling in 30 polling stations spread across several constituencies. Only 'the massive dimensions of the rigging in the Barrackpore constituency' was overlooked.[19] Jyoti Basu in an article in the *Peoples' Democracy*,

3 days before the 16th March poll, alerted people about the efforts to rig the election in 1977 also. He had written letters to Chief Minister Siddhartha Shankar Ray drawing attention to how the meetings of CPI(M) leaders were being disturbed, their party leaders were threatened, and cadres were attacked. But these letters were dismissed as concocted or exaggerations. Some of the constituencies where such muscle flexing were rampant included Malda, from where Pranab Mukherjee was contesting, Calcutta South (Priya Ranjan Dasmunshi was the sitting MP), Jadavpur (Somnath Chatterjee was contesting), and Diamond Harbour which was the constituency of Jyotirmoy Basu who was a prominent critic of the Indira Gandhi government in the Lok Sabha.[20]

During the 5-year period from 1972 to 1977 the Left parties had suffered miserably. Only 3 parties, the CPI(M), Forward Bloc and RSP, which had some local influences somehow survived while other smaller Left parties like RCPI, Workers' Party, etc., were consigned to history. The Lok Sabha election was a test case for the Left to check how much of its past penetration was still there. It was politically prudent for CPI(M) to tie up with the Janata Party which was a mixture of all sorts of ideologies – right, left, socialism, Hindutva – essentially a collection of anti-Indira forces in Indian politics. In the loss of the Congress the prayer of the CPI(M) in West Bengal fructified – the Left forces got the much needed respite from the administration-backed atrocities on their cadres. The assembly election of 1977 had set the future course of politics in the state, the final separation of state politics from that of the national mainstream.

The electoral adjustment of the Lok Sabha election could not be repeated in the assembly election held a few months later. Given the political ideologies of the Janata Party and CPI(M) such an alliance was not expected, nor was it desirable to elect a government that would not last for 5 years. Political leadership in West Bengal was more mature in 1977 than it was in 1967-69. Also pure electoral arithmetic had shown how the scenario was in favour of the Left. A veteran leader and master of legislative politics Jyoti Basu could not have given up the lure of forming a government at last. The factional fights within the Congress coupled with the ideological contradictions in the Janata Party, and its lack of any cadre support in West Bengal were strong enough reasons for the CPI(M)-led Left Front to contest the 1977 state assembly election for a kill. On 3 June 1977 Jyoti Basu appealed to the people to vote for the Left Front. That was the first time under the Morarji Desai government political parties were given time to speak on the government-controlled Doordarshan and All India Radio. Basu had explained how the local unit of the Janata Party was not keen on a coalition with the CPI(M) and its Left alliance. The Janata Party felt that people were afraid of the Left. He regretted that a coalition government with the Janata Party would have helped the state but it did not happen.[21] The failure of such a coalition was a loss for the Janata Party and a gain for the Left Front. In many seats due to tri-corner contests the Left Front candidates sailed through. However the Janata Party felt that without the 'baggage' of the Left it would sweep to power in the state. Meanwhile the Congress and the CPI broke its alliance, mostly due to the insistence of the West Bengal unit of the CPI.

The Left Front swept to power. While it was not a surprising result the scale of the victory was astounding. The Left Front bagged 230 seats out of a total of 293, for which polling was held. The Congress won 20 and Janata 29 seats – clearly the year 1977 marked a sweep of West Bengal by the Left forces. The massive victory perhaps was not even expected by the CPI(M) since it had attempted, before the election, to form coalition with the Janata Party which rejected the proposal. Perhaps the hibernation of 5 years that CPI(M) had suffered after the ouster in 1972 made it shaky of its strength. Had the assembly election been an extension of the anti-Indira vote of the Lok Sabha poll, the Janata Party should have received more votes than it eventually did. Clearly there was a strong support for the CPI(M) and sympathy for the party due to the violence it faced for 5 years. Forgotten by then was the fact that the party was no less responsible for the inter-party political violence that had engulfed West Bengal. One must acknowledge that the CPI(M) too had learnt its lesson. Post-election the Left Front government ensured containing political violence. West Bengal saw a peaceful transition to the Left. With its short-sighted politics the Janata Party led by the former chief minister Prafulla Chandra Sen lost its chance to come to power in coalition with the Left. That was the last opportunity for any national political party to knock at the gate of the Writers' Building. Though CPI(M) was recognised as a national political party on paper, in reality it was a regional party of West Bengal, Tripura and Kerala with West Bengal as its strongest base. The isolation of West Bengal from the national political mainstream received its final seal with the sweeping victory of the CPI(M)-led Left Front in 1977.

Immediately on winning the election and coming to power Chief Minister Jyoti Basu was busy presenting the picture of an efficient administration. Basu used the administrative machinery to effectively counter any possible political violence. He warned the Naxalites who were released from jails that they would be dealt with firmly if they went back to their old ways. Basu did not hesitate to use the police when a section of MBBS students resorted to hooliganism during the examinations. 'The party seems to be preoccupied with the concern for disarming its, to use a very mild term, critics, in the various chambers of commerce and in the South Block in New Delhi,' wrote the Left-leaning magazine the *Economic and Political Weekly*.[22] Jyoti Basu was pragmatic in pointing out the limitations of a state government in the national political economic system.

Clearly his initial moves illustrated his determination to run the Left Front government in the state for a longer period than seen in the past. Immediately after coming to power, messages issued from the Left Front government declared that the state was keen to welcome investment, even if it came from the multinational or Indian capitalist houses. This militated against the CPI(M) policy of checking the colour of money and it was rumoured that Promode Dasgupta did not entirely subscribe to the policy of welcoming capitalists of all classes irrespective of their pedigree. However Basu prevailed over him with the argument that for the state and the newly elected government it was advisable not to go into such dialectics. It was later in the year suggested that West Bengal could seek investment from the Eastern Bloc countries. There was talk of investment in the proposed Haldia petrochemical complex.

Without much delay the Left Front government went on to amend the much-criticised West Bengal Land Reforms Act 1955 and placed the West Bengal Land Reforms (Amendment) Bill. It was passed by the state assembly on 29 September 1977 after stiff opposition and eventual walk out by both the Congress and the Janata Party. The bill attempted to plug a loophole used by the landowners and defined owner cultivation. Now it meant that cultivation of the land had to be done by the owner or by use of family labour. It aimed at tackling the problem of absentee landlords. Anybody tilling land for a landowner was defined as 'bargadar' and the onus of proving that the person was not a bargadar was on the landowner. The new act, Operation Barga, ensured that the Left Front retained its political supremacy over rural Bengal.[23]

The next reform brought on the table was about administrative decentralisation. In 1977, the Panchayati Raj was introduced in order to fight rural vested interests and to tilt the relationship between different classes in favour of the mass of poor people.[24] The Left Front Committee recommended to the state government to hold the panchayat election in the state around the month of March of 1978. This, it was felt, would extend democracy to the grassroots. At the village level, distribution of surplus land and issues regarding barga, etc., could be handled by the panchayat. Thus the village-level problems which often enough created powerful vested interest groups could be tackled to a great extent through the decentralised Panchayati Raj system. On 4 June 1978, West Bengal held the first three-tier panchayat election. The two measures of Operation Barga and Panchayati Raj system created a firm root for the Left Front in West Bengal's politics.

The other important political decision of the Basu government was to demand a reform in the Centre-state relation. The state felt this would strengthen the nation, weaken the autocratic tendency as was seen during the promulgation of emergency, and help equitable distribution of resources for growth. The Left Front Committee recommended to the state government on 21st November to take up the issue of the need for modifying the Centre-state relation. Accordingly, on 1 December 1977 the state cabinet adopted the proposal on the Centre-state relation and the same came up for discussion before the state assembly on 25 March 1978. Before that on 4th November Basu issued a statement that during his stay in J&K he had detailed discussions on Centre-state relation with the state's chief minister Sheikh Abdullah. In order to seek support, the Left Front government had already circulated the Memorandum on Centre-State Relations among 'Ministers of the Union Government, Chief Ministers of States, Members of Parliament, Members of the State Legislatures, jurists, educational and cultural institutions, mass organisations and other representative bodies'.[25] The state assembly adopted the resolution demanding changes in provisions of the Centre-state relation. There is no record that any other state had joined the issue aggressively in support of the Left

Front government. West Bengal under Jyoti Basu opted to remain in isolation from the mainstream national politics as soon as the Left Front came to power.

The political isolation was clear in the Lok Sabha election of 1980. When election took place next, after the failure of the Janata experience, Indira Gandhi swept back to power with 353 seats, improving her record-breaking win in 1971 by one seat. But from West Bengal her party could bag just 4 seats, 2 from North Bengal, 1 from Calcutta and 1 from the industrial belt of Asansol. CPI(M) bagged 28 seats and its partners Forward Bloc, RSP and CPI took the remaining 10 seats. In the Lok Sabha CPI(M) emerged as the second largest opposition party, next to Janata Party (Secular). Clearly none of the political parties having support in the Hindi heartland had any influence in West Bengal. The isolation could also be seen when the Indira government came up with the Prevention of Black Marketing and Maintenance of Essential Supplies Bill. Pranab Mukherjee wrote,

> Jyoti Basu in his characteristic manner, challenged the government and boasted that the communist governments in three states would not implement the law. I firmly pointed out that it was the constitutional responsibility of the central government to ensure the implementation of the law passed by Parliament, the highest national forum of the country.[26]

This kind of bravado had become a regular routine of the West Bengal leaders. What Basu said was not expected from a person holding a constitutional post. In the Indira Gandhi cabinet in 1980 West Bengal had two cabinet ministers in Pranab Mukherjee and A.B.A. Ghani Khan Choudhury (known as Barkatda to his supporters). Both the leaders were willing to work for the people of the state. In fact, Ghani Khan was known for bringing in the NTPC thermal power plant at Farakka and also developing Indian Railway facilities in his constituency of Malda. Also he was instrumental in providing jobs and business opportunities to young people in Malda. Had the Left Front government adopted more conciliatory attitudes towards such ministers, the state would have gained. Curiously political differences took the form of isolation which harmed the common people in the long run.

In 1978 the displaced persons from erstwhile East Pakistan who were rehabilitated at Dandakaranya in Odisha started moving into a place called Morichjhanpi in the Sundarbans. Since the political stance of CPI(M) was that all refugees from East Bengal could be accommodated in West Bengal they felt that with the party coming to power they could then move back into the state. Earlier during the Congress rule the CPI(M) had taken up the cause of the displaced persons and demanded that they be resettled within West Bengal. Jyoti Basu, the leader of the opposition, while protesting the bill on eviction of people from occupying land illegally, had said that it would not be easy for the administration to evict people.[27] It is claimed that as late as 1974 Jyoti Basu had demanded in a public meeting that the Dandakaranya refugees be allowed to settle in the Sundarbans. In 1974-75 leading members of the subsequent Left Front government, including Ram Chatterjee, the minister of state for home (civil defence), had assured the refugees that if the Left Front came to power they would arrange for their resettlement in West Bengal, and at a meeting of the 8 Left Front parties in 1975 it was resolved that the refugees would be settled in the Sundarbans.[28] The West Bengal government in 1975 had cleared the mangrove vegetation at Morichjhanpi, an island in the northern-most forested part of the West Bengal Sundarbans, and replaced these with coconut and tamarisk plantation to increase state revenue. Since 1975, refugees who had been sent to Dandakaranya started to move to Morichchak which was part of Morichjhanpi Island under the Gosaba police station. The trickle turned into a deluge after Ram Chatterjee visited Dandakaranya on 30 November 1977. His companion Satish Mandal had reportedly referred to the Left Front government's 'decision' to develop the Sundarbans and assured the refugees that they would get land there. His slogan 'Sundarban Chalo' triggered the large-scale movement to the Sundarbans. The chairman of the Dandakaranya Development Authority rushed to Calcutta to brief the government. Immediately the state relief minister, Radhika Ranjan Banerjee, led a team of MLAs from all parties to Dandakaranya and told the refugees that West Bengal had no land to offer for their resettlement. 'The whole story is indeed a sordid one of broken promises, of missed trysts with fortune and of unprincipled exploitation by politicians of an unfortunate mass of people desperately seeking compassion,' wrote the *Economic and Political Weekly* in July 1978, much before the state administration had to use force to evict the refugees.[29]

On 9 February 1979, the matter was discussed in the West Bengal legislative assembly. Jyoti Basu denied the allegation that he had said, when on tour to Bhilai, that he would rehabilitate those suffering at Dandakaranya. Samar Mukherjee, his party MP, had raised the issue several times in the Lok Sabha. He also had blamed a section of politicians both from the Congress and the Janata Party for fomenting trouble, distributing land illegally and preventing the police from enforcing law and order in the island. Basu wrote to Prime Minister Morarji Desai that the deserters from different camps from outside West Bengal had taken shelter at the reserve forest area, claiming, 'They have created a sort of free zone for themselves in Marichjhanpi and have expressed their determination to resist by force any attempt to repatriate them … a number of organisations like Unnayan (OXFAM), Nikhil Banga Nagarik Sangha etc. are actively helping and instigating the deserters.' In response Prime Minister

Desai supported Basu on the actions he had taken or proposed to take.[30] Basu wrote the letter on 24th January and on 26th the police action started. Police launches blocked the island, tear gas was used, huts and tubewells and fisheries were destroyed. The casualty figures due to police actions varied. Annu Jalais mentioned only 25 per cent of those who came could return, while Basu had mentioned only two deaths in the assembly and had announced financial compensation for the family as well. It is claimed by subsequent researchers that the people who attempted to come belonged to the lower caste. The gentleman communists had no sympathy for them. They took up the cause of ecology and saving the reserve forest in order to keep the upper caste voices from Calcutta in good humour. Some even suggested that since several persons died and their bodies floated around the rivers, the tigers of the Sundarbans turned into man-eaters. However this subsequent observation of researchers like Jalais or Mallick seems biased. Basu had expressed anguish at the media reports from Calcutta on the issue. Calcutta's media was run by and for the 'bhadralok', who they felt, wanted the Left Front to take harsh action against the refugees deserting camps in Madhya Pradesh or Odisha. The fact remains that as chief minister Jyoti Basu had adopted similar high-handed methods used by the Congress regime in tackling the refugee settlement issues. Morichjhanpi remains a dark spot in the Left Front administration. The fact that this did not receive any coverage beyond Calcutta illustrates that the problems of rehabilitation of displaced persons due to the Partition did not generate interest outside the state. It remained confined within a specified circle of academicians working on the issues of subalterns as a case study of how refugees of the lower caste were ill-treated even by a Left government. Annu Jalais went further and wrote how the Morichjhanpi incident encouraged Sundarbans tigers to turn into man-eaters. Jalais wrote,

> The villagers explained that tigers, annoyed at the disturbances caused by the unleashed violence in the forest had started attacking people and that this was how they ended up getting a taste for human flesh. Others argued that it was the corpses of killed refugees that had floated through the forest that had given them the taste. Morichjhanpi was a turning point after which man-eating became part of the tiger's 'nature' or 'behaviour'.[31]

Such extreme views aside the fact remains that the Morichjhanpi episode remained a blot on the image of the Jyoti Basu-led communist government.

West Bengal was passing through several economic issues when Basu took over as chief minister. The fate of Haldia-Calcutta port was one such burning issue. The headwater discharge from the Farakka Barrage depended on the international agreement between India and Bangladesh. Water discharged, hydrologists said, was inadequate to flush the river. This apart, there were competing ports coming up on the eastern coast. West Bengal had certain assurances from the Janata government on developing a ship-repairing unit at Haldia. But such economic issues require negotiation particularly in the face of competing claims from other states. The isolationist political behaviour of successive West Bengal governments since 1977 in particular had placed the state at a disadvantage in competing with other states.

The state's economy had another nagging problem – load shedding. This was a problem which Basu had inherited but the result was slow withering of West Bengal as an industrial state. The nagging power shortage made industries opt for their own generators and also to move production to other parts of India. In the state assembly Basu spoke on 25 March 1980 about the problem his government had inherited. He pointed out the lack of investment made in power generation and how several projects were delayed or ignored. On the third anniversary of the Left Front government Jyoti Basu wrote in a party magazine *Deshahitaishi* how a large part of the economic activities in the state – rail, post, defence establishments, post offices, banks and central PSUs – were outside the control of the state government and how their independent plan of work affected the operation of the state government adversely. Clearly this was the prelude to the standard refrain that the Left Front had used a few years later – Deprivation by the Central Government (*Kendrer Banchana*) which used to be prominent in all its political campaigns.

Law and order continued to be a problem area in West Bengal. A letter from Basu to Prime Minister Indira Gandhi written on 29 November 1980 mentioned how the internal squabbles in the Congress was adding to the law-and-order problems in the state. Basu listed several instances where the various factions owing allegiance to Somen Mitra or Subrata Mukherjee fought with each other. Basu requested Mrs Gandhi to address the problem of inner party rivalry within the West Bengal Congress. Killing of political rivals was by then a part of West Bengal's daily life. Among the issues that Basu wrote about on the occasion of the Left Front government completing 4 years, was how the central government was acting against the interest of the state government. The Centre had stopped providing wheat for West Bengal's food-for-work programme. Supply of sugar, cement and kerosene was inadequate and irregular. There was hardly any progress on the setting up of the petrochemical complex, nor was the Centre keen on solving the Calcutta and Haldia port issue. The Centre objected to the setting up of an electronics complex in the state on the ground that it was a border state. Basu pointed out how the state was at a disadvantage even in framing laws. 'This requires approval from the President which means approval of the Central government.'[32] Thus the state government had limitations wrote Basu in another party magazine in 1981. Clearly the chief minister was preparing for the forthcoming state election in 1982. His message was simple. The central government had different political-economic views and wanted the Left Front government to be replaced.

The five-year rule of the first Left Front government was coming to an end. The reasonably stable administration and the government's success in Operation Barga made the Left Front feel confident of electoral success. The state cabinet formally adopted a resolution recommending an early election – by 15th March instead of the summer month of May. However the opposition in the state, the Congress, continued to be divided despite efforts made by the prime minister herself. The kind of suggestions which came in response to the Left Front government's recommendation of preponing the poll indicated that the party was still suffering from the nostalgic rigging of the 1972 elections. The Congress factions agreed on one issue – the state election should be held under the President's rule in the state. This could be done either by dismissing the Left Front government or after its term expired. The qualitative change in West Bengal politics with an ideologically cohesive Left Front government with massive majority in power made it difficult for the Centre to even think of any undue intervention in the state government. Finally the assembly election was held along with that of other states in May 1982.

There was one problem which the state government had not addressed – that of the handling of the police department. The recalcitrance of the police force went to such an extent that on 29th March the metropolitan magistrate of Calcutta, K. Ganguly, reprimanded the officer-in-charge (OC) of Taltola PS for intentionally and repeatedly flouting court directives. The magistrate observed that some of the OCs of different police stations in Calcutta had become so powerful that they did not bother to heed the orders of the court. They did not even report in time to the court about arrests made. There were several such instances and even a memorandum was submitted to the governor of West Bengal, B.D. Pande, by the Association for the Protection of Democratic Rights (APDR) highlighting several instances of police highhandedness in the state.

There was no doubt about the Left Front victory in the 1982 assembly election. Perhaps the only element of surprise was the scale of the victory. The Jyoti Basu-led Left Front bagged 238 seats out of a total of 294 – 81 per cent of seats, 9 more than the last assembly. While the Front had spectacular support in the rural and industrial areas, it failed to impress the voters in Calcutta. Two of its stalwarts – finance minister Asok Mitra and I&B minister Buddhadeb Bhattacharjee – lost in the city. The election result had revealed polarisation of the state between the Left and anti-Left. The Congress emerged as the rallying force of all anti-Left votes. There were complaints of rigging by the Congress and some media houses. The reason cited was the sharp increase in polling percentage. Compared to 56.15 per cent votes polled in the 1977 assembly elections, the polling percentage in 1982 was 20 per cent higher at 76.61. Points worth remembering are that in 1977 Lok Sabha polls the polling percentage was 60.24 per cent while it was 70.62 per cent in the 1980 Lok Sabha elections. Judging by just 6 per cent increase in polling it would be difficult to conclude that there was widespread rigging across the state.[33] Credit for increased voter turnout should go to the election machinery of the Left in the state. Their cadres knew like the back of their hands the voters booth wise and who would vote for them. Even many absentee voters in every booth were ensured of proxy votes. It is impossible for any election pundit to expose this kind of quiet systematic handling of polling. This was a standard feature of elections in the state. Unlike the poll result of the Lok Sabha constituency of Barrackpore in 1977, polling in West Bengal was never so openly manipulated again but managed scientifically.

Historically the reason for the existence of the comprehensive and systematic election machinery in the state can be traced back to the massive rigging during the 1972 state assembly polls. In a volatile state like West Bengal political survival depended on cadres keeping an eye on the party's prospects. With the introduction of local-level democracy like panchayat elections and increased emphasis on local polls political parties in West Bengal had no other option but to remain organised at the grassroots level. One important offshoot of such local-level political activity is that those who oppose the dominant political party too exercise their franchise energetically. The long queues that polling booths in West Bengal experience are the result of such political polarisation. This was seen across the state. For instance, the Left Front swept the districts where there was little reason to nurture grievance against the government by the majority of voters who in any case supported the kind of rural reforms which were initiated by the Basu government. Four districts of Cooch Behar, Jalpaiguri, Nadia and Burdwan only elected candidates fielded by the Front, and Darjeeling gave all but one seats to the Front. Even in the two largest districts of the state, 24 Parganas and Midnapore, with 55 and 37 seats, the Front won 48 and 32 seats, respectively. The strength of the non-Left opposition remained nearly unchanged at 54. Most of the Front candidates won with huge margins, of over 10,000 votes. But the election machinery of the Left Front was evident in the success of a little-known CPI(M) nominee, in the bye-election for the Diamond Harbour Lok Sabha constituency with a margin of more than one lakh votes. In Calcutta however the Front had to taste reverses when two of its prominent ministers had to bite the dust. Evidently Calcutta had no reason to be enamoured of Operation Barga or the Panchayati Raj system. The election result had shown the fault lines that the Left Front had to address. The last mile delivery of the benefits brought by the government had to be improved. In certain cases the state was dependent on support from the Centre – food for work for example. It was expected that the Centre ruled by the Front's principal opponent in the state would not be generous in extending such a support. The question was once the novelty of the Operation Barga and the food-for-work programme wore off, how would the Left Front keep charming the voters.[34]

Endnotes

1 'Behind the Violence,' *EPW* Annual Number January 1971, https://www.epw.in/system/files/pdf/1971_6/3-4-5/west_bengal_behind_the_violence.pdf.

2 Ibid.

3 Basu, *Nirbachita Rachanasangraha* vol. 2, p. 70. Incidentally the author was a schoolboy staying in the same locality, familiar with the two younger brothers of the five members of the Sain family and is an eye witness of the incident. There was absolutely no attack made on the procession of the CPI(M) by any of the Sain brothers.

4 Election Commission website.

5 Basu, *Nirbachita Rachanasangraha* vol. 2, p. 123.

6 'Politics of Mass Murder,' *EPW*, August 21, 1971, https://www.epw.in/system/files/pdf/1971_6/34/west_bengal_politics_of_mass_murder.pdf.

7 'Liquidation of the Left,' *EPW*, December 4, 1971, https://www.epw.in/system/files/pdf/1971_6/49/west_bengal_liquidation_of_the_left.pdf.

8 Biplab Dasgupta, 'The 1972 Election in West Bengal,' *EPW*, April 15, 1972, https://www.epw.in/system/files/pdf/1972_7/16/the_1972_election_in_west_bengal.pdf.

9 In 1969 when the Congress split, the party led by the old guard was called Congress O (O for Organisation) and the other led by Indira Gandhi was known as Congress R (R for Requisitionists). Ordinarily they were referred to as Old Congress or Adi Congress and New Congress or Naba Congress.

10 Basu, '*Paschimbange Sansadiya Ganatantra Dhangsa*' in *Jyoti Basur Nirbachita Rachanasangraha* vol. 2, pp 154-91.

11 Bala, "Dominance to Marginality 1947-1977".
12 Mukherjee, *Dramatic Decade*.
13 Bala, "Dominance to Marginality 1947-1977".
14 Ibid., quoted from Saroj Chakraborty, *My Years with Chief Ministers*.
15 'The Five-Year Emergency,' *EPW* Annual Number, February 1977, https://www.epw.in/system/files/pdf/1977_12/6-7-8/west_bengal_the_five_year_emergency.pdf.
16 Election Commission database.
17 Kalyan Chaudhuri, '1972 More than a Memory,' *EPW*, February 26, 1977, https://www.epw.in/system/files/pdf/1977_12/9/west_bengal_1972_more_than_a_memory.pdf.
18 Ibid.
19 Ajit Roy, 'Gains for the Left,' *EPW*, April 2, 1977, https://www.epw.in/system/files/pdf/1977_12/14/west_bengal_i_gains_for_the_left.pdf.
20 Basu, *Nirbachita Rachanasangraha* vol. 2, pp 264-8.
21 Ibid.
22 Ajit Roy, 'Not a Negative Vote,' *EPW*, July 2, 1977, https://www.epw.in/system/files/pdf/1977_12/27/from_our_correspondents_west_bengal_not_a_negative_vote.pdf.
23 Ratan Ghosh, and K. Nagaraj, "Land Reforms in West Bengal" in *Social Scientist* 6, no. 6/7 (1978), pp 50–67, www.jstor.org/stable/3516543 (accessed June 19, 2020).
24 Proshanta Nandi, 'Communism through the Ballot Box: Over a Quarter Century of Uninterrupted Rule in West Bengal,' in *Sociological Bulletin* 54, no. 2 (May-August 2005), pp 171-94 (Sage Publications, Inc.), http://www.jstor.com/stable/23620496.
25 Speech of Jyoti Basu before the state assembly on 25 March 1978, reprinted in Basu, *Nirbachita Rachanasangraha* vol. 2, pp 25-37.
26 Mukherjee, *Dramatic Decade*.
27 Ross Mallick, "Refugee Resettlement in Forest Reserves: West Bengal Policy Reversal and the Marichjhapi Massacre," in *The Journal of Asian Studies* 58, no. 1 (1999), pp 104–25, www.jstor.org/stable/2658391(accessed June 20, 2020).
28 Annu Jalias, 'Dwelling on Morichjhanpi When Tigers Became "Citizens", Refugees "Tiger-Food",' *EPW*, April 23, 2005, https://www.epw.in/system/files/pdf/2005_40/17/Dwelling_on_Morichjhanpi.pdf.

29 Kalyan Chaudhuri, 'Victims of Their Leaders' Making,' *EPW*, July 8, 1978, https://www.epw.in/system/files/pdf/1978_13/27/from_our_correspondents_west_bengal_victims_of_their_leaders_making.pdf.

30 Basu, *Nirbachita Rachanasangraha* vol. 3, pp 57-67.

31 Jalias, 'Dwelling on Morichjhanpi.'

32 Basu, *Nirbachita Rachanasangraha* vol. 3, pp 132-46.

33 'Un-arithmetic of "Rigging,"' *EPW*, June 26, 1982, https://www.epw.in/system/files/pdf/1982_17/26/west_bengal_un_arithmetic_ofrigging.pdf.

34 'Clear Polarisation,' *EPW*, May 29, 1982, https://www.epw.in/system/files/pdf/1982_17/22/west_bengal_clear_polarisation.pdf.

DARKNESS UNDER THE LAMP

The Left Front started its uninterrupted 'democratic' rule in West Bengal with a monotonous slogan that the Centre treated the state very 'shabbily'. In his second full-year budget in 1979 the West Bengal finance minister Ashok Mitra told newsmen how the state was being treated shabbily by the Centre. He pointed out that the Left Front government would tell the people of the state of the National Plan incongruity, organise them to rise and fight against it. He tried to cite the partiality of the Centre against the Eastern Zone with some statistics. During the 7-year period of 1969–76, the per capita bank credit advanced was only Rs 24 for Orissa, Rs 40 for Assam, Rs 19 for Tripura, Rs 38 for Bihar, and Rs 146 for West Bengal. By contrast, the figure for Punjab was Rs 346, for Maharashtra Rs 308 and for Tamil Nadu Rs 203. The Life Insurance Corporation's per capita investment during the same period was Rs 16 for Assam, Rs 23 for Orissa, Rs 5 for Tripura, Rs 14 for Bihar and Rs 17 for West Bengal; against these, the amount for Gujarat was Rs 52 and for Haryana Rs 55. The distribution of loans from term-lending institutions also conformed to the same pattern.[1] The theory of *Kendrer Banchana* (Centre's deceit) without looking at the reasons and possible remedies was used as a cloak by the political communication savvy Left Front leaders.

After winning the second term there was some lip service from the top leaders of the Front on stepping up investments in the state. In the first public meeting that he addressed soon after being sworn in as the chief minister for the second term, Basu noted that during the past 15 years or so, there had been hardly any fresh investments in the state's large-scale sector.[2] Curiously Basu mentioned that his government would continue to hold dialogues with industry chambers for investment. When other states were busy wooing industrial houses for investment the state remained confined to a system with a rigid, inattentive administrative set-up. Investment decisions are made not merely on the basis of policies enacted but the alacrity with which policies are implemented to suit an investor. But this did not find much merit in the appeal of the Left Front government. In fact, Promode Dasgupta, the chairman of the Left Front and the other power centre, said that so long as workers were not cheated by the industry, West Bengal was the best place in the country for investment. Clearly the appeal for investment was from the perspective of workers' rights, which might sound attractive to his politics but certainly not for an investor. What is more, while wooing investors Jyoti Basu had pointed out discrimination by the Centre in giving permission to MRTP and FERA companies[3] to set up new industries in West Bengal. The reason why immediately after coming back to power the Left Front leaders took up the issue of investment was their awareness that the biggest problem of the state would be the burgeoning unemployment. It was beyond the capacity of the state exchequer to provide unemployment benefit and food-for-work programme in perpetuity. If only issuing statements could attract investment West Bengal could have been the most successful state during the 1980s.

The 1982 elections had shown how the Left Front had by then mastered the art of winning elections by a strategy of controlled and disciplined mobilisation of the people aimed at manufacturing consent in its favour and at delegitimising and decimating the very idea of a legitimate opposition.[4] When the Lok Sabha election was held in December 1984 the popular sentiment across the nation was completely in favour of the Congress due to the assassination of Mrs Indira Gandhi. That Rajiv Gandhi, her son, would win was beyond any doubt. The only issue was how many seats would the party fetch. For the CPI(M) in West Bengal it was a contest for retaining its supremacy at a time when the party was losing its charm with the electorate and also had to meet the challenge of sympathy wave in favour of the Congress. However, the Left Front could benefit from the strong factional fight in the Congress – there were two strong cabinet ministers at each other's throats – Pranab Mukherjee and Ghani Khan Choudhury. As far as Ghani Khan was concerned, he was popular in Malda, his home constituency, due to projects he had brought into the district. Pranab Mukherjee was a non-resident Delhi-centric politician with no base anywhere in West Bengal. His search for a safe seat in Calcutta did not materialise due to the factional fight. For the Congress the 1984 Lok Sabha election was a huge success – the party bagged 16 seats, the highest after 1962. What is more, the Congress swept all the seats in Calcutta and its outskirts. The most notable electoral loss for the CPI(M) was that of Somnath Chatterjee at Jadavpur where a fresh young candidate Mamata Banerjee won. Apart from Chatterjee, stalwarts of the Forward Bloc (Chitta Bose), RSP (Tridib Chaudhury) and CPI(M) leaders Niren Ghosh and Samar Mukherjee lost. The Congress received 48.16 per cent of votes and the four Left Front partners polled nearly the same – just 48.43 per cent votes. The Left Front won 26 seats with the CPI(M) bagging just 18 seats. The feeling of anti-incumbency towards the Left was visible in the success of the Congress in the 1984 Lok Sabha election. The Left Front paid closer attention to election management after this debacle. Jyoti Basu in his assessment stated that people were influenced by the false promises made by the Congress of providing employment to West Bengal youth and opening of factories which were closed in the state apart from the sympathy factor. He maintained his argument that the central government had in the past deprived the state and would still do the same.[5] Subsequent election management in West Bengal should be read in the context of this close encounter of the 1984 Lok Sabha polls.

In 1987 when the state assembly election fell due, the Congress hoped that this was its chance to come back to power. Prime Minister Rajiv Gandhi came to West Bengal for an intense campaign. He promised that he would provide one million new employment opportunities and kickstart development in the state. His whirlwind tour was matched by Jyoti Basu traversing the state in an organised and systematic manner. If there was factional fighting in the Congress, so was there in the CPI(M) and among other Front partners. Basu defended the 10-year track record of his government by highlighting the failure of the Rajiv Gandhi government in the last 3 years of power. In the end the election result was determined by the organisational supremacy of the Left Front.

Rajiv Gandhi's dream of creating a *Natun Bangla* (New Bengal) ended up in a dream victory for the Left Front which won 251 seats in the 294-member assembly. The Congress won just 40 seats – a loss of 13 seats from the 53 seats it had bagged in 1982. The Left Front bagged 51.06 per cent votes against 41.41 of the Congress. In 1982 the Front had 50.73 per cent votes. The election machinery of the Left Front, CPI(M) in particular, could not be challenged in West Bengal. It proved invincible even in the face of a challenge led by a popular prime minister, who only 3 years back had swept to power with record victory or visible feeling of anti-incumbency among the electorates of the state. The stunning victory of the Left Front in 1987 could not be attributed either to the land distribution of the first term or to any spectacular economic development brought in by the Basu government. There was no visible wave in favour of the ruling Front.

Yet it could retain its vote share per constituency on an average.[6] It was the victory of a well-oiled election machinery that the Left had created in the state. This stunning election machine helped the Left Front in four more assembly elections. The political isolation of West Bengal was supported by such magnificent election machinery.

There were many heinous incidents and murders committed in public view in West Bengal. A prominent one, that was never investigated, had been the lynching of 17 Ananda Marga members (16 monks and one nun) on the morning of 30 April 1982. When the 17 Ananda Marga renunciates were travelling to their headquarters at Tiljala to attend a conference they were dragged out of taxis at Bijon Setu, railway overbridge at Ballygunge station. They were beaten to death and then set on fire. Curiously nobody was arrested. Jyoti Basu said that it was done to defame his government. However, he took no steps to arrest and punish the perpetrators. Then the officer in charge of the Tiljala police station, Gangadhar Bhattacharya, was killed in broad daylight on 31 October 1983. The deputy commissioner of police in charge of the Calcutta port, Vinod Mehta, and his bodyguard were killed on 16 March 1984. A suspect arrested for the murder was killed in the lock-up of the police headquarters in Calcutta. Perhaps this helped to protect the conspirators. These were some high-profile cases of murder in the state capital Calcutta. If this was the scene in Calcutta one can well imagine how peaceful the rural areas were.[7] Organised political violence is what makes West Bengal a unique example in the largest democracy of the world.

The rape and murder of health officers on 30 May 1990 had painted a frightful picture of the state's law and order situation. Three health officers were returning to Calcutta after inspecting an immunisation programme in Gosaba. The team consisted of Anita Dewan, the deputy district extension media officer of the West Bengal Health Department; Uma Ghosh, a senior officer of the Health Department;

and Renu Ghosh, a representative of the UNICEF's World Health Organisation office in New Delhi. Around 6:30 pm when they had reached Bantala near the Eastern Metropolitan Bypass, a group of 4-5 youths stopped their car near the CPI(M) party office. The driver Abani Naia made an attempt to escape, but he lost control and the car overturned. In the meantime, another gang of 10-12 youths arrived at the spot, who pulled one of the ladies out of the car, while the others pulled out the other two ladies. The attackers killed the driver and set the car on fire. The lady officers were taken to a nearby paddy field and raped. One of the ladies who tried to resist the rapists was killed. The police brought the naked bodies of the officers to the emergency department of Calcutta National Medical College at around 11:30 pm. Initially they were presumed to be dead, but later two of them was found to be alive and were admitted for treatment. The dead lady officer had a metallic torch inserted in her vagina. Even the word 'gruesome' fails to describe the barbarity of the acts. Health Minister Prashant Sur and Chief Minister Jyoti Basu attempted to dismiss the incident lightly and said this did not indicate breakdown of law and order in the state. Clearly the CPI(M) was living in denial. Not that the other constituents of the Left Front bought into this. On 3rd July, the state's minister for agriculture, Kamal Guha (of the Forward Bloc) alleged connivance of the police with dacoits in Cooch Behar in North Bengal. On 11th July, a CPI(M) MLA, Chittaranjan Biswas, made similar allegations in connection with a spate of dacoities in Karimpur in the eastern district of Nadia. On 17th July, during the elections to the Calcutta Corporation, the city saw widespread violence and rigging, prompting at least one Left Front constituent, the CPI, to publicly deplore the incidents.

Incidences of rape and murder, often in clear complicity with the police, were plenty. Soon after Bantala, between 6th to 8th June, inside the Singur police station in Hooghly, three policemen raped a young girl. When the local people surrounded the station to protest, the police opened fire on them killing one person. On 18th July, near Birati railway station in North 24 Parganas, a band of smugglers and hooch-den owners raided the neighbouring shanties and gang-raped seven women who were refugees from Bangladesh. Both in Bantala and Birati, the local police stations were situated within a stone's throw of the affected spots but the police chose to turn a blind eye to the incidents. All through May, June and July of 1990, news of dacoities from different parts of the state poured in through media reports.[8]

That the CPI(M) did not care much could be gauged from the reactions of its leaders. Basu had support from his comrades. Two CPI(M) MPs, Biplab Das Gupta and Malini Bhattacharya, expressed satisfaction with the police for their investigation into the Bantala incident. Another CPI(M) member, Shyamali Gupta, who was then heading the party's women's front, Ganatantrik Mahila Samiti, felt that the Birati incident was invited by the women since 'one of the Birati women is of ill-repute'.[9] What is more, Lakshmi Sen, secretary, Calcutta district committee of CPI(M) even discovered a Congress conspiracy behind the Bantala incident. The secretary of the state CPI(M), Sailen Das Gupta, was less imaginative and blamed 'police inaction and nexus between the hoodlums and the police for such incidents'.[10] Clearly by 1990 the CPI(M) had turned the state of West Bengal into a den of hooligans. The ruling party had built up its deep network with the lumpen elements which in a politically charged-up state was a sure shot route to continued power. West Bengal had good reason to remain isolated from the rest of the nation.

The Lok Sabha election of 1989 saw the second occasion, again short lived, when a coalition of opposition political parties replaced the Congress at the Centre. The election saw the ruling parties losing everywhere across India with the singular exception of West Bengal. The Left Front secured 37 seats out of 42 Lok Sabha seats in the state. The Congress polled 41.8 per cent votes while the Left Front won 51 per cent out of 79.7 per cent polling witnessed in the state. Clearly the Front wielded its magic wand for any election in the state. By splitting hair, analysts noted that in the 1989 Lok Sabha poll the Congress had maintained its lead in 60 assembly constituencies compared to just 40 that the party could win in 1987, just 32 months later. It was therefore concluded that the Congress did better than earlier. The media highlighted the election result of the Jadavpur constituency – the seat bagged by the young and upcoming leader Mamata Banerjee in 1984 went back to the Left Front 5 years later. What was the reason for the electoral success of the Left Front? The state's economic parameters were no shining examples enticing enough for the voters. The advantage that the CPI(M) had over any other political party was its disciplined and robust organisational structure where the success of cadres to leaders was dependent on the seamless system laid out from the village panchayat to the Writers' Building in Calcutta. The local committee offices of the party were more powerful than the local-level administrative machinery. The active involvement of the party cadres in the everyday life of the people gave the party a strategic advantage in election campaigns.[11] The presence of the party was so pervasive that it had a nearly foolproof system of information gathering and taking preemptive actions. No other political party in the country had this kind of organisational network. Partha Chatterjee wrote,

> … Especially in the rural areas, a large part of that party's cadre is in any case engaged on an everyday basis in political work at the village level in connection with the running of the panchayats. The party can, even at short notice, without

> much difficulty, set up an effective machinery for a door-to-door campaign in almost every constituency in West Bengal.

One major outcome of the Left Front rule in West Bengal was the death of the autonomy of 'civil society'.[12] The Left Front government had successfully maintained its hegemony over the civil society in the state through careful manipulation and coercion. The tools used were simple but effective. Anybody aspiring for a position had to pass through a process of selection and verification to determine if the person would cause trouble and militate against the party line. Thus a dominance was ensured in perpetuity. The Left Front had continued for 10 years now yet the civil society in West Bengal remained shackled in its past, isolated from the rest of humanity.

The other instrument used by the Left Front administration in ensuring its control over the grassroot level was decentralised planning. This empowered its local-level cadres and turned them into rent seekers, an intelligent way of lubricating the party machinery. Land redistribution and Operation Barga had laid the foundation which was effective in turning village panchayats into vibrant bodies for the rural economy.

> In West Bengal, the experiment at decentralized planning (initiated from 1985-86) was preceded by the politicization of the panchayat elections (in 1978 and 1983), by the introduction of land reform through the panchayats, and finally, the implementation of programmes like the IRDP, NREP, Drought Relief Programme (and other rural development and employment programmes) through the panchayats.[13]

The Left Front used all centrally sponsored schemes and low-interest loans available from banks for the benefit of its supporters. The party was shrewd enough to use every possible fund made available under central government schemes and at the same time ensuring that the beneficiaries remain obligated to the party. The rural people also knew that by defying the well-laid-out system they would be deprived hence continued to remain loyal to the system. This complete dominance of politics in everyday life had ensured that West Bengal remain isolated politically.

The three levels of local administration – the gram panchayat at the village level, the panchayat samiti at the block level, and the zilla parishad at the district level – brought in a new type of socio-economic balance in the West Bengal rural scene. These bodies were involved in activities relating to the planning of developmental and infrastructural works, the appointment of staff and extension workers, the execution of centrally sponsored poverty alleviation programmes, and the implementation of state-initiated reform programmes, such as land reforms and Bargadar registration. The elected leaders at the village level had a dominant say in earmarking the funds available from departmental outlays, district plan funds and special programme outlays such as the IRDP, NREP and RLEGP.[14] In addition, the panchayats had a decisive role in the distribution (and recovery) of bank loans. Panchayats took responsibility for formulation of schemes under IRDP and implementation of the same in collaboration with banks. They identified the persons eligible for getting loans under IRDP and sponsored their cases to the banks as also the sharecroppers. All beneficiaries had to be selected by a joint commission of the government administration, i.e the BDO, the panchayat *pradhan* and the bank officer.[15] Therefore the party was keen on maintaining its hold over panchayat election – the reason why such elections even now are decided on the strength of the local-level hooligans. Caste has been replaced in West Bengal by political muscle flexing.

In a case study of human rights and state politics in three states – Assam, West Bengal and Punjab – researcher Koyel Basu made an apt observation,

> The most powerful conduit of left authoritarianism is disempowering the people by immobilizing them politically. It involves the crushing of any independent or autonomous political initiatives of any individual or group. Where fear or inducements did not work the left resorted to spectacular displays of violence and arson to retain its rule. History has shown that there is a major transformation of the left when it comes to power. Outside of power it is a militant champion of democracy and rights; but when it is comfortably ensconced in power it often becomes a status quoist and conservative force.[16]

Thus in West Bengal terror came back within a few years of the Left Front government taking over. The police were resorting to firings in various parts of the state and by 1982, West Bengal earned the distinction of having the highest number of incidences of police firings in the whole country. It was becoming apparent that the Left Front government was in no way different from any other government.[17]

The election results in the state illustrate the claustrophobic grip that the election machinery of the CPI(M) had in West Bengal. The state remained immune to the national sentiment mostly, an exception being the 1984 assassination of Prime Minister Indira Gandhi who was hailed as the architect of Bangladesh, an emotional issue for West Bengal. Barring the 1984 election, the charm of Mrs Gandhi over the electorates of West Bengal could not be ascertained, since the elections of 1971 and 1972 were held under a different political atmosphere which was decided more by power than passion of the ordinary voters. The Lok Sabha poll of 1989 was held in the backdrop of the Ram temple agenda in the Hindi heartland and saw a revival of the BJP nationally which had just two seats in the 1984 Lok Sabha. Even in West Bengal the BJP made some mark, in terms of votes polled, though at 1.67 per cent of votes polled it was insignificant politically. One characteristic of polling in West Bengal is the higher voter turnout compared to any other state of similar size. In 1989 against a national average turnout of 61.95 per cent West Bengal recorded 79.67 per cent polling. In the next 4 Lok Sabha polls the polling percentage in West Bengal compared to the national average had been uniformly higher – ranging between 15 per cent in 1999 to 24 in 1996.[18] Evidently election engineering in West Bengal was in an advanced stage. Left Front cadres – to be more specific, those belonging to the CPI(M) – were familiar with voter profiles in every locality. The party was always prepared to meet any electoral challenge. From 1989 to 1999, in 5 Lok Sabha polls the seats captured by the Left Front varied between 29 (lowest in 1999) and 37 (highest in 1989 and 1991). Of these the CPI(M) captured 21 (the least in 1999) and 27 (highest in 1989 and 1991). Clearly the election wave in West Bengal moved only in one direction – a stark example of political isolation of the state. Meanwhile in two state assembly polls, held along with the Lok Sabha election, the Left Front maintained its lead with the CPI(M) capturing absolute majority on its own in both 1991 and 1996. The only element of surprise occurred in 1996 when the Congress recovered from a low of 43 seats in 1991 to 82 seats – a near doubling of seats. If one looks at the poll percentage, the Left Front maintained its 45+ vote share with CPI(M) taking 35+ and the three partners collectively winning the remaining 10 per cent polled by the Left Front. The anti-Front vote was stuck at over 35 per cent, touching 40+ occasionally but the equation changed with the arrival of the Trinamool Congress (TMC) in 1998. Both in 1998 and 1999 the total opposition votes touched 50 per cent with the Congress vote share touching 15 and 13 per cent only. Clearly to West Bengal electorates a national political party had less appeal than a homegrown regional party. The arrival of TMC and its instant electoral success illustrate the isolation of West Bengal from the national mainstream politics. A splinter group, separated from the Congress, could immediately win a larger share of opposition votes which had otherwise been going to the Congress so long.

That politics, power to be precise, was at the root of all decisions of the Left Front government since its victory in 1977, was best demonstrated by its decision to abolish teaching of English from the primary level. In 1980 in its education policy the government concluded that English was a stumbling block for the rural poor to strive further in studies, hence the language should be taught only at the post-primary level, say from class five, when the student has reached proficiency in the mother tongue. There were intense debates for and against the decision but the government did not budge. Looking back, the decision helped creating a generation of students who were deprived of the opportunity to compete in the fast-changing market economy. This helped the party to maintain the supply of cadres who would swallow whatever was dished out to them. The education policy was aimed at creating faithfuls. English learning could return to the primary stage, from class one onwards, only 24 years later. By then, elsewhere in the country, information technology (IT) had emerged as the fastest source of employment. In fact, if one looks at the anecdotal experiences the crux of the political philosophy of the Left Front government was to keep people at a subsistence level so that the vote bank created meticulously remained unimpaired. The stiff opposition to introduction of computers in West Bengal, too, had its origin in the same idea of staying away from progress. Only then the people, living at just above starvation level, would remain subservient to the command of the party. A three-term CPI(M) member of the Lok Sabha from Diamond Harbour constituency, Amal Dutta, had to learn a bitter lesson at a late stage in his experienced life. Dutta was a member of the public accounts committee of the parliament. He saw in course of his visit the prosperity of the flower farmers in Bengaluru. Since the soil quality in his constituency Diamond Harbour was similar, he wanted to introduce flower farming to help increase the earnings of the people in his constituency. The party wanted him to place the idea before the panchayat leaders who dismissed his idea. They said that the support to the party was inversely proportional to the income of the people. It was therefore necessary to keep them just above the poverty trap.[19] The same principle of maintaining the party hegemony led to the Left Front protest against introduction of computers in the state. It was said that computers would reduce job prospects while the huge prospect of IT sector employment was completely ignored. How much this decision ensured the political continuation of the Left Front is less important than the economic loss that West Bengal faced. A state which had the prospect of leading the Indian IT and ITES sector remains handicapped even today due to missing the opportunity when the time was ripe.

The curious political outlook of the leadership was exposed during an inner conflict in the Left Front in West Bengal. The problem was exposed to the public glare on 18 September 1988 when a Bengali newspaper in Calcutta splashed on its front page facsimiles of two confidential notes exchanged between Chief Minister Jyoti Basu and PWD Minister (and RSP nominee) Jatin Chakravorty. The notes related to the subject of according preference to a Calcutta-based electric lamp manufacturer, Bengal Lamp, in procuring the government's requirements of electric lamps and fluorescent tubes.

The chief minister's note had mentioned the lamp manufacturers' representation on this and his recommendation to the PWD minister to consider 'the prayer along with other manufacturers' of lamps. Jatin Chakravorty mischievously wrote in his response that Basu's son had earlier met him with the request. The notes were leaked and created a controversy. Even the opposition Congress jumped at the issue to demand Jyoti Basu's resignation. While the immediate outcome of the controversy was the resignation of Jatin Chakravorty from the ministry, the practical issue that was ignored during the unnecessary controversy was the closure of the company factory. In any administration, protecting a running establishment and about 500 jobs would have received priority but not in West Bengal. Even the unchallenged leader of the Left Front could not help a sinking company. Leaders who were expected to rejuvenate the state's economy were unconcerned about their primary responsibility – completely isolated as they were from reality. The *EPW* commented that this was no sudden development rather '... it is the logical outcome of all the unprincipled slide down and laxity that has been the feature of the functioning of the left parties in the state during the last 10 years.'[20]

The fault lines were in open display when the Left Front started its third term, after a sweeping election victory. Analysts argued that the mess into which West Bengal had plunged could be traced to two factors.

> First, right from the beginning, in the daily running of the state administration, the party had demonstrated a rabidly partisan and a curiously unprofessional attitude along with a pathetic inefficiency in functioning. Following the line of least resistance, it has allowed employees in government offices and other establishments (most of whom are members

of CPI (M)-led unions) to shirk work and indulge in graft and other corrupt means of satisfying their private ends.

The second and unavoidable effect of such a relaxed administration was 'the emergence of lumpen underworld as a powerful arbiter both in politics and civil society.'[21] These two factors, partisan politics by the ruling party and use of lumpen elements to thwart any political challenge, plagued West Bengal since then. Even today the same elements are present overwhelmingly as can be seen more than 30 years later. Though the Left Front, architects of the downfall, have fallen by the wayside and a new class of political power has taken over, the same architecture that the Left Front had built carefully remains unimpaired in West Bengal.

When the only goal of the political leadership was to somehow stick to power and win elections, the necessary step would have been to weaken the civil society and institutions meant to protect the rule of law. The Left Front had successfully completed this objective within 10 years of its rule. The membership of the party was a good enough defence against anything. When party was supreme nothing moved in the corridors of government office without a party recommendation.[22] This helped corruption to flourish. The low plant load factor in the state-owned power plants resulting in such indiscipline became a source of perennial power failure in the state. All public services like repair and maintenance of roads or clearing garbage were dead but the employees entrusted with the task could earn their living while enjoying all benefits of trade unionism. Such an atmosphere affected the police department. The incidents at Bantala and elsewhere mentioned earlier were the result of such lax policing in the state.

The relentless pursuit of power resulted in muscle power replacing ideological debates. Naturally the underworld enjoying protection from the ruling party became decisive factors in certain areas, effective gate keepers for anybody not stamping on the party symbol. Of course their spheres of operation expanded beyond politics and extended to the daily social life of the citizens. The longer the Left Front ruled the more deep rooted the arrangement turned. Even Arun Prokash Chatterjee, a leading lawyer and a former standing counsel of the Left Front government, said that as a member of the CPI(M), he had found that 'often the number of the "auxiliary groups" trained in the use of arms was more than the real party members.'[23] The sway of the underworld was once again established during the Calcutta Corporation election in 1990. Calcutta's media flashed reports of booth capturing and violence but CPI(M) leaders congratulated the people for a peaceful election. 'False voting,' said a CPI(M) leader who was a mayor of the Calcutta Corporation, 'is part of bourgeois democracy.'[24]

The condition of West Bengal was well presented by Sumanta Banerjee in his 'anticipatory' post-mortem of the state of politics in West Bengal,

> CPI(M) leaders, as we have seen so far, tend to react with anger whenever faced with uncomfortable realities. But we wonder how the dedicated CPI(M) members working at the grassroots level ... and the CPI(M) intellectuals ... rationalise the present trend in West Bengal. Discussions with people at both these levels reveal a peculiar sense of ambivalence and helplessness. Some among them have chosen to follow the old Russian adage: 'When you're living with the wolves, howl like the wolves!' Others, who still choose to remain loyal to the party out of either ideological commitment or past emotional ties, have opted for the role of sleeping partners in party committees or 'panchayats.' In private conversations,

> party workers often confess their fears about the organisation being hijacked by the lumpen underworld. But they are reluctant to voice these fears in public, trained as they are in the party norms which dictate that any public criticism of party functioning will provide a handle to the class enemy (the Congress (I) in this case). It is the same old Stalinist norm which prevented Communist veterans like Togliatti and Dimitrov from revealing the crimes that were being committed in the Soviet Union during the 1930s, although they knew all along what was happening.[25]

The only point Banerjee did not mention was the socio-economic compulsion of the intellectuals that made them remain silent and change colour when the death knell of the CPI(M)-led government sounded. Clearly the 34 long years of the Left Front rule was not, as many argue, due to successful land redistribution and Operation Barga but because of a careful mixture of political hooliganism with suitable party colour and slogan and rigging elections with tacit support from the intellectuals. The support increased manifold with the increasing popularity of the Bharatiya Janata Party in the Hindi heartland. To the generation next who were shunted out of erstwhile East Pakistan due to religious differences, curiously anything supporting the cause of Hinduism was more abominable than some electoral rigging, corruption or muscle flexing here and there in the life of ordinary people.

West Bengal had been the hotbed of radicalism in the country. The stability that CPI(M) brought in with its policies such as local self-governance, rule of party cadres over the lives of ordinary people, control over education system at all levels, and total politicisation of the administrative system sounded the death knell for new ideas. These policies effectively ended the most vibrant characteristic in a

Bengali – that of adapting new thoughts from across the world. After observing the first 13 years of the Left Front rule, Bhabani Sengupta observed how the 'Left intellection has waned conspicuously.'[26] It was evident that the Left rule had tended 'to build a divide between Bengal and the rest of India … Left rule has also alienated the non-Marxist intellectuals … from the state regime, and from the leftist intellectuals, and their supporters from the Centre.'[27] The Left Front promoted intellectuals who knew well that the policy of the government was to cater to friends and supporters and trained themselves to remain so while the non-left academicians stayed away from trouble. The harassment that Dr Santosh Bhattacharya, vice chancellor of Calcutta University, faced was an example. Dr Bhattacharya was selected by the governor of the state A.P. Sharma from a panel of three. Bhattacharya was included in the panel of three by the non-CPI(M) members of the Calcutta University senate. Sharma as chancellor, selected Bhattacharya, a well-known economist and excellent educational administrator who had successfully steered the university's economics department which he headed away from the chaos prevailing in the main campus. The economics department was one of the very few departments which ran its courses on time and could boast of a galaxy of prominent teachers cutting across ideological divide. As vice chancellor, Dr Santosh Bhattacharya had to face regular dharnas, gheraos and blockades by the CPI(M) affiliated staff, students and teachers. The party was setting an example for anybody who were not from within the CPI(M). Credit goes to Dr Bhattacharya who had refused to step down and retired as vice chancellor of Calcutta University in 1987. Naturally in such an atmosphere there was hardly any polemics between the two sides – the friends and not-so-dear-friends of CPI(M). Sengupta had noticed that there were no theoreticians or intellectuals of 'any persuasive timbre' among the communists, starkly visible after the collapse of the Berlin wall. As far as CPI(M) in West Bengal was concerned, the party was more concerned about maintaining its stranglehold on the electoral system and also the affluence it had acquired with so many years of power. 'Certain larger issues are also responsible for the significant waning of Bengali radicalism in the last 15 years or so,' wrote Sengupta. 'A single newspaper house dominates the intellectual-literary life of Bengal. Few have ever made it in Bengal creative literature without the approval and blessing of this house.' In short, the gentrification of communists and the virtual monopoly over creativity did not provide an atmosphere of competitive rise of radical ideas. Sengupta summed up that a Bengali would remain a soft and mellow rebel since 'Bengali radicalism cannot feed on the pale residual orthodoxies of Vietnam and Cuba. It needs a more vitalizing diet which is not available for import, nor producible at home ...' [28]

The 1991 election was an important turning point in national politics as well as for West Bengal. Though there was a Congress government at the Centre, the party lacked absolute majority in the Lok Sabha and the party had lost its control over the entire Gangetic valley. 'Its unrealistic strength in the Lok Sabha is the gift of an assassinated Rajiv Gandhi who, alive, could hardly have shored up as many seats ... Rajiv Gandhi's gift is much smaller than what he had received from his departed mother.'[29] The tenth general election had only one successful political party – BJP, which came second. Clearly the future political rivalry in the country was destined to be between the BJP and its allies and the Congress. West Bengal had no presence of the BJP. The Left Front still faced the Congress as its main rival. But the rise of BJP signalled to the Left Front that it had to prepare itself for a potential political realignment which eventually would reach West Bengal as well. Analysts concluded that though BJP did not win a single seat in West Bengal it played a major role by splitting the opposition votes. Left Front had reasons to feel indebted to the BJP as quite a number of seats both in the Lok Sabha as well as the state assembly went to them only because of the BJP attracting non-Left votes. BJP increased its share of aggregate votes in West Bengal from 5.3 lakhs in 1989 to 35 lakhs in 1991, that is from 1.7 per cent of the total to about 12 per cent. Emergence of the BJP was a threat that needed some new political thinking for the Left.

The other development was the new economic policy adopted by the Narasimha Rao government. The restrictions on business licensing were being dismantled. It meant states, too, had to wake up to the reality of market economy and rerail its policies. The economic liberalisation turned the standard complaint of stepmotherly treatment of West Bengal by the Centre stale and the Left had to rework its political outreach. But the network that the party had created for electioneering could continue for a few more years. What, however, hurt the Left most was the fast advances in the television network. Private channels started operations. Even the state-owned Doordarshan opted to hand over time slots to private companies for news and current affairs programmes. The socio-economic changes which took place in phases after 1991 had a huge effect on the politics of the nation. West Bengal too witnessed changes.

The demolition of the Babri Masjid in 1992 had a profound influence on India's politics. All of a sudden, the central government woke up, nabbed some 130 odd Bengali migrants from *jhuggis* in Delhi and deported them across the border to Bangladesh. More than the number of deportees sent across for being illegal immigrants what mattered was the alacrity of the response of the Congress government, evidently to dampen the sharp attack of the rising force of the BJP. For the Left Front government in particular this was an important political development. Its major power centre was in West Bengal where in the 20 odd years since the liberation of Bangladesh, infiltration across the border into West Bengal continued at more or less an even pace. When economic conditions deteriorated in Bangladesh resulting in drop in employment opportunities, the pace of border crossing into West Bengal increased. The Border Security Force (BSF) did not make much effort to stop it and more often than not facilitated the movements for a consideration. Political elements in West Bengal were not concerned since the newcomers were treated as vote banks. The people in West Bengal, intellectuals in particular, were hospitable to the down-and-out elements.[30] They also did not want to shake the apple cart managed by the Left Front government and were equally apprehensive of criticising the Bangladesh government for failing to stop such infiltration. Bengali intellectuals counted on support from Bangladesh, the only independent nation with Bengali as the national language. Thus the porous border between West Bengal and Bangladesh coupled with an administrative system benevolent towards the migrants saw a demographic change in West Bengal. Post Babri Masjid demolition the charged up communal condition had reduced the easy flow of such infiltrators to other parts of India though they could procure without much ado the necessary documents, ration card for instance, as proof of Indian citizenship. The simmering communal tension in the mainstream national politics had its effect on West Bengal also but as before with a different result, illustrating the state's political isolation. Thus in 1996 when the Congress was on a losing track everywhere it won more seats in West Bengal – 9 against 5 in 1991 and 82 seats in the assembly against 43 earlier. A look at the election results reveal that constituencies where Muslims had substantial presence voted for the Congress, expecting the party to safeguard their interest against a rising BJP nationally. Despite the Muslim community's reported dislike of P.V. Narasimha Rao, the Muslim-dominated seats in Malda, Murshidabad and North Dinajpur among others went with the Congress. This was seen in some assembly segments in Calcutta too, such as Cossipore, Entally, Chowringhee, Vidyasagar and Kabitirtha. Apart from the national factor two local issues made the Muslims suspicious of the Left Front. One was the continued imprisonment of *satta* don Rashid Khan and the other being the scandal regarding sale of Wakf property which involved the assembly speaker Hasim Abdul Halim. For the leader of the Left Front, the CPI(M), it was a wake-up call that the support of the Muslim community could not be taken for granted any longer.

But the party loved to remain in isolation. To the extent that when in 1996 the opposition chose Jyoti Basu to head a coalition government at the Centre it failed to accept the same. The opportunity came when the party's political prospect was stagnant at best. Basu later called it a historic blunder. In an interview given to *The Indian Express* (January 18, 2010) he said,

> Yes, I still think it was a historic blunder. Why historic? Because such an opportunity does not come. History does not give such opportunity. Knowing who I am a Marxist, a Communist, in the party here, for so many years I have been in politics, they invited me because they had no other prime minister in view. So we thought that even if we last for one year in that coalition with myself as the prime minister and our party joining it, then people would understand backward sections. In many places, they don't even know what we are all about.

The decision of the party not to accept the offer indicates that the political isolation of West Bengal was largely due to the ruling CPI(M). The party knew how it was in power year after year in the state. It had failed to break into any other state other than Kerala and tiny

Tripura exposing its political limitation. They knew well that their strength came from the large number of seats they won every year in West Bengal. Clearly the party did not want to sacrifice their only charismatic leader for the sake of national prominence. The CPI(M) knew well its limitation especially in a world where its old economic formulas were junked everywhere. Given its internal limitations the CPI(M) denied Jyoti Basu the opportunity that nobody from West Bengal perhaps would receive ever – the price of isolation the state pays. The party could retain its power in West Bengal for two more terms before fading out even from its 'Red Fort' in Calcutta.

In 1977 when Jyoti Basu came to power he realised that the Janata government at the Centre was not a homogeneous entity like the Congress. Also the emergency promulgated by Indira Gandhi was fresh in public memory. To take advantage of the confusion Basu had submitted a 16-point memorandum to the Centre for restructuring the Centre-state relation leaving only few national issues with the central government and transferring the rest to the states. Prime Minister Morarji Desai was a rigid constitutionalist and paid no attention to the memorandum. When the Congress returned to power within the next two years the document was lost from public discourse. The document subsequently became a campaign tool for the Left Front government, that of stepmotherly treatment of the state. It was easy to impress the electorates in West Bengal since the state had a strong sense of being neglected by the Centre since its partition. For the Left Front there was the memory of the unceremonious dismissal of the first United Front government by the then governor Dharamvira. The governor being the administrative link between the Centre and the state the Left Front was particularly sensitive to who was appointed in the state. It objected to the removal of T.N. Singh after Indira Gandhi came back to power in New Delhi. It was suspected that the Congress would like to remove the Left Front government.

But it seemed that the then business community, mainly the leading Marwari business houses, did not want the state government to be disturbed. They had seen enough of the chaotic days since 1967 and opted for stability that Basu brought. There was once again problem brewing between the governor and the state government in January 1984 when Governor A.P. Sharma as chancellor of Calcutta University selected Dr Santosh Bhattacharya as the vice chancellor over the CPI(M) nominee Ramen Poddar. The Left Front government started boycotting the governor as a consequence. Even the next governor Umashankar Dixit attracted the ire of the Left Front government a few months later when he appointed a pro-vice chancellor at the recommendation of Vice Chancellor Bhattacharya. For the Left Front, particularly its leading partner the CPI(M), any deviation from the party's wish was a part of conspiracy against the people, a tradition firmly planted in the state since then. While in public discourse the state government mentioned the policies on freight equalisation and industrial licences, etc., in reality small matters of the nature mentioned above had bothered the politicians of the Front the most.

The Centre's procrastination over two projects – Haldia Petrochemicals and Bakreshwar Thermal Power Plant – had pushed the state backwards but helped the Left Front politically against its main rival, the Congress. Even in his farewell interview to the party's newspaper *Ganashakti,* Basu had recalled bitterly how the Centre sat over the Haldia Petrochemicals project for 13 long years. The Centre had suggested that the state should involve NTPC to work on the Bakreshwar thermal power project. The reason cited was that only then the loan granted by the Russian government could be used for the project. But Basu rejected the proposal since that meant the state would receive only 30 per cent of the electricity generated. 'State government decided that it would do the project on its own. The party cadres even donated blood to raise funds. That was the symbol of people's support,' said Basu.[31] There were differences over handling of the Gorkhaland agitation also. The Congress used the agitation to win political support in the Darjeeling district. The political isolation of the ruling CPI(M), therefore of the state of West Bengal, had worked against the state's political-economic interests.

The split in West Bengal Congress in 1997 was a new chapter in the politics of the state. The Congress in the state had split on many occasions before but post-Independence only two persons had hurt the party's electoral prospects. First was Ajoy Mukherjee separating from the Atulya Ghosh-run Congress and becoming the rallying point for the entire non-Congress opposition parties in the state. The next was Mamata Banerjee leaving the Congress in July 1997 and forming her own party. Ajoy Mukherjee had left the then ruling Congress while Mamata left a party which was consigned to play the role of not a significant opposition in the state. But what she brought with her was the reputation of being the lone anti-Left leader in the Congress fold. The other leaders were seen as retaining their seats with the tacit help of the Left so as to warm the chair of the opposition, a much-needed spectacle in a parliamentary form of democracy. Mamata left the Congress at a time when the BJP was gaining strength nationally and was then the largest party in the Lok Sabha. It had even formed a government for a few days by virtue of being the largest party in the lower house. It was believed that India had then entered the coalition era since no political party was expected to win absolute majority in the Lok Sabha. The BJP, too, was looking for alliance partners so as to form a coalition government in an impending election. Not only the CPI(M) but even intellectuals associated with the party found Mamata as virulently anti-communist. Ashok Mitra wrote in *EPW* after Mamata's loss in the Lok Sabha election in 1989, 'She in her persona exhibits some of the worst aspects of plebianisation, as opposed to proletarianisation, of national politics. She is coarse; loud-mouthed, given to dramatics and, of course, virulently anti-communist ...'[32]

There was a reference to Mamata Banerjee again when she was the Union railway minister in the Atal Bihari Vajpayee-led NDA government by the same eminent columnist. Jyoti Basu vacated the chief minister's seat and Buddhadeb Bhattacharjee took over as the chief minister few months before the state assembly election in 2001. There was apprehension that the assembly election would not be a cakewalk for the Left Front as before. The columnist wrote,

> These latter elements were for the past few months nourishing high hopes that the lady holding the railway portfolio at the centre, who flaunts the right mixture of authoritarian behaviour and vacuous populism, would be able to wrest power from the CPI(M) at the next assembly elections scheduled for 2001. These hopes were further sparked by the marked consolidation of the lumpenproletariat on the side of the lady.[33]

Clearly the Congress's split or to be precise Mamata Banerjee leaving the party which was sidelining her was seen as a potential threat even for the strongly entrenched CPI(M) government. Due to complexity of national politics the Left Front government survived the 2001 election and the one in 2006 thereafter but intellectuals supporting the CPI(M) had realised that the rise of the lumpenproletariat was a potential threat to the party's government in West Bengal. The isolation of the state from the national mainstream and the resultant failure to rejuvenate the state economy had created the lumpenproletariat. It was the inability or could be the unwillingness due to political shortsightedness of the CPI(M) that West Bengal continued to remain isolated not only from the national mainstream but also from the theatre of development seen across the world since the 1990s when India too embraced the competitive economic development model.

The Left in West Bengal had a foothold initially due to industrial workers and its trade unions. But this was city and industrial hub centric and needed to be expanded for the communists to win enough number of seats and come to power. This led the CPI(M) to expand in the rural areas through its farmer-centric organisations. Given the widespread disparity of land distribution and population pressure rural West Bengal was sitting on a powder keg that did not require much effort to ignite. The politics in West Bengal was a story of this strife between the landowners and landless and marginal farmers which often ended up in violence. There was a brief interlude to this when the Congress manipulated the election in 1972 and the entire state became a den of violence. This naturally could not have lasted long in a democratic society. In 1977 the Congress was ousted for good from West Bengal and a cohesive coalition of Left parties led by the CPI(M) came to power. Realising its political imperatives the Left government from the outset put emphasis on land reform, tenancy reform and Panchayati Raj institutions. The last one was a tool for the first two and also ensured the hegemony of the party over the economy of rural West Bengal. In a democracy a political party cannot just come at regular intervals and contest elections. The political parties must connect with the people on a regular basis which needs a large number of cadres. These cadres look for economic survival as well, therefore a regular flow of income and progress in political career over a period. The Panchayati Raj institutions ensured both these requirements for the cadres of the Left Front government. The Congress, a political party of the top-down mode, lacked the people connect and was destined to lose elections which it did at regular intervals. For the ruling Left Front it was equilibrium of sorts as far as maintaining political hegemony in the state was concerned. Jyoti Basu, the experienced politician as he was, knew that to remain in power this equilibrium should not be disturbed. This feeling was deeply rooted in the politics of the party as was the experience of its Lok Sabha member from Diamond Harbour, Amal Dutta. But that pertains to its rural sector. Dipankar Basu came to the conclusion that

> … the type of land reforms that was implemented in West Bengal after 1977 under the leadership of the CPI(M), in fact, creates the conditions for the emergence of fascism in contradistinction to strengthening the anti-fascist forces in rural areas. The replacement of one class of rulers (the 'large') with another (the 'middle') only postpones the time for the resolution of the most basic contradiction of a pre-capitalist rural economy: the contradiction between the rural proletariat and the landed classes.[34]

The struggle of the poorest, that is the proper proletariat, could be postponed with the rule of the middle farmers who wielded the political sceptre. Basu concluded that this, the revisionist politics of class collaboration, managed to blunt the class consciousness of the rural proletariat. But this was actually a fault line waiting to be exposed sooner than later. The emergence of Mamata Banerjee brought in the prospect of using this weakness in the system meticulously developed by the Left. Mamata, as Ashok Mitra had written, represented this lumpenproletariat. True Mitra used the term in the context of the urban lumpen elements but in reality rural Bengal too had many such people, rural proletariat, who could fall in the category of lumpenproletariat surviving on the benefits doled out by the leadership of 'middles'. Studies conducted in 1994 found out that close to 50 per cent of the *bargadar*s had not managed to register themselves till then and the legal share of 75 per cent of the produce for the tenant was hardly ever obtained by them. This was a clear indication of the problem that was waiting to explode.

Urban Bengal was no better since industry in the state was only withering. There was no service sector worth speaking of. With political dogmatism over introduction of computers, banks and other services did not have much scope for expansion in the state. Job opportunities for the young were shrinking. Struggles related to the Haldia Petrochemicals project or the Bakreshwar thermal power plant made good headlines for the political leadership but did not contribute to job creation. The issue was about offering gainful occupation to the burgeoning job seekers. The party had developed a system of paid cadres. It also kept funding clubs for young people to remain busy with some activity or other. Various fairs organised in urban centres too helped generating some man-hours. But all these innovative systems had their weaknesses too. Not everyone could dislodge the well-entrenched in the system and thus created the class which Mitra called lumpenproletariat. The industrial policy of the Left Front government could be broken into three phases.[35] The first one was loaded against the state – between 1977 and 1991. Only two coalition governments which came to power at the Centre were supportive of the Left Front government but the Congress was mostly combative. The other phase was between 1991 after the Centre adopted the liberalised economic policy and 1994 when West Bengal too adopted a new industrial policy. This was when the Left Front was critical of the Centre's policy and was mostly busy generating intellectual opinions against the same. Finally, in 1994 Jyoti Basu realised that isolation would not help and his government adopted a new economic policy too. A policy on industrial development was prepared and presented before the state assembly on 23 September 1994. A look at the document still reveals the stale thought process of a status quoist regime. It spoke among other things about the revival of sick public sector undertakings and mentioned lack of adequate financial support from the central government to revive the industries. On the subject of revival of sick private sector undertakings again the thrust was on packages from the financial institutions.[36] There was no mention of an exit policy – exiting from unviable units, developing a service sector especially in IT and emerging ITES sectors. It was the same old wine of political dogma repackaged in a new bottle. The document is proof positive of how deep was the isolation of the state's government and political think tank from the reality of the future economic growth.

Endnotes

1 'Centre's Inequities,' *EPW*, March 24, 1979, https://www.epw.in/system/files/pdf/1979_14/12-13/from_our_correspondents_west_bengal_centres_inequities.pdf.

2 'Wooing Industrialists,' *EPW*, June 12, 1982, https://www.epw.in/system/files/pdf/1982_17/24/from_our_correspondents_west_bengal_wooing_industrialists.pdf.

3 Monopolies and Restrictive Trade Practices (MRTP) and Foreign Exchange Regulation Act (FERA).

4 Koyel Basu, 'Human Rights and State Politics in India: Case Studies of West Bengal Punjab and Assam 1970-2000,' https://shodhganga.inflibnet.ac.in/handle/10603/197598.

5 '*Nirbachan Prasanga o Bamfront Sarkar*,' speech by Jyoti Basu delivered on 27 February 1985, reprinted in *Jyoti Basur Nirbachita Rachanasangraha* vol. 4, pp 1-7.

6 Ajit Roy, 'Deep-Rooted Stalemate,' *EPW,* April 18, 1987, https://www.epw.in/system/files/pdf/1987_22/16/reports_west_bengal_deep_rooted_stalemate.pdf.

7 Tathagata Ray, *Bampantha Bhyankari* (Mitra & Ghose, 2020), pp 100-3.

8 Sumanta Banerjee, 'West Bengal Today: An Anticipatory Post-Mortem,' *EPW*, August 18, 1990, https://www.epw.in/system/files/pdf/1990_25/33/reports_west_bengal_today_an_anticipatory_post_mortem.pdf.
9 Ibid
10 Ibid.
11 Achin Gupta, 'Left Front Rule in West Bengal: Domination without Hegemony,' *EPW*, November 10, 2001, https://www.epw.in/system/files/pdf/2001_36/45/Left_Front_Rule_in_West_Bengal.pdf.
12 Ibid.
13 Arun Ghosh, 'Decentralised Planning: West Bengal Experience,' *EPW*, March 26, 1988, https://www.epw.in/system/files/pdf/1988_23/13/special_articles_decentralised_planning_west_bengal_experience.pdf.
14 Integrated Rural Development Programme (IRDP), National Rural Employment Programmes (NREP), and Rural Landless Employment Guarantee Programme (RLEGP).
15 G.K. Lieten, 'Panchayat Leaders in a West Bengal District,' *EPW*, October 1, 1988, https://www.epw.in/system/files/pdf/1988_23/40/special_articles_panchayat_leaders_in_a_west_bengal_district.pdf.
16 Basu, 'Human Rights and State Politics in India.'
17 Ibid.
18 National poll percentages were 61.95 (1989), 56.73 (1991), 57.94 (1996), 61.97 (1998), 59.99 (1999) against West Bengal's record 79.67 (1989), 76.73 (1991), 82.66 (1996), 79.27 (1998), and 75.05 (1999) – Election Commission Data.
19 Ray, *Bampantha Bhyankari*, pp 32-3.
20 'Crisis for Left Front,' *EPW*, October 1, 1988, https://www.epw.in/system/files/pdf/1988_23/40/west_bengal_crisis_for_left_front.pdf.
21 Banerjee, 'An Anticipatory Post-Mortem.'
22 This writer has personal experience of handling applicants in the Telecom Ministry between 1999 and 2001. Applicants from West Bengal used to come to the office of the minister which was under the supervision of the writer. They used to come for telephone exchange, telephone connection or medical attention at AIIMS. The applicants could reach the DOT headquarter without any trouble and get their applications approved by a BJP minister but they could not get any letter of recommendation from their local MP unless the local party recommended the same. Even CPI(M) MPs who knew the author well had admitted their helplessness in taking decisions without local party approval.

23 Banerjee, 'An Anticipatory Post-Mortem.'

24 Ibid.

25 Ibid.

26 Bhabani Sen Gupta, 'The "Radical" Mind of Calcutta,' in *India International Centre Quarterly* 17, no. 3/4 (1990), pp 24–41, www.jstor.org/stable/23002451 (accessed June 26, 2020).

27 Ibid.

28 Ibid.

29 Bhabani Sen Gupta, 'Power-Shift,' *EPW*, June 29, 1991, https://www.epw.in/system/files/pdf/1991_26/26/capitalscope_power_shift.pdf.

30 'Operation Pushback,' *EPW*, November 7, 1992, https://www.epw.in/system/files/pdf/1992_27/45/operation_pushback.pdf.

31 Jyoti Basu's interview in the *Ganashakti* on 6 November 2000, the day he retired as chief minister of West Bengal, reprinted in Basu, *Jyoti Basur Nirbachita Rachanasangraha* vol. 5, pp 283-90.

32 Ashok Mitra, 'Calcutta Diary,' *EPW*, January 6, 1990, https://www.epw.in/system/files/pdf/1990_25/1/calcutta_diary.pdf.

33 https://www.epw.in/system/files/pdf/2000_35/47/Calcutta_Diary.pdf.

34 https://www.epw.in/system/files/pdf/2001_36/16/Political_Economy_of_Middleness.pdf.

35 Jørgen Dige Pedersen, *India's Industrial Dilemmas in West Bengal* (Asian Survey, 2001), https://watermark.silverchair.com/as_2001_41_4_646.pdf?token=AQECAHi208BE49Ooan9kkhW_Ercy7Dm3ZL_9Cf3qfKAc485ysgAAAo8wggKLBgkqhkiG9w0BBwagggJ8MIICeAIBADCCAnEGCSqGSIb3DQEHATAeBglghkgBZQMEAS4wEQQMtbvhQgrEjCXUicjkAgEQgIICQmYMK5HoV5RUmX0SOrSNJwAK_c-1ykH0pFpPOkgdoEoITg9OiFSf33duXdIbUbTIeHKUgc407O6zOYfs_qlEgnStat.

36 Statement on Industrial Policy placed before the assembly on 23 September 1994, reprinted in Basu, *Jyoti Basur Nirbachita Rachana Sangraha* vol. 5, pp 291-301.

THE LEFT CITADEL CRUMBLES FINALLY

The state of politics in West Bengal could be encapsulated in the incidents that unfolded during the bye-election in the Ballygunge assembly constituency of Calcutta on 8 June 1992. It 'revealed in all its luridness the seamier side of West Bengal politics' as practised by the two main rival political parties the CPI(M) and the Congress. The election was fought bitterly though nothing was at stake for the existence of the state government. Apart from the two principal rivals from the CPI(M) and the Congress, there was a rebel candidate put up and supported by the CPI(M)'s expelled faction from the Calcutta district committee. Badshah Alam was the chief election agent of the rebel CPI(M) candidate. He was said to be the leader of the CPI(M)'s muscle brigade in Calcutta with influence inside the police headquarters. His brother Lalu Alam was the main accused in the murderous assault on Mamata Banerjee on 16 August 1990.[1] The bye-election was a prestige issue for the CPI(M) while it was an occasion to show its strength by the opposition Congress. First the Congress candidate and next the rebel CPI(M) one withdrew from the election alleging massive rigging. By the afternoon Congress supporters turned violent, set fire to state transport buses and did some target practice with brickbats on the police. The Calcutta police retaliated, resorted to tear-gassing and then to firing. Two innocent persons died of bullet injuries – one on the spot and the other later in the hospital. During

> … the course of the tear-gassing part of the police operations, a few gas canisters, accidentally or otherwise, found their way into the second floor central election office of the Congress party, facing the main venue of the violence wherein the leader of the opposition in the state assembly and a former chief minister of the state, Siddhartha Shankar Ray, and the redoubtable leader of the state Congress and a union minister of state Mamata Banerjea, were talking to some news persons.[2]

As was the standard operating procedure in West Bengal in those days, first the Congress called for a 12-hour bandh on 10th June in Calcutta and Howrah, and next the CPI(M) joined with a 24-hour bandh call on the same day protesting against suspension of counting of votes by the Election Commission. Those were the days of TV channels beaming reports with visuals which had shown how a police bullet killed the innocent man and how the police dragged the body and washed the blood on the street. Due to TV visuals the administration could not pass off the death as caused by a bomb attack. This started the second round of political drama, farcical but a common enough exposition on West Bengal state politics. Mamata Banerjee rushed to the residence of the deceased person on the day his last rites (*shradh*) were being performed, handed over a cheque of Rs 10,000 and also promised a monthly payment to the family. She had claimed the victim as her party supporter, though it was denied by the family. Not to be outsmarted in the game of showering competitive benevolence, Chief Minister Jyoti Basu called the widow who was pulled away from the *shradh* ceremony to Calcutta. Basu assured the widow with several charitable promises who was overwhelmed by the tug of war between the two political leaders. While the Left Front government was collecting accolades for showcasing the success of an elected communist government, the reality was the rush towards the bottom in the quality of the state's politics which could be seen in the light of this incident. The other point that emerges from this incident, particularly the way Chief Minister Basu had to drag the widow to his office, was that even within the CPI(M), Mamata was seen as a threat to its continued power.

In the 1998 Lok Sabha election Mamata had a lifeline in the rising national force of the BJP. After failing to attract any alliance partner in the short-lived government of 1996 the party was careful this time. The BJP offered an alliance to Mamata Banerjee's newly formed Trinamool Congress. For the first time after 1967, West Bengal saw a tri-cornered contest in the Lok Sabha polls. While the Left Front maintained its position with 33 seats, the Congress could win only 1 due to Mamata bagging 7. Even the BJP made history by winning the Dum Dum Lok Sabha seat, the first seat it won in the state after the party's founder Dr Syama Prasad Mukherjee was elected in 1952. For the CPI(M) this meant a competition had arrived on the scene. The Lok Sabha poll next year, in 1999, saw the TMC-BJP alliance improving the tally – BJP won 2 and TMC 8. Even the Congress could bag 3 seats with the Left Front winning 29 seats. The state assembly election due in two years did not seem any longer an easy win for the CPI(M) like on previous occasions. The new political equation forced the CPI(M) to strategise afresh. There were three problems for the Left Front. First, the electronic media, particularly the privately owned news telecasters on the state-run Doordarshan. This made muscle flexing, a common tool used in elections, difficult. Second, the Election Commission had turned vigilant, a development initiated since the days of T.N. Seshan in the early 1990s. There were voter ID cards to keep in check false voting. More importantly the commission was alert and vigilant in ensuring law and order during the election. Furthermore, since 1998 the commission had introduced electronic voting machines which were used to conduct the assembly elections in 2001. Electoral malpractice, rigging of polling, were easier in case of paper ballots. Clearly elections since 2001 went into an uncharted territory. The old system of election management had to be reworked and despite the abhorrence of the CPI(M) for anything machine related it could not stay isolated when nationally systems changed. The major decision that the CPI(M) took before facing the 2001 election was changing its chief minister. Veteran Jyoti Basu retired in November 2000 and Buddhadeb Bhattacharjee took over as the new chief minister. Despite the enthusiasm of media barons and election analysts over possible change in government, the Left Front won the election though with less number of seats for the CPI(M) – 143 seats against 157 won in 1996. The Left Front won 192 seats, 10 less than the 202 seats it won in the previous election. Clearly those who were excited at the prospect of Mamata-led TMC replacing Left Front in 2001 lacked a clear idea of the national political equation. For the Congress the bigger political enemy was the BJP. Therefore the wish of anti-Left Bengal intellectuals for a grand alliance of the Congress-TMC and BJP was a mirage which naturally did not take place. Also, though the Congress for the sake of state politics tied up with Mamata, in national politics the CPI(M) was a more reliable ally than Mamata's TMC in its contest with the BJP. This was also seen when certain Congress leaders having local influence helped their own candidates in contests against TMC candidates. Mamata had used the Tehelka spy camera incident to leave the BJP-led NDA since she felt that with more than 25 per cent Muslim votes she had a better chance to win the state without the baggage of BJP. Such prompt political camp changing might influence arm-chair analysts but ordinary voters cannot be fooled so easily. Mamata's flip-flop was not taken very kindly by a large section of the people. Even the BJP at the Centre was aware that there was little electoral prospect of a TMC-led government in West Bengal and contested 266 seats for its

5 per cent committed votes. The votes polled by TMC and Congress were 38.6 per cent, nearly 10 per cent less than what the Left Front received. The euphoria by a section of Bengal's media over the possibility of a Left Front defeat in 2001 was yet another reflection of their isolation from the emerging equation in the national coalition politics. The slogan of the opponents – *Ebar noye never* (This time or never) – was not attractive enough, at least not in 2001.

A curious hope was generated in West Bengal that the voters of the state, frustrated with the failures of the Left government, would buy the populist promises trumpeted by the Trinamool leader Mamata. But the fact that Mamata was a loose cannon without either any ethical norms or ideological moorings – allying with the BJP today and with the Congress the next day – turned voters away from her. This was the reading of the BJP too since in 2001 despite Tehelka there was still some popular support for the Vajpayee government. In any case the question of money taken either by the BJP president Bangaru Laxman or allegedly by Samata Party's Jaya Jaitley was viewed by many as part of the trappings of politicians who need funds to run their political affairs. By promptly jumping out of the NDA Mamata tried to paint herself as a picture of honesty but for the ordinary voters in Bengal her theatrics did not have much impact. What is more, to the educated Bengali 'bhadralok', Buddhadeb Bhattacharjee seemed a better choice to be given an opportunity at this stage. Bhattacharjee, the very picture of 'bhadralok' norms of modesty, was any time more attractive than 'the uncouth manners of the pugnacious Mamata'. As for the vast constituency of the rural poor, caught as they were in the socio-political trap of Panchayati Raj institutions, neither Mamata's populist slogans nor Buddhadeb Bhattacharjee's 'bhadralok' image had any influence. The point that the analysts fervently hoping to replace CPI(M) with TMC missed was the reality of the national politics. The CPI(M) was losing its national reach by this time but by virtue of its formidable presence in West Bengal (a state with 42 Lok Sabha seats) had then acquired the image of an arbiter of sorts at the Centre. The Congress needed its support to bring together the non-BJP opposition against the NDA government. Clearly the Congress's coalition with TMC for the West Bengal assembly was just a short-term regional political tactic, at least at that point in time. The failure to recognise this was a clear sign of the distance of Bengali discourse from the national political scene.

Commenting on the Congress-Mamata coalition, Debabrata Bandyopadhyay, a former bureaucrat and later TMC Rajya Sabha member, wrote,

> Their (Congress) objective was not so much to capture power but to cut her to size and lead her to a cul-de-sac so that in future she would have no alternative but to merge with the Congress ... The Congress sacrificed them to pander to her whims. Like a Czarina she nominated whomsoever she liked in constituencies with which they had no connection whatsoever. It created strong local bickerings. But she would listen to none ... The TMC posters and festoons bore only her picture. She had no real manifesto. She had no programme. She projected herself as the programme, the party and the future of the state putting to shame any high-handed autocrat having some vestige of democratic pretension. She succeeded in creating a Mamata-fatigue among the intelligent electorate.

Why did Bengal stick to the Left Front? A very interesting observation of Bandyopadhyay was,

> Bengalis are very fond of their 'macherjhol-bhat' (fish curry and rice). Fish bones getting stuck in the throat often cause

> a great deal of irritation and discomfort. But they would not give up their staple diet for such inconveniences. In spite of their failings and deficiencies, the electorate here has got so accustomed to the enduring status quo of the LF that they feel more comfortable with it than with any other party. It is the incumbency factor in fact which returned the LF to power in West Bengal for the sixth consecutive term.[3]

The change of guard in West Bengal saw a change of direction in the economic policy of the Left Front government. The party realised that in order to continue its political supremacy the government had to attract some new investment. The focus turned to urban areas and self-introspection led the party to believe that there was need for change of work culture. Several leaders including the chief minister stated that 'irresponsible' trade union activities would no longer be tolerated and that the revival and setting up of industries was one of the government's top priorities. The state government could no longer cry hoarse about the stepmotherly treatment of the Centre. The NDA government at the Centre had no reason to act against the state administration as did the Congress government. The BJP was still a marginal party in the state and needed to build goodwill among the voters. For Bhattacharjee the time was right to look afresh and adopt steps to plug the loopholes. A group of Bengali economists had expressed their views just before the state assembly election: 'Though much has been achieved in the area of agricultural growth, limited land reform, and decentralization through the panchayat system, West Bengal has steadily lost ground over several decades in various areas, especially in the industrial sector'. They had published their paper on the strategy for economic reform in West Bengal in which they opined, 'the state has fallen behind in other sectors - industry, higher education, and state of public finances, particularly

- to an extent that is seriously worrying.' Their suggestions, nothing earth shaking and some even called these banal and statement of the obvious, could be summed up as:

> With regard to industrial revival, it stresses public investment in transport and communication, measures to improve higher education, foster industry-university collaborations, and help small-scale industries overcome specific market imperfections (access to credit, technology and distribution channels). In public finance, emphasis is placed on raising tax revenues (especially with regard to the service sector), limiting losses of public sector undertakings, and widening the scope of land taxes and user fees. In the agricultural sector, the need for a greater role of the government with regard to biotechnology, extension services, irrigation and flood control is emphasized, along with suggestions for encouraging and regulating contract farming with MNCs. Finally the article urges greater empowerment of panchayats with regard to social service delivery and agro-business development, and administrative reforms to enhance accountability of state government employees.[4]

These economists expressed the hope that,

> Given that the new Chief Minister has expressed serious interest in economic reform, we hope our discussion will not only stimulate public debate but result in action. Even in areas where reform may be difficult, it is important to identify the key problems and recognize that they exist. Our discussion has been motivated by this pragmatic need to confront the facts as they are and to get the state's economy moving again.

Unlike hardnosed Jyoti Basu, the new chief minister Buddhadeb Bhattacharjee was emotion driven and wanted to sincerely work towards rerailing the state's economy. He had realised that there was no other option but to bring in new industrial establishments to create employment in the state. His new economic policy, at least the intent, generated a new class of well-wishers for the Left Front government. Encouraged by these signs, prominent economists too published a version of their paper which was a collation of several articles they had published in the Bengali newspaper *Ananda Bazar Patrika* as also in the same group's English newspaper *The Telegraph*. Bhattacharjee embarked upon a new economic policy which eventually led to the political loss of the party at the hands of the lumpenproletariat leader Mamata Banerjee. The political failure of Buddhadeb Bhattacharjee is definitive proof of a curious isolated political character of the state.

In Buddhadeb Bhattacharjee the state of West Bengal had a leader who wanted to rise above his political dogma and work generally for the good of the state keeping in mind the national interest. In other words, here was a chief minister who was not averse to ending the state's isolation, at least economic isolation if not political.

After the 9/11 terrorist attacks the international community became alert and unified on the issue of terrorism. On 22 January 2002, a few months after the state assembly election, Islamic terrorists attacked the American Center in Calcutta. At least 5 policemen died and 20 were injured. The global opinion was that the madrasas were indoctrinating the young and influencing them to commit such crimes. Immediately after the attack on the American Center Buddhadeb Bhattacharjee warned the state's 'unaffiliated' madrasas against carrying on anti-national activities. He was referring to the 'khareji' madrasas that have not been recognised by the West Bengal Board of Madrasa Education and which teach mainly Islamic and

Arabic literature. He also spoke of the terror network being set up by Pakistan's ISI in coordination with these madrasas on the porous India-Bangladesh border. He expressed his worry over the unabated influx of illegal immigrants from Bangladesh. But such plain speak was political suicide in a doggedly 'secular' West Bengal which saw no fault in Islamic militancy.

The Congress joined several fundamentalist Islamic groups in protest. A little-known organisation, Jamait-i-Ulema-i-Hind, organised a demonstration in Kolkata and urged the chief minister to tackle problems such as unemployment plaguing the Muslim community instead of creating new ones. The stealing of the secular platform away from the CPI(M) and its Front partners was deeply embarrassing. Their pressure compelled Bhattacharjee to backtrack eventually and sacrifice good governance at the pedestal of 'good' politics as practised in West Bengal.[5]

Buddhadeb Bhattacharjee came at a time when both his party and the opposition had a new set of leaders. The national politics was divided along communal lines and so was the international scene after the 9/11 attack in New York. The NDA's economic policy was a new phase of liberalisation, something that had stopped effectively after Narasimha Rao's defeat in 1996, and there were some signs of economic activity in the country. The growth in communication system, mobile telephony, IT and ITES sector as also the national highway development started a new phase of growth and expectation. West Bengal too was restless. The past performances of the Left Front government were under scrutiny, an important reason why Buddhadeb Bhattacharjee moved away from the well-trodden, successful, status quoist policies of Jyoti Basu.

One such study concluded that West Bengal's primary education system was in a dismal state.

> It appears that two decades of left rule in West Bengal was not all that bliss, particularly, for primary education, despite the entrenched panchayat system and a decentralised structure of primary education administration. In fact, both political and administrative bureaucracy were in full command despite the so-called administrative decentralization ...[6]

wrote Poromesh Acharya in *EPW* on the basis of field studies on the impact of Panchayati Raj system and elementary education in the state. The panchayats were not made responsible for implementing the task of universal elementary education. The District Primary School Council (DPSC) was formally entrusted with the task of universal primary education, at the district level. There was the West Bengal Board of Primary Education above the DPSCs. Panchayats and DPSCs were meant for implementing the command from above. Theoretically as also in practice a political party based on the principle of democratic centralism would not allow decentralised administration, in any area of social activity. More importantly, in West Bengal the structure was used more for electoral advantages and political control than any interest in experimenting on decentralised development. Since the party represented the people, its diktat was viewed as the 'true expression' of people's will.

Acharya concluded that two decades of Panchayati Raj in West Bengal had done more harm to the village society than good, by destroying the 'village solidarity' which was replaced by party solidarity. The spate of violence in rural West Bengal and strong arm used in local elections had been the result of such politicisation of rural lives. He observed,

> Through this system of party panchayat a class of new mandarins have emerged in the village society, who are

> unscrupulous to the extreme and heinously power hungry. Unfortunately, primary teachers, being a major group of panchayat members, are also involved in this unholy power game. This has also vitiated the primary system.[7]

It is not surprising then that West Bengal in 2002 was at a dismal 18th position in literacy rates among 35 Indian states and union territories.

The Pratichi Trust headed by Amartya Sen studied three districts of the state – Bankura, Birbhum and Purulia. It found that the rate of literacy among the Scheduled Caste communities was low, at 42.21 per cent. Almost 15 per cent of the population in the age group 6-11 were out of school in 1997-98. The student-teacher ratio was 54:1 against 40:1 claimed by the government. The value of primary education, the report pointed out, was widely appreciated even by illiterate parents not only for its implications for employment or income generation but as a necessary tool for social change. And only 41 per cent of parents said they were satisfied with the work of teachers in primary schools. There was greater absenteeism in schools with a majority of children from Scheduled Castes and Scheduled Tribes (75 per cent), compared with other schools (33 per cent). In some schools with children from 'lowly' families, teaching hours were arbitrarily reduced. The persistence and intensification of class barriers in the schooling system, even in a state ruled by the communists for 24 years, was a matter of special concern. The report recommended the revival of the school inspection system and the formation of school-based parent-teacher committees. The Pratichi report also made a strong case for a 'proper' midday meal to replace the prevailing system in which primary school children receive three kgs of rice every month.[8] The state of the education system clearly reveals that the Left Front government was concerned only with maintaining its political power and it neglected empowering people at the bottom of the pyramid. The party knew well enough that any development, social or economic, beyond a point would disrupt the political hegemony it intended to build. What it missed to note is that at some stage the perpetually deprived too can rebel. In the later stages the Left Front government faced this revolt which hastened its process of moving out into oblivion.

The disgruntled elements within the Left found in the TMC a new channel to vent their opposition. In a politically polarised West Bengal, any opposition required some strong backing of a political power. In the TMC many saw that support. The defeat of the Left Front candidate in the Lok Sabha bye-election in June 2000 made the CPI(M) cry hoarse against violence in West Bengal politics. The party felt that the election was manipulated since only

> … a couple of weeks ago, the people of West Bengal had given their verdict in the elections to the 79 municipalities, clearly reposing their confidence once again in the Left Front. The result of the Panskura by-election, therefore, does not reflect the popular mood of the people, but appears to have been manipulated.[9]

The CPI(M) bitterly complained of violence against its party members,

> … 42 members of the CPI(M) were done to death by murderous gangs of the Trinamul. Five more party cadres were killed in the run-up to the elections. As a result of this unprecedented terror, in many areas, particularly in the Keshpur and Pingla assembly segments, polling agents of the Left Front were prevented from entering the booths and ordinary citizens were prevented from casting their votes.

That booth-level manipulation had been an important factor for the election result in West Bengal was illustrated by the Lok Sabha bye-election of Panshkura. The ruling CPI(M) in the state bitterly complained about how booth-level manipulation helped the TMC to defeat the Left Front candidate. The party cited examples of certain booths with reference to the election result. Booth no. 40 registered cent per cent polling; not a single person was indisposed or had died since the electoral roll was prepared at least some months before the election. In the booth, mentioned the CPI(M) release, out of a total of 822 votes, the TMC got 812 votes and the LF got only 7 votes, while 3 votes went to others. Similarly, in booth no. 158, which also had 100 per cent polling, out of the total 818 votes the TMC got 812, the LF 4 votes and others 2. In booth no. 110, out of the 616 votes polled, the TMC registered 614 and the LF 2 votes. In a total of 54 booths, the Left Front got 1,019 votes and TMC got 36,821 votes. The clean sweep against the well-entrenched Left from a constituency which used to elect veteran CPI leader Geeta Mukherjee regularly was curious indeed. Similarly, in the Pingla assembly segment (which had a sitting Left Front MLA) 8 booths recorded 100 per cent polling. Of the total 4,840 votes from these 8 booths the Trinamool got 4,443 votes while the Left Front got only 331. Occasional booth-wise election result analysis where the Left Front had recorded similar sweeps too had revealed similar near complete preference of booths in favour of the winning Left Front candidates. The rise of the TMC in West Bengal and the CPI(M)'s press release on the Panshkura bye-election were just clues left for future researchers. The other interesting point that emerges from a cursory look at the analysis of West Bengal elections is the complete silence about election manipulation. Politics in West Bengal was a contest between rival political parties in ensuring the hold over a locality using muscle power through intimidation. That is why local elections witnessed intense violence right from the time of filing of nomination till making life miserable for any opposition cadre or victor. This is a well-documented story that even witnessed the apex court pulling up the state election commission for malpractices in the panchayat election of May 2018.

Small-scale violence resulting in only one or two deaths had become routine in the state but when 11 persons lost their lives at a village called Suchpur under Nanur police station of Birbhum district, this could not be passed off as lynching of armed robbers by the villagers. The violence was a result of the CPI(M) trying to recover its lost ground in the area to TMC – *Elaka Dakhaler Larai* (fight to win over a locality) as a Bengali would put it. The 11 landless persons aged between 25 and 40 were brutally murdered on the morning of 27 July 2000. Ten years later, on 9 November 2010, the lower court pronounced 44 persons guilty of the crime. Among them were several CPI(M) office bearers. That such gruesome killings were perpetrated with the political objective of recovering the lost political hegemony in the locality was seen in the assembly election outcome in 2001. Suranjan Das analysed the violence after the Left Front victory in 2001 with the casual nonchalance of an academic,

> Some political commentators refer to TMC's bid to break the CPI(M)'s rural dominance by mobilising the 'jotedars' who had naturally suffered material loss following the Operation Barga. Events such as the killings in the village of Nanur (Birbhum district) are cited as manifestations of this strategy. But this TMC tactic failed in the 2001 election – as is evident from the victory of the Left in Nanur. Again, the infamous 'Panskura line' which enabled the TMC to wrest the Panskura (Midnapur) Lok Sabha seat in a by-election following the death of the legendary CPI leader Gita Mukherjee backfired. This is evident from the Left victories in the assembly

> segments within the Panskura Lok Sabha constituency. Keshpur, the area in Midnapur district which had been hitting the headlines for recurrent political violence, too, returned a CPI(M) candidate by a margin of over one lakh votes.[10]

That politics in West Bengal was an arena of brutal violence where political supremacy depended on the ability to assemble hooligans to drive out the rivals found little mention in the intellectual discourse. West Bengal's political isolation has been no less facilitated by the refusal of the intellectuals to provide narratives based on reality.

During the 2004 national elections it was evident that Mamata Banerjee was not a trusted partner in an era of coalition governments. In fact, after leaving the NDA with the belief that she would dethrone the CPI(M) in 2001, Mamata Banerjee landed herself in political wilderness. More so due to her impulsive behaviour. She met the President K.R. Narayanan along with Congress leader Priya Ranjan Dasmunshi to complain against the ruling Left Front for rigging the 2001 polls. Mamata had blamed the state government, the Election Commission and the central government for the rigging. She also developed strained relations with veteran leader Ajit Panja. Reports surfaced that she wanted to rejoin the NDA cabinet and was seen trying to embarrass Railway Minister Nitish Kumar so as to get back the portfolio she had left. The panchayat election of 2003 was another blow – her party came third in a three-horse race – behind the Left Front and the Congress. She even expelled Sudip Bandyopadhyay, one of the founders of the TMC. Politically she was completely isolated at this point. Finally, a few months before the 2004 national election, Mamata was accommodated as coal minister in the NDA government. There was more in store for her. In the 2004 election Mamata was the only elected member to the Lok Sabha from the TMC-BJP coalition out of 42 seats in West Bengal. The Congress bagged 6 with Pranab

Mukherjee winning an election for the first time in his long political career. The CPI(M) and the Congress contested separately but with some tacit adjustments which saw a complete rout of the TMC-BJP coalition in the state. Mamata's political exile that started with her resignation in 2001 from the NDA cabinet would have lasted longer but for a major political blunder by the CPI(M) over the Indo-US civil nuclear deal.

After the BJP-led NDA could bag only 182 seats in the Lok Sabha, a coalition government led by the Congress with support from the Left Front and other non-BJP political parties formed the government. In the UPA government 59 members of the Left Front constituted an important group and had huge influence over the government. Problems started when the CPI(M) wanted the government not to go ahead with the Indo-US civil nuclear deal, an important milestone for the country which was put together after a long negotiation that started during the previous government led by Atal Bihari Vajpayee. When the CPI(M) withdrew support on the deal and BJP sensed it could unseat the government, it went for a no-confidence motion. There was some difference of opinion even within the BJP with a section wanting to help the government with the much-needed deal. The Manmohan Singh government won the trust vote. The political hara-kiri of the CPI(M) in 2008 was the single most important factor behind the party's eventual loss in West Bengal.

Till the time the CPI(M) was a coalition partner with the UPA it was arguably at the height of its political influence. The state assembly election in 2006 was yet another easy victory with the Left Front winning 235 seats (out of 294) and the CPI(M) alone getting back its absolute majority in the house with 176 members. The Congress got 21 seats and the TMC bagged 30. The TMC had a vote share of 26.6 per cent, second to the CPI(M)'s share of 37 per cent. The Left Front had won half of the total votes (50.6 per cent). The assembly election in 2006 was different from any previous election held in the state. One crucial deviation from earlier elections was the activism of the Election Commission. The administration went under the overall supervision of the commission for almost two months in order to ensure free and fair poll. Secondly this was the first time when the EC took the complaint regarding bogus votes in West Bengal seriously and checked the voter list carefully. Election observers who inspected the voter list weeded out 1.3 million bogus voters from the list. According to D. Bandyopadhyay this was but the 'visible tip of the iceberg'. Bandyopadhyay estimated that there were around 10 million bogus voters in the state's electoral rolls. He blamed a pliant state bureaucracy for the presence of huge numbers of false voters in the electoral rolls.[11] The point that cannot be denied is that despite increased vigilance and supervision by the Election Commission the election result in 2006 was among the two best results ever managed by the Left Front. It fell short of the result of 1987 when the Front won 251 seats. The election result, argued forcefully by Ashok Mitra, proved wrong the presumptions of the Election Commission that the higher rate of participation of people in the election process in West Bengal was due to electoral malpractices. Mitra argued that the three postulates of the commission were proved incorrect by the election results. Mitra had summed up the hypothesis of the commission that

> (a) a state where voter registration as a proportion of the state's population is higher than the national average is likely to carry a relatively higher load of bogus voters; (b) in case the proportion of votes cast to the aggregate number of votes registered in a constituency or for a particular polling station happen to be higher than national average, the poll in this constituency or polling station should be subjected to close scrutiny; and (c) similarly, if in a constituency or a polling

> booth, a candidate received as high as 85 to 90 per cent or more of the votes cast, the count must be subjected to rigorous checks and rechecks, and, if necessary, a re-poll ordered.[12]

It may be recalled that even the CPI(M) had argued on the basis of similar polling result at Panshkura Lok Sabha bye-election in 2000 that the election was rigged. One may also argue as Bandyopadhyay did that the mere 1.3 million false voters identified in a hurry was just the tip of the iceberg. The well-organised party machinery of the Left Front constituents, in the absence of any competing political set-up, managed to use their elaborate and well-laid election management system to score a record victory. The important point to note is that there was no opposition to the Left Front in 2006.

In the context of the 2003 panchayat election in the state Bandyopadhyay wrote, 'The CPI(M) undoubtedly has a well-oiled election machinery. It uses all the electioneering tricks often laced with a bit of villainy and roguery which others also do. But they did not anticipate that what they would do others also would learn and practise.'[13] The same applied in the 2006 assembly poll also. The stranglehold of the Left Front could be understood if one took a look at the huge number of seats (6,800 or 11 per cent of the total) which the Front bagged without any contest. Only in 1988 did the Front take 8 per cent seats (4,200) uncontested. The point to be noted is that in 1987 the Congress under Rajiv Gandhi had made an effort to unseat the Left Front from the state. Evidently in 1987 the election machinery was activated which helped it in the 1988 panchayat poll as well. Clearly the efficiency of the election management varied directly with the perceived threat the party faced. In 2006, however, the threat was not from any political rival but the Election Commission persuaded by political rivals and a section of the civil society including the media. Increased vigilance, an aggressive media coupled with disgruntled foot soldiers entrusted with the job of election management finally brought an end to the Left Front government in the state.

Hidden in the massive victory of Buddhadeb Bhattacharjee was the virus that eventually exterminated the Left Front from the state. Bidyut Chakrabarty had captured the problem that the government would face.

> Unless a mechanism of 'checks and balances' is internalised, the Left Front government is likely to drift away from the ideological goal that accounts for a massive popular mandate in its favour... There is no doubt that the West Bengal chief minister has captured the lost ground in urban areas on the dream of what a liberalised economy can bring to the state. Now he has to sell this brand of 'economics' to those 'hardcore' members of the party who are still critical to the organisation.[14]

The election victory was largely due to the robust party structure. But there was a contradiction between the party structure and the commitment Bhattacharjee made to the people. Chakrabarty sensed that unless this contradiction is addressed 'the euphoria that was translated into positive votes for the Left Front will evaporate in no time.' In his address to the media, Bhattacharjee had identified three important tasks he had to accomplish. First was to continue to accord importance to the agricultural sector. The second task was tricky, to match the improvement in agriculture by similar growth in the industrial sector. The third task was the mission to ensure an overall growth of the state so as to bring relief to those still below the poverty line. Chakrabarty rightly mentioned that it was a tightrope walk for Bhattacharjee who was following an ideological path similar to the European social democrats. Buddhadeb Bhattacharjee was the first Left leader post liberalisation in 1991 who admitted 'we cannot avoid liberalisation because we live in a time where we have to work according to the market conditions'. He was critical of 'isolationism' which was, according to him, responsible for the breakdown of the former Soviet Union. In conformity with 'the Chinese reformist ideology', Bhattacharjee never found any contradiction between the private or even the foreign sector with the state sector when the primary mission was to 'ensure economic well-being of the people'.[15] Chakrabarty refused to predict what would be the outcome of this tightrope walking that the chief minister was undertaking. But Ashok Mitra had sensed that the problem would come from the issue of acquisition of land. In his post-election analysis Mitra saw how 'the issue of conversion, at state initiative, of arable land for commercial exploitation', needed to be handled with circumspection. From the 2006 poll results Mitra could see how in the rural belt of South 24 Parganas,

> … the Left Front lost in just a single constituency, Bhangar, partly because of the involvement of this location in the controversy. Similarly, while the Front made a clean sweep of the rest of the seats in the district of Howrah, it failed to win in two constituencies where the issue of land sales had cropped up.[16]

The diversion of resources to capital intensive industries which according to Mitra were economising on labour would not find much enthusiasm among the 7 million unemployed. The defeat of the labour minister in 2006 was a curtain raiser of sorts for the Left Front. Clearly amidst the euphoria of the massive election victory of 'Brand Buddha' was hidden the warning signals for the Left Front.

Failure to contain the issue of land acquisition and the political failure of the CPI(M) central leaders in deciding not to support the Centre on the Indo-US civil nuclear deal finally ended the Left Front rule in West Bengal.

The rich farmlands of Singur, a place some 40 kms away from Kolkata, buried two dreams. One was that of Buddhadeb Bhattacharjee to bring West Bengal back on the map of industrialisation, therefore economic growth. And the other was that of the mighty Tata group chairman Ratan Tata's dream of making a low-cost four-wheeler for the people driving two wheelers, a dream that was tracked even by the global manufacturers. The dream project did not take off at Singur. It saw the Tatas moving out and eventually succumbing to market forces by stopping production of the low-cost car. It also ended the last sincere effort of bringing industry and private investment into West Bengal. It proved to be a big disappointment both for West Bengal and the Tata group. The shattering of the dreams however fulfilled one person's hitherto unfulfilled dream, that of Mamata Banerjee to replace the Left Front and lead the state of West Bengal as its chief minister. The land acquisition saga at Singur remains a case study in political economy for future students of democratic governance.

The Bhattacharjee government was keen to attract the much-talked-of small car project of Ratan Tata to West Bengal. There were good reasons too. The laggard West Bengal had to make good the lost time and compete with advanced states like Maharashtra, Tamil Nadu, Gujarat, etc., in attracting investment. One big bang project like the Tata small car would have immediately helped the state to cover a large part of the perception gap. It also would have helped the state which was once the leader in automobile manufacturing in the country in reclaiming the lost glory. Apart from succeeding in the race for investment the state badly needed a boost for economic rejuvenation. It had done all that could be done in the rural sector. It was pointless to talk of revival of the sick industries. Those were outdated in 2006. The other standard suggestion of the Leftist intellectual leaders like Ashok Mitra was to stick to public sector-led industrial growth. Ashok Mitra wrote in *EPW*,

> Above all, the mandate the Left Front has won, in the view of a vast number of its rank and file, is a mandate for Left principles. Any deviation from these principles, such as a diminution of the role of the public sector in the development agenda, could meet with fierce internal resistance. The seventh Left Front government therefore must continuously watch its steps.[17]

But in the year 2006 there was no public sector investment planned nor did the state have money or management capacity to invest in some large industrial project. Therefore, the Buddhadeb government rightly did not try to chase a mirage as suggested by Mitra. Meanwhile Chakrabarty felt that one reason for the sweeping success of the Left Front in the 2006 assembly election was its industrialisation programme.[18] The economic policy had attracted the younger voters to the Left Front fold.

Problems started over the Left Front government decision to acquire some 997 acres of agricultural land at Singur for the Tata Motors project. The state government claimed that the majority of the landowners at Singur had given consent to part with their plots for the project. Ignoring the agitation it was facing the state government went on to acquire 10,000 acres of farmland at Nandigram for a proposed chemical hub to be set up by the Salim group from Indonesia. In his zeal for setting up industry in West Bengal and to make good the time lost, Chief Minister Buddhadeb Bhattacharjee seemed to be embarking on a risky course of weakening the very foundation on which the CPI(M) was standing in the state. Such politically naive decisions compounded by several other administrative mistakes helped the lone opposition leader of West Bengal to embark on what she was best at doing – creating agitation. This time the scenario was loaded in her favour. More so since the Left Front leadership in the state as well as the national leaders of the CPI(M) had no clue of the changing mood of the people of the state.

At Singur the state government claimed that the majority of the landowners had submitted letters giving consent to the sale and along with their registered sharecroppers had collected compensation too. The problem was that of the unregistered sharecroppers and agricultural labourers. The sharecroppers who did not have registered deeds but had been living on the land they were tilling lost their livelihood. The government offered them a future opportunity of reskilling and working in the factories which would come up. The problem is that dreams fail to get digested in hungry stomachs. They were more concerned with their next meal after losing the land than about a job in a factory a few years later. Getting a job in a factory and ancillary factories which would come in future was not their priority but surviving till then was. These people needed someone to lead in their fight for survival. In Mamata Banerjee they had an ever willing and experienced leader to fight for their sake. The CPI(M) leaders, perhaps because of their pathological dislike for Mamata Banerjee, failed to read the writing on the wall and use political tact to engage with the disgruntled agriculturists. It was evident that there was a complete lack of will on the part of the administration to engage with the land oustees. Apart from Mamata, civil society activists backed by the Maoists and the CPI(ML) descended on the scene. They set up a panel with Mahashweta Devi, Medha Patkar, Justice Malay Dasgupta, Dipankar Dasgupta et al. as members who held a public hearing in one of the affected villages. They had invited the administration to join them and reserved chairs for them. No one attended thereby signalling a clear reluctance to listen to the aggrieved villagers. During the hearing the villagers complained of inadequate compensation, police atrocities and coercion to part with fertile land. In any public hearing on land acquisition such complaints are common. What was expected from the Left Front government was engaging with the disgruntled elements in order to expedite the land acquisition process. Accustomed to muscle flexing the state government failed miserably in diffusing the crisis. Curious political innocence was exhibited by the state government. It even failed to perceive the effect such coercive steps would have on its rural support base of sharecroppers and agricultural workers. Maybe the party thought that since it was a seat belonging to its opposition, the Trinamool Congress, there would be no impact on its core support elsewhere in the state. Blinded by their political parochialism the Left Front leaders did not even consider the chances of the entire class of sharecroppers and farm labourers joining in a class struggle. In fact, these were the deprived ones in the Left Front's twin policy of Operation Barga and Panchayati Raj system. Dipankar Basu in an article titled 'Political Economy of Middleness' (*EPW*, April 21, 2001) had warned how the Left Front government and 'its subsequent agrarian reforms programme, alienated large sections of the rural poor. It was these sections which proved amenable to fascistic mobilisation by the TC-BJP combine from the mid-1990s onwards.' These were the rural 'lumpenproletariat', to borrow the phrase used by Marx in the context of urban poor workers waiting to revolt. At Singur the Left Front government ignited the fire in them.

As if Singur was not enough, next came Nandigram which was the strong base of the CPI(M). Mitra wrote,

> The Left Front was in fact strangely entrenched in Nandigram, but the threat of compulsory land acquisition caused large-scale disaffection among its erstwhile supporters, many of whom crossed over to the opposition and drove out by force those who wanted to stay loyal to the CPI(M). For a number of months following the police firing, Nandigram was the happy hunting ground of disparate anti-CPI(M) parties and groups. The state government was seemingly in a state of atrophy; it decided to withdraw police personnel from the area, thereby reducing it to a 'free' zone. With the administration taking leave, conditions slid into near-anarchy ... Armed cadres of the ruling party streamed into and 'recaptured', through assertion of might, lost ground in Nandigram and restored land and homestead to party loyalists who had been driven out earlier.[19]

Not a flattering picture of an efficient administration. The Buddhadeb Bhattacharjee administration in its blind pursuit of industrial investment sacrificed its primary responsibility of administering the state and maintaining law and order.

In the meantime, the administration compounded its misfortunes by seeking out several more avoidable issues. The death of Rizwanur Rehman (on 21 September 2007) who married a Hindu girl from an affluent business family (the Todis) snowballed into a major controversy and shook the political foundation of the Left Front government. The Muslim community was up in arms and resorted to violence against the police. Mamata Banerjee, who excels in agitational politics, did not miss the opportunity. On the day of the festival of Eid she organised a rally in sympathy for Rizwanur and called Buddhadeb Bhattacharjee a foolish and arrogant chief minister who did not even visit the family of the deceased. Evidently the Calcutta police commissioner Prasun Mukherjee was the suspect. Mukherjee was then the president of the Cricket Association of Bengal (CAB) and had the support of the chief minister to replace the veteran cricket administrator Jagmohan Dalmiya from the post. It was alleged that Snehasish Ganguly, brother of Saurav Ganguly, former India captain, was the conduit between the Todis who were his business partners and Prasun Mukherjee. Buddhadeb made the cardinal mistake of sticking to the side of the Calcutta police commissioner. It was rather late when he admitted to the media, 'The incident has touched people's hearts. I am not defending any (police) officer. You have seen the social impact and there are several dimensions to this case. There is money power and there is also a communal angle. The government will not compromise.'[20] But by then Mamata Banerjee had managed to wipe off her sin of partnering with the BJP in her earlier days. There were more troubles in store when on 21st November the predominantly Muslim All-India Minority Forum called for blockades on major roads in the city demanding expulsion of Taslima Nasreen, the controversial feminist writer from Bangladesh, from Calcutta. In addition, they demonstrated against police action on Muslims in Nandigram. The state government sent Taslima packing from Calcutta to win back the support of the Muslims. Ashok Mitra wrote how the failure of the administration exacerbated the problems faced by the party,

> Both the issue of land acquisition, which caused concern to sections of the Muslim peasantry, and the ineptitude of the state authorities in handling the Rizwanur Rehman case created large-scale discontent amongst the minority community. The hustled exit of the Bangladeshi writer, Taslima Nasreen, following a day's violent show of wrath at her presence in the state by angry fundamentalists, was

> connived at by the state government anxious to regain the trust of Muslims. This gesture however alienated further liberal-minded constituents of the middle class, many of whom were already considerably worked up over Singur and Nandigram.[21]

While the West Bengal unit of the CPI(M) was caught in one issue after another, its general secretary Prakash Karat led the party politburo to withdraw support from the Manmohan Singh government objecting against the Indo-US civil nuclear deal. In a press release on 9 July 2008 the CPI(M) announced the withdrawal of support,

> The Congress-led government was supported by the Left parties on the basis of a commitment that it would follow an independent foreign policy in contrast to the pro-American stand of the BJP led Government. That commitment has been violated. Hence, the Left parties will have to disassociate from the government.[22]

Somnath Chatterjee, the speaker of the Lok Sabha, refused to resign and was expelled from the party as a result. Many in West Bengal including Chief Minister Bhattacharjee were against the decision of withdrawal of support. This decision helped Mamata Banerjee to form a coalition with the Congress in West Bengal and eventually ended the more than three decades long Left Front rule. The CPI(M) central leadership compounded the party's problems in West Bengal by alienating the ruling party at the Centre and effectively handing over the Congress support on a platter to Mamata Banerjee. This myopia of the CPI(M) arose out of their confidence in the isolation of West Bengal from the national mainstream – something the party had successfully nurtured over its three decades long rule.

Just a few weeks before the suicidal decision in New Delhi, the ruling Left Front in West Bengal received a jolt in the panchayat election. In 2008 the CPI(M) lost 5 districts to the opponents – the Congress and the Trinamool Congress. CPI(M) had one consolation, that of wresting the Murshidabad Zilla Parishad from the Congress by a wafer-thin majority. But the panchayat samiti and village panchayat level results were more alarming than the zilla parishad results. The Left Front was virtually wiped out in the districts of East Midnapore, 24 Parganas (North), 24 Parganas (South), Nadia, and North Dinajpur. Even in quite a few of those districts where the Left Front had been able to maintain its domination in the zilla parishads, the Congress and the Trinamool Congress did exceedingly well at the panchayat samiti and gram panchayat levels. Clearly there were deep inroads into the Left vote bank by the TMC and the Congress. The result had shown beyond a shred of doubt that a coalition of the Congress and the TMC would poll more votes than the Left Front for the first time since 1977. Despite such a scenario the Left leaders in New Delhi stuck to some archaic concept and withdrew support from the UPA government thereby facilitating a possible TMC-Congress pact in West Bengal. Political foresight was not a strength of the Left politicians in India.

The 2008 panchayat election result was another big warning signal for the ruling Left Front government. There was significant erosion in the Left Front vote bank among the minorities and the poor farmers and farm labourers. Clearly the failed land acquisition effort of the state government misfired since this had harmed the interest of the economically lowest strata the most. Singur and Nandigram were lessons they remembered. The Left Front in its arrogance of more than 30 years of continued power failed to read the writing on the wall. The mayhem perpetrated by the CPI(M) cadres backed by the police at Nandigram to recover the party's dominance was a big blow to the image of the party and the government. Such muscle flexing and even collection of speed money and nepotism had been going on quietly but Nandigram brought this under public glare. The emperor lost his clothes. The Left Front had created a halo of sorts around its electoral stranglehold in the state. Any appraisal of the West Bengal government used to eulogise the success of the Panchayati Raj system, Operation Barga, and land redistribution policies. Few cared to look deep into the oppression and see the political economy of middleness that had been affecting the village economy. Chakrabarty mentioned this constant reign of terror in the rural areas.

> There is no doubt that the success of the Left Front was built on formidable and pervasive party machinery ... The grip of the party eventually became so complete that little could happen in the rural areas without its approval. As a result, many of the party activists turned into extortionists.[23]

There had been several complaints from poor villagers about how the party cadres used to charge for everything from throwing a feast during marriages to repairing a thatched roof or growing and harvesting of crops. Chakrabarty also mentioned the extortions by the party cadres for giving work under the NREGA scheme of the Centre – the tradition of cut money dug the grave of the Left Front deep among the rural poor. The party by then was a hostage to the system. To cure it of such evil was beyond the capacity of Buddhadeb Bhattacharjee or Biman Bose. They were helplessly presiding over the final rites of the Left Front rule.

The Sachar Committee report on the state of the Muslims in the country was used against the Left Front government to highlight its failure in uplifting the minority communities in the state. The Sachar report had mentioned that only 4.2 per cent of government jobs went to Muslims who constituted 25 per cent of the state's population. It was seen earlier that a similar argument was used before Independence by the Muslim League government. This campaign and the mistakes committed by the administration at Nandigram and in the Rizwanur Rehman case turned the minority community critical of the Left Front. What is more, the withdrawal of support from the UPA government too worked against the Front. In the communally divided politics of the nation, Muslims viewed the Congress as an insurance against a BJP government while the Left Front was merely a regional force. Also the views of the chief minister both on infiltration from Bangladesh and the poor quality of madrasa education did not make him popular among a section of the minority community.

The rot within the Left Front was deep. As a result, there was an exodus from among the grassroots workers, first from the smaller constituents like the RSP and the Forward Bloc. All the Front constituents had lost touch with the common people because of corruption, high handedness and petty factional politics within their party and the coalition of the Left Front. Failure to implement the National Rural Employment Guarantee Scheme and failure in preparation of the below poverty line (BPL) list at the village level sealed the fate of the Front in the Lok Sabha election of 2009. The usual malady of a political system where the party rules over everything and removes any barrier between the party and the administration was deeply rooted in West Bengal. The panchayat election was a curtain raiser; the Lok Sabha election of 2009 was the trailer of what was in store for the Buddhadeb Bhattacharjee government. Out of 42 seats the CPI(M) could win just 9; along with other partners the Left Front managed just 15 seats against 35 in 2004. The Congress along with its coalition partner TMC and SUCI could win 26 seats – the Congress received 6 and TMC 19. Though the state assembly election was due two years later, effectively the Left Front government in West Bengal turned lame duck from this point onwards. Chakrabarty had shown how votes shifted away from the Left Front. For instance, in case of Muslim votes there was a 9 per cent shift away from the Left Front to the TMC-Congress alliance. The Left Front received an estimated 37 per cent of Muslim votes against 58 per cent of the alliance.[24] This shift was substantial particularly in a state where 25 per cent electorates were Muslims, a community which had a record of high percentage of polling. In vote share the CPI(M) won 33 per cent with TMC close on its heels with 31 per cent votes. The Left Front received 43 per cent votes against TMC alliance's 47 per cent votes. In the Lok Sabha the CPI(M) and its partners had lost their position – the party had a total of 16 members against 19 of the TMC.

The events at Singur and Nandigram had started alienating the Bengal intellectuals from the Left Front. Since the only alternative to the Left Front was Mamata Banerjee, her TMC received the much-needed stamp of approval from writers, educationists and artists. TMC's leader Mamata earlier was at best a pariah to Bengal's intellectuals, most perhaps quietly agreeing with the assessment of Ashok Mitra: 'She in her persona exhibits some of the worst aspects of plebianisation, as opposed to proletarianisation, of national politics. She is coarse; loud-mouthed, given to dramatics and, of course, virulently anti-communist.'[25] When everyone was looking for an alternative to the Left Front, she was the only one on the scene. Her perseverance in opposing the CPI(M) finally worked in fulfilling her dream. The Lok Sabha election result was a clear enough indication that 'Ma, Mati, Manush' would come to power in the next assembly election in 2011.

Endnotes

1 Lalu Alam was acquitted of the charges by the Alipore court on 12 September 2019 for want of proof and delay in prosecution. The incident at a busy junction near her residence made the one-term Lok Sabha member who had lost her seat in 1989 election an instant hero of all anti-CPI(M) forces in West Bengal politics. For CPI(M) too she became the enemy number one. This helped her immensely in later day politics.

2 Ajit Roy, 'Competition in Low Politics,' *EPW*, June 13, 1992, https://www.epw.in/system/files/pdf/1992_27/24-25/competition_in_low_politics.pdf.

3 D. Bandyopadhyay, 'Enduring Status Quo,' *EPW*, May 26, 2001,https://www.epw.in/system/files/pdf/2001_36/21/West_Bengal__Enduring_Status_Quo.pdf.

4 Abhijit Banerjee et al., 'Strategy for Economic Reform in West Bengal,' August 5, 2002, http://econ.lse.ac.uk/staff/mghatak/My%20Papers/westbeng.pdf.

5 'Spotlight on Madrasas,' *EPW*, February 16, 2002, https://www.epw.in/system/files/pdf/2002_37/07/West_Bengal__Spotlight_on_Madrasas.pdf.

6 Poromesh Acharya, 'Education: Panchayat and Decentralisation Myths and Reality,' *EPW*, February 23, 2002, https://www.epw.in/system/files/pdf/2002_37/08/Education_Panchayat_and_Decentralisation.pdf.

7 Ibid.

8 'Schools out of Shape,' *EPW*, October 26, 2002, https://www.epw.in/system/files/pdf/2002_37/43/West_Bengal__Schools_out_of_Shape.pdf.

9 'Panshkura, a Manipulated Verdict': Press Release by CPI(M), https://cpim.org/content/panskura-manipulated-verdict.

10 Suranjan Das, 'New Left Has to Please All,' *EPW*, June 16, 2001, https://www.epw.in/system/files/pdf/2001_36/24/West_Bengal__New_Left_Has_to_Please_All.pdf.

11 D. Bandyopadhyay, 'Elections and the Bureaucracy in West Bengal,' *EPW*, April 15, 2006, https://www.epw.in/system/files/pdf/2006_41/15/Elections_and_the_Bureaucracy_in_West_Bengal.pdf.

12 Ashok Mitra, 'Suffrage in West Bengal,' *EPW*, May 27, 2006, https://www.epw.in/system/files/pdf/2006_41/21/Suffrage_in_West_Bengal.pdf.

13 D. Bandyopadhyay, 'The Caucus and the Masses West Bengal Panchayat (Amendment) Act, 2003,' *EPW*, November 15, 2003, https://www.epw.in/system/files/pdf/2003_38/46/The_Caucus_and_the_Masses.pdf.

14 Bidyut Chakrabarty, 'Left Front's 2006 Victory in West Bengal Continuity or a Trendsetter,' *EPW*, August 12, 2006, https://www.epw.in/system/files/pdf/2006_41/32/Left_Fronts_2006_Victory_in_West_Bengal.pdf.

15 Ibid.

16 Mitra, 'Suffrage in West Bengal.'

17 Ibid.

18 Bidyut Chakrabarty, "The Left Front's 2009 Lok Sabha Poll Debacle in West Bengal, India: Prospective Causes and Future Implications," in *Asian Survey* 51, no. 2 (2011), pp 290–310, www.jstor.org/stable/10.1525/as.2011.51.2.290 (accessed July 4, 2020).

19 Ashok Mitra, 'Eyeless in Bengal,' *EPW*, February 23, 2008, https://www.epw.in/system/files/pdf/2008_43/08/Eyeless_in_Bengal.pdf.

20 Rajashri Dasgupta, 'Why Did Rizwanur Rehman Have to Die?' *EPW*, October 20, 2007, https://www.epw.in/system/files/pdf/2007_42/42/Why_Did_Rizwanur_Rehman_Have_to_Die.pdf.

21 Mitra, 'Eyeless in Bengal.'

22 On Withdrawal of Support to the UPA Government press statement on July 9, 2008, https://cpim.org/content/withdrawal-support-upa-government.

23 Chakrabarty, "The Left Front's 2009 Lok Sabha Poll Debacle in West Bengal."

24 Ibid.

25 Ashok Mitra, 'Calcutta Diary,' *EPW*, January 6, 1990, https://www.epw.in/system/files/pdf/1990_25/1/calcutta_diary.pdf.

CHANGE IN GOVERNMENT ONLY, NOT IN ISOLATION

The Left Front's myth of invincibility was finally busted in the 2011 assembly elections. The curtain raiser Lok Sabha poll of 2009 translated into a sweeping win for the Congress-Trinamool alliance in 2011 which bagged 228 seats against 62 of the Left Front. This was near reversal of the election result of 2006. Even Chief Minister Buddhadeb Bhattacharjee lost his Jadavpur seat by a huge margin of 17,000 votes. For the first time a regional party came to power in the state winning absolute majority. Five years later the TMC improved its performance and won 211 seats. The Congress and the CPI(M) formed an alliance for political survival and managed to win a total of 70 seats – the CPI(M) won 26 seats, 14 seats less than in 2011, and the Congress won 44, still 2 less than in 2011. Meanwhile in the Lok Sabha polls of 2014, TMC had shown its complete control over the state by winning 34 seats. The CPI(M) managed to win just 2 seats, down from 15 in 2009. This was the end of the CPI(M)'s political domination in West Bengal. The 2019 Lok Sabha poll exposed weaknesses of both the Congress and the CPI(M) in the state. The Congress managed to win just 2 seats while the CPI(M) got none. For the first time there was not a single Left member in the Lok Sabha from West Bengal. The TMC managed 22 seats against its slogan of winning all 42 seats. The BJP emerged as the second largest political party from West Bengal. It won 18 seats and more than 40 per cent of votes polled, just 3 per cent less than the state's ruling TMC. The Lok Sabha election result opened up the possibility of a national political party emerging as the principal opposition party in the state assembly election of 2021, an indication of sorts that the isolation of West Bengal from the national political scene, which was reflected in electoral outcomes since 1967, might finally come to an end.

West Bengal has certain conspicuous political characteristics – some of which could be seen since the dawn of modern education during the British rule, and the rest acquired by the state and its political leadership in course of the evolution of India's political economy. The obtrusiveness of West Bengal's politics has come into the national glare since the meteoric rise of Mamata Banerjee. There are good reasons for the same. Mamata Banerjee rose as a pure West Bengal leader with no baggage called national politics. To begin with, she could take a stand which appealed to her support base only, the Singur-Nandigram agitation being a case in point. Secondly, she had no qualms about niceties or even parliamentary protocols. Once she had thrown a shawl at then speaker Purno Sangma. In 2005 Mamata Banerjee was angry at the ruling of the then speaker and her political rival Somnath Chatterjee. She had said, 'Illegal migrants from Bangladesh are also part of the voters' list in West Bengal. The state government has done nothing about it. Therefore, the issue must be discussed,' and it was denied. A visibly disturbed Mamata threw some papers at the chair – Deputy Speaker Atwal who was then presiding.[1] More than her behaviour as an MP, one may take note of the topic she wanted to raise: infiltration from Bangladesh and inclusion of such people in the state's voter list. This took place more than a year before the land acquisition agitation in Singur and Nandigram which propelled Mamata as the head of the resistance which included a sizeable Muslim population.

Mamata Banerjee held high the flag of rebellious Bengal. She opposed all institutional procedures and even supremacy of the Union cabinet in taking decisions which were the Centre's prerogative. When Dinesh Trivedi of the TMC was made the railway minister in 2011 after Mamata stepped down from the post to become the chief minister of West Bengal, there was a big tussle over the hike in passenger fare in the Railway budget presented in March 2012. Mamata vehemently opposed it and finally Dinesh Trivedi was removed from the post of railway minister and the hike was rolled back.

Tensions between Mamata Banerjee and the Centre started almost as soon as she took charge in Kolkata. There were many issues – the debt burden left on the state exchequer by the Left Front government and the need for a bailout package from the Centre was one. But more than that Mamata was keen on protecting her political turf. This made her turn ultra-Left, more Left than the Left was. Once her objective of ousting the CPI(M)-led Left Front was achieved she initiated a series of moves to entrench her political gains, strengthen her organisation and cut the support bases of both the CPI(M) as well as the Congress. Even before the elections, large sections of the CPI(M) rank and file and cadres of the Left Front partners had joined the TMC. These elements had been instrumental in helping Mamata Banerjee ousting the 34-year-old Left Front government. With the cadre base which handled the election machinery of the Left switching to the TMC, political fortune also shifted. The first task of Mamata Banerjee was to cement this shift and to break the hold of the CPI(M) on the state's institutions and public spaces. An expert in creating a spectacle, she returned the Singur land, which had been given to the Tatas and on which they had already constructed large buildings, to the original owners (who could never grow anything there nor put it to any use). Mamata Banerjee knew well how the Left had created and nurtured a vote bank to keep itself in power. The TMC had to address this section of Bengal's voters who were brought up on the staple diet of populism of the communists. Hence Mamata's TMC turned more populist and more Left than the CPI(M). This zeal had made Mamata pressurise the Centre to roll back a railway fare hike. She championed all the causes the Left had adopted, like opposition to foreign direct investment in retail, issue of pension funds and also the issue of protecting the states' rights in the Lokpal Bill. She wanted to send across the message that she was a fiercely independent leader looking after the Bengali ego of independence. With absolute majority in the state assembly assured and knowing fully well that the Congress in West Bengal did not have the cadre base to compete with her, Mamata Banerjee could chalk out her complete isolationist policies which she was confident would ensure her continued rule in the state of West Bengal. Mamata effectively wore two hats – one that of the ruling party in West Bengal and the other, which was more important, that of the opposition to the Centre, a party ruling and opposing at the same time. This removed the Congress as well as the CPI(M) as competition for the TMC. Isolation helped her, effectively erasing any opposition from the state.

She knew well enough who would be her ally in the political battle for supremacy. There is a large section of people who had crossed the border from Bangladesh and had managed to possess voter ID cards and were opposed to the Bangladesh prime minister Sheikh Hasina who has been ruling since 2008. Mamata knew her politics well despite the expensive sari gifted to her by Sheikh Hasina when she visited New Delhi in January 2010. She thus did not hesitate to embarrass Indian Prime Minister Dr Manmohan Singh when he was scheduled to visit Bangladesh along with 5 state chief ministers which included Mamata. Just before the trip she withdrew from the delegation resulting in the putting off of the most important issue – that of the Teesta water-sharing treaty between India and Bangladesh.

The Teesta rises in Sikkim, flows through North Bengal into Bangladesh where it finally joins the Brahmaputra at Teestamukh.

The contentious water-sharing issues revolve around requirements during just 4 dry months, from December to March, when farmers in both countries rely on irrigation water. The rest of the year this region receives adequate rainfall and the river is in full flow. Bangladesh Prime Minister Sheikh Hasina, under immense pressure from the opposition in her country, needed an agreement over the Teesta river so as to show that she was not soft towards India. Mamata Banerjee needed to show to her constituents in North Bengal that she would not compromise their concerns and also to the vast sections of the minority community who fled from Bangladesh that she would not help Sheikh Hasina, a liberal face of Bangladesh.

Mamata Banerjee espouses the worst aspects of the politics of plebianisation. She won the election in 2011 on the back of the support from the lumpenproletariat, the landless and marginal farmers who lost out or were stuck at the lowest strata under the Left's rural economic policy and rule of panchayat. She also received support from the so-called 'Sushil Samaj', the intellectuals who were perturbed over the changed policies of the Left Front government. She had the backing of the Maoists too who were engaged in a bloody battle with the Left administration. The support of the Sushil Samaj, the well-meaning intellectuals, helped her immensely in her image makeover – Mamata was transformed as a potential leader capable of addressing the faults of the Left Front rule, a different image from the volatile street activist.

This Sushil Samaj formed the face of civil society and were out on the streets, pointing to the Left Front's deficits. The image makeover process involved sidelining the lumpen-based party organisation of the Trinamool Congress, which had not been accepted earlier by the people, and bringing the elite to the forefront of the election campaign.

> So there was a silent alliance of the anti-left, particularly anti-communist, elite and the party faithful. Both sections calculated on overthrowing the other after victory and Banerjee did nothing to dissuade them. In addition, this being the age of neo-liberal policies, Banerjee had the support of domestic capitalists, who, encouraged by the much-discussed potential of "Look East" policies, were interested in investing in the state.[2]

Dipankar Sinha, a professor of Political Science in Calcutta University, called the politics of West Bengal as 'same side goal politics'. Enumerating further he said: 'In it the concerned actors in politics would act in such a manner that they themselves would put their own party in a disadvantageous position, rather than letting or waiting for their competitors to do so.'[3] Sinha cited two examples of scoring self-goals by the ruling TMC. One was the death of a student activist of the CPI(M) student wing in police custody, and the other was the handling of the Kamduni rape and murder case. The unfortunate death of the student was called a 'small affair', and the young women who protested the Kamduni crime were denigrated. Evidently the TMC had no use of the Sushil Samaj any more. It also had no use of the Congress government at the Centre since by 2013 it was clear that in the 2014 election the party would find it difficult to retain its power. With the emerging face of Narendra Modi as BJP's candidate for the top job Mamata Banerjee saw an opportunity to strengthen her hold in national politics. She knew that if the TMC could bag a substantial number of seats from the state, in case of a hung Lok Sabha she would call the shots, like the CPI(M) had done in the past. She even sought support from Anna Hazare who was used by Arvind Kejriwal. Using Anna Hazare and his ability to fast, Kejriwal came out of nowhere and managed to become the chief minister of Delhi and was next testing the waters for a crack at the post of prime ministership in 2014. He even took a dip in the Ganga, visited some temples and went on to contest against Narendra Modi. Mamata planned for a rally in Delhi after obtaining endorsement of Anna Hazare but Anna skipped the rally since there was hardly any crowd. He even backtracked on his endorsement of Mamata as a potential prime ministerial face. Mamata's political naivety was seen earlier also when she landed in the national capital to canvass Dr A.P.J. Kalam as the President for the second term. She claimed that Mulayam Singh Yadav would join her in endorsing Dr Kalam. Mamata's personal dislike of Pranab Mukherjee who was then emerging as the frontrunner for the post led her to more theatrics. After getting snubbed by the Congress, she wrote in a Facebook post, her maiden appearance on the medium, seeking support for Dr Kalam. She even suggested the name of former West Bengal governor Gopalkrishna Gandhi as well as Meira Kumar – anybody but Pranab seemed to be her politics. Finally, she had to fall back on supporting Pranab Mukherjee realising that the people in West Bengal would like to see Pranab babu as the nation's President. Impetuousness had been the hallmark of Mamata's politics. These hasty, ill-conceived steps also show how isolated Mamata Banerjee had been from the national political trend.

Power was a new experience for Mamata Banerjee. The international exposure she received for defeating the Left Front made her dizzy with success. Perhaps to maintain the tempo, Banerjee kept on resorting to theatrical moves, one after another. Such moves, perhaps, she felt would make people hold her in awe and deprive the media the power of argument. Opinion leaders of West Bengal could not have questioned Mamata's prime ministerial ambition. The sub-national spirit, always present in suitable doses in the state, could not be insulted. In suggesting Dr Kalam or Gopalkrishna Gandhi,

Mamata tried to present a picture of a national politician who was not parochial to a potential Bengali candidate.

The TMC faced a major crisis when Sudipto Sen, the chairman of the Saradha Group of companies, was arrested in Kashmir on 23 April 2013, for allegedly defrauding lakhs of depositors who had invested in various schemes floated by his companies. The still unsolved chit fund scam in West Bengal resulted in loss of crores of hard-earned savings of the middle and lower middle-class people of the state. After the Saradha Group went bust, Mamata Banerjee told the duped investors, 'let go whatever has gone'. Realising her mistake within two days she announced Rs 500 crore relief package for the hapless investors. While Saradha started its operation in 2006 when the Left Front was in power, it expanded its presence manifold with the change of government. Sudipto Sen started shifting his loyalty to the Trinamool Congress when the 'winds of change started blowing across Bengal after the 2008 panchayat elections'. The political link got strengthened in the next few years as the media business launched by the group tried its best to give legitimacy to the new regime. The Saradha case bears testimony to close ties between the media, politics and chit funds. The group promoter Sen had supported the 2011 campaign of the TMC. In 2011 Mamata Banerjee distributed ambulances, motorcycles and bicycles donated by the Saradha Group in Jangalmahal. It is also reported that Sudipto Sen bought a painting of Banerjee for Rs 1.86 crore. The TMC transport minister, Mr Madan Mitra, was appointed the president of the employees' union of the group. Its MP Kunal Ghosh was the group's media head. In 2010 the Left Front government had asked SEBI to investigate the group. While the Left Front government too did not take enough steps to stop the company or alert the depositors of the trap they were walking into, the Mamata government emerged as a big support for the group. The growing proximity between the ruling party and the Saradha group on the other hand helped in increasing the latter's credibility. West Bengal had been a breeding ground for chit funds running Ponzi schemes. The central government in reply to a question in the Lok Sabha had given a list of 73 companies from West Bengal which were running Ponzi schemes.

How much money did such Ponzi schemes collect could be seen from the quantum of fall in small savings deposits in West Bengal. In 2006-7, the net collection from small savings was Rs 6,238.93 crores, it increased to Rs 8,985 crores in 2009-10, was Rs 8,409 crores in 2010-11. In 2011-12 small savings deposit collection turned negative, there was a net outflow of 987.22 crores in 2011-12. The annual flow of around Rs 9,000 crores did not go to small savings schemes but moved to various Ponzi schemes under the watchful eye of the state government.[4] There was an elaborate effort by the West Bengal government to keep control over the investigation but in 2014 the Supreme Court transferred the scam case to the Central Bureau of Investigation (CBI) due to the inter-state nature of the scam. This led the state chief minister adopting desperate steps to derail the investigation. It reached its height in January 2019 when a CBI team went to West Bengal to interrogate a senior police officer Rajiv Kumar who was heading the special investigation team (SIT) appointed by the state government to investigate the scam. The CBI officers were detained by the state police. Mamata Banerjee sat on a sit-in protest against the central government because the CBI was trying to interrogate Rajiv Kumar.[5] This was an unprecedented move by a state chief minister to derail an investigation ordered by India's apex court. With such impulsive moves she not only weakens her political stature but also isolates the entire state from the national mainstream. The state administration's use of the police for its political schemes has made the entire law-and-order system suspect. This had been started by the United Front government when Jyoti Basu became the home minister and steadily things have come to a pretty pass. In West Bengal FIRs are used liberally to tame any opposition including the leading opposition party members.

The success of the new TMC government in eliminating the Maoist insurgency in the Jangalmahal area of the state was viewed critically by many having sympathy for the Maoists. This is cited as an example of how smoothly TMC stepped into the shoes of the Left Front as also as betrayal of her electoral promise. One must admit that once in power, Mamata had a responsibility of exterminating lawless insurgency. This she carried out effectively criticisms notwithstanding. As part of *poriborton*, Mamata Banerjee had promised the withdrawal of the joint forces, the unconditional release of all political prisoners, especially the hundreds of their own folk arrested and dumped into jail in the course of the police operations, and a dialogue with the Maoists. On assuming power, the state government reneged on all of these pledges, some perhaps rightly so. Instead Mamata put emphasis on addressing the basic needs of the people. As she saw it, the root cause for Maoists in the state in the Jangalmahal districts of West Midnapore, Purulia and Bankura was the neglect of those areas. Her administration initiated welfare projects in Maoist strongholds under her direct supervision. She ensured that potable water was available to all. Along with this, everybody in the area was provided 16 kg of rice, every month. The local organisation of the TMC, which had spread throughout the area in Banerjee's days in the opposition, began acting as a vital source of information while also acting as vigilante groups. Youths in the area, desperate for employment, were utilised as informants and special police officers (SPOs), who gathered information and showed security forces the way to get to the Maoist hideouts. Simultaneously, security forces conducted raids on the basis of specific information from former Maoists, who had been swayed by

Banerjee's rhetoric. Her administration's 'development package' with 'surrender' sops, the redeployment of the joint forces, the setting up of police training facilities in jungle warfare and a strengthening of the state's counter-insurgency force yielded results. Though many questions were raised about the encounter killing of Communist Party of India (Maoist) politburo member Kishenji, the fact remains that those who live by the gun will die by the gun. Even the Maoist sympathisers accepted that the Maoists had to give serious thought to ending the murder of adivasis and popular activists of mainstream political parties in Jangalmahal.

In the meantime, Mamata Banerjee had anticipated the disenchantment of the Sushil Samaj and was not unduly perturbed by it. Continuing her tirade against the media on its coverage of the West Bengal dengue outbreak in September 2012, Chief Minister Mamata Banerjee claimed that it was now cooking up cases of shortage of beds in hospitals. 'I think the media needs counselling, the way they resort to distorting comments,' she said. Since the media did not accept the counselling, she had to issue similar statements time and again with one minor change, that of replacing CPI(M) with BJP being the carrier of 'fake news'. This was the result of the BJP occupying the second slot in West Bengal replacing the CPI(M) as well as the Congress in the Lok Sabha election of 2019.

The Lok Sabha election of 2014 had given an opportunity to TMC to show its hold over the state of West Bengal like the CPI(M) had done earlier. This, logically enough, resulted in many incidents of violence. On the eve of the last round of elections, some spectacularly violent incidents took place in Kolkata and its neighbourhood. In most of the cases, the tough men associated with the ruling party, the Trinamool Congress, led such attacks against the CPI(M) leaders and functionaries. The incidents illustrated the deep-rooted criminalisation of the public sphere and partisanship of the police force which had its origin from the late 1960s onwards. This process became a common enough tool in the 1970s under the Congress rule, got perfected under the Left Front and finally switched in favour of TMC since the lumpen elements shifted sides. Criminalisation of the public sphere and politicisation of the police became an organic part of everyday governance in West Bengal. Politics in West Bengal had moved from the realms of freedom of choice to guided freedom of those having muscle.

How did Mamata Banerjee keep the muscle under her control? Just take a look at the budget of the cash-strapped state. Within one year of coming to power, Mamata Banerjee gave an amount of Rs 2,00,000 each to 26,000 clubs across the state. Since then, these clubs have received grants worth Rs 1,00,000 every 3 years. Every club thus receives Rs 5,00,000 from the state government in 4 years. Thus the state government paid out Rs 1,300 crores for these clubs over every 4 years. The *Business Standard* reported on 28 January 2019 that the state government had sanctioned Rs 2 lakhs each to 4,300 clubs across the state. She said at an event, 'Our government is providing a yearly aid of Rs 2 lakhs to 4,300 clubs across Bengal. Also, these clubs would be eligible to get financial assistance of Rs 1 lakh every year for the next three years if they submit their annual audit report.'[6] On 13 March 2020 the chief minister handed over grants for 2019-21 to the clubs. In a similar function in January 2018 the chief minister said, 'The Left Front ignored sports. Its budget allocation for sports in 2010-11 was only Rs 74 crore. We have hiked that to more than Rs 450 crore in 2017-18.'[7] The allocation for sports and youth affairs rose to Rs 514 crores in the state's budget for 2020-21. Apart from the triennial grants to the clubs, the government also provides a sum of money to 28,000 clubs for organising Durga Puja every year. In 2018, the state government gave Rs 10,000 each to 28,000 clubs before the festival. In 2019, this amount saw an increase of 150 per cent.

The clubs received an amount of Rs 25,000 each before Durga Puja. It doubled in 2020. Why does the government support these local clubs? The chief minister had asked young club members to protect the fairer sex – mother, sister and young girls – of the area from goons and against antisocial atrocities. The clubs were also directed to build the character of the younger generation. In short, the 'para' clubs were handed over responsibility of a locality with their writ running in the neighbourhood with permissions of sort to interfere in the lives of the locals as and when required.[8]

This unofficial sanction from the chief minister helped the unemployed members of such clubs to extort from the locals. Not that the extortion racket started only after the TMC came to power. The system of organised extortion, the 'tola' system in Bengali, had its origin during the Left Front rule. For all local economic activity, say construction or renovation of a house, or setting up of a shop, etc., one had to pay the local party boss. Under the Trinamool, the single-window system got replaced with turf wars involving different factions of the same party. Local dadas now dominate the localities and citizens live in anxiety and fear of humiliation. The tola system thus dominates an individual's life in West Bengal.

People getting employment under the Mahatma Gandhi National Rural Employment Guarantee Act (MGNREGA) in the state are forced to share their meagre payment. Unskilled workers who, under this scheme, get paid 6 to 8 months late, find extortionists waiting right outside the bank to take a hefty cut from their earnings. The direct benefit transfer of Prime Minister Modi ensured money reached their bank accounts but could not check extortion when the beneficiaries withdrew the same from their accounts. During the rule of the Left Front, CPI(M) had ensured that benefits of the welfare schemes were denied to political opponents. This tradition continued in the case of distribution of new digital ration cards and also when funds were released through panchayats for various rural development projects. The hiring of civic volunteers presented another example of widespread nepotism in the state. Even the Calcutta High Court declared that the appointment process of civic police volunteers in West Bengal was 'a sham with systematic malice' and ordered the state government to cancel all such appointments by the end of 2016.

The smooth running of the rent-seeking market economy under the TMC government would have continued but for Prime Minister Narendra Modi during the 2019 Lok Sabha election campaign referring to the triple T – Trinamool Tolabazi Tax. The election result of 2019 – where BJP surprisingly bagged 18 seats – scared Mamata Banerjee. She sought advice from Prashant Kishor, a much-hyped election strategist. He created a campaign for Mamata – 'Tell Didi' (*Didike balo*) and thus opened up the Pandora's Box. Earlier while addressing Kolkata's civic body leaders, Banerjee asked those who took 'cut money' or commissions from common people to return it. She admitted that some TMC leaders didn't even spare the dead and charge Rs 200 for releasing the sum of Rs 2,000 the state government gives to poor people to cremate family members. The Tell Didi campaign started receiving complaints of extortion. In certain areas people were so angry that the police had to intervene and arrest certain TMC leaders and thus saved them from lynching. Many left the locality and were afraid to return. Mamata could not stay above the filth of her cadres since her nephew and Lok Sabha MP Abhishek Banerjee faced several allegations of making money beyond his known sources of income. In the Kolkata airport the customs authority had detained Banerjee's wife Rujira Naroola for allegedly carrying excess gold without a declaration on the intervening night of 15-16 March 2019. The West Bengal police came and got her released and filed a charge against the customs officers for extortion.

The customs authority had issued summons to Rujira Naroola on 26 March 2019. The Calcutta High Court set aside the summon in June 2020 on technical grounds. In any case, when the election comes such allegations hurt like the mention of the triple T by Modi did in 2019.

While the TMC had a cakewalk in the Lok Sabha election of 2014, the assembly election could have proved a tough battle for survival for Mamata Banerjee. She was helped by an external development – the coming together of the Congress and the Left Front to contest the election. This created a new realignment of forces. For the BJP a victory of the Congress-CPI(M) would have meant a weak base for the 2019 national election. The party could not have conceded West Bengal, a state with 42 Lok Sabha seats, to its national rival the Congress. This softened the BJP campaign felt many analysts.[9] It was noticed that Mamata had reduced her stringent attacks on the BJP while the BJP helped in appointing West Bengal finance minister Dr Amit Mitra as head of the GST panel. Disturbances in the campuses of JNU and Jadavpur University did not emerge as a flashpoint between the BJP and the TMC, an unlikely silence on the part of the West Bengal ruling party. The tacit understanding was seen in the delay in investigation of the Saradha chit fund scam. The opposition Congress and the CPI(M) even approached the Supreme Court for expediting the probe. A delay would mean Mamata Banerjee would be spared several uncomfortable questions.

The TMC government, to its credit, has initiated several welfare measures during its rule. These schemes include food rations at subsidised rates for a large section of the people, the Kanyashree scheme of cash transfers for girl students, cycles for students of classes nine and ten in rural areas, and potable water in villages under the Sajaldhara scheme. Better roads and improved supply of electricity too are considered feathers in the cap of the ruling TMC government. 'There is no denying that these programmes, however faulty in their implementation, created certain goodwill for the ruling party among the rural poor.'[10] But these were viewed as too little and full of faulty delivery effectively not reaching the beneficiaries in full. The tola economy or cut money economy came in between. But then this cut money helped the TMC to sustain its party cadres and ensure electoral muscle flexing.

Sumanta Banerjee compared the Bengali electorate's race for prosperity under Didi with a famous poem called *Khuror Kol* (Uncle's Machine) by Sukumar Ray. The accompanying illustration by Ray showed a man, with a rod strung to his neck, and a bag hanging at the front-end of the rod, and the man running to reach it. 'The Bengali voters have elected Mamata for a second term, hoping for the "nourishment" of their immediate selfish economic needs, without bothering about the long "distance" that they are expected to run, forever trying to catch the elusive fruit that is being dangled by their didi ...'[11] For how long will they run is the question. Similar efforts by the Left Front lasted for 34 years, while Mamata has already managed two terms. But the problem is that the change in communication technology has made people more aware than before. In today's world nothing can be hidden from public scrutiny. The Left Front's well-concealed scientific electoral manipulation finally got exposed in the days of new technology. For the TMC there is hardly anything to conceal. Still, due to political alignment, it managed to sweep the 2016 assembly election. One important element for any change is availability of an alternative. In 2016 there was none.

By the end of 2016 Mamata Banerjee sensed an opportunity to launch herself as a national alternative to Prime Minister Narendra Modi. She attempted to emerge as the principal political campaigner against the decision to demonetise Rs 500 and Rs 1000 notes, 86 per cent of India's currency. She attempted to test the waters in poll-bound Uttar Pradesh. Addressing a rally in Lucknow she blamed the prime minister for pushing the people of the country, especially the poor farmer, deprived and downtrodden, to pain and agony in the name of demonetisation.[12] She even led a march in New Delhi and submitted a memorandum to President Pranab Mukherjee. As late as during the 2019 Lok Sabha polls Mamata continued on the plank that demonetisation had helped the BJP to convert black money into white. Mamata's tirades against demonetisation can be judged from the huge cash economy in her state. During the demonetisation the then CEO of United Bank of India Pawan Bajaj told the *Business Line* that West Bengal and the North East region of the country had

> … the maximum affinity to cash. This region had the highest CASA (current account, savings account) ratio of over 40 per cent as against the national average of 31 per cent. CASA is the ratio of deposits in low-yielding current and savings accounts to total deposits. Add to this, low incidence of cashless transactions in the region, the nation has little clue to the money trail and the reach of the tax net is impacted. In West Bengal - which records the lowest tax-to-GSDP ratio of 4 per cent among major States - the entire jute sector was run on cash till this month. While salaries will now go to the cashless mode, raw jute is purchased from farmers in cash.[13]

In fact, during the demonetisation period West Bengal became the centre for transferring cash hoarding into assets – mostly illiquid assets like real estate, *benami* transactions through 'Hundi', an instrument used for trading with Bangladesh. Demonetisation and a few months thereafter the introduction of GST had shaken the peaceful cash-based transactions of West Bengal. In a report dated December 30, 2019, the *Business Standard* said that the Income Tax Department and Serious Fraud Investigation Office (SFIO) had identified close to 30,000 shell companies in Kolkata. Most of these companies were used to launder unaccounted money after the note ban and some of them did not even possess a PAN (permanent account number). Directors of 15,000 shell companies are also directors of 15,685 companies, all from Kolkata. The Income Tax Department found that almost 90 per cent of shell companies were located in Kolkata. In a state where a large section of the people live on extortion it will certainly spawn new ways of converting cash into legitimate assets.

The result of the Lok Sabha poll 2019 indicates that the BJP has emerged as the competing force for the TMC in West Bengal. The party bagged 18 Lok Sabha seats and 40.25 per cent votes – just 3 per cent less than that of the TMC which could win 22 seats against its target to sweep all 42 in the state. What is more, Mamata Banerjee had campaigned on the plank that in the event of a coalition government at the Centre she would take a shot at the PM's chair. Despite her best efforts to capture votes on the sentiment of regional nationalism the people of the state opted for the BJP. Breaking up the election result in terms of assembly constituencies TMC still had a lead in 164 seats (out of 294) while BJP led in 121 seats. In a national election where the BJP leadership paid much less attention to the state, a lead in 121 assembly seats indicate an ominous future for the ruling TMC. But it will not be proper to compare the 2019 Lok Sabha poll with the one in 2009 when the CPI(M) realised an assembly election defeat was staring at it. Post the 2009 poll debacle the Left Front government turned effectively into a lame duck. In contrast the TMC is very much active and even attempted to change the course. The campaign titled 'Tell Didi' was one such effort though it paid no dividend and created inner party problems instead.

The point one must remember is that the Lok Sabha poll was between incumbent Prime Minister Narendra Modi and a state chief minister who intended to take a shot at the chair. In the duel between Narendra Modi and Mamata Banerjee, naturally Modi had the advantage as the nation's choice to lead the Centre. He had a track record of delivery, he could appeal to nationalism, and what is more he had the advantage of highlighting TMC's 'cut money' economy. Modi even termed Banerjee as the speed breaker in Bengal's development. This led to more political polarisation than a communal one, though analysts brand the BJP as a Hindutva party having adversarial relations with the Muslims. The Centre for the Study of Developing Societies (CSDS)–Lokniti pre-poll survey of end March 2019 and the post-poll survey of May 2019 had revealed that the net satisfaction with the BJP-led National Democratic Alliance (NDA) government at the Centre registered a sharp rise while the net satisfaction with the incumbent TMC government in West Bengal registered a comparatively smaller growth.[14] There is sharp political polarisation in West Bengal. This polarisation, judged by the Lok Sabha 2019 result, seems to be between two parties – the TMC and the BJP. In other words, the BJP is the new force for the anti-TMC voters. From the National Election Survey data it seems that political polarisation has taken the form of communal polarisation also. Barring the Muslim community all others voted for BJP in large numbers. Among the Muslim community 70.4 per cent of voters supported the TMC while a mere 3.8 per cent voted for the BJP.[15] Given the fact that Muslims hold the decisive votes in a majority of West Bengal assembly constituencies Mamata Banerjee seemed to be starting with an advantage.

Predictably therefore Mamata Banerjee had passed a resolution in the West Bengal state assembly in January 2020 against the Centre's Citizenship Amendment Act (CAA) which eased citizenship for people of minority communities from three Muslim majority neighbouring countries – Pakistan, Bangladesh and Afghanistan – displaced on grounds of religious persecution. CAA and a possibility of introduction of National Registry of Citizens (NRC) like in Assam have been two contentious points for Muslims in West Bengal, many of whom are illegal migrants to India. Mamata Banerjee pampers this community since the BJP is called a Hindu communal party working against the Muslims. The TMC should emerge as the natural choice of the minority communities in West Bengal. Once assured of more than 25 per cent of electorates, Mamata needs only another 15 per cent or so to retain her power in 2021.

Dipankar Sinha has argued that 'the high level of politicisation and consequent political polarisation in West Bengal suck in the potential members of emergent civil society, thereby leaving lesser scope for creation of a durable civil society.'[16] This trend is seen in the arguments made by the members of civil society. They find no communal angle in the blatant pampering of the minority communities by the administration while they find fault with legislations like the Muslim Women (Protection of Rights on Marriage) Act, 2019 passed in August 2019 which criminalised triple talaq declared illegal by the Supreme Court and made it punishable. They conveniently ignore that the public opinion against triple talaq was created by Muslim women in the first place. Sinha called it a 'pop-up civil society'.

> It is single issue-centric and it requires a specific issue to emerge, to be picked up by the media with all publicity blitz and laid on the table as a suitable item for orchestrated debate. The issues are highlighted as 'leads' in newspapers and on prime-time television-based panel discussions for a certain period of time, but they recede into background soon after.[17]

Since the civil society takes up issues highlighted and played up in the media the government ensures that it controls the media's work on its 'agenda setting function' so as to help the ruling party. Since the state government provides a major part of the advertisement to support media houses, the agenda is set by West Bengal media to suit the ruling entity in the state. This is what the media did even during the Left Front rule and they are continuing along the same lines to support the TMC now. If there is a change in government the media might not take much time to defend the new government. But there is a threat for the mainstream media from the online space. Information can no longer be suppressed. This is an added problem for all political parties in India, a major one for the TMC which has many skeletons in its cupboard.

A very curious policy of the state government is not to launch any central government scheme but to create similar schemes only with state government funds. One reason for non-implementation of certain prominent central government schemes beneficial to the common man could be the publicity value. The state government wants to present a picture of an unsympathetic central government. It wants to show that any benefit accruing to the people comes from the state alone. This is a curious stance since during the Left Front government the constituents of the Front used to ensure that benefits of popular schemes like IRDP or DRI loans go to their members. During the days of Loan Melas in the early 1980s, Left Front members made it a point to corner the loan mela application forms, interact with banks and ensure that 'their' people receive benefits. Why did TMC leader Mamata Banerjee fail to introduce such central schemes for the people of West Bengal? Even the prime minister made reference to such curious decisions of the state government. He told a gathering in Calcutta on 12 January 2020 during the 150th year celebration of the Calcutta Port Trust how the people of the state were being deprived of these benefits.

> Till now around 75 lakh poor people have received free treatment under Ayushman Bharat scheme. Around 43,000 crores have been transferred directly to the bank accounts of 8 crore farmers under PM-KISAN scheme. There are no middlemen and syndicates. Why will anybody implement these when the schemes do not support middlemen and syndicates?

Modi asked the state government.[18] While the prime minister scored a political point the fact remains that Mamata Banerjee by her stance is missing out on the fund the central government provides for such schemes. The TMC depends on strong local leaders in distributing benefits to the people. Unlike a party-based control as was during the Left Front rule, the TMC handles issues with strong leaders having local networks and command over local administration.[19] They are the new mediators and protectors of people's interest. The central schemes handled through such a network would have expanded the number of beneficiaries and helped the TMC in the elections. Despite that Mamata Banerjee refuses to use the benefits. The problem of such local leader networks was seen during the distribution of free rations during the ongoing Covid-19 pandemic. Local leaders hijacked the rice and grain from the ration dealers, made their own packets and distributed them under their relief banners. As a result, benefits earmarked did not reach the target beneficiaries. Even during the relief provided to those affected by the devastating cyclone Amphan there were several such incidences of pilferage of relief materials. Clearly in the absence of an organised party network to tame such local-level power brokers, the intended beneficiaries suffer and in the process the party in power generates strong hatred. The other problem of such a model is that local power brokers have allegiance only to money and safety. In case of trouble they jump the ship as did many local-level operators from the Left Front in 2011. All these operators look for is safety in case a regime changes. The TMC thus is sitting on an active volcano which may erupt any time.

Violence in the state has increased due to lumpenisation of the society by the local dadas owing allegiance to the TMC and the police force surrendering to such elements. Corruption and extortion are part of the life of an average resident of Bengal. There is hardly any work, even for unskilled workers who move to other distant states seeking livelihood. According to Census 2011, between 2001 and 2011 an estimated 5.8 lakh people moved outside the state in search of work. This was the fourth highest in the country after Uttar Pradesh, Bihar and Rajasthan. This number has increased substantially during the next 10 years since then. A ball park estimate of the number of migrant workers from West Bengal is around 12 lakhs. During the Covid-19 pandemic there was a rush of such migrants to go back to their native places. Other states had arranged quarantine and transportation for their migrants while the West Bengal government had shown reluctance to allow them to enter the state. When special trains were run to transport migrant workers back to their homes West Bengal had requisitioned the least number of trains. Initially it even refused permission to the Indian Railway to let such trains enter the state. Politically such gestures cost dear. When the central government launched a special scheme – the 'Garib Kalyan Rojgar Abhiyaan' – in select 116 districts of six states (Bihar, Madhya Pradesh, Uttar Pradesh, Rajasthan, Jharkhand and Odisha) at an outlay of Rs 50,000 crores West Bengal was not included. Though the state protested it was revealed that when the Centre had sought data the state did not provide the same. It woke up when the launch of the scheme became public and as a measure to divert attention took objection for ignoring West Bengal. Clearly in a competitive environment West Bengal cannot remain aloof. There had been umpteen instances when government officials from the state had failed to attend important meetings at the Centre for fear of antagonising the chief minister. A former state vigilance commission member admitted that he had skipped many deliberations in Delhi since travelling to the national capital was viewed unfavourably by the state. The state's behaviour seems like declaration of its independent identity – isolated from the nation.

Endnotes

1 *The Telegraph* Calcutta, August 4, 2005, https://www.telegraphindia.com/india/mamata-casts-shame-at-house-paper-throw-at-speaker/cid/860298.

2 Ishita Mukhopadhyay, 'Moving towards Semi-Fascism in West Bengal,' *EPW*, May 26, 2012, https://www.epw.in/system/files/pdf/2012_47/21/Moving_towards_SemiFascism_in_West_Bengal.pdf.

3 Dipankar Sinha, "'Same Side Goal' Politics West Bengal's New Brand Image?" *EPW*, July 27, 2013, https://www.epw.in/system/files/pdf/2013_48/30/Same_Side_Goal_Politics.pdf.

4 Subhanil Chowdhury, 'The Political Economy of Shadow Finance in West Bengal,' *EPW*, May 4, 2013, https://www.epw.in/journal/2013/18/web-exclusives/political-economy-shadow-finance-west-bengal.html.

5 *The Economic Times*, November 29, 2019, economictimes.indiatimes.com/news/politics-and-nation/sc-notice-to-ips-officer-rajeev-kumar-on-cbis-appeal-challenging-his-anticipatory-bail/articleshow/72289250.cms.

6 'Mamata provides financial aid to 4300 clubs in Bengal,' *Business Standard,* January 28, 2019, https://www.business-standard.com/article/news-ians/mamata-provides-financial-aid-to-4300-clubs-in-bengal-119012801206_1.html.

7 *Hindustan Times*, January 24, 2018, https://www.hindustantimes.com/kolkata/have-donated-rs-600-crore-to-neighbourhood-clubs-since-2011-mamata-banerjee/story-gFdo0KQp7aRuciAI8skt8L.html.

8 'Mamata Banerjee's Bengal: Clubs take over neighbourhoods,' *India Today*, January 24, 2018, https://www.indiatoday.in/india/story/mamata-banerjee-s-bengal-clubs-take-over-neighbourhoods-1153593-2018-01-24.

9 Rajat Roy, 'Why the BJP and the Trinamool are Going Soft on Each Other,' *The Wire*, February 23, 2016.

10 Rajat Roy, 'Nothing succeeds like Success in West Bengal,' *EPW*, May 28, 2016, https://www.epw.in/system/files/pdf/2016_51/22/CM_LI_22_28052016_2016_State_Assembly_Elections_Rajat_Roy.pdf.

11 Sumanta Banerjee, 'West Bengal Elections: Myopic Popular Verdict in a Political Vacuum,' *EPW*, September 3, 2016, https://www.epw.in/system/files/pdf/2016_51/36/West_Bengal_Elections_0.pdf.

12 *The New Indian Express*, November 29, 2016.

13 *The Hindu Business Line*, November 25, 2016.

14 Jyotiprasad Chatterjee and Suprio Basu, 'A New Trajectory of Politics in West Bengal,' *EPW*, August 3, 2019, https://www.epw.in/system/files/pdf/2019_54/31/CM_LIV_31_030819_Elec_Spl_Jyotiprasad_Chatterjee.pdf.

15 Ibid.

16 Sinha, "'Same Side Goal' Politics."

17 Ibid.

18 'PM Modi hits out at Mamata Banerjee for not implementing Central Schemes,' *India Today*, January 12, 2020.

19 Suman Nath, 'Everyday Politics and Corruption in West Bengal,' *EPW*, May 27, 2017, https://www.epw.in/system/files/pdf/2017_52/21/CM_LII_21_270517_Suman_Nath.pdf.

ISOLATION UNCHECKED – WILL IT END SOMEDAY?

Bengalis have come a long way since the early days of the British rule and the espousal of English education to the rule of a regional political party led by the first female head of the state, from the days when the rich and the landed gentry used to command respect to the present days when one must pay obeisance to the local mastans for peace, from the days when people from across the vast country used to come to the state's capital Calcutta (the second largest city of the British empire next to London), to today when the young flock out of the state for education and livelihood, from the days when Bengal was the thought leader and educated the rest of the Indians on nationalism to now when West Bengal and its local leadership is viewed as laggards in a progressive India. This is a story of the descent of a state – a state which even the other day saw one of its boys receiving the Nobel memorial prize in Economics, a state whose poet was the first Asian honoured with the Nobel prize, a place which was the *karmabhumi* of Nobel laureates Ronald Ross, C.V. Raman, and Mother Teresa, the land that nurtured the philosopher Sarvepalli Radhakrishnan, and produced Satyajit Ray, the first Indian filmmaker receiving accolades in the global cinematography scene, and Pandit Ravi Shankar, the first Indian to win the Grammy. The children of this state shine in their adopted countries and rise to the top. The bright young people of this state today feel relieved when they manage to migrate and move out. This is the history of a state living in and taking solace from its past and feeling happy when migrants from the state win laurels. West Bengal is a story of an unending descent – economically, culturally and politically. It is the story of a state that has lost its plot.

In the early days when Calcutta was the centre of the Indian renaissance it saw persons with orthodox education like Raja Rammohun Roy taking up learning of English so as to serve the dual purpose – that of getting close to the new rulers and also to pick up the knowledge that gave the Europeans the mastery over such a distant land. A Bengali did not remain isolated, confined in his own narrow sphere but learnt, questioned and provided answers to the future mixing its past with the present. Thus there were social reformers, educators, financiers who followed their instincts of laying the foundation of a great nation and even enriched Bengali their mother tongue in course of learning English. The development was fast enough so as to match the more developed European language even in the field of literature within less than one hundred years of its initiation into the modern era. It saw one of its young monks enthralling a global galaxy of preachers with his oratory and positioning firmly the Hindu philosophy on the global stage. Even today the bitterest critic of a Bengali will admit that Bengal was the unchallenged thought leader in the subcontinent. It was Bengal which had planted the seed of nationalism, germinated it and turned it into a sapling that eventually led to the creation of the largest democracy in the world.

History is moved by no individual but the collective efforts of people under an individual who assumes the position of a leader by virtue of knowledge, sacrifice and the capacity to influence. While the narrative of the political twists and turns of Bengal attempted to capture the events and outlined the roles of certain individuals it would be appropriate to single out certain prominent personalities who played significant roles and evaluate how they fared in the overall context of the Indian political evolution. Though in the context of Indian nationalism Bankim Chandra's 'Vande Mataram' and his novel *Ananda Math* are referred to as the point of inception, the sense of nationalism in Bengal had its origin much before. Bankim Chandra articulated the same with his mastery over Bengali literature. Historically speaking Bengal's first point of departure with the rest of the nation was seen during the times of the Sepoy Mutiny in 1857, arguably India's first struggle for freedom. If that was the case, it needs to be accepted that Bengal's products of the renaissance did not find much merit in the movement though it had its first spark on the soil of Bengal. It was a matter of difference between two outlooks – one looking at the future and the other intending to reverse the changes and remain in the status quo of the days before the British stepped in. Bengal was somewhat torn between the two regimes – the British and the Muslim rulers. It was evident in what Raja Rammohun mentioned in his 'Appeal to the King in Council', that under the Muslim rule, 'the natives of this country enjoyed every political privilege in common with Musaalman …' But under the British rule despite loss of political consequence, the natives 'were consoled by the more secure enjoyment of those civil and religious rights which had been so often violated by the rapacity and intolerance of the Mussulmans …' The violation of civil and religious rights of the Hindus was the issue between the Muslim rulers and the Hindu subjects. The novel *Ananda Math* and the song 'Vande Mataram' should be interpreted in this context. As far as political discourse is concerned one has to place Bankim Chandra as a literary figure, not a political leader.

Surendranath Banerjee was the first Bengali who had assumed the role of a political ideologue. It was his influence that saw Bengali youth wake up to the need of having a say in how they are being governed – that is what politics aims to do. Till he channelised the spirit and energy of the young in Bengal towards the need for political intervention they were caught between, as Bipin Chandra Pal mentioned, the factions of the Brahmo Samaj. Some were even influenced by Sri Ramakrishna and spent time at the Dakshineswar temple of Goddess Kali. The most prominent personality to emerge from there was Swami Vivekananda who was responsible for inculcating a sense of pride among the Hindus nationally. Though Vivekananda was not involved in politics his contribution to the development of Hindu nationalism was immense. As far as direct political role is concerned it was Surendranath Banerjee who led and he was reverentially referred to as Rashtraguru (the teacher of the nation). In 1876 a 28-year-old Surendranath was the star orator at the first meeting of the Bharat Sabha or Indian Association. The Indian Association preceded the Indian National Congress and was the leading forum where Indian voices used to be articulated. In fact, the first session of the INC in Mumbai was of less significance in size and influence than the Indian Association session that took place around the same time in Calcutta. The point that cannot be missed is that the first session of the INC did not have any prominent face from Bengal, an omission that saw Rabindranath Tagore lamenting 'Where are you Bengali' (*Koi re Bangali koi*) in the poem '*Awhangeet*' (Song to join the call). To a sensitive mind this was an insult to Bengal which was at the forefront of the nation; yet the first session of the Congress had no significant presence of prominent faces from there. If one judges merely by political prominence at that time, Surendranath deserved to be the first president of the Indian National Congress. This had hurt Tagore and he wrote, 'The world over the trumpet has been sounded, hearing it, so many have come with their flags, but where is the Bengali?' The poet was crestfallen at the insult meted out to Bengal but did not give up hope. He wrote, 'Rise the poet of Bengal, give life afresh in the mother tongue, the people of the world will drink nectar in that language.' (*Utha bangakabi, maer bhasay mumurshere dao pran, jagater lok sudhar ashay se bhasa koribe pan.*) It was a call to Bengali pride, to its sub-nationalist identity in order to show its leading stature to the rest of India.

Surendranath, however, did not take it as a snub. He wrote in his autobiography that since the session of the Indian Association too was at an advanced stage of preparation when the plan for the Congress session came to light, Surendranath could not join the session in Bombay. It was generous of Surendranath to not express any bitterness and also to disband his Indian Association and work for the Congress when Hume approached him. Objectively speaking one cannot dismiss the discomfort of Tagore. In the first place, Calcutta was the seat of all activity including the capital of the country. Planning an event in Bombay, instead of Calcutta, was clearly an effort to bypass the already vibrant capital city. In fact, the second session of the Congress had to be brought to Calcutta next year. A stronger view would be that there was an effort on the part of Hume and his friends to isolate Bengal when planning for the Indian National Congress was at the drawing board stage.

Surendranath was, at the dawn of political India, the tallest leader who had the cause of the nation deeply rooted in his heart. When Hume approached him, Surendranath had readily helped the Congress to organise its first successful though its second session in 1886 in Calcutta. Even later-day historians like Irfan Habib who were critical of Bankim Chandra's *Ananda Math* and 'Vande Mataram' for his unflattering portrayal of the Muslim rulers, highlighted the role played by the forceful presence of Surendranath. Irfan Habib had acknowledged Surendranath as a proponent of early liberal nationalism, especially appreciating Surendranath's denial that there was any antagonism between the two great races who inhabit this vast continent and who together form the Indian nation. It was Surendranath who led the birth of secular nationalism in the country. He was the Rashtraguru who was not given his due regard by the others in the early stages of political India. The rightful choice to lead the first session of the Indian National Congress should have been Surendranath not W.C. Bonnerjee, and it should have been held in Calcutta, not in Bombay.[1] Therefore the birth of political India witnessed an undercurrent of discomfort with Bengal and the tall leaders of the state.

With the passage of time the concept of nationalism took a different turn. The annual sessions organised in the western style with representatives behaving as if they had come from heaven to deliberate on issues did not find much favour with many. Some like Rabindranath, Bipin Pal and Aurobindo did not hesitate to express their disapproval of the manner in which the Congress was being steered. The disconnect of the leaders with the people, particularly the deep-rooted elitism of the Congress leaders, was not looked upon favourably by many. They felt that the Congress leaders had lost touch with the masses. The Partition of Bengal in 1905 was perhaps the first point of departure between the political thoughts of Bengal and other leaders hailing from outside Bengal. Gopal Krishna Gokhale who is often referred to in Bengal for saying something along the lines of 'what Bengal thinks today India thinks tomorrow' was the most anxious among them to bring about a rapprochement with the British. Surendranath, too, belonged to the moderate section of the Congress. When Aurobindo had drafted a pamphlet titled 'No Compromise' and the same was brought to Surendranath, he had refused to support the same. The Congress was split ideologically between the old guard like Gokhale and the neo-nationalists like Aurobindo. Bal Gangadhar Tilak was among the prominent faces in the neo-nationalist group. Surendranath remained a prominent leader among the moderates. He was a minister in the provincial ministry in Bengal when under the Government of India Act of 1919 councils were created but lost in his re-election bid when the Swarajya party entered the contest. That was the end of the public life of one of India's first successful nationalist politicians. Surendranath's public life was fairly long, more than 50 years, from the 1870s till 1924, though he lost prominence with the rise of the neo-nationalists.

Bengal's leadership was deep rooted and it remained the nursery of nationalism and also witnessed its evolution into neo-nationalism. The neo-nationalists found no reason to follow the path of compromise as was being preached by the likes of Gokhale. While the Congress remained under the influence of the old leaders, in political India these leaders were becoming less relevant. Aurobindo had brought in the most dramatic change in Bengal's politics with his idea of revolutionary struggle. His presence in politics was brief – just about 5 years. But during this brief period he had laid the foundation of terrorist groups which took such a deep root in the politics of the state that even after the failed Quit India Movement this spirit had seen creation of independent areas in the district of Midnapore. Aurobindo's presence in politics coincided with the British government's decision to partition Bengal. This was the first major movement of the people against a government decision. There was no single leader, no party organisation, particularly no role of the INC, yet the British administration found it difficult to contain the spontaneous movement in Bengal. True, the intensity of the movement died with the passage of time and by 1911 when the same was revoked it hardly mattered. In the brief period of 5 years Aurobindo had shaken up political Bengal. In a way, he was the political avatar of religious leader Swami Vivekananda, the monk from Bengal, who arguably had an electrifying influence in India and helped the political Hindu to have a sense of pride in his own past.

Aurobindo had seized upon the idea and applied it to politics. He had recognised the arrogance of Westernised Bengal and preached that the Bengal after Ramakrishna Paramahansha was different. The capacity for belief was what had saved Bengal, said Aurobindo. And this belief came from the teachings of several religious men, 'men whom the educated world would not have recognised'. Aurobindo claimed the superiority of Bengal in spreading political idealism in India. In that sense he was the first Bengali politician in the national scene – unlike Surendranath he did not hesitate to claim his superiority or express his views without hesitation. Aurobindo's idea of underground movements caught the fancy of Bengal and arguably culminated in Subhas Chandra Bose leading the Azad Hind Fauz onto Indian soil along with the Japanese forces. Aurobindo was the rebel who transformed the rebellious youth of Bengal into a new political tool that later had continued friction with the Gandhian idealism of the Congress. This resulted in Bengal getting sidelined in the national mainstream politics. Aurobindo was a person of ideas and acted from behind the scenes. He was instrumental in the breaking up of the Congress in 1909 and did so even without consulting Tilak, as he had admitted later. He saw through the politics of the likes of Gokhale and referred to him as 'Bibhishan' of the *Ramayana*. Clearly Gokhale had a long-term vision about the role of the Congress which was different from the strong, emotional and rebellious thoughts of Bengal. It is interesting to note that it was Gokhale who brought in Mahatma Gandhi to steer the Congress in subsequent years. Perhaps he had seen in Gandhi the exact leadership qualities which Gokhale felt were necessary. The short-lived presence of Aurobindo in the political life of Bengal was in a way a blessing in disguise for the type of public movement which the stalwarts of the Congress had envisioned and which eventually served as the foundation of modern political India.

The third tall leader from Bengal who shone in the national scene was Chittaranjan Das. Chittaranjan rose as the defence lawyer of Aurobindo, the revolutionary leader. He came in close contact with the revolutionaries of Bengal and joined politics later. He too had a very short stint in politics, less than 10 years. Chittaranjan joined the Congress in 1917, the year when Gandhi too joined the party. Both emerged as the top leaders of the party with differing views on occasions. When Gandhi formally joined the Congress party, he had to contend with two formidable personalities – Bal Gangadhar Tilak and Chittaranjan Das. Tilak and Das had unanimity on many issues while Gandhi had different views. Chittaranjan was a modern political person who knew the value of legislative politics while Gandhi was a person dedicated to the traditional ideals and felt council entry would not serve the nation. The other major point of departure between the two was Chittaranjan's sympathy for the revolutionary terrorists of Bengal. After all, Chittaranjan's public life even in legal practice started with the Alipore Bomb Case in which he defended Aurobindo, the main accused. Mahatma Gandhi, in contrast, had helped the British war effort during the First World War before coming to India from South Africa. Gandhi's movements in South Africa concerned obtaining civil rights from the government there. He had even assisted the British during the Boer war. Das came into politics with the background of offering legal defence to revolutionaries of Bengal while the Mahatma entered Indian politics from the background of extracting privileges for the deprived people in collaboration with those who denied the same. There was a difference in their approaches which was increased by Gandhi's steadfast refusal to endorse anything remotely violent. The two different political philosophies were bound to turn antagonistic and it came to a head over the hanging of Gopinath Saha. This was the point of departure of Bengal from mainstream India which kept on widening since then. Bengal never really reconciled to Gandhian politics wholeheartedly. In fact, even in later years the devoted Gandhians in the Bengal Congress could never win leadership positions and had to remain content as a faction. The isolation of Bengal's most popular leader in the decision-making process of the Congress, as was seen in the refusal of Gandhi's followers to accede to council entry, was the beginning. This gulf kept on widening since Bengal did not have any leader to sway the national sentiment and challenge the unquestioned leadership role of Gandhi. The illness and sudden death of Chittaranjan Das ended the leadership position of Bengal which had taught India its rudimentary lesson of nationalism.

Politics of council entry brought in its attendant complexities. First, there was an inevitable tussle for the leadership position. The post for the chief executive of the Calcutta Corporation was hotly contested among the three followers of Chittaranjan – Birendranath Sasmal, Jatindra Mohan Sengupta and Subhas Chandra Bose. Sasmal lost and even left politics eventually. Jatindra Mohan had the baggage of not giving up law practice during the Non-cooperation movement. Eventually Bose received the support of the Calcutta elites of the Congress and the erstwhile revolutionaries and members of the Jugantar party. This was the precursor to the factional feuds within the Congress. In the council emerged a group of successful professionals and landed aristocracy to dominate. This was another reason for internal feuds in the Congress. The other unavoidable problem of politics was the emergence of Muslim politicians with whom came communalism in Bengal's politics. With a domineering figure like Chittaranjan passing away there was nobody influential enough to nip the huge emerging problem in the bud.

The post-Chittaranjan phase of Bengal politics was one of internal squabbles. An intense power struggle between the two protégés of Chittaranjan saw various factions siding with one or the other and in the process weakening the political muscle of Bengal. Mahatma Gandhi who emerged as the unchallenged leader of the Congress could not douse the fire of dissent in Bengal since a large section of the members of the Congress came from the erstwhile revolutionaries. Many of the Bengal Congress leaders had maintained contacts with the underground terrorist movement and did not hesitate to support the causes of this category of freedom fighters. But for the Mahatma the means, that is strict adherence to non-violence, was more important than the objective of freedom. This was the basic conflict between Mahatma Gandhi and Bengal's freedom movement. The ardent followers of Gandhi could never influence Bengal's youth so as to emerge as the dominant most in Bengal politics. Only Subhas Chandra enjoyed this position but he had to confront many detractors – the British administration as well as the Gandhian leaders in the Congress. After Chittaranjan's demise Mahatma Gandhi had the advantage of recasting the Bengal Congress leadership since Subhas was then interred in faraway Mandalay jail. But once he was released from prison the leadership of Gandhi's chosen disciple Jatindra Mohan did not last. Even the former revolutionaries were in favour of Subhas since they were not keen on Gandhian non-violence.

In a curious turn of events Gandhi had come to Calcutta and stayed as a guest in the house of Sarat Chandra Bose, 'mejda' or older brother of Subhas Chandra in 1937. Gandhi then, as observed by Nirad C. Chaudhuri who was secretary to Sarat Bose at that time, was an unchallenged king who could command respect and even *dakshina* from anybody. Rabindranath Tagore was unwell during that time. Nevertheless he came to meet Gandhi – a fact that Nirad babu did not appreciate. The members of the Congress who accompanied Gandhi were full of themselves – the Congress was to them a power centre parallel to the British Raj. Bengal, the pioneer of nationalism and the nationalist movement, was by then one of the many provinces with little influence to sway political India. Subhas Bose became the Congress president at this juncture in 1938 with the blessings of the Mahatma. To his credit he had command over the Congress members though the top leadership, in which Sardar Vallabhbhai had control over finances, was neutral to antagonistic towards Bose. Sardar Patel harboured an animosity towards Bose over the will of his elder brother Vithalbhai Patel. That was at a time when undivided Bengal had non-Congress governments where there was greater influence of the Muslim League and other Muslim leaders. The policies which were being framed were against the interests of the Hindus. The communal divide between the Hindus and Muslims was not much hidden but the Congress had chosen to turn a blind eye at the dangerous turn in Bengal, just a province outside its politically more important Hindi heartland. The isolation of Bose in the Congress underlines the isolation of Bengal from national politics. Though the Congress president was then a de-facto rubber stamp of Mahatma Gandhi the president had certain authorities. What is more he made the unpardonable mistake of contesting against the Mahatma's candidate and defeating him. Naturally it was a matter of time before he was removed from the Congress. With his ouster the Congress lost its Bengal unit – the entire Bengal Congress sided with Subhas Chandra as was seen in the election of the Calcutta Corporation. In any case by then Bengal politics had turned adversarial to the interest of the Hindus. This brought Syama Prasad Mukherjee into politics.

Subhas Chandra was elected Congress president 16 years after his political mentor Chittaranjan Das. And he was the last Bengali to assume the post. Atulya Ghosh who was a top member of the CWC could never receive the nod of his colleagues to become president of the Congress. Post-Independence West Bengal was insignificant in national politics. The Union cabinet did not have any tall Bengali presence who could wield power and tilt decisions in favour of the state. Much later A.B.A. Ghani Khan Choudhury had emerged as a person who used his influence to bring in projects for his home state. In the arena of competitive politics West Bengal was a loser, a reason which made it to look inwards and remain politically isolated.

Syama Prasad Mukherjee was a whiff of fresh air in Bengal politics. He was a roadblock to the unhindered prominence of the Muslim leadership, a natural outcome in a Muslim majority state. Prominent Bengalis like Nalini Ranjan Sarkar, judged by his record of holding office, were focused more on attaining some important office or the other than furthering the cause of ordinary people of Bengal. The Indian National Congress had less time and energy for Bengal though leaders followed Gandhi in later days when riots became a near regular event in parts of the state. There was no prominent Muslim face from Bengal in the Congress who could have counselled and helped in bringing the two warring communities together. There was a political vacuum in Bengal. Lack of interest of the Congress in Bengal was strikingly illustrated by the complete silence of Gandhi during the famine of 1942-43. Clearly the Indian national leadership had written off Bengal, the state that taught India nationalism.

The Congress under Gandhi had little interest in shaping its politics according to the need in a particular province. Thus in 1936 when Fazlul Huq, the leader of the Krishak Praja party, had evinced interest in forming a coalition government in Bengal, Congress leaders stuck adamantly to its decision that it would form government only where the party had won a majority. In a Muslim majority state like Bengal it would have been prudent to join hands with Huq but Gandhi, in particular, did not agree. Later when Subhas Chandra again pressed for a coalition with Huq, Mahatma Gandhi went by the prudent advice of businessman G.D. Birla, career-hunter Nalini

Ranjan Sarkar, and Maulana Azad, a non-entity in Bengal. Not only were popular voices from Bengal ignored, the top leadership of the Congress, Gandhi in particular, cared to be surrounded by opinions of persons who had no people support. It was a two-way isolation – isolation of the top leadership from the ground-level situation in Bengal and also the failure of the Bengal leadership to press for a pragmatic attitude from the Congress top brass.

Syama Prasad Mukherjee came into politics alarmed over the proposed education policy of the provincial government. He had also noticed the anti-Hindu legislative efforts of the Huq-League coalition government. He tried to build a collective opinion of leaders but at that point Subhas Chandra was the Congress president and had no interest in opposing the provincial Bengal government for fear of losing support from the Muslims. Later when he was shunted out of the Congress he created a movement for removing the Holwell Monument, viewed as a symbol of Nawab Siraj-ud-daula's oppression of the English in Calcutta. Meanwhile Syama Prasad formed a coalition with N.C. Chatterjee who was the Hindu Mahasabha leader then. The only time the Bose-led faction sided with Syama Prasad was in joining Huq to form a ministry. Subhas Chandra was desperately looking for some political foothold and had even contested the Calcutta Corporation election with the Muslim League accepting the post of an alderman – a Congress president turned an alderman of a city corporation. But for his heroic move to lead the Azad Hind Fauz, Subhas Chandra would have met with an inglorious end to his eventful political life in Bengal.

The Hindu Mahasabha did not have much political influence and in the provincial election of 1945 it lost badly when the Congress leaders were released from jail. But once again the Muslim League had the numbers to form the government. Post 1945 was the darkest period in the politics of Bengal. It saw several Hindu–Muslim riots, the prominent one being the well-engineered one in Calcutta. This was the period when Indian independence was a matter of time and the only point that was required to be negotiated was how the nation would be partitioned. As a Muslim majority province, the question of Bengal remaining part of India run by the Hindu leadership of the Congress was improbable. There was the option of Bengal remaining an independent country – an idea that Sarat Bose propagated with support from Suhrawardy. This was an effort to separate the port and industry city of Calcutta from India. Bose fell for the idea that originally the communists had propagated. The entire idea was impractical and devoid of ground realities. By then the Hindu–Muslim conflicts were flaring, especially in the Muslim-majority eastern part of Bengal where mostly vulnerable sections of Hindus – lower caste and poor – lived. Syama Prasad had some kind of premonition and with Chatterjee he lobbied for a separate homeland of Hindu Bengalis which would be part of the Indian union. The move received approval in the Bengal legislature to the discomfort of the communists and the Muslim League. The steadfast refusal of leaders to address the rising problems of communalism had resulted in partition of the province, untold suffering of Bengali Hindus living in the eastern part, and also complete failure of leaders from West Bengal to extract support from New Delhi for rehabilitation of the refugees. If there is a strong dislike in West Bengal today for the politicians of the Hindi heartland, the events of 1930-50 should be studied closely.

Syama Prasad's presence in politics was also short-lived – for around 14 years. Of this he was in the national political scene for just 5 years. His idea of India was in conflict with that of Jawaharlal Nehru. Nehru's dislike for Syama Prasad, who was thrust into his cabinet by Gandhi, is well documented. There was a campaign against Mukherjee stating that he was treating Bengali officers favourably in his ministry. Such an issue came up for discussion in the parliament also. It is difficult to conclude if it was Nehru's dislike for Bengalis in general or for Syama Prasad in particular that led to such incidences. Syama Prasad stood out among all the politicians from Bengal for his uncluttered thoughts. He knew that Bengali Hindus were being persecuted – before Independence by the then elected governments of Huq, Nazimuddin or Suhrawardy. He also had objected to the harsh police action on Bengal's freedom fighters in Midnapore. Once working in the cabinet, he knew the value of modern industry and tried to introduce the same in the country. He did not hesitate to bring in the locomotive factory to West Bengal. As cabinet minister (supported in no small measure by Dr B.R. Ambedkar) he was instrumental in getting the tripartite agreement between West Bengal, Bihar and the Centre signed for the launch of the Damodar Valley Corporation on the lines of Tennessee Valley Authority. It was left to Dr Bidhan Chandra Roy to take the project forward. He realised the futility of the Nehru-Liaquat Pact and knew well enough that the persecution of Hindus in East Pakistan would not end with the pact. That his resignation had shaken the central government could be understood from the extensive campaign that Prime Minister Nehru had launched through All India Radio. The pact and the campaign which included speeches by Sardar Patel as well are testimony to the neglect of the Centre in ameliorating the distress of the displaced persons from East Pakistan on the same footing as those who came from West Pakistan. Even Dr Bidhan Roy had expressed his frustration through his official communications. Independence had brought in a new type of stepmotherly treatment for West Bengal. Syama Prasad had realised the need for a national political party, not as parochial as the Hindu Mahasabha, but a party committed to the needs of the Hindus. He had arguably the plight of the East Pakistan displaced Bengalis in mind but the party took off with the support of the refugees from West Pakistan. The Bharatiya Jana Sangh (later BJP) could not find its roots in West Bengal and finally ended up being ridiculed in the native state of its founder.

After ousting Subhas Chandra Bose, the Congress leadership attempted to rejuvenate its Bengal unit and entrusted Maulana Azad, a rank outsider, to do that. In the faction-ridden Bengal Congress this launched the game of teeter-totter that led it on a political suicide mode. The first choice of the Congress for the position of chief minister (then the position used to be called 'Prime Minister') was Dr Prafulla Chandra Ghosh, a hardcore Gandhian. But he could not survive the factional fight and also had earned the displeasure of Sardar Patel for refusing to accommodate ministers recommended by the Marwari business community. Dr Bidhan Roy was the natural choice as his successor. Dr Roy had the requisite stature as a leading medical practitioner, had been leading member of the Swarajya party when it entered the council, and was even Bengal Congress chief when Subhas Chandra was not in India. Due to his stature, he was acceptable to both Pandit Nehru and Sardar Patel. There were several attempts by the Jugantar faction led by Surendra Mohan Ghosh and the Gandhians under Dr Prafulla Ghosh to topple him but he survived because of his stature and equation with the central leaders, particularly Prime Minister Nehru. During this period two prominent political faces from West Bengal were Dr Roy and Atulya Ghosh. No other factions in the state Congress could penetrate their alliance and the Congress government under Dr Roy had offered a stable administration despite several problems like rehabilitation of refugees, food crisis, employment generation, etc. The crisis helped the communists to lay a deep foundation in the state's politics. Dr Roy, the tallest politician from West Bengal, was content with the responsibility of managing the state. His presence helped the Congress to win three consecutive elections till 1962. But after that neither Prafulla Sen nor Atulya Ghosh had the ability to stem the rot. What is more, the factional fight forced Ajoy Mukherjee, a Gandhian and respected freedom fighter, to leave the party. This was the end of the road for the Congress in West Bengal. The party could come to power only once thereafter that too through electoral rigging and muscle flexing.

West Bengal came to the forefront of the national stage with its struggle for independence in East Pakistan. That was when the state had no politician of national stature. Ajoy Mukherjee was a weak, confusing figure, Atulya Ghosh was a nobody, Siddhartha Shankar Ray emerged due to his equation with Prime Minister Indira Gandhi, and Pranab Mukherjee was at the Centre but was at the beginning of his political career. The only politician in West Bengal who was a leader in his own right was Jyoti Basu but his party was yet to emerge as the first choice in the state. The state was full of lawlessness with Naxalite hooliganism ruling everyday life in West Bengal. This gave an opportunity to the Congress under Siddhartha Shankar Ray to use muscle power and establish a 5-year rule of the Congress. The method adopted by the Congress prevailed with fine tuning by the subsequent governments in the state. It also ensured that the Congress would never emerge as the ruling party in West Bengal again. The only occasion after 1972 when the Congress had some impact was the Lok Sabha election of 1984 after the assassination of Indira Gandhi. The Congress on the back of a wave of sympathy had bagged 16 seats from West Bengal.

Jyoti Basu came into legislative politics in 1945 as an elected member when Suhrawardy was the chief minister. There were two members from the communist party, both had voted against the partition of Bengal. The communist party wanted borderless Bengal yet had managed to win support from the refugees from East Pakistan. Predictably so since they offered a dedicated vote bank.

The communists had taken up issues dear to this community. The communist politics was purely aimed at expanding their sphere of influence with no intention of looking for a durable solution for the displaced persons from across the border. Jyoti Basu, due to his mastery over legislative politics, emerged as the tallest regional politician during his time. He was even offered the post of prime ministership of the country but his party, due to its fear that this would weaken its grip on West Bengal, did not accept the offer. That was the only opportunity for Bengal to have its own man as prime minister of the nation. The other leader from the state was Pranab Mukherjee who remained in national politics and had failed to win any election despite contesting the Lok Sabha on several occasions. However his command over legislative issues and grasp over rules and procedures to be followed in a democratic set-up made Pranab Mukherjee an indispensable person for the Congress. The brief estrangement he had to suffer due to internal rivalry was a loss for Rajiv Gandhi as well who was deprived of a sane advisor when he needed him most. Pranab Mukherjee's political life was tragic. He had all the abilities, perhaps he was more able than many who occupied the chair, to become prime minister and run a competent government. But his ability to deliver came in the way when Sonia Gandhi had to select a prime minister in 2004. Pranab Mukherjee, judged by his long experience and proven competence, should have been the obvious choice. But he was probably viewed as a person who would not accept backseat driving by anybody and therefore was not chosen by the Gandhi family. In hindsight had Pranab Mukherjee been the prime minister perhaps the Congress would not have lost as miserably as it did in 2014. The most competent politician from West Bengal who spent his life in national politics finally had the consolation of becoming the nation's president, a post he managed with competence and left his mark in the Rashtrapati Bhavan.

Jyoti Basu was effectively the leader of a regional party which had a strong hold in West Bengal, some presence in Kerala, and also in the small state of Tripura. Its political behaviour too was regional, acting as the opposition in New Delhi and ruling the state. This branding was so deep rooted among its office bearers that they could not think of any future for the party had they allowed Jyoti Basu to take up the job of prime ministership of India. The CPI(M) was so satisfied with its scientific electoral manipulation and control over West Bengal that it did not even think of the issues which might come up due to such a myopic politics. Thus when problems started coming into the open the party was at its wit's end and failed miserably. Not only did the party lose in 2011, it simply got erased from the state and in 2019 the communists failed to win a single seat in the Lok Sabha. The failure of the CPI(M) is even more glaring since it lost to a force which was not ideologically superior to it or offered any better leadership than even in the last stages of the Left Front rule.

Since 1977 West Bengal's isolation from the national political scene is complete. Both the Left Front and the TMC could run the state unchallenged by any national alternative due to the deep-rooted political isolation of West Bengal. The evolution of politics in West Bengal had four phases broadly. First was from the dawn of exposure to modern thoughts till the period when Bengal had enjoyed a leadership role in India – roughly this ended with the death of Chittaranjan Das. It is not that Bengal's superiority was unchallenged during this phase. It was seen that the first annual session of the Congress was organised without taking the top Bengal leaders into confidence. But Surendranath Banerjee and the members of the Bharat Sabha (Indian Association) were magnanimous in wishing success to the Congress session. It was also noticed that there was opposition to Bengal perhaps due to arrogance born out of knowledge as Aurobindo had said in his speech in Poona. But the link between the rest of India and Bengal was a non-politician sanyasi, Swami Vivekananda, who had inculcated a sense of superior confidence in the ancient Indian philosophy. When Chittaranjan Das came into the national scene he had the support of Bengal as well as leaders like Bal Gangadhar Tilak and Motilal Nehru. Mahatma Gandhi accepted Chittaranjan as a strong leader and after the failure of his first non-cooperation movement even followed the council entry line of Das. In fact, during a brief period it was the Swarajya party that had been the face of the Congress. Bengal's dominance in national politics ended with the passing away of Chittaranjan Das. Gandhi did not have to look over his shoulder for any possible challenge after the untimely death of C.R. Das.

The second phase of Bengal's role in national politics was a period of reconciling to the idea of following a leader, both in ideology and management. It was the period when Mahatma Gandhi had rejuvenated the Indian National Congress. Nothing could move in the Congress without his consent. There was not a single person from Bengal, barring perhaps the financier of the party, G.D. Birla, who had any influence on the Mahatma. In Bengal the provincial leaders were caught in their own concerns of dominating local activities. This applied even to Subhas Chandra Bose who was then fighting with his principal rival Jatindra Mohan Sengupta. However, Jatindra Mohan had won support from Mahatma Gandhi. His untimely death saw his wife Nellie Sengupta elected as Congress president in 1933. Subhas Bose was made president of the Congress in 1938. Before him Jawaharlal Nehru had occupied that post three times. Clearly in the freedom struggle phase between 1926 and 1939, when Bose was finally removed from the Congress, Bengal had no role in the national leadership.

The third phase was the battle for the survival of the province. Bengal was leaderless after Bose left India in 1940. In any case after Fazlul Huq had formed a coalition with the Muslim League, politics in Bengal was fast moving along communal lines. There was no question of seeking a leadership role though certain parts of the state had excelled in spontaneous movements against the British government. The freedom movement was not exactly what Mahatma Gandhi would have liked it to be – violence was part of the movement in Midnapore. When the Congress leaders were in jail, the Quit India call remained leaderless, and the freedom movement was run by Bengal's youth and the Azad Hind Fauz, forces put together by Rashbehari Bose and led by Subhas Chandra Bose, the former Congress president, suspended for defeating Mahatma Gandhi's nominee. This was the period when the reluctance of the national political leadership to acknowledge Bengal was starkly visible. Poor people dying of hunger, going without clothes due to rampant black marketing, facing communal riots were lost in the more pressing task of negotiating Partition and formation of a Congress government. Mahatma Gandhi visited Bengal on a few occasions but his efforts to inculcate sense among the rioters failed with Hindus remaining at the receiving end in Noakhali. This was when young men in Calcutta had even demonstrated against Gandhi. Since the late 1930s it was a struggle for survival for Bengal.

This struggle and the Centre's reluctance to support the hapless refugees from East Pakistan laid the foundation of the fourth phase, that of isolation that one witnesses in West Bengal today. The failure to provide adequate relief turned people towards the communists who had strengthened their political base by opposing the government. Since the Congress was ruling the state then, the anger against the national government helped the opposition to channelise it against the state Congress. In 1967 more than the failure to win majority, the electoral defeat of Chief Minister Prafulla Sen and party boss Atulya Ghosh had hurt the Congress the most. As far as electoral support is concerned that was the end of the Congress. West Bengal shifted away from national political parties.

The emergence of the BJP in the national political scene exacerbated the sense of isolation. The strong Muslim vote bank in the state helped both the Left Front and later the TMC in maintaining their isolationist politics. The dominant ideology in Bengal has always been liberal. Even the Hindutva that Swami Vivekananda had preached was liberal. The distress faced during the Partition had turned Bengal towards communism. The failure to address their rehabilitation added strength to this conversion to communism. Repeated food crisis and incompetent rationing system had turned the people against the Congress. Only the communists were active among the common men. Naturally the Leftists emerged as the choice of the people. The issue was consolidating the fragmented Left. The muscle power used by the Siddhartha Ray government aided this consolidation. The lack of touch with political reality in the Janata Party leader and former chief minister Prafulla Sen hastened the process of Left Front rule. There was a distinct possibility of a Janata-Left coalition government which could have delayed the doomsday that West Bengal faced. Perhaps it could have postponed that predicament indefinitely depending on the quality of governance. The problem was that the elitist politics of the Congress was deep rooted – whether the leaders were Gandhian or whether they hailed from some elite heredity, the background was immaterial. Though the party had attracted new and young leaders in the 1970s, they were encouraged to fight with each other, thanks to factions in the Congress. Discipline is one element hopelessly absent in Bengal politics. That is why leaders who had the personality to keep the flock together had managed to control politics in the state. As was seen in the past, even the occasional visits of Gandhi to the state did not win him any durable base here. Politics here is a continued daily action, not merely being visible before the election season or during some events. This was the basic difference between the CPI(M) and the Congress and saw the latter out in the wilderness. This failure to maintain touch with the people could be one reason why Bengal leaders had failed to maintain their position in national and state politics at the same time. The defining quality of Mamata Banerjee as a leader is that she understood the need for people connect and visited the districts regularly. This helped in addressing certain grievances of the people and also to tame the local muscles in the party. The highly politicised society in West Bengal demands in-depth local connect. Without such a link it is difficult to administer the state. In order to maintain such grassroot-level people connect, West Bengal leaders fail to build their national-level political rapport. Unlike many other Hindi heartland states where there is some deep-rooted connect with national politics, strong regional leadership is a necessity in states like West Bengal. Where a national figure like Mahatma Gandhi had drawn a blank it was natural that the charisma of successive prime ministers like Indira Gandhi and Rajiv Gandhi did not help the Congress in West Bengal.

The isolationist tendency of politicians in West Bengal has its dangers as well. Matters of national significance – water sharing with neighbouring countries, transport of goods vehicles, exchange of enclaves and such issues had given rise to disagreement between West Bengal and the Centre in the past when both the Centre and state had the same party government and afterwards when West Bengal shunned the national party. In the past the Congress was successful in many states since the party in effect was a broad coalition among the nationalists from provinces and the provincial leaders had their voices on the national stage. This was seen even in the decisions of the finance commissions appointed to adjudicate on distribution of financial resources between the Centre and states. West Bengal had faced isolation due to the extreme stances by its local government starting with the Left Front government. The setting up of the Bakreshwar thermal power plant and Haldia Petrochemicals are two examples from the Left Front rule. However the Front government was level headed enough to utilise the central schemes for the benefit of its support base, as was seen during the Loan Mela days. This has taken an extreme turn under the TMC government. Now beneficial schemes of the Centre are shunned since the state too has to share in the funding of such schemes. But in the process the state loses out on the money earmarked by the Centre. The political mileage from any populist scheme comes from the targeted distribution. The Left Front leadership was smart enough to realise that the name of the scheme whether prefixed with 'Prime Minister' or 'Chief Minister' does not matter. Had it been so, the Congress, which had used the names of a particular family in anything that could be named, would not have faced the political wilderness it faces today.

Economists with roots in West Bengal, well established in their respective specialisations elsewhere, come at intervals and suggest how the state can improve its economy. But their sincere advices have failed to take note of the apparently minor but in effect most critical aspect of the West Bengal society, therefore the economy. The point of departure with the rest of India is the isolation – it is not merely isolation in political terms. Take Tamil Nadu for instance. There is no presence of any national political party in the state but its economy moves in tandem with the growth of the nation, using all the policies to its advantage. Tamil Nadu is also an inward-looking society like West Bengal and has huge migratory population in many parts of India and the world. A special feature of such migrants from Tamil Nadu is that once retired many of these professionals go back and settle in their home state, unlike the Bengalis from West Bengal. The reason for the tendency of such migration from the state should be studied carefully for any policy prescription. One also needs to examine how much cross-border economic activity takes place between West Bengal and Bangladesh. Let us take one example. In West Bengal's border areas illegal cultivation of poppy is undertaken in abundance. Farmers indulge in it by paying protection money to the local political mastans. This has been going on since the days of the Left Front rule. Poppy seeds come from Bangladesh, and the finished product goes back to Bangladesh. Poppy cultivation in India is regulated and needs permission. In West Bengal this is violated with impunity. One major fallout of illegal trade is a law-and-order issue – it takes place because of weaknesses in the administration and increases and nurtures such lacunae of the system. In effect the state ends up being a den of lawlessness, an important reason to remain isolated from the rest of the country. The political system is so devised as to maintain such isolation so as to reap the benefits of the illegal economy. A detailed look at the use of informal trade with Bangladesh in converting banned currency notes during the 2016 demonetisation drive has not been delved into. Only certain shell companies have been identified and served notices by the Income Tax authorities. But in a relaxed administrative structure even the central government offices get equally contaminated. The maintenance of isolation is imperative for the rent-seeking economy that has taken firm root in West Bengal.

When reputed economists recommend policies for economic growth of the state they do not go into the details of ailments in the state's socio-political-administration system. The economy is a sum total of orderly or disorderly systems prevailing in a particular place. The political system in the state has developed in such a manner that corruption and muscle flexing are the main ingredients of survival. The presence of local-level leadership with total command in the area of their sphere of influence explains the fragmentation of the state's economy. One simple example may not be out of place. The auto rickshaws in Calcutta run point to point. They follow a system of rigid pick-up-and-drop points. There is no scope of enterprise beyond what is laid down since localities are run by different power brokers. Crossing one and moving into another to maximise income and opportunity is a criminal offence. The economic system has so developed that even local area trade and service are regulated by the needs of local area muscle power who for their survival join the ruling political power. When this happy co-existence breaks, as it did after 2007-08, the government's survival is challenged. This saw replacement of the Left Front with the TMC government in 2011. Unless one studies in depth the muscle-flexing, local-level equilibrium trap that is the rule in West Bengal one cannot predict the future – political or economic – of the state. This very structure of the economy and society of West Bengal explains the reason for the behaviour of its political leadership. What is incongruity in the politics of Mamata Banerjee to an outsider is perfectly synchronised to one looking into the state minutely. Mamata Banerjee has no intention of suffering the fate of Buddhadeb Bhattacharjee who attempted to bring in industry competing with other states and thereby managed to upset the apple cart.

Since 2016 there have been several changes in the political landscape of West Bengal. The surprising political penetration of BJP in the 2019 Lok Sabha poll has brought in a national political party face to face with a well-settled regional leader and her party in a political slugfest. There had been efforts by Rajiv Gandhi in 1987 to dislodge the Left Front government. But the problem was that the Congress did not have any populist rhetoric or delivered product. In contrast Narendra Modi thrives on what is branded as populism, schemes meant for the benefit of the economically disadvantaged. Post re-election in 2019, the central government quickly took several decisions on sensitive matters aided by favourable judgments from the apex court. The interesting characteristics of such decisions had been calculative thinking which outsmarted the entire opponents to the ruling BJP.

> In such calculative thinking, members of the ruling party tend to use the 'ordinary human being' first as raw material to be exploited for election purposes and later on as an entity to be kept entangled in a series of political as well as socially necessary illusions. Those who have vested interests in perpetuating their rule normally work through the calculative rather than the reflective mode of thinking about politics.[2]

Such decisions came up for discussion in the politically sensitive West Bengal too but the limits of such commentaries in the media lie in the fact that they analyse developments in a superficial and selective manner. More often than not pre-decided allegiance of the people as reflected in the media and social media they follow guide the thought. More often than not such thoughts are anti-incumbency in nature. The calculative politician keeps on moving from one decision to another in quick succession, not pausing to give others a chance to think through before the next one is thrust on the people. This is a new kind of politics – democracy managed through populism. In West Bengal for the first time perhaps a national party led by a calculative populist leader is pitted against a local populist leader. In the process the local leader gets trapped in isolation and ends up losing the plot.

A major problem in political isolation is corruption and nepotism. During the Left Front rule, the top leadership was reasonably blemish less though the same could not be said of the second tier and the others managing the grassroots under them. This had weakened the foundation on which the power structure was built. TMC inherited the same structure with corruption shifting from the party apparatus to local-level party mafia. Friction within such a system arises over the issue of distribution of the loot or enticement for collecting more from elsewhere. The point to remember is that the loyalty of such political musclemen lies with making money and saving the loot amassed. They don't hesitate to bite the hand that fed them once. There are such characters aplenty in West Bengal while in political discourse political analysts see 'that a model based on a strong government which has marginalised the opposition and rules the state under a stable, populist, benevolent, autocratic leadership is generally succeeding in the peripheries of India'.[3] Ranabir Samaddar had argued after the spectacular election victory of Mamata Banerjee in 2016 that 'the results of the assembly elections point to the subalternisation of politics in the face of the opposition's hollow campaign to restore democracy'.[4] In other words, it is believed that Mamata Banerjee represents the subalterns unlike the Left Front and the Congress which were the principal rivals in 2016. Nemai Karan felt that the politics for the subaltern was essentially a politics of populism. And the opposition in 2016 had called for restoration of democracy in the state. The election result, therefore some would like to say, was a victory of populism over democracy.[5] A closer analysis, however, punctures such an argument. Karan noted that the two political groups – the Left Front-Congress-save-democracy coalition and the TMC had retained their respective areas of influence. The only difference was the transfer of some 5 per cent votes of the BJP to the TMC. In other words, Karan said, 'The impact of populism is not so tremendous to affect all political segments of the state. It implies that there is no sociopolitical turmoil. It is rather a verdict of political status quo in conformity with the political tradition of the state.'[6] The status quo of 2016 was a reflection of the state's isolation from national mainstream politics, a factor that made BJP consider the assembly election more as an opportunity to keep a tight leash on its major national-level adversary the Congress than making the TMC face some humiliation or improve its own poll prospect. 'The post-poll reactions of the Akhil Bharatiya Vidyarthi Parishad and the Hindu Sanhati Manch are indicative of the possibility of tactical voting by a section of the supporters of the BJP and the Rashtriya Swayamsevak Sangh to defeat candidates of the Congress–Left Front alliance.'[7] Jan-Werner Muller, a professor of Princeton University, wrote, 'Conventional wisdom has it that populist parties are primarily protest parties and protest cannot govern since one cannot protest against oneself.' But this doesn't mean that once in power populists will fail.[8] Once in power populists can easily pass on all their failures to behind-the-scene activities of the elites – as did the Left Front government, and the reason why it never joined the coalition at the Centre. Mamata Banerjee came to power in coalition with the Congress which was then governing in New Delhi but did not spend a long time with the UPA once she won the mandate to govern West Bengal.

Why does populism succeed? According to Muller, populism assures people the deliverable which a democratic system cannot provide. But nobody ever officially announced the promises a democracy must fulfil. They are more like what is sometimes called the 'folk theory of democracy'. The question that comes up during electoral debates is how much such intuitive expectations could be fulfilled and whose fault was it for the gap between expectation and achievement. In such a discourse the better storyteller scores more points. In a state like West Bengal which remained aloof from the national mainstream for such a long time it is necessary to use special narratives to match against the local populism. Rajiv Gandhi had failed when he confronted Jyoti Basu in 1987. What is critical in populism which built nearly 44 years of isolation from the mainstream national political economy is the quality of messaging.

We are living in the age of populism. Populism, wrote Nemai Karan, is tending towards the far right to give social legitimacy to the neo-liberal order. It is essentially racist, xenophobic, suffering from colour prejudices and anti-immigration. In the Indian context, populism thrives on identity politics based on caste, religion, etc.[9] But the policies of the BJP have so far been pro-poor which helped Narendra Modi to a sweeping electoral victory as also indulge in formulating calculative policies. Even the TMC government in West Bengal, otherwise having people connect, was outwitted. Not only that, its steadfast isolationist agenda had helped the BJP and its associates to spread their tentacles and strengthen their foothold. According to Karan, the indulgence given by the state government to religious matters had enabled the BJP and its associates to sustain their momentum. The typical brand of TMC's political populism in the long run will strengthen the neo-liberal order which may finally end the long isolation of the state from the national mainstream politics, by bringing a national party in power.

Endnotes

1 W.C. Bonnerjee was a leading lawyer in Calcutta as well as in London. As a non-domiciled Bengali he was not viewed as part of Bengal by the elites including Rabindranath Tagore. The reason for his being selected as the first Congress president could be his association with Dadabhai Naoroji, who was the second president in 1886.

2 'Problems in Thinking about Politics', editorial, *EPW*, August 17, 2019, https://www.epw.in/journal/2019/33/editorials/problems-thinking-about-politics.html.

3 Ranabir Samaddar, 'West Bengal Elections: The Verdict of Politics', *EPW,* June 11, 2016, https://www.epw.in/journal/2016/24/commentary/west-bengal-elections.html.

4 Ibid.

5 Nemai Karan, 'Populism, Democracy and Development', *EPW*, March 18, 2017, https://www.epw.in/system/files/pdf/2017_52/11/DI_LII_11_18032017_Nemai_Karan.pdf.

6 Ibid.

7 Ibid.

8 Jan-Werner Muller, *What is Populism?* (Penguin, 2017), p. 41.

9 Karan, 'Populism, Democracy and Development.'

POSTSCRIPT
REGIONAL PRIDE HOLDS SWAY

The result of the 2021 West Bengal state assembly election is a confirmation of the deep-rooted political isolation of West Bengal from the Hindi heartland. Regional pride is not confined to West Bengal alone. Many other states – Kerala, Tamil Nadu, Telangana, Odisha and Andhra Pradesh for instance – have seen strong regional political parties keeping the national parties at bay. What separates West Bengal from the rest of the states is its constant rift with the Centre. The extreme political bitterness between the TMC and the BJP escalated during the 2021 state election and it continues to play out even after the election.

In tune with her core political theme, the Mamata Banerjee-led TMC campaigned for the 2021 assembly election by focusing on the role of 'outsiders'. Bengalis were repeatedly told that people from Gujarat, the home state of Prime Minister Modi and Home Minister Amit Shah, who had no clue about the rich culture of the land of Tagore, Vivekananda and Subhas Bose were trying to destabilise the state. In the heat of the electoral battle even the officers of the Election Commission and the supporting central forces were branded as outsiders – *Bohiragato* in Bengali. The TMC's campaign slogan was 'West Bengal wants its own daughter' (*Bangla tar nijer meyeke chay*).

The Narendra Modi-led BJP uses nationalism as its trump card in all political matters. Perceived as outsiders in West Bengal, the party challenged the regional identity cocoon and hoped to turn the tables on the TMC. The bitter electoral battle was fought between two political parties trying to grab power, one propagating itself as neo-nationalist and the other strongly entrenched in regional pride – *Bangalir Ashmita* (literally 'vanity', but commonly used as 'identity'). Caught amidst it were many a stalwart in agreement, disagreement and even confusion.

A prominent case in point being Amartya Sen's comments during a PTI interview. Asked to comment on the 'insider-outsider' debate started by the TMC, Sen said it is 'certainly a bad thing' as Bengal has, historically, been tolerant to outsiders.[1] At the same time, Sen stretched the argument to find the origin of the *bohiragato* debate in the politics of the challenger BJP: 'When one of the major political contenders … portrays a part of the "insider" population of Bengal – in particular, Bengali Muslims – as less deserving of support, while deriving their strength from the support of Hindu activists coming originally from outside Bengal, the dividing lines are hard to be kept pure.'[2] That the identity issue would figure in electoral propaganda was not surprising, according to Sen, but what he found disturbing in the 2021 election had been that it went 'further than Bengali sub-nationalism.'

The question is how did the people in West Bengal react to the bitter political rhetoric. This was evident in the election outcome. The TMC swept back to power capturing 48 per cent votes and 213 seats leaving BJP a distant second with 77 seats and 38 per cent votes. For the BJP the vote percentage was less than what it could bag in the 2019 Lok Sabha poll, underscoring the point that regional aspirations cannot be steamrolled under one ideology.

In the 2019 Lok Sabha elections the BJP emerged as the major challenger to the hegemony of the ruling TMC by winning 18 seats. The windfall gain of 18 seats enthused the BJP, the party from the Hindi heartland, to challenge the TMC in the next assembly election. However, the BJP had two factors to contend with. First, due to the presence of nearly 30 per cent minority votes in the state and the axiom that minorities always vote against the BJP, it was presumed that in 2021 the ruling TMC would have another easy victory like in 2016. Second, and no less important, was the political society prevailing in rural West Bengal since the days of the Left Front rule. 'Here political parties tended to displace other competing channels of public transaction – such as civil societal associations – which made the rural situation ontologically different from the urban political society. Indeed, political parties in rural West Bengal largely transcended caste, religion or ethnicity-based organisations, which have a greater salience in struggles for social justice in other parts of the country,' argued Dwaipayan Bhattacharyya.[3]

In fact, Bhattacharyya noted in February 2021 that the scale was tilted towards a TMC victory in the upcoming assembly election. He wrote: 'The BJP's entry signals deep changes in West Bengal's political culture. Despite occasional flare-ups on religious lines and post-partition trauma, West Bengal by and large avoided any communal split for seven decades or so. Instead, there were deep divisions on party or class lines mounting over caste/religious identities. By pushing its rhetoric of "minority appeasement", the BJP hopes to maximise support in 70% Hindu voters.'[4]

Buddhadeb Bhattacharjee, the last Left Front chief minister, who attempted to lift the state out of the morass of stagnation, mentioned in his autobiography *Phire Dekha*[5] how stiff resistance by just a small section of people supported by the 'intellectuals' stalled his sincere efforts to bring investment to the state. Economic issues have since then taken a backseat in the political discourse of the state.

It cannot be denied that the genesis of BJP's interest in the state was communal in nature. The BJP felt that Mamata Banerjee had been playing the dangerous game of minority appeasement in the state. In electoral politics, as seen in earlier chapters, seeds of communalism were sown in this very Gangetic plain, and then dispersed elsewhere. For Mamata Banerjee maintaining communal harmony in a charged-up situation was a priority.

The Hindutva brigade were looking for an opportunity to strike at what they considered to be Mamata's appeasement of minorities. In March 2017, the highest decision-taking body of the RSS passed a resolution on the 'Grave concern over the unabated rise in violence by Jihadi elements in West Bengal'.[6] Evidently the Sangh Parivar now seemed to be ready to take their discontent into the open.

A few weeks after the resolution passed by the RSS, the state witnessed massive Ram Navami processions, in which bike-riding youngsters wearing saffron bandanas chanted 'Jai Shri Ram'. The processions triggered a backlash from Bengalis, who alleged that the Sangh Parivar, an umbrella term referring to the RSS's numerous affiliates, was trying to impose 'North Indian culture' on Bengal.[7] This is how the debate witnessed in course of the 2021 state assembly election took shape.

The 2019 Lok Sabha campaign was a curtain raiser of sorts. The BJP had strengthened its base in West Bengal by inducting into its folds disgruntled leaders from the TMC. The first one to defect was Mukul Roy, who was among the founding members of the TMC. In the 2019 Lok Sabha election several TMC turncoats such as Saumitra Khan, Arjun Singh, Nishith Pramanik among others were given tickets. Before the state assembly election, the Adhikary family of Midnapore led by Suvendu Adhikary, a state minister, switched over to the BJP. While the BJP opted for local leaders, not all of them had clean public images. This provided ammunition to the TMC to criticise the BJP for accommodating the leftovers of the TMC. Moreover, these opportunist moves did not find favour with the common people and came handy for the TMC in shedding the weight of anti-incumbency against the party. The TMC took this opportunity to paint the deserters as the reason for hiccups in its delivery system.

The BJP was banking on anti-incumbency as its trump card in the state assembly elections. What the party did not take into account was the personal popularity of Mamata, her minority vote bank, her tremendous appeal to the women voters, and the strong sense of identity (*ashmita*) of a Bengali. In addition as an outsider the BJP did not study how politics in West Bengal was structured – the power rested largely on the local youth, whom Mamata has cultivated well.

In order to gain from the anti-incumbency factor, the BJP campaign focused on the concept of a 'double-engine Sarkar' (a government with two engines) – development pulled by the state and the Centre in tandem. But communicating such an alien concept to the people of West Bengal was not easy. More so in a state where people are largely dependent on doles and state support in the absence of a flourishing economy. 'What Modi did not realise was that wooing voters of Bengal with showmanship, muscle and money power will not work. Traditionally, communal harmony is always given importance in Bengal,' opined *Business India*.[8]

The unfettered growth of regional politics in West Bengal has seen rampant use of electoral violence preventing any party to stake a claim without local muscle. Gopalkrishna Gandhi, a former governor of the state, wrote, 'Bengal has known electoral violence for years now ... that violence has brought discredit to the state ... it needs to be addressed ... the Election Commission of India has to make note of it and factor it into its scheduling of elections in Bengal.'[9] Such concern brought about an unprecedented eight-phase election and a retinue of central forces along with experienced election observers to ensure free and fair election in 2021. At a time when the deadly second wave of the Covid-19 pandemic was rearing its head in India the eight-phase drawn-out election did not find favour with the people of Bengal and ultimately worked against the BJP. The overwhelming negative feeling that it generated may pose a problem for the BJP to overcome in the near future.

The BJP made a serious effort to establish a strong political footprint in West Bengal 2016 onwards. It did its homework but from the point of view of an outsider. It summed up the key issues plaguing Bengal's development as: Politicisation of administration, criminalisation of politics, and institutionalisation of corruption. While they may be good pointers for armchair discussions they are not useful in grassroot politics. Mamata Banerjee knew well enough that such a critical analysis would not influence ordinary people who are dependent on state support for their livelihood, and her government has been generous on that score. She did not try to match the blitzkrieg of the BJP campaign and relied on her personal popularity and her track record of delivery.

The BJP also failed to attract any major public intellectual or influencer from Bengal and had to bring in successful, erudite Bengali faces from outside the state. Barring one, all of them lost the election. No challenger in West Bengal can be successful without first carefully tackling the sensitive issue of regional pride.

Maitreesh Ghatak wrote in an article that 'while some voters are clearly committed to specific parties, a large fraction of the voters are floating or swing voters. Depending on the specific election, they can switch their allegiance from one party to another'. He also felt that identity politics in terms of religion and caste, generally, was not a salient issue in West Bengal elections, but regional identity, particularly Bengali vanity, had played a role.[10] Clearly the politics of neo-nationalism coupled with anti-incumbency were not strong enough to outweigh the regional identity issues – 'Bengali pride', 'locals vs. outsiders', and *Bangla nijer meyeke chay* campaign.

Voters in Bengal are accustomed to accepting the same political order year after year. They prefer status quo over a new set of unknown elements affecting their daily lives as is common in the state since the Left Front days. In the end, West Bengal saw 81.87 per cent polling – nearly the same number polled in the Lok Sabha election 2019 (81.76 per cent) while it was a little less than the polling figure in the assembly election 2016 (83.02 per cent). The reasonably free and fair polling – which saw re-poll in only one booth, a record of sorts – proved to be a new element in West Bengal elections. But in the end the contest was between the BJP and the anti-BJP forces. As a result, all the committed voters of the Left-Congress ecosystem, who were apprehensive of the BJP, opted for the TMC. Thus the vote share of the Congress and the CPI(M) came down to just 8 per cent. Extreme polarisation ensured that the entire minority vote went to the TMC. Meanwhile the BJP failed to create complete Hindu consolidation, as was expected in a politically sensitive West Bengal. The BJP could not impress upon the voters of West Bengal that the party had any agenda other than 'Hindutva'.

The prime minister's attempt to use Bangla during the election rallies backfired due to poor pronunciation; it ended up creating hilarious memes. The party had also failed to project any leader from the state. The feeling that the 'one size fits all' oratory of Narendra Modi would sway West Bengal was proved wrong. Firstpost wrote, 'Modi and Shah's amateurish attempts to speak Bengali and appropriate "Bengali icons" just makes things worse, compounded further by the serial gaffes made by the Bengal BJP on a number of pretty basic cultural facts. In other words, a sub-nationalist strategy could work better for the TMC than for the BJP.'[11] In fact, by trying to cash in on the regional sentiment angle the BJP might have ended up hurting its future prospects in the state.

In the final analysis, Mamata Banerjee's personal popularity in heading the state was stronger than the visiting Modi-Shah duo who had a set narrative. The BJP could not sell its ambitious manifesto to the people who felt that the proverbial one bird in hand was better than the BJP's promised two in the bush. And finally the age-old antipathy of West Bengal towards the Hindi heartland narrative – an undercurrent that even Mahatma Gandhi had faced in his heydays – was too strong for Prime Minister Modi. Politically West Bengal has opted for isolation from Hindi heartland politics, thereby holding aloft its distinct regional identity.

Endnotes

1 Interview with Press Trust of India, updated on April 19, 2021, https://www.ndtv.com/india-news/bengal-should-not-be-party-to-national-degeneration-amartya-sen-241714.

2 Ibid.

3 Dwaipayan Bhattacharyya, 'Of Control and Factions: The Changing Party Society in Rural West Bengal', *EPW*, February 28, 2009, https://www.epw.in/system/files/pdf/2009_44/09/Of_Control_and_Factions_The_Changing_PartySociety_in_Rural_West_Bengal.pdf.

4 Dwaipayan Bhattacharyya, *EPW*, vol. 56(6), February 6, 2021, https://www.epw.in/journal/2021/6/comment/whither-west-bengal.html.

5 Buddhadeb Bhattacharjee, *Phire Dekha,* Part II (Kolkata: National Book Agency, 2017), 56-65.

6 RSS ABPS-2017 Resolution: 'Grave concern on Jehadi Violence in West Bengal', Coimbatore, March 21, 2017. RSS's Akhil Bharatiya Pratinidhi Sabha #RSSABPS2017 passed a major resolution expressing grave concern over the violence by Jehadi elements in West Bengal, https://samvada.org/2017/news/rss-abps-2017-resolution-grave-concern-on-jehadi-violence-in-west-bengal/.

7 Snigdhendu Bhattacharya, 'Behind West Bengal's Identity Battles: Rising Population & Economic Pressure', India Spend, March 26, 2021, https://www.indiaspend.com/west-bengal/west-bengal-election-identity-battles-rising-population-economic-pressure-738077.

8 Sajal Bose, 'Mamata regains Bengal, emerges the credible torchbearer: Bengal rejects Modi and renews faith on Mamata Banerjee,' *Business India*, May 21, 2021, https://businessindia.co/magazine/mamata-regains-bengal-emerges-the-credible-torchbearer.

9 Gopalkrishna Gandhi, *Hindustan Times,* April 15, 2021, https://www.hindustantimes.com/opinion/elections-and-violence-do-not-make-bengal-its-history-and-people-do-101618401885782.html.

10 Maitreesh Ghatak and Bishan Basu, 'West Bengal: The Dilemma that Left-Leaning Voters are Facing in this Election', The Wire, April 3, 2021, https://thewire.in/politics/west-bengal-dilemma-left-leaning-voters-assembly-elections-tmc-bjp.

11 Suhit K. Sen, 'West Bengal polls 2021: Top Guns alone won't win BJP State; Mamata's Populism a Hard Barrier to Break,' Firstpost, February 23, 2021, https://www.firstpost.com/politics/west-bengal-polls-2021-top-guns-alone-wont-win-bjp-state-mamatas-populism-a-hard-barrier-to-break-9337651.html.

INDEX

Y

Z